WIRELESS IMAGINATION

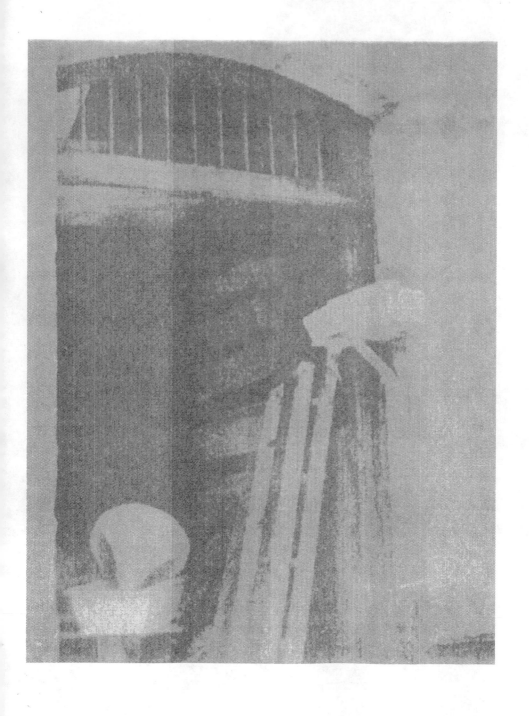

WIRELESS IMAGINATION
SOUND, RADIO, AND THE AVANT-GARDE

edited by Douglas Kahn

and Gregory Whitehead

The MIT Press

Cambridge, Massachusetts

London, England

First MIT Press paperback printing, 1994
© 1992 Massachusetts Institute of Technology

This book was set in Bembo and Futura by Compset Inc. and was printed and bound in the United States of America.

Library of Congress Cataloging-in-Publication Data
Wireless imagination: sound, radio, and the avant-garde / edited by
    Douglas Kahn and Gregory Whitehead.
        p.   cm.
    Includes bibliographical references and index.
    ISBN 0-262-11168-3 (HB), 0-262-61104-X (PB)
    1. Sound in art. 2. Arts, Modern—20th century. 3. Avant-garde (Aesthetics)—
History—20th century. I. Kahn, Douglas, 1951- . II. Whitehead, Gregory.
NX650.S68W57 1992
700'.9'04—dc20

10 9 8 7 6 5 4

92-3066
CIP

CONTENTS

The human ear offers not just another hole in the body, but a hole *in the head*. Moreover, the absence of obstructive anatomical features such as earlids would seem to assure a direct and unmediated pathway for acoustic phenomena, with sonic vibrations heading straight into the central nervous system. Yet the privileged access afforded to sound waves has left little impression on one conspicuous area of brain activity: it remains almost unheard of to think about sound. Although aural notions of silence, noise, groove, transmission, and the universal parasite of interference have all received widespread currency inside the various domains of contemporary theory, they are most typically employed like migrant workers, obliged to cultivate somebody else's juicy literary analogies before being trucked off to the next field.

Not surprisingly, the deafening silence of sound-in-thought is mirrored by the absence of anything remotely resembling a coherent tradition of audio art. Instead, we are left with an odd assortment of isolated moments and cultural marginalia: the fantastic acoustic scenarios projected through the texts of Raymond Roussel; the impossible aural objectives of Marcel Duchamp; Dziga Vertov's proposal for a phonographic "Laboratory of Hearing"; the zaum language and Radio Sorcery pronounced and promoted by Velimir Khlebnikov; the brazenly iconoclastic castaways of F. T. Marinetti's and Pino Masnata's *La Radia;* the antimusics of the Surrealists; the noise bands of Russolo, Foregger, and Cage; the contorted radio talk show delivered by Antonin Artaud; the labyrinthine inner journeys invoked by German Hörspiel; the razor contamination and cut-up ventriloquism of Gysin and Burroughs.

Rather than simply starting to pull theories of aurality out of a hat, we have chosen to ground *Wireless Imagination* in the more modest intent of documenting and charting sonographic resonances among the above existing histories, strangely dissonant and cacophonous as they may strike the naked ear. From there, by uniting the isolated gaps, silences, minutia, and marginalia into a polyphonous chorus (with every voice its own part), we hope that the book might literally *give another sense* to the broader contours of cultural history. How could our understandings of modernism, the avant-garde, and postmodernism *not* be transformed by the audition of such diverse voice migrations, phonography, and noise; by overhearing the varied mutations of acoustic space imagined and installed; or by tuning in the degenerative pulse of artist radiophony?

Over the several years it has taken to assemble *Wireless Imagination,* we have come to appreciate why uncharted wilderness so often remains uncharted: at times, the lack of landmarks made it difficult to find our bearings, and there were certainly times when we felt altogether lost, or when the excitement of some fresh discovery would be paid for the next day by an exasperating dead end. The resulting diversity and even discordance of the contributions reflect their halting articulation and assembly, leaving us with a *Wireless Imagination* that is by no means comprehensive. As one example, we decided to bypass sound poetry, which is a related but distinct history requiring its own excursion, along lines quite different from those pursued here.

We have seeded the book with a few documents attached to the essays that immediately precede them (although the Villiers selection relates as much to Kahn's essay); we can only leave these as teasers to a comprehensive collection of documents that might be taken up at some other time by someone else. Further, with the idea of compiling a future volume on more contemporary disruptions in the "regime of the visual" (from Fluxus to Hip Hop), we have limited the chronological scope of the book to a period ending in the 1960s with Burroughs, Cage, and German Hörspiel. Finally, as both of us are audio artists, it is inevitable that our selections, focus, and emphasis should be shaped to some extent by our own interests and inclinations, though we have tried hard to keep our ears clean.

In short, *Wireless Imagination* should be read not as the Last Word but rather as a collection of first utterances still looking for an autonomous language. At the very least, it should be clear that the deafening silence surrounding sound was made to be broken. Let the clamor begin!

DOUGLAS KAHN

One would expect to find amid the accumulation of studies of modernism, post-modernism, the avant-garde, and postwar experimentalism a more faithful attendance to the cultural preoccupations of hearing—one of the two major senses, the "public" ones, as John Cage described them for their ability to make contact from a distance—especially when one remembers that there are few arts that are mute. It would also be reasonable to expect a stronger curiosity about earlier artistic responses to the audio- and radiophonic technologies that so success-fully submerge us now in a mass-media din. Yet the literature on the arts of recorded and broadcasted sound, and of conceptual, literary, and performative sound, is scant at all levels, from basic historical research to theoretical modelings. Thus, while other historical fields may be busying themselves with things more detailed, the study of the relationship of sound and radio to the arts is open to a full range of investigations, including the most general.

Only recently have individuals begun to describe themselves as sound and sound installation artists, audio and radio artists. Only recently have they been self-identified with projects such as the radicalization of sound/image relationships, or of acoustics in architectural, environmental, or virtual space. These individuals demand knowledge of their predecessors, and a history and theory of sound in the arts. Without it artists will remain deaf to the spinning sound of reinvented wheels, for there is no easy artistic escape from deficient discourse. As part of this project historians might undertake, in the spirit of their own absence from the field, an investigation of what could have happened but didn't, that is, a *nonhistory*. Given developments within the avant-garde as a whole, given certain discursive, technological, and institutional conditions, why didn't certain practices ensue? This line of questioning—found in Rudolf Arnheim's 1936 *Radio* or Carlos Chavez's 1937 *Toward a New Music*, in which the fact that artists did not take advantage of the new possibilities presented by optical sound film, phonography, and archives of recorded sound stands as a source of bewilderment—needs to be pursued. Similarly, events that are usually excluded or trivialized in historical research should receive their due; after all, misguided aspirations, the oddest of infatuations, failed attempts, and unintentional accomplishments can often be more provocative than complete, final, and flawless realizations. Most of the events central to a history of sound have been nothing but marginalia on conventional historical agendas.

But this history presents problems at all levels, beginning with the fact that, despite the cultural pervasiveness of sound, there was no artistic practice outside music identified primarily with aurality. What took place was required to do so under other auspices: Marcel Duchamp was an antiretinal artist who focused on sound; Antonin Artaud was many things before he became involved in radio; Dziga Vertov took up film after his attempts to found a phonographic "Laboratory of Hearing" were frustrated; Piet Mondrian found time to ruminate at length on Luigi Russolo's noise music; William Burroughs was a writer who cut up audiotape; etc. There is no history of a self-described and autonomous art in the way one might think of the history of sculpture, no facade of a purposeful unity and linear continuity, no ongoing biographical intrigues and libidinal exchanges of influence. As a historical object, sound cannot furnish a good story or consistent cast of characters nor can it validate any ersatz notions of progress or generational maturity. The history is scattered, fleeting, and highly mediated—it is as poor an object in any respect as sound itself.

Another problem has been the privileging of music as the art of sound in modern Western culture.[1] Modernist and avant-garde artists admired the disjunctiveness and simultaneity that music could by its very nature perform, the "nonobjective" nature of its autoreferentiality, the dynamics between the rule of musical law and the sublime it administered, the mystical associations music holds, etc. In terms of many of the artistic agendas at hand, music had already auspiciously *arrived* and, therefore, suffered few challenges to its dominion—with one major exception: the French Surrealists' antipathy to music. Western art music proved at best awkwardly disposed to changes in mass culture and mass media, to new technological developments, to complex interaction with folk, subaltern, and non-Western cultures, and to overturning its most basic signifying presuppositions to the degree that other arts would, ironically, undertake in its name. Even this century's most noted radical attacks upon music—conducted, as they were, under the sign of noise and sound—ultimately returned to music. Luigi Russolo's "art of noises" was recuperated immediately into the goal of "a great renovation of music"; Edgar Varèse's "liberation of sound" was a motto of retreat when compared to Russolo's position; and at the core of John Cage's emancipatory project was a will to impose musical precepts upon all sounds. The main avant-garde strategy in music from Russolo through Cage quite evidently relied upon notions of noise and worldly sound as "extra-musical"; what was outside musical materiality was then progressively brought back into the fold in order to rejuvenate musical practice. This strategy was, of course, exhausted at the point when no audible sound existed outside music. But for a sound to be "musicalized" in this strategy, it had to conform materially to ideas of sonicity, that is, ideas of a sound stripped of its associative attributes, a minimally coded sound existing in close proximity to "pure" perception and distant from the contaminating effects of the world. This discursive block, bountiful in writings on Western art music, has inhibited the fusion of artistic ideas and activities with sociopolitical realities, with trenchant critiques and rapturous moments culled from aurality in general, with operations of the body and psyche, technological im/machinations, institutional workings—all that might be encountered beyond musical materiality.

Yet another problem exists in merely thinking about sound within a culture that so readily and pervasively privileges the eye over the ear. Visuality is so embedded that attempts at redress seem doomed to tautology. Many contemporary theories and philosophies, in fact, invoke aural, sonic, musical, and preguttural metaphors at the points where they are unable to speak, at the limits of language.[2] How can we then rely on the same theories and philosophies to query the very sounds heard during such moments of inarticulation? How, for instance, can listening be explained when the subject in recent theory has been situated, no matter how askew, in the web of the gaze, mirroring, reflection, the spectacle, and other ocular tropes? Visually disposed language, furthermore, favors thinking about sound as an object, but sound functions poorly in this regard: it dissipates, modulates, infiltrates other sounds, becomes absorbed and deflected by actual objects, and fills a space surrounding them. And the very attempt to establish a historical object, to understand the scattered, fleeting, and highly mediated history of sound, leads to an uncharacteristic state for sound itself. We are dealing here, however, with historical events that by their nature do not exist in inviolable perceptual or phenomenal states. They are necessarily cultivated amid the clutter of the sensorium and episteme. It is the task in these circumstances, then, to keep an eye on how at any specific moment the culture of visuality impinges upon the realms of sound and hearing as we speak about them. In my own attempt to underscore some larger attributes of the history of sound and radio in the avant-garde, I will first point to various artistic links to sound recording technologies and then propose a schema of three figures of sound operative in the arts since the late nineteenth century. These two approaches are not meant to displace the more complex analyses that occur at local levels but are instead offered here as other means of

Douglas Kahn

exploration, ones that I hope will result in generating understanding closer to the topic at hand.

It is no coincidence that the essays in this volume deal primarily with sound mediated by technology. From the beginning of the modern artistic fixation on sound, which was concurrent with the phonographic capture of sound in the late nineteenth century, to contemporary media arts, the connection between sound and technology has endured. In fact, we only begin to really hear *about* sound as a cultural entity with the introduction of Cros' paleophone and Edison's phonograph right into the midst of ascendant modernist and avant-garde culture. The timing of the two was perhaps no coincidence, for here was a machined fusion of orality and literacy, the completed artistic/cultural incidence of sound per se and thus a foregrounding of the isolation of other perceptual objects and operations, the first articulate return of the selfsame voice as had been experienced with the mirrored face since the first self-consciousness of the species, the totalizing cornu/copia of all and every sound, a plenitude that true to its course would expansively reproduce itself through exchanges amid its newfound elemental state—a technological incursion into apperception and communication during the heyday of imperial expansion.

The phonograph provoked many responses from within the arts, no matter whether or not it could be employed as a technology in the making of art. The ideational mission of the phonograph, in fact, totally outstripped any practical application for decades to come, for its conceptual implications were much more accessible, mobile, and workable than its actual mechanics. Save for rare instances, the phonograph was simply not taken up in the arts as a topical concern; there were no portraits; instead, by making the boundaries between humans and machines, writing and voice, human sounds and worldly sounds, music and noise, much more problematic, it lent itself to more important matters: if a machine like the phonograph could now talk, mock subjectivity, and invoke the dead, it followed that humans could record the previously unrecordable, the technologically inaccessible regions of consciousness or the mysterious. Voices could thus be installed to complete existing circuits of dread or desire, one example being how the famed *fin de siècle* misogyny so readily intersected with phonography. Apparently, the spectre of a technologization of humans sparked by the phonographic animation of voice proved to be a perfect outlet. Very soon after his friend Charles Cros placed his patent for his pre-Edisonian phonograph, Villiers de l'Isle-Adam began writing his novel *L'Eve future*, in which a fictional Edison, so-named, constructs a gynoid whose intelligence is given voice by two phonographs located where her lungs would have normally been and beneath where the synthetic breasts are. In Marcel Schwob's *La Machine à parler*, discussed in Charles Grivel's essay, a horrible monster operated by a woman from a keyboard frightens the narrator with its even more horrible phonemes. That the phonographic voice could live on after the body that had originally given rise to the voice had died provided the themes of reanimation of the dead found in both Maurice Renard's *La Mort et le coquillage* and Raymond Roussel's *Locus Solus*. Some phonographic literature incorporated the machine's technological attributes into their own operations. The violence of Alfred Jarry's *Phonographe* is simulated in the text itself, which skips into repetition like a faulty phonograph; we can also detect phonographic relations in Roussel's writing method, in his youthful ecstasy, and certainly in the scene in *Locus Solus* where a psychiatric patient of sorts attempts to write phonographically the voice of his daughter, who had been trampled to death by bandits.

Between how acts of writing were disposed to technology and how technology was later used in the arts, there was an inclination for authors and artists to internalize the attributes of phonography, to move it from representation closer to experience. For instance, Surrealism's founder André Breton brought principles of recording into his own body as a form of psychotechnics, implanting a trope into the brain where actual technology could not go. He used the term "modest recording instruments" in the 1924 *Manifesto* to speak of, among other things, automatic writing, that quasi-scientific transcription, the faithful recording of the incessant murmuring of the unconscious. The term had been derived, through the autoanalysis of French Dynamic Psychiatry, from telecommunications practices in the late nineteenth century, as noted in Christopher Schiff's essay in this volume.

Italian Futurism's founder, F. T. Marinetti, also technologized his body. In "Destruction of Syntax—Wireless Imagination—Words in Freedom" he clearly stated that deep-seated effects of modern technology upon body and soul were, in fact, inescapable. "Those who use the telephone today, the telegraph, the phonograph, the train, bicycle or automobile, the ocean liner, dirigible or airplane, the cinema or a great daily newspaper (the synthesis of a day in the whole world) do not dream that these diverse forms of communication, transportation and information exert such a decisive influence upon their psyches."[3] In 1911 Marinetti covered the Italo-Turkish War in Libya as a war correspondent for *L'Intransigeant* of Paris, and then, about a year later, he was in the Balkan War. His report from the trenches of Adrianopolis was an example of *parole in libertà* (words-in-freedom) that would appear in the 1914 collection *Zang-tumb-tuum, Adrianopoli, ottobre 1912* as "Bombardment." In it Marinetti takes on the role of the phonograph by enacting an onomatopoetic reportage of the *ZANG-TUMB-TUUUMB* of the cannons, the *taratatata* of the machine guns, and other sounds interspersed with musical instructions. As he eagerly recounted, "I finished that short synthesizing noise-making poem while witnessing the machine-gunning of three thousand horses ordered by the Turkish general who was the governor before the fortress fell."[4] The widespread influence of this poem, especially in its relation to the whole genre of *parole in libertà*—"Words-in-freedom were born on two battlefields Tripoli and Adrianople"[5]—can be followed into two important trends within the subsequent avant-garde: noise music and sound poetry. Luigi Russolo's 1913 "The Art of Noises" manifesto contained Marinetti's report from Adrianopolis under the guise of a personal correspondence and used it as a key rhetorical element; in fact Russolo's 1916 book of the same name contains a chapter entitled "The Noises of War." Likewise, in Zurich in 1916, with the war all around, Hugo Ball had Marinetti's *parole in libertà* as an inspiration for his famous Dada sound poetry performance at the Cabaret Voltaire. Thus, to the myriad of other less unseemly influences already acknowledged by historians that had a formative role on the avant-garde, experimental music, *bruitisme,* and sound poetry in this century, there must be added Marinetti's phonographic celebration of militarism.

The validity of utilizing actual phonographic technologies within artworks was recognized by many artists central to the history of the avant-garde, as it has been written. Among them was Guillaume Apollinaire, who, in his last major essay before his death, "The New Spirit and the Poets" (1918), criticized Marinetti's onomatopoetic practices of carrying the "new spirit to excess."[6] Excess ostensibly results from the reduction of poetry to a "kind of imitative harmony that would not even have the excuse of being exact."[7]

I, at least, cannot conceive of a poem consisting merely of the imitation of a noise that cannot be associated with any lyrical, tragical, or emotional meaning. If some poets indulge in this game we must see in it no more than an exercise, a kind of rough sketch of elements to be included in some given work. The "brekekekex coax" of Aristophanes' Frogs is nothing if it is separated from the play from which it derives its comical and satirical connotations. The "iiiii" of Francis Jammes's bird utters for an entire line is a paltry imitative harmony if it is divorced from the poem whose fantasy it helps enhance.[8]

Douglas Kahn

"Why," asks Apollinaire, "would anyone want to verbally imitate worldly sounds such as the Futurist-like 'whirring of an airplane' when auditive reality will 'always be superior?'"[9] If one were truly interested in creating an illusion of auditive reality, the phonograph could better perform the task. "Conceivably, imitative harmony might play a certain role, but it can serve as foundation only for an art that will make use of machines. For instance, a poem or a symphony in which the phonograph will play a part might well consist of noises artistically chosen and lyrically combined or juxtaposed."[10] Apollinaire, perhaps because of the phonographic quality of his "conversation-poems," foresaw a future where the "new spirit" would be tied up with technology, where the phonograph and cinema would "be the only forms of reproduction, and when as a result poets will enjoy a freedom hitherto unknown."[11]

The inevitable march of technological devices also informed Kurt Weill's attitude toward radio, but instead of providing new tools or conditions to set free a certain class of artists, as Apollinaire thought would be the case for poets, Weill felt that an entirely new art form would come into existence. The meteoric rise of radio in the Weimar Republic prompted Weill to write in 1926, "Within a remarkably short period of time, radio has become one of the most essential elements of public life. Today, it is one of the most frequently discussed topics among all segments of the population and in all organs of public opinion."[12] Yet it was still too early to "foresee what new types of instruments and sound-producing devices may develop," but there could be no "doubt that the preconditions for the development of an independent artistic genre of equal stature [with the other arts] are present." Just as radical proponents of sound film warned against using it simply to reproduce theater, Weill argued that radio must resist "reproduction of earlier artistic achievements" and instead work to develop an autonomous "radio art."[13]

Yet artists who attempted to incorporate technology directly into their work were guaranteed neither technological nor artistic success. In the avant-garde milieu in Petrograd during 1916, the young Dziga Vertov drew upon his background in writing and music and directed it "into an enthusiasm for editing shorthand records [stenographs] and gramophone recordings. Into a special interest in the possibility of documentary sound recording. Into experiments in recording, with words and letters, the noise of a waterfall, the sounds of a lumbermill, etc., a 'Laboratory of Hearing.'"[14]

He attempted to launch his laboratory with a 1900- or 1910-model Pathéphone wax disc recorder. "I had the original idea of the need to enlarge our ability to organize sound, to listen not only to singing or violins, the usual repertoire of gramophone disks, but to transcend the limits of ordinary music. I decided that the concept of sound included all the audible world. As part of my experiments, I set out to record a sawmill."[15] Presumably, he became frustrated with the poor sound quality, the nonplasticity of the medium, or the stricture of one generation; indeed, he spoke of his transition to film in terms of an inadequacy of phonographic technology.

Upon returning from a train station, there lingered in my ears the signs and rumble of the departing train ... someone's swearing ... a kiss ... someone's exclamation ... laughter, a whistle, voices, the ringing of the station's bell, the puffing of the locomotive ... whispers, cries, farewells ... And thoughts while walking: I must get a piece of equipment that won't describe, but will record, photograph these sounds. Otherwise, it's impossible to organize, edit them. They rush past, like time. But the movie camera perhaps? Record the visible ... Organize not the audible, but the visible world. Perhaps that's the way out?[16]

His inability to "phonograph sounds," in Edison's words, resulted in a desire to "photograph these sounds." Thus, the famed Kino-Eye, the fetish of much post–World War II experimental film, was ironically the result of a frustrated ear.

Douglas Kahn

László Moholy-Nagy also met with technical difficulties. In his 1922 *De Stijl* article "Production—Reproduction," he expressed a desire, already quite common among technologists in the 1880s, to read and write sound through the graphic figures inscribed into a wax record by a phonograph needle.

An extension of [the phonograph] for productive purposes could be achieved as follows: the grooves are incised by human agency into the wax plate, without any external mechanical means, which then produce sound effects ... The primary condition for such work is laboratory experiments: precise examination of the kinds of grooves (as regards length, width, depth etc.) brought about by the different sounds; examination of the man-made grooves; and finally mechanical-technical experiments for perfecting the groove-manuscript score. (or perhaps the mechanical reduction of large groovescript records.)[17]

He later attempted to realize this idea using the visible lines of recorded sound that run along the edge of optical sound film. In *The Sound of ABC*, one attempt in a genre of "drawn sound films" in the European avant-garde during that time, graphic figures such as letters, lines, and profiles were scratched onto the sound track and then played back through the projector. He was known to ask people, "I wonder how your nose will sound?"[18] A film in which drawn sound was employed, along with other techniques of manipulating sound, was *Romance Sentimentale* (1930), certainly the first sound film made *by* Russians, if not *in* Russia. It was made in France and is usually attributed only to Grigori Alexandrov but, arguably, Sergei Eisenstein was also quite involved, even though he persistently tried to dissociate himself from the film because it was such a failure.[19] In particular, the film's opening visual montage of nature scenes, very much in the style of Eisenstein, runs parallel to a radically constructed sound track. The American film critic Harry Potamkin talked with Alexandrov about his use of sound; in these comments we can find, as in the work of Moholy-Nagy, the long-standing desire to merge the technologies of phonography and writing into a new vocal form of sound synthesis.

[Alexandrov] has done in this film a number of things I have thought basic in "playing with sound," such as: running the sound-track backwards, inscribing or designing the sound (sound is after all only inscription). He cut the sound inscription.

... A lexandrov, so he told me, has played with the designs of sound by inscribing it directly on the negative and allowing light to make the final registration. ... By studying the inscriptions closely one may come to an exact knowledge of these inscriptions and read them as easily as one reads musical notes for sound. The inscription for speech and that of sound differ only in the composition of the intervals and a close student will come to recognize the peculiarities of the different impressions. Actually sound will be created without being uttered![20]

Optical film sound was used more successfully, if less adventurously, during the late 1920s in the Weimar Republic for radio works created by Walter Ruttmann ("Weekend") and Friedrich Walther Bischoff ("Hello! You're Tuned to Radio Earth!!"), as discussed in Mark Cory's essay. Similar techniques were used in the 1930s for American animated cartoons and in France beginning in the late 1940s with the *musique concrète* compositions of Pierre Schaeffer, who had begun composing with phonographic disc-cutting equipment before (reluctantly) moving on to magnetic audiotape. Obviously, with the precedence of phonograph lathes and optical sound film in the 1920s, the inheritance from the German military of the magnetic audiotape recorder by post–World War II composers and artists did not have the technologically determinist effect upon artistic practice so often attributed to it; that is, its mere availability did not spontaneously engender an art appropriate to it. Yet there was indeed at least a quantitative increase in activities, ascribed by artists themselves to the easier access and availability of the tape recorder. Most of the activities in the 1950s, however, were restricted to musical practice, for instance, the works of Pierre Schaeffer, Pierre Henry, and others with the *Groupe de Recherche de Musique Concrète*, John Cage, or, within popular culture, the novelty cut-ups of Bill Buchanan and Dickie Goodman and others.

Douglas Kahn

In contrast, the audiotape cut-up collaborations of William Burroughs and Brion Gysin, as discussed in Robin Lydenberg's essay, took a literary tack. The cut-ups were derived from reworked Dada collage techniques, but Burroughs' ideas surrounding them, set forth in his novels, essays, and audiotapes, elaborated a new system of recorded sound that metaphorically extended the idea of recording from a psychobiological *recording* at the level of genetic code—formed by the cipher of the four DNA bases—on out to the larger realms of political conspiracy and spiritist forces. This writing could tie together the proliferating genetic material of viruses, the syntax of language, and the contagion of ideologies, the segmentations of bodies and systems. Audiotape bore an unreadable inscription of reconfigured metallic particles upon its surface that could manifest action at other locations of writing, from genetic code to the clandestine and coded actions of conspiracy. Just hearing certain recorded sounds could change bodies and move people into unwilled action. Although involved in the production of many audiotape cut-ups, Burroughs nevertheless did encounter technical difficulties while moving from metaphor to artistic technology. In the literary cut-ups of newspapers and other texts, Burroughs was able to "write across" the cut, that is, he was able to interject his own words as a bridge or to pare down adjacent words to suture a cut. He could thereby generate and select richer texts, highly resonant in their fragmentation, to introduce as elements within certain novels. He was unable, on the other hand, to write across the cuts of audiotape; a cut severely impaired any mobility of sounds and voices, and any literary impulse, to be productive, had to be surrendered to the winds of chance and to the overlays of profusive interpretation that would furnish it with significance.

The literary and musical activities during the 1950s using magnetic audiotape were accompanied by artworks that manipulated phonograph records themselves, precursors to the avant-garde and hip-hop scratch artists of today. Experimentation continued in the decades following, in cinema, experimental music, das Neue

were not entertained through concepts of objecthood and corporeality, as commonly done within technological discourses during the same time. And the idea of an autonomous "sound" had to wait for the leverage of phonography to be felt within culture. A decade into the twentieth century, at the cusp of the major cultural incursion of inscriptive figures, Marcel Duchamp, in his conceptual approach to sound and aurality, satirized the inability of vibrational space to generate objects and bodies with his idea for an acoustic Venus de Milo, a life all her own but existing in neither stone nor flesh.[22] Raymond Roussel similarly satirized synesthesia; in one of his novels, the names of flowers called out into a ravine echo back accompanied by their respective scents. This, of course, did not prevent the concurrent or subsequent repetition and elaboration of synesthetic ideas within the arts.

Although most figures of vibration evaporated out into the heavens, it should be noted that an exception can be found in "Ka" (1915), a story by the Russian Futurist poet Velimir Khlebnikov. The story employed the type of determinism and universality found in synesthesia, but at least it was sufficiently eccentric and ecological that it managed to stay on earth. Ka is a mythic figure, a time traveler capable of taking different forms, "the soul's shadow, its double, its envoy to the world some snoring gentleman dreams of."[23] Well into the story Ka is a bird flying near the source of the Nile, where he joins a circle of apes who sit around a fire reminiscing about the Roc bird. Then Ka fashions an oracular lyre, a remarkable instrument using a Pythagorean correlation between musical tone and historical chronology, derived from Khlebnikov's "Tables of Destiny," a set of calculations mapping the temporal relationships of past events.

Ka set an elephant tusk on end and at the top, as if they were pegs for strings, he fastened the years 411, 709, 1237, 1453, 1871; and below on the footboard the years 1491, 1193, 665, 449, 31. Strings joined the upper and the lower pegs; they vibrated faintly.[24]

Douglas Kahn

Ka asks a beautiful female ape to sing, and she takes up the lyre and begins singing a song of the Fates.

She moved her hand across the strings; they sounded the thunder boom of a flock of swans that settles as one body onto a lake.

Ka observed that each string consisted of six parts, each part consisting of 317 years, 1902 years in all. And also that the top row of pegs indicated years when the East attacked the West, while the pegs at the lower end of the strings indicated an opposite movement, the West against the East. In the top row were the Vandals, Arabs, Tatars, Turks, and Germans; below were the Egyptians of Hatshepsut, the Greeks of Odysseus, the Scythians, the Greeks of Pericles, the Romans. Ka attached one additional string: between the year 78, the invasion of the Scythians of Adia Saka, and the year 1980—the East. Ka studied the possibilities of playing on all seven strings.[25]

INSCRIPTION

While figures of vibration head for the heavens, figures of inscription pull sounds down to earth, much like Rabelais' "frozen sounds" that sit, the size of plums, upon the ground in a variety of colors, waiting for the spring thaw. One thing that attached inscripted sound to the earth's surface was its tie to technology. There was no effectively new technology associated with figures of vibration; it depended instead on the old technology of the ancient Greek monochord and other stringed instruments for its elaboration. Figures of inscription, on the other hand, were associated with the phonograph of the late nineteenth century and the phonautograph not too long before it. The cultural implications of phonography were profound for the reasons stated in the previous section (see also my essay on Raymond Roussel and phonography in this volume), and these implications could be as evident as the jagged line that the stylus etched onto lampblack, paper, tin, or wax. First of all, the acoustic events in synesthesia only carried weight in concept because in actuality they consisted merely of conventionally pitched musical tones and phonemes. An inscripted sound could be any sound, even a very distant or dead one, and the whole process of inscription was in no way limited to the prosaic sounds rehearsed within synesthetic systems. Inscripted sounds were, on the contrary, apperceptual, empirical, scriptural, and technological, capable of being seen, read, written, and drawn directly.

That the mechanical etching of any acoustic event could be seen spawned the idea in the late nineteenth century that the markings could be read and written and, therefore, could constitute a mechanically precise alphabet of *all sounds,* all that had been withheld and unexplored, an onset of plenitude that signaled anything from an unprecedented candor to the new imperial order. The notation of sound in musical notation and phonetics was crude in comparison, dependent as it was upon culture and interpretation, whereas phonography appeared to be the direct product of mechanics. Even conventional alphabets appeared to be superseded by the phonographic collapse of speech and writing into visible speech and vociferous graphemes. This hope against hope, premised on earlier ideas of universal alphabetics, themselves based upon the hope that the Biblical lost language had just been misplaced, was confirmed by the way sound was finally brought into the visualist and scriptural logic of Western culture. The phonograph promised that all and any sound whatsoever could be created "without being uttered!" as Alexandrov enthused.[26] "Without being uttered" meant not spoken, not played musically, especially not by wind instrument. Inscripted sound, in other words, meant something distant from the conceit of nothing-but-consciousness, from the necessity of human agency and metaphysical presence. This was a sound that could be given up to the content of the world exceeding human concerns alone, capable of invoking an ostensible "nature" that was not uttered within the familiar bounds of human speech or musical performance, while at the same time being subjected even more effectively to the machinations of material culture.

Douglas Kahn

There is obviously a major distinction, however, between the work of someone like Raymond Roussel and others during the early avant-garde, where sound is written on the *surface* of objects, and that of William Burroughs after World War II, where writing occurs submerged within a secretive *interior,* such as the site of genetic code, or in a way not easily readable, such as the reconfigurations of metallic particles on magnetic audiotape. It becomes difficult, after all, to read things at a subcellular scale without an electron microscope; but it is just this type of scientistic thread that can enhance any agenda: anything can grow from a seed you can't see. There is another important relationship between the submerged inscription of sound and objects and bodies: inscription establishes the concreteness of "surfaces" in the interior that, in the process of reading or writing, may break through the skin or reconfigure the body (note the anomalous bodies in Burroughs' writings). Furthermore, as with genetic engineering, writing is a seed from which entire bodies may grow, but there also exists the possibility of severe mutation, injury, and destruction, set off simply by the act of reading and writing, of bringing the text to light, of turning a body inside out to expose the inscription, a violence that accompanies the technologization of the body and the abeyance of sonic movement.

TRANSMISSION

The most pronounced impression produced by figures of vibration was that of spatiality, whereas inscription reduced space into impressions upon a surface. Despite the fact that vibrational space was ultimately an ordered one and could exist in idealized representation alone, it did simulate the acoustic space that sound both creates and inhabits. The problem was that actual acoustic space included bodies and objects rarely positioned in harmonic relationship with one another, and rife among real acoustics were noises that raise havoc with any attempt to structure a system. Inscription technologically incorporated noises and mundane sounds of actual objects and bodies but at the expense of diminishing the "vibrancy" of space, its expansiveness and mobility, its objects and bodies, into cipher, stasis, and autonomy. Figures of vibration lived in the space of an imaginary world, whereas figures of inscription destroyed the space of the real world.

Figures of transmission combined aspects of both vibration and inscription, fusing the spatial features of vibration with the objecthood and corporeality of inscription, but exceeding them both in terms of complexity. Transmission could situate objects and bodies in inharmonic, noisy, and terrestrial relations without consuming their autonomy. In the harmonics, chromatics, and syllabic/phonetics of vibrational space, the autonomy of an object was always consumed by the existence of another object being manifested through it from a distance; whereas in transmissional space the object was ostensibly replicated in itself as it was transported over an equivalent distance; that is, disem*bodi*ment meant that an object or body existed in two places at once, as opposed to object or body referring to a corresponding color, tone, affect, etc. Vibrational space that had existed only in representation was given breadth and depth once again by a *signal* silently crisscrossing space, bearing both sonic content and the objects that had been demobilized by inscription in a variety of manners, internal and external, point-to-point and centripetal narrowcast, broadcast, to and from an isolated inscription, to and from inscripted objects and bodies, to and from objects and bodies, and to and from the spaces they inhabit and that inhabit them. In other words, transmission was basically the return and invigoration of objects and bodies that had been fixed by inscription to the space implied by vibration.

Transmission also implied a proliferation and differentiation of objects and situated them in a totalizing notion of space. This particular characteristic can be explained by distinctions between phonography and wireless/radio. Phonography established the objecthood of sound and the ability to replicate a myriad of objects, but it did not strongly imply sounds from a distance.

Wirelessness immediately meant great distances, thus all the references to the expanses of the oceans, to crowds, to other lands, and to the otherness of the unexplored globe. This globalness was finally determined, however, within the framework of where the technology was footed politically and historically. Yet, this newfound and newly populated space was not acoustic; the distance between replicated objects was a vacuum that collapsed space to an ideal of instantaneous transmission and reception, a communication without mediation. Sound existed at either end(s), but in between there was nothing but silence, reduced to the trajectory of a signal. This structure was anthropomorphized in several accounts of radio and transmission in general to ideas of unmediated communication, thought transference, and signal as corporeal sensation. A technology that had already been heavily invested with human fears and desires was elevated to vitalistic, prosthetic, and necrotic tropes as when, for instance, F. T. Marinetti and Pino Masnata, in their 1933 *La Radia* manifesto included in this volume, proposed an artistic materiality that would be "a pure organism of radio sensations," or when Khlebnikov in "The Radio of the Future" foretells of long-distance synesthetic healing without medicine and the transmission of an anthem of strength in production: "It is a known fact that certain notes like 'la' and 'ti' are able to increase muscular capacity, sometimes as much as sixty-four times, since they thicken the muscle for a certain length of time. During periods of intense hard work like summer harvests or during the construction of great buildings, these sounds can be broadcast by Radio over the entire country, increasing its collective strength enormously."[27]

Obviously, that transmission was restricted to earthly air did not mean that its was immediately wrested from the cosmos; instead, in early encounters one can find quick recourse to the spiritist notions of vibrational space. The Polish artist Stefan Themerson was capable of recuperating radio noise in a figure of vibration: "When I was 14 (in 1924) I built myself a wireless-set ... what fascinated me ... more than the fact of hearing a girl's singing voice coming to my earphones from such strange places as Hilversum, was the *noise,* to me the Noise of the Celestial Spheres, and the divine inter-ference-whistling when tuning. It became an instrument for produc-ing new, hitherto unheard sounds, which at the time no person would have thought had anything to do with 'music.'"[28]

In another instance, André Breton, writing his "Ode to Charles Fourier" in 1945, late in the age of radio, teased the grand harmonies of Fourier down from the stars and navigated them across the diapasonic seas of an invocatory keyboard:

> *Fourier what have they done with your keyboard*
> *That responded to everything with a chord*
> *Setting by the movements of the stars*
> > *from the capers of the smallest boat on the sea*
> > *to the great sweep of the proudest three-master*
> *You embraced unity you show it not as lost but as totally attainable*[29]

Just thinking about this oceanic expansion to all ends of the earth and the possibility for its instantaneous and simultaneous communication to a single moment of consciousness meant that the potent force of an unstructured, chaotic space was sent hurtling down onto individual means of expression, splintering them into fragments. Marinetti's "wireless imagination" credited wireless telegraphy with the collapse of syntax and analogy in *parole in libertà.* All conventions of relationality, traditionally confined as they were to local and man-ageable structures and comparisons, would break down once they were bombarded with a global infinitude of possible relations, all arriving at once with a newfound speed having "no connecting wires."[30] Wirelessness also operated less violently in Guillaume Apollinaire's 1916 story "The Moon King." In it a traveler seeking shelter is drawn into the subterranean passages of a mountain, where he hears sounds from a remote room. He finds there an elderly man he recognizes as King Ludwig II of Bavaria, thought to be drowned, sitting at an unusual keyboard instrument. When a key is pressed, Japan at dawn is heard.

Douglas Kahn

The flawless microphones of the king's device were set so as to bring in to this underground the most distant sounds of terrestrial life. Each key activated a microphone set for such-and-such a distance. Now we were hearing a Japanese country side. The wind soughed in the trees—a village was probably there, because I heard servants' laughter, a carpenter's plane, and the spray of an icy waterfall. Then another key pressed down, we were taken straight into morning, the king greeting the socialist labor of New Zealand, and I heard geysers spewing hot water. Then this wonderful morning continued in sweet Tahiti. Here we are at the market in Papeete, with the lascivious wahinees of New Cytheria wandering through it—you could hear their lovely guttural language, very much like ancient Greek. You could also hear the Chinese selling tea, coffee, butter, and cakes. The sound of accordions and Jew's harps.[31]

Then a train in the United States, urban noises of Chicago, vessels along the Hudson, prayers for Christ in Mexico, carnival in Rio, a teacup in Paris, a chorus in Bonn, hand games in Naples, and finally ten o'clock in Tripoli. Then the "king's fingers ran over the keys at random, simultaneously raising all the sounds of this world which we, standing still, had just toured aurally."[32]

Edgar Varèse aspired unsuccessfully to use the radiophonic space that Apollinaire could only imagine in his unrealized symphony *Espace*, initiated in Paris in 1929 and occupying him for over a decade. In an argument sketched out in 1941, he wrote,

Voices in the sky, as though magic, invisible hands were turning on and off the knobs of fantastic radios, filling all space, criss-crossing, overlapping, penetrating each other, splitting up, superimposing, repulsing each other, colliding, crashing. Phrases, slogans, utterances, chants, proclamations. China, Russian, Spain, the Fascist states and the opposing Democracies all breaking their paralyzing crusts.

... I suggest using, here and there, snatches of phrases of American, French, Russian, Chinese, Spanish, German revolutions like shooting stars, also recurring words poundingly repeated like hammer blows or throbbing in an underground ostenato, stubborn and ritualistic.[33]

In his biography of Varèse, Fernand Ouelette went a little further in explaining his plans: "Varèse had imagined a performance of the work being broadcast simultaneously in and from all the capitals of the world. The choirs, each singing in its own language, would have made their entries with mathematical precision. The work would have been divided up into seconds, with the greatest exactitude, so that the chorus in Paris—or Madrid, or Moscow, or Peking, or Mexico City, or New York—would have come onto the air at exactly the right moment."[34] Similarly, the practice of German Hörspiel during the Weimar Republic is replete with works that use the radio to collapse disparate reaches of the world into a unity, as discussed in Mark E. Cory's essay, and many works that play themselves out over the ocean for purposes spanning global solidarity to radiophonic *Lebensraum*.

In transmission the unknown expanses of the psyche were as intriguing and explorable as those of the earth. They two were brought together in the psychotechnics of Surrealist automatism. Inscriptive, stenographic practices took down the "magical *dictation*" from the "mouth of darkness" (Breton), the noisy gate to the unconscious,[35] but the action of the unconscious itself, its "voice," was delivered to the Surrealist by way of a radiophonic narrowcast. Even the literary voice privy to having overheard the unconscious could be described along these lines: in his *Treatise on Style* (1928), Louis Aragon detailed the physiognomy of someone unable to hear such a voice:

... your ear trimmed with a festoon of broderie anglaise, your ear the color of calves' feet, your tender ear of rubber, your ear, ever as waxy and buzzing as a hive, your little dirty cartilage that looks more like a poorly puffed fritter than a phonograph horn ... [36]

But when the ear that can hear is equipped with a sensitivity that radiophonically spans the oceans,

... more and more able to grasp in the grassy hollow of sentences the clear tinkling of a clinked glass that causes a man to die at sea each time, and the

same ceremony takes place, the sailors line up at the flag at half-mast, plop!
the bag in the waves carries the sleeper away.[37]

Likewise, the underground oracular voice of the unconscious was radiophonically transformed into a vast subterranean region that could be heard residing on the other side of the earth's surface. In discussing the "timbre" of Lautréamont's style ("I confer a very elevated meaning on the word style"[38]), Aragon describes the work of the intellect as an acoustic mining:

When the worker who was digging into the bowels of the earth—whether in knotty Asia or near the Italian sea, where the dust is lightest because it is made with the powder of statues—when this worker suddenly hears the steel of his pickax ring strangely, he bends over, questions the distant depth, and thinks he hears a dirge. To the bottom of the pit he glues an ear that is used to romances. What is this perpetual rumbling? A monstrous parade, an enormous troop which nothing wearies. Profuse resonance of subterranean carriages. The ebb and flow of hidden waters, where everything merges.[39]

Aragon's mining strikes an aqueous metaphor, which continues to flow while he describes the automatic speech of the poet Robert Desnos during the Surrealist "period of sleeps": "He spoke like no one speaks. The great common sea suddenly found itself in the room, which was any old room with its surprised utensils."[40] Here, the subterranean waters "where everything merges" are themselves transmitted into the room through the buccal spigot of a "sleep talking" Desnos, as though he were but a puncture on the surface of the earth and of consciousness, a breach through which can be heard "the echo of what we are tempted to consider as universal conscience" (Breton).[41] Desnos was such an avid "sleeper" that he eventually pressed the patience of his listeners too far, as evidenced by the episode when an intolerant Paul Eluard, to awaken Desnos, emptied a jug of water onto his chest. In 1932, several years after leaving the Surrealist ranks, Desnos replaced the transmission technology of his own body for that of radio broadcasting proper, working in

Information et Publicité to create what he thought of as either an extension of poetry or a return to it: radio advertising. "I threw myself passionately into the almost mathematical, yet intuitive, work of adapting words to music, of fabricating sentences, proverbs and mottoes for advertising, the primary exigency of this work being a return to the people's taste in the way of rhyme."[42] As his wife, Youki Desnos, recounts, "Robert's ambition—and how many times he repeated it to me—was outside of his pure poetic work, to create songs which could sweep through the streets, to be whistled by a boy pedaling a carrier tricycle, for example, or murmured from ear to ear by lovers."[43] In other words, Desnos abandoned the "universal consciousness" that populated the unconscious for the crowded unconscious of "the People." Goods and services lodged in the bodies of jingles and songs were recorded into the minds of thousands of French people in order to be irrepressibly repeated. Desnos thereby socialized himself by radiophonically transmitting an entirely denatured "period of sleeps" and extending the transmitter from the psychotechnical device of his own body to the crowd.

In terms of historical sequence, figures of transmission might seem like a return of sorts to the space of vibrations and objects and bodies of phonography, had these very figures themselves not been available since the late nineteenth century as well. A more complete account of their histories will have to wait for another occasion. They have been proposed here, along with the outline of art and phonography, as methods to cohere a wide range of scattered events and ideas; the cohesion need not be a narrative one. The following essays certainly supply enough information and analysis to gain further bearings on this history and will hopefully provoke research into the field of sound and aurality, sound recording and radio in the arts, that will delve into greater detail, propose other ways of theoretical and historical understanding across the arts in general, and engender a complex sense of artistic possibility among practitioners.

Douglas Kahn

NOTES

1. For a discussion of the discursive and technological relationship of music to the aural arts see Douglas Kahn, "Track Organology," *October* 55 (Winter 1991).

2. This line of thought has been introduced by Frances Dyson in "Notions of Acoustic Truth," the unpublished abstract for her Ph.D. dissertation from the University of Technology, Sydney, 1990.

3. F. T. Marinetti, "Destruction of Syntax—Wireless Imagination—Words in Freedom," *Lacerba*, 11 May and 15 June 1913, translated in Richard J. Pioli, *Stung by Salt and War: Creative Texts of the Italian Avant-Gardist F. T. Marinetti* (New York: Peter Lang, 1987), p. 45.

4. F. T. Marinetti, *Selected Writings*, ed. R. W. Flint (New York: Farrar, Straus and Giroux, 1972), pp. 332–333.

5. F. T. Marinetti, "From the Café Bulgaria in Sofia to the Courage of the Italians in the Balkans and the Military Spirit of Désarrois," in *Selected Writings*, p. 332.

6. Guillaume Apollinaire, "The New Spirit and the Poets," published as an addendum in Francis Steegmuller, *Apollinaire: Poet Among the Painters* (Freeport, NY: Books for Libraries Press, 1971), p. 280.

7. Ibid., p. 281.

8. Ibid., pp. 281-282.

9. Ibid., p. 282.

10. Ibid., p. 281.

11. Ibid., p. 279.

12. Kurt Weill, "Radio and the Restructuring of Music Life" (1926) in *Writings of German Composers*, ed. Jost Hermand and James Steakley (New York: Continuum, 1984).

13. Ibid.

14. Dziga Vertov, *Kino-Eye: The Writings of Dziga Vertov*, ed. Annette Michelson (Berkeley: University of California, 1984), p. 40.

15. Dziga Vertov, "Speech of 5 April 1935," cited in Seth Feldman, *Evolution of Style in the Early Work of Dziga Vertov* (New York: Arno Press, 1977), p. 13. For an astute comparison to Russolo's work, a source which influenced Vertov, refer to Feldman's comments on pp. 12–15.

16. Ibid., p. 40.

17. See Krisztina Passuth, *Moholy-Nagy* (New York: Thames and Hudson, 1985), p. 289.

18. Sibyl Moholy-Nagy, *Moholy-Nagy: Experiment in Totality* (New York: Harper & Brothers, 1950), pp. 68, 97. Although it is unfortunate that this film is lost, the sound generated by this technique would probably have resembled a bird whistle of sorts, alternating with thin, scratchy sounds.

19. Luis Buñuel concurs: "Eisenstein's friends have tried to blame Alexandrov for the debâcle of the dreadful and shoddy production of *Romance Sentimentale*. But I saw Eisenstein making it with my own eyes, since he was shooting it on the stage next to me when I was making *L'Age d'or*." (Cited in Francisco Aranda, *Luis Buñuel: A Critical Biography* [New York: Da Capo, 1976], p. 87.) A full accounting of Eisenstein's participation in this film, along with his other early failures and frustrations relating to sound film, could not only fundamentally disrupt notions of Eisenstein's position on sound film but could also, because of his reliance on aural, musical, and synesthetic metaphors throughout his theoretical writings, require a reformulation of much more.

20. Harry Potamkin, "Playing with Sound," in *The Compound Cinema: The Film Writings of Harry Alan Potamkin* (New York: Teachers College Press, Columbia University, 1977), pp. 86–88.

21. Synesthesia exists only in a privatized articulation and even then within select few individuals, as evidenced by the variation of synesthetic systems listed in Gordon's essay. The attempts to socialize these solitary perceptions into a communicative mode could only survive among ideologies of the artist as an innate generator of languages.

22. See Douglas Kahn, "Acoustic Sculpture, Deboned Voices," *Public* (Fall/Winter 1990/1991), pp. 23–34.

23. Velimir Khlebnikov, "Ka," in *The Collected Works of Velimir Khlebnikov, Volume 2: Prose, Plays and Supersagas*, trans. Paul Schmidt, ed. Charlotte Douglas (Cambridge, MA: Harvard University Press, 1989), p. 56.

24. Ibid., p. 67.

25. Ibid., pp. 67–68.

26. Harry Potamkin, "Playing with Sound," p. 88.

27. Velimir Khlebnikov, "The Radio of the Future," in *The Collected Works of Velimir Khlebnikov, Volume 1: Letters and Theoretical Writings*, trans. Paul Schmidt, ed. Charlotte Douglas (Cambridge, MA: Harvard University Press, 1987), p. 395.

28. Stefan Themerson, letter to Henri Chopin, reprinted in the review *Ou* 36–37 (c. 1969).

29. André Breton, "Ode to Charles Fourier," excerpted in Marcel Jean, ed., *The Autobiography of Surrealism* (New York: The Viking Press, 1980), p. 404.

30. Marinetti, *Stung by Salt and War*, p. 48.

31. Guillaume Apollinaire, "The Moon King," in *The Poet Assassinated*, trans. Ron Padgett (San Francisco: North Point Press, 1984), p. 80.

32. Ibid., p. 81.

33. Dorothy Norman, "Edgar Varèse: Ionization—Espace," *Twice a Year*, (Fall–Winter, 1941), pp. 259–260.

34. Fernand Ouellette, *Edgard Varèse* (London: Calder & Boyars, 1973), p. 132.

35. André Breton, "Entrée des médiums" (1922), excerpted and translated in *The Autobiography of Surrealism*, ed. Marcel Jean (New York: The Viking Press, 1980), p. 101.

36. Louis Aragon, *Treatise on Style* (1928), trans. Alyson Waters (Lincoln: University of Nebraska Press, 1991), p. 106.

37. Ibid.

38. Ibid., p. 105.

39. Ibid., pp. 103–104.

40. Ibid., p. 104.

41. Breton, "Entrée des médiums," p. 101.

42. Quoted from Robert Desnos, *Etat de veille (Waking State)* in Mary Ann Caws, *The Surrealist Voice of Robert Desnos* (Amherst: University of Massachusetts Press, 1977), p. 9.

43. Youki Desnos, "Desnos poète populaire," *Simoun*, "Robert Desnos" issue (1956,) pp. 52–54, quoted in Steven Kovács, *From Enchantment to Rage* (Rutherford, NJ: Fairleigh Dickinson University Press, 1980), p. 52.

CHARLES GRIVEL

THE PHONOGRAPH'S HORNED MOUTH

translated from the French

by Stephen Sartarelli

The phonograph's horned mouth; the twisted mouth of someone expressing himself. Grimaces, frowns, contractions of cheekbones, laughing and not laughing, grinning. The voice passing through a body, a conduit, the fact of pipes. Surfacing, skimming, blossoming: bulb. The deforming voice. The relation of the speaker to his voice, his body, imaginary or not. The sort of spasm that the production of a sound provokes in him. He expresses himself by excretion, constriction of the organs and muscles. His expression does not come without contortion of his appearance. Puckering, damage.

The one speaking is someone else; the one speaking does not recognize himself, and yet is only that. I have never been able to tolerate the sound of my own voice, nor the appearance that this voice—when so displaced, so forced, so unrecognizably come from without—suggests to me, or seems to have. Division of speech, split of self from self: someone else who speaks is inside me. I can hear the mechanism he starts up, the tick-tock and the key winding up, the sound of chains and wheels, elongation, spring, song yet the censure of song, the abruptness committed, inside the flesh.

From a rupture to the body, by way of its ear.

A machine is a mass; it has a form, a shape, a body. We only invent machines that are bodies; we invent machines after our bodies; we recognize ourselves through them, in them, in their form: machines. *Machine-mirrors*. Machines that give back to us a portrait, the secret project, of ourselves. General thesis: man only invents in his own image. He only discovers that which resembles him. And only to this end: resemblance. Doing so that what did not exist comes to be and corresponds. Making an identity with the self arise from nothing. This was not that, and this becomes me. The inventor or engineer in me operates in the organs of a body required to be analogous to the one I possess, which I don't have. The goal is to identify oneself. To invent identity for oneself, to add it on, to give good weight: the more it is lacking on one side (economics), the more it adds on to the other (person). So here I am, endowed with an imaginary carcass (with an element of carcass) of sure profitability. The industrial and lucrative function of a machine is not in question: we note only that the mental investment it represents contaminates its form as well as every operation it is expected to perform. It carries, for example, a sound: but why sound? How? What inventiveness, what skill makes it possible to capture it? The machine is a medium: I make it say a bit more about my desire, a bit louder, a bit deeper. Or better yet: as subject, I can turn anything to account; everything comes at the right moment in my project of generalized appropriation: the vegetable and animal realm, and everything else I can imagine myself adding to it. The more a society uses me to these ends, the more—conversely—I stick to employing symbolically the means of production implied in the process for my own benefit. Identification as opposed to de-individualization. I imagine against everything that is done to me. Of course, it is an artificial opposition: if a machine produces everything it wishes (its uses and my work), it is because it provides, in other respects, something to satisfy me (my imaginary pleasure).

Let us take the phonograph. One of the possible machines. At least one of those come from afar, having spanned all of History, now ending up in our room, inseparable from ourselves. Ulysses, long ago, bound to his mast, his ears stripped of their wax plugs, represents to us this fascinating hand-to-hand combat with a noise come up from the depths, imperceptible, irresistible yet unknowable: so who's talking in the song I hear?

The phonograph, invented by Cros and Edison in 1877, a mechanism for reproducing voices, sounds, tones, and music, a set of forms given to what it does: a pavilion (an ear), a horn (a mouth or beak), a record (a tongue), claws and talons (fingers): a machine with a body. An animal machine, grasping, clasping, cannibalistic. Symbol "become life," that is, substance, of a being articulated like a sex (or rather like two!) and violently applied upon the listener. Machine par excellence, which its user applies to himself and recognizes.

At just about the same time, Rimbaud was writing that *"je est un autre"* (I is someone else), Mallarmé that a blank volume is his expression, Lautréamont that poetry is made up of everything and by everyone, and Nietzsche, of course, that since God is dead, the voice, without reservation, dissolves. A machine arrives in the nick of time to capture all this and give it an appearance. It is reproduced, and one can see that it is reproduced: a box with wheels tells us so. The visualization of the process implies its irreversibility, its irremediability. The repeating machine inside poetry: inspiration seemed to come from elsewhere, a breath seemed to span from top to bottom, descended from Olympus—henceforth, this inspiration goes of itself. If someone speaks, it's of himself. A voice comes from a voice comes from a voice comes from a voice. Generic transmission. An infinite sense bursts forth from an organ given a body *outside the body*. Respondence is produced, desire is produced. (It's the love cycle: Cros himself says this in a story—*La Science de l'amour;* the recording machine is the culmination.)

Man doesn't hear himself. Not too well. Never tires of hearing himself. He lacks self, the transfer to self. Everything that would enable him to respond to himself. Not enough mirrors around me, he says; my image is never sufficiently my image; it lacks signs, views, corroborators. The self only exists as long as it can be shown to me. In full, on the surface, sound-matter, flux, substance. From inside out, then—inversely—from outside in: the road back is reproduction; I displace myself in returning, I come back.

If I write, it's by consolation. Sculpting, painting, photographing in order to bring back an appearance and a name. I hone my techniques and instruments with the same gesture, out of insatiability with myself: the self is what is most cruelly lacking in me, since I am tied down to it. Eighteen fifty: an ideology of the subject-citizen-worker is in place, but, in the opposite direction, so is an economy of the consumer denatured to programmed needs. Oneself is of course that with which one endows it in language (it is legitimate to freely draw one's own conclusion therefrom), but also that of which one strips it in reality (no positive science, and no market system, is based on an individuality). Result: the social awaits the contrivances capable of certifying for the subject the existence of the subject. Reproducing mechanisms that would reduce anxiety, in short: photography, panorama, phenakistoscope, and many others—typewriter, railways, cablecars, steam-engines, wheels. Intellectuals and inventors are hard at work: accelerating the circulation of goods, accelerating the certification of personhood. To the extent that goods multiply, the means to producing the identity necessary for guaranteeing their consumption are also multiplied. Objects on the one hand, symbols on the other, they for me and I for them. Less to disalienate an individual henceforth given to the pursuit of better-being, than to add in him (like him) the symbolic unity fit to endow him by virtue (but also by fiction) of a nature justifying his desires. So desire comes from without? Fine, an identificatory mass will prudishly cast the veil and constitute the untouched point of origin from which it emanates. The reproduction machine is for beginning this: giving the subject an origin, making it symbolically first, automatically engendering ego to the ego. The machine causes me, since in a reverse take of its action I discover myself in memory, in eye, vision, basis. As if it were true that I am.

Charles Grivel

Thesis: The phonograph emphasizes the self in the lack of subject. This machine bears a paradox: it identifies a voice, fixes the deceased (or mortal) person, registers the dead and thus perpetuates his living testimony, but also achieves his automatic reproduction *in absentia:* my self would live *without me*—horror of horrors! "The pavilion of a person's ear is the larger, the less this person can hear," writes Breton.[1] Thus the phonograph, to begin, is an enormous adventitious ear added to a body lacking in perception— one that does not perceive itself well. This sort of perfected ear trumpet thus compensates for a deficit in the symbolic body that I am: I never have enough ear, for I am never enough myself. I dream of myself, therefore I invent. And in inventing this mechanical form, I graft upon myself the irremediable impression of my death.

Interdependence between what I do and think, in memory and in reality. Double orientation of the objects I take, objects come from far behind the driving forces I recognize in them, objects fit to accomplish the tasks for which I believe them to be made. A phonograph seduces doubly every time: it fulfills its little nasal function and roots me in reality as I cannot imagine. It reproduces and it symbolizes, the one with the other, the one inside the other, inseparable. "The force of the tools that a society provides itself and that of its imagination are never dissociable."[2] What exists outside of us, like a machine increasing the power of the hand or the ear, also works its damage mentally. Projection, but also retrojection: what I see represents me, what I form fulfills me; I invent, but I invent myself. A machine corresponds necessarily to a call of the imaginary, the determined inventor's patience is the file between his fingers; it tends to provide the imaginary solution that his self-entangled mind cannot bring itself to formulate. Better yet: a machine corresponds to what its user expects of it but also provides him with an unprecedented, unformulated response of which it is itself the idea. This machine is representation; I recognize in it the principle of representation at work—I discover it as an organ, an element of the body added to my body; it speaks to me and adapts itself, meshes, grafts itself. Something of representation has joined itself, materially, from this angle, to me.

Mechanical investment. I recognize my machines a bit as if they were animals, with the same mixed feeling of familiarity and fear. I touch them and I read them—and I rejoin myself in them: they are what I am (more able, but also cruder), they are where I am not, they fulfill my request and deliver it to me point blank. I decipher in their action and their form an improvement and a lack, as in any mediatized system of expansion: they give back to me more than I thought I could ask of them, yet less than they demand that I desire. Machine terror: I see them giving back to me that which I didn't dare think.

A perfect example, in this regard, is that of the phonograph. I note that the launching of this device on the market at the turn of the century was symptomatically accompanied by a frantic, delirious literarization.[3] As if the machine itself, such as it appears, its form, its nature, its emergence, were not enough. As if it were still necessary to digest it or exploit it symbolically. As if the (visible) necessity of its invention were perforce accompanied by an irresistible tendency to the imaginary revision—and relaunching—of the device. No sooner is the machine available than I rewrite it. It is offered to me and I refuse it. It becomes, as soon as it is in my hands, the alarming object of a desperate reformulation. I am very desirous of this machine, thus I ask it immediately what it (and its engineers) planned to provide.

A critical and revealing point: this machine arose from the depths of time against time, beyond the systematically negative literary implementations that, as we shall see, welcomed it into the world. My questions will be the following: how does a society react in order to achieve the utopia of reproduction of what is fleeting, personal, forgotten, forgettable, and mortal? Especially when it attains it wrongly and, so to speak, in spite of itself, precisely where it never expected to? What does a society that becomes suddenly "mistress of its own memory" do with all the distancing mirror effects that this implies? What to do—and this is what this phonographic invention teaches me—with a memory that I, as subject, can not only formulate and fix but also and above all constitute at will, a mechanical memory, infinitely extensible, practically limitless and outside of myself?

In the beginning was the word, okay. Now I can finally, and without end, reproduce, phonographically, the original situation—the one where this word supposedly was spoken (without me, for me). I can start the beginning again—start over, hence erase. Question: What is a subject whose origin is incongruously postponed?

Phonography: suppression of time, suppression of divinity, suppression of creatures! Thus have we become phonographically of the creative species. "God is dead," but the living voice of the apparatus makes me equal, wretched me, to his eternity. It's my revenge—revenge through sound.

In the beginning is an image—in the beginning of analysis, the beginning of the world, the beginning of me. A primitive image— Urbild! Something that I haven't seen and that I must have always seen. A perfectly incomprehensible image. An image I've not been able to do without, though I could in fact look at it only belatedly, in the autumn of 1986, while skimming through *Minotaure*, André Breton's review, by chance dated the year of my birth, or almost. This image is a phonograph, shown amid what it signifies. I've had a phonograph in my mind for many years, without really knowing what it wants to tell me. This is another reason why I'm talking about it now. This image comes from a text—a text in an image in my head or in reverse order, an order impossible to retrace. The reversibility of words in icons and vice versa, of the head in the word and vice versa—we'll have to talk about this later. Anyway, I've had this text in my mind for twenty-four years: twenty-four years ago I was reading for the first time "Phonographe," a story by Alfred Jarry, in *Minutes de sable mémorial,* which I had the dangerous foresight to put in the syllabus for the class I was teaching in order to "explain" it. With no real success. I was hearing, without understanding, something that wasn't speaking. For twenty-four years I have thus found myself in search of an unfinished understanding of an image in a text because of what the image and the text do to ME in my mind.

What does the image say on this side of the image, with and without the words that accompany it? What does the machine say in the representation that it is? What does the idea of the reproduction of sounds in sight contain for the consumer of those sounds even when the latter is under the spell of a new fear?

This deep-seated, driving image is a photograph by Manuel Alvarez Bravo, a Mexican friend of the Surrealists, entitled *Ladder of Ladders,* dated 1932.[4] The plate (see frontispiece) shows several ladders leaning or suspended, a pile of coffins for children, as well as a phonograph with its horn rising up against the dark background of a joiner's workshop. The machine is sitting in one of the boxes in the foreground. Obscenity, rupture: one cannot place death and life side by side in this fashion. One cannot mix the two principles in this manner, one cannot use a coffin with such nonchalance, as one would use a window-box, the future corpse cannot tolerate the noisy flourishing of the sounds that have the impudence to burst forth!

Breton's commentary, in the margin: Alvarez Bravo manages to make us perceive "the extreme poles of sensation.... The relation of light to shadow, of the pile of boxes to the ladder and the grid, and the poetically explosive image obtained by the introduction of the phonograph's horn in the lower coffin, are superbly evocative of the sensitive atmosphere in which the entire country is steeped."[5] To say that this image is "sensitive"! To find nothing better to say— and Breton is usually not spare with words!—than that it is "sensitive"! How can one not know at this point what such a plate asserts! On the other hand, the commentary disturbed the commen-

Charles Grivel

tator himself, since we read, immediately after the passage just cited and on the subject of another image by the same photographer, the following remark: "It's the whole constituted by a mummified head and hand: the pose of the hand and the spark endlessly produced *by the proximity of the teeth and the fingernail describe a suspended, teeming world prey to contradictory instances*" (my emphasis).[6] A very curious remark, for the paradoxical combinations of the head and the hand, of life and death, of a celestial vault—both happy and threatening— and a sound, constitute the very center of Jarry's poem to which I previously alluded.

I am not saying that Breton is copying Jarry; I am saying simply that phonography is imaginarily ingrained in the subject, as much in relation to sex as in relation to death: it phonographs sex and does it morbidly. This will be demonstrated. What formerly I didn't understand but heard nevertheless is nothing other than the contradictory and irresistible message that a machine, invented by me and for me, conveys to me. This machine spoke the way I hear it. This too will be demonstrated. I believe, in fact, that literature has taken upon itself (in its time, in my time) to give vent to this message, this contradiction, this incomprehension. The library is full of what was not supposed to be seen.

Literature is overflowing with phonographs. One need only have a look, and one will find them there: this is a first point to consider. The wish for phonography more or less fills literature, from Homer to Rabelais to Porta to Becher, to Grundel and Nadar, to Cros and Villiers, etc. As one may suspect, it involves a desire to preserve: "One can distract oneself for an hour or two by phonographing a few fragments of conversation in one's memory"—this from the morgue of Gourmont.[7] The machine that Bealu discovers in his attic cries out, in perfect keeping with its nature, "May it last forever!"[8] Recall and rebirth. Preserving that which is in the process of occurring and whose memory is lacking—ego, the identity of ego, this ego's extreme particularity in the process of falling short. The phonograph contains the one who has departed; it reproduces the one no longer there; it noisily presents his mark. Man phonographically recovers what he had lost: primordial eternity. The machine tells me I am audible, possible beyond the circle in which I keep myself, beyond here and now, outside of time, absent or dead. It's a rather nice, utopian vindication.

Literature, however, no less often plays an entirely different tune in this regard: the systematic negation of the device that, in other connections, it seems to call forth in its wishes with such insistence; the phonograph "in flesh and blood," if I may call it such, has no sooner appeared than its symbolic abolition is set in motion: Villiers, Schwob, Renard, Leiris, and even Jarry turn the phonograph into a monster—a system of aggression of which I am the victim. Phase 1: the demand. Phase 2: the invention. Phase 3: the liquidation of the invention—whether by renewal of the imaginary or by a banalization of the machine's functions: it apparently does not suffice, or only suits prosaic uses (like the dictaphone). Everything happens as though (and this is a general phenomenon, the phonograph being hardly the only victim of such conditioning) demand and suppression went together, the desire to preserve the voice and anxiety generated by the spectacle of one's own self (its excessive coherence, its "eternity"). Thus it is the device, man's revelation to man through the material he foments or inspires, that leads to suppression; however, its *technique* has secondary, inappreciable, and unexpected effects. The phonograph is an original object of matter in which my mind has steeped. The return shock of the one on the other triggers the negative reaction, and the machine is put on trial.

But the mechanism has several foundations, and literature represents, moreover, through interposed denial, the broadening of the original demand and the radicalization of the phonographic utopia. Regularly, with the appearance of every somewhat profound invention, voices are raised for the fine folk who mean no harm by it;

Charles Grivel

voices are raised against (somber spirits); voices—literary ones, this time—lift up the debate, take the machine seriously (or take the phonograph at its word), and ask it to conform in actual fact to the unformulated desire that justified its original appearance. Literature's provocation: demanding the fulfillment of the desire because our ears are soothed by it—the actual restitution of the voice (not its mere simulacrum), since that's what we've been promised. A bit more (I imagine this bit more): the nasal being-voice of the machine should come out of the box, mix with the living, walk among them like a double, indistinguishable from them (which is the real one, the being or its perfect reproduction?).[9] Literature thinks beyond the phonograph. It imposes on the machine supplementary demands for which, perhaps, the latter was conceived, but which its engineers are very careful not to reveal: the phonograph finds itself *literarily* charged with reproducing not only the sounds of the voice or of song but also those of the soul, the very intonation of identity—self. I do not only want it to repeat me, but more than this, to capture me and find me—invention within repetition. Mechanical accession to being—yes, that's really what I want.

I am thus claiming that literature explores phonographic desire to the point of utopia; it recasts this desire somewhere else (farther away, in any case), rather than on its foundations. It reveals the real nature of a technical invention by denying its possibility, on the one hand, even while demanding, on the other hand, nothing less than the impossible. Literature declares that the machine is thinkable—it need only be the thought that realizes itself as thought, and the thought will be its fulfillment, fateful and happy. Thought is possible once it is thinkable: Machines to your posts!

But the machine will not be set against the mind: what I invent is also what I am. Technology will not be set against literature: what I write brings the apparatus, denied in usage, unfailingly back to its proper ends and acknowledges them.

What is desired is intolerably so; one takes exception to it, also intolerably. Twofold, alternate gap between desire and real-

The Phonograph's Horned Mouth

ization, memory and machine. There is a profound mechanical reason in this (among several others, about which I shall remain silent): technology does not attain perfection; even the most sensitive apparatus always leaves something to be desired. For example, the phonograph (of days gone by!—nowadays its flaw lies elsewhere) makes nasal sounds; the vocalizations or tirades of my great-grandmother are metallic, hard, ringing, even thin and raspy, not easily identifiable, poorly accentuated, monotone: the machine ruins the voice of my ancestress. In short, the marvel of the phonograph misses its mark and for this reason detects the flaw from which identity flees. Basic thesis of common opinion: it is by fixing identity that one comes to master it (identity is a fix). Counterthesis of literatures (also basic, after the invention of the device): it does not reproduce (itself), not enough, not what is called for, not in the right way, never well, never more. The fiction of mimetic modulation becomes phonographically sensible, unavoidable. Literature insists on this illusion, and often draws a mad apocalypse from it, as we shall see.

The phonograph, at that primitive moment of its existence, is paradoxical: on the one hand, it simulates sounds (approximately but sufficiently, since we do recognize them), on the other, it mechanizes this sound; its murmur is material—its voice is horrible, mine too. This voice is a falsetto, the voice of a *castrato*, feminized or masculinized as the case may be, but never in the right way. How to escape the paradox of a machine that performs without performing what we ask of it, that carries out its program even while altering its data? Forcing it, breaking it, embodying it…. We shall see what strategies enjoyed literary currency in this regard.

I would now like to propose a selection of quick readings; I skim through the phonographic series, go from book to book to try and see what's been done. In my library in order of increasing complexity, aside from past technical elaborations, which I've presented and discussed elsewhere,[10] there are the following works:

1. Charles Cros, "Procédé d'enregistrement et de réproduction des phénomènes perçus par l'ouïe." As well as "Note au sujet du phonographe de M. Edison (1877–1878)."[11]
2. Villiers de l'Isle-Adam, *L'Eve future* (1886).[12]
3. Marcel Schwob, "La Machine à parler" (1892).[13]
4. Maurice Renard, "La Mort et le coquillage" (1907).[14]
5. Michel Leiris, "Perséphone: Gorge coupée."[15]
6. Alfred Jarry, "Phonographe" (1894).[16]

A few points of reference before getting to the readings.[17] We have always wished we could stop the flow, the direction, of what passes intolerably then disappears, the voice that dissolves after having resonated, the past that vanishes after having been lived, the present time—"if only it would suspend its flight!" We wish to counter dissemination, dissolution, the end. To make it rise again. Giovanni Battista Porta, 1589: "I have devised a way to preserve words, that have been pronounced, inside lead pipes, in such a manner that they burst forth from them when one removes the cover."[18] F. Grundel, a Nuremberg optician, according to the letters of J. J. Becher, suggested enclosing words' echoes inside a bottle; by agitating the stem of a spiral, one could carry them for a whole hour, and in reopening the device, one could supposedly hear them again.[19] Nadar, three centuries later but along the same lines, exclaimed, in regard to Edison's 1877 invention, that we have lived "this extraordinary hour in which the phonograph [has made] the fantastic chapter of Rabelais pass from the imaginary to the real— gathering and setting down synoptically and synacoustically on paper, with no need of thawing, all the words caught in flight and fixed in air by freezing."[20] The phonograph is a hot medium! Grabby and liquefying. Heating up particles that a memory had stopped and garnered beforehand. Hearing is proportional to the halt it was necessary to produce. It is repetition, but a repetition mediated two or three times. Important fact: it is obtained by friction, first from the mechanical force of the sound applied to the wax, again when it comes back out of the spool (or disc), and again when it strikes the tympanum. Thus there is no solution of continuity between speaking, memorizing, playing back, hearing. The apparatus is an organ placed outside the head, and the head effervescently mechanizes its own circuits.

I shall now look at six successive essays on the device:

1. Charles Cros calls it a "paleograph": "you will write what has (already) taken place," says man to his machine, "you will rewrite, you will remember me." The phonographic wish is accompanied by the idea that the person is restored to himself at the moment of listening. The word, a modulated fragment, is only of interest as long as it lends itself to refraction. The *echo machine*—which was able to capture sound, to freeze it in its impression and revive it, simply by reviving this impression—surpasses in power the *word machine* (or the "song machine"), though it only seems to be a takeoff of it. Indeed, the reproductive apparatus, through mimetic impression, begets (if you will) the incontestable reality of the sign it utters "in its brass throat." What is real is not what I articulate, nor its impression, but its substantive mechanical reproduction: the phonograph completes the reality of the sign—thanks to it, the truth returns to simulacrum. It speaks to me much better than I myself could: it still expresses itself when I am already silent: you will listen to me in it after I am gone.

It is no surprise that this device's fantastic power should astonish its inventor. That he should be compelled, as a result and metaphorically speaking, to give it the very form of the human body in his descriptions follows from the same reasoning: the Crosian phonograph is made up principally—and I quote the texts we have at our disposal—of an "index"

Charles Grivel

(finger); it is "phallic" and capable (I'm still quoting) of "embracing."

2.   As we know, *L'Eve future* (*The Future Eve*) of Villiers de l'Isle-Adam, is a story about Edison himself—"the Phonograph's papa!"—who is shown in utopian and ironic fashion in quest of absolute reproductive perfection: his Eve is supposed to imitate *and improve upon* the woman with whom the suicidal hero is so desperately in love. Repeating what has already been uttered, says the novel's Edison, is child's play; what really needs to be done is to succeed in expressing the unheard of, what cannot be repeated—the inexpressible itself. To bring the unconscious into speech—as into my own voice—into the inner voice, deep and personal. To phonograph the antecedent principle, the nonexistent, the inappropriate, that which I renounce or repress or replace, which has no stability of its own, which is different from itself—that which the tongue keeps back: these are the novel's stakes, and its triumph.

The author's reflections justify this audacious project in full: first of all, because nothing is any longer worth recording in the present day (the invention having arrived too late in a degraded world), and then because phonographic sound depends on the listener's *ear*. Indeed—and this is the unforeseeable catastrophe of the historical Edison—the inner sentiment of the sounds of the past (the phonograph is always that which speaks in someone's or something's "absence"), to which the "analytical" understanding of contemporaries has become deaf, is only and barely *and morbidly* set in motion by the machine: I do not know how to listen, and therefore I hear only dead sounds.

The total phonographic weapon that Villiers is ironically proposing thus skirts the obstacle in the following manner: the perfection of a feminine robot (Eve) serves as medium of an appropriate text (phonographically recorded) for an appropriate listener (who is absolutely in love, that is, capable of listening in accordance with the nature of the message transmitted)—the mainstay of this ironic construction obviously being the rather particular character of the recording enclosed in the breast of the lovable robot:

Here are the two golden phonographs, inclined at an angle toward the center of the breast, Hadaly's two lungs. Each passes to the other the metallic leaves of her harmonious—and I should say heavenly—conversations, a bit the way printing presses pass the sheets for printing. A single tinfoil ribbon can hold seven hours of her words, which have been imagined by the greatest poets, the subtlest metaphysicians, and the most profound novelists of this century, geniuses whom I solicited and who provided me, at the price of diamonds, with these forever original marvels.

This is why I say that Hadaly has replaced an intelligence with Intelligence itself.[21]

Of course, as a precaution that we can well understand, these "eternal words" were recorded beforehand by the (human, all too human) woman with whom the hero is in love. And they were recorded unbeknown to her. A complementary cylinder, in addition, contains, "in relief," her expressions, her walk, and her demeanor. Hadaly is an irresistible duplicate substance. In fact, on the other side of the medium, if I may say so, the lover really drinks up words that have become for him (and for him alone) more authentic in their echo than those he may have heard formed by the ordinary mouth of the real Eve whose acquaintance he had the misfortune to make. The moral: the machine is the right one! But she is only the right one if I am her unconditional lover!

The outrageousness of the utopian condition lived by Villiers' characters of course bursts apart in the epilogue: the boat burns, the

Charles Grivel

goddess sinks—forever mad, I shall forever miss her unique repetitive voice!

3.   The mechanism's weakness is that it has to repeat: the machine logically comes (according to a certain logic, by which one becomes aware of having to take one's leave) in second place. It is thus slave to what, beforehand, must have taken place. The ideal would be for it to speak of it "by itself" and thereby to produce, spontaneously, that by which *desire*—not reality—exists: ego-identity, ego-identified, of the subject replete with itself. Villiers filled his Eve through a "medium" and phonographically interposed "poets" with that of which only the idea is manifest: an ideal of words, of voice, of language and person, adapted to a *single* listener. Hence its fragility. Schwob, in the same vein but in a completely different manner, makes a parable centered around an ideal—and murderous— talking-machine:

> *I followed the man who was heading toward the door. We passed through busy thoroughfares, turbulent streets, then ended up on the outskirts of the city, as the gas-lamps began to light up one by one around us. Before the postern of a blackened wall, the man stopped, and pulled on a bolt. We entered a dark and silent courtyard. My heart filled with anxiety: I heard groans, gnashing cries and syllabized words that seemed to bellow forth from a gaping throat. The words had no inflection, just like the voice of my guide; with the result that, in that boundless enlargement of vocal sounds, I could recognize nothing human.*
>
> *The man had me enter a room that I could not bear to see, so terrible did it seem to me because of the monster that stood at its center. For there, rising up to the ceiling, was an enormous throat, long and speckled, with folds of black skin that hung and bulged, a breath of subterranean squall, and two huge lips trembling above. Amid the creaking of wheels and the screech of metal wire, one could see these heaps of leather quivering, the gigantic lips gaping hesitantly; then, at the red bottom of the yawning gulf, an immense, fleshy lobe wriggled, swaying, stretching up, down, to the right and to the left; a blast of wind burst from within the machine, and articulated words spewed forth, uttered*

by a voice beyond the human. The explosions of the consonants were terrifying; for the P's and B's, sounding like V's, came out directly flush with the edges of the swollen, black lips: they seemed to spring up under our very eyes; the D's and T's shot out from under the snarling upper mass of leather curling up; and the R's, long in preparation, had a sinister roll. The vowels, bluntly modified, spouted from the gaping maw like trumpet blasts. The lispings of the S and CH sounds exceeded the horror of even those prodigious mutilations.[22]

Now it turns out that there's a woman who, both servant to the ingenious inventor and slave to the monstrous "mechanical mouth," operates the horrific device from a keyboard. And it must count for something that what throbs beneath her expert fingers is her sex itself. At the keyboard this woman—is she submissive, or will she rebel in the end? This is a subject the tale takes care not to broach—interprets a language "without nuance," an absolute, hence soulless tongue, developed by the inventor. This universal machine language is a pure language of sounds:

Its notes are stammerings, its scales and exercises the A E I O U of grammar-school, its studies the fables of my composition, its fugues my lyric pieces and poems, its symphonies my blasphemous philosophy. You see the keys that carry, in their syllabic alphabet, on their triple row, all the miserable signs of human thought. I produce at once, without damnation's intervention, the thesis and antithesis of the truths of man and his God.[23]

This language, in the mind of its creator, is supposed to replace the other, which is a lie: the machine's language is the language of matter. The inventor's stroke of genius—or of madness—is to have dared to make a machine speak in man's place, in order to fulfill the reality of his language better than he, thereby discharging him of his burden of soul.

The machine is conceived to carry out blasphemy; that is, to deny the soul, to deny the language, of the soul, to deny the word of God, to deny God even while denying his action within language; and this machine that speaks matter as reality without remainder carries out the negation of the famous, orthodox "In the beginning was the Word," substituting in its place a disgusting "I created the word," which it applies to itself and which the outraged ears of the witness-narrator consent, with great difficulty, to hear.

The story's catastrophic epilogue: the machine explodes at the very moment it is repeating, upon dictation, the horrible blasphemous affirmation, at the same time striking its inventor dumb. The loss of "nuance," the triumph of matter, the ablation of the supplement of soul, was fatal. It matters little, in the end, that a woman was at once, in a way, the invisible double of the ignoble machine and the instrument of divine vengeance: one man alone, and even imaginary, refused on the one hand what he nevertheless had granted himself on the other. A movement minus a movement is still a movement.

4. Maurice Renard. Another work of affirmation-denial of phonographic power. Literature, apparently, never stops repeating that it is possible to hear the inaudible, but also that its real hearing, once it is achieved, "kills" or "maddens" he who achieves it. As if the point were, yet again—though this time by means of the interposed machine—that of not overcoming the taboo by which language is marked, "thou shalt spare the soul"; "thou shalt not express that by which one's own is fulfilled"; "thou shalt commit to God the enjoyment of His own."

This sort of commandment, accompanied by its furious denial, informs "La Mort et le coquillage" ("Death and the Seashell"). The parable relates the following: a musician listens to the recorded voice of his deceased friends; he's a very melancholy man; the refinement of his musical ear and his grief compel him to seek the means to hear directly, without phonography and without recording, the voices of his dear departed. "What the mouth of a seashell says": this phrase opens up horizons for him in this regard. His idea is to write down at the piano, without intermediary, to reproduce with his hands and with musical notation, from breath to art, with and without a machine, this primordial, definitive, funereal sound. But such an operation, unfortunately, proves impossible. What does the phonograph (here, the "graphophone") do? It reproduces intonations from beyond the grave. What does the seashell produce "with the pink lips of its valve"? It reproduces, in the ear of he who listens, the death-agony of the mollusk that secreted it. What does the composer's music do? It does not succeed in carrying out this task of reproduction:

Nerval seized the miraculous shell from me and ran to the piano. For a long time he tried to write down its divine sexual clamor. At two o'clock in the morning, he finally gave up. The room was strewn with blackened, torn sheets of paper. "You see, you see," he said to me, "I can't even transcribe the chorus under dictation!..."

He went back to his armchair, listening, despite my efforts, to the venomous paean. Around four o'clock, he started to tremble. I begged him to get some rest. He shook his head, and seemed to lean over an invisible abyss. At half past five, he fell, forehead on the marble of the hearth: dead. The seashell broke into a thousand little pieces.

The "melody's poison" has done its work: it is not possible to hear what is not supposed to be heard: it is not possible to reproduce it mechanically and musically. Nothing has its equivalent, the tale tells us: something cannot represent something else. This happens only within an "own," an essence, that cannot be assimilated or appropriated, and is inaccessible, inexpressible: thou shalt not touch the essence, it also tells us, even while letting us read into the hollow of the commandment it articulates in the contrary sense: thou shalt make every effort, thou shalt appropriate, thou shalt put as much as thou canst in thy ears, etc.

5.   The withdrawal of the voice. The taboo of the voice. The taboo of the reproduction of the voice. There is no reproduction without horror. This is said in life, it is said in texts. Michel Leiris. A phonograph is a device for reproducing voice—dictated, spoken, or sung. This device refers back: one finds in oneself what one gave oneself. Mirror. It answers me with me: I hear myself (and even see myself) as identical and different. Dream accomplished: there without being there. Person without person. Horror and rapture, engendered by this miracle. Even if it has become routine to us. Infinite medium of sounds. Telephone, gramophone, dictaphone, records, screens, videos: endlessly producing voice. We are never done hearing ourselves speak; we no longer hear ourselves speak. Let us examine this double relationship: a pleasure augmented by a horror, more or less in one fell swoop. Our current machines—glossy, built-in, dissimulated—might seem innocent to us. The form and *literary* power they once possessed, archaeologically, sufficiently demonstrate their true nature.

We identify by means of voice. It is impossible to modify (perfectly) one's voice; there is no mistaking it; one emerges from it ineluctably, lies within it, prisoner of the sounds one emits, in an unfathomable innermost depth. A voice is a signature. And yet, this undeniable imprint is more invisible than the one I leave with my fingertips, less apprehensible, immeasurable—it is, in short, the pure essence that a sound is.

Voice contains me. I am the content of my voice. This voice constitutes at once my material and spiritual medium. Fluid or impalpable substance of the core of being. I am the breath that I respire, aspire, expire, which I am capable, incomprehensibly, of modulating (it varies, but I remain in it).

Now the problem: the invention of the phonograph comes to expose the artificiality of the process. At first, of course, it passes for an excellent certifier: the incorrigible innocent puts his ear to the horn so as to recognize himself therein; however, this self is mechanically fixed by something, mechanically reproduced, produced and reproduced: I see before me a machine that speaks me. I am buried in its entrails (or it is in me): I am the equal of this imitating device. When it speaks to me, it also represents to me, outside of me and without me, the absence of subject: it repeats me without my being there. A voice coming from no one, meaningless and empty, devoid of soul, vacant. The first consequence of the mechanical reproduction of the voice was to break the bond unifying sign and person, the self and its support or medium. I am no longer characterized, I am dispossessed of my character, I am missing the sign of truth: voice, the soul. Who will not say I have been dissolved?

The invention of the phonograph means that the person is not capable of fulfilling his identity, nor of efficaciously or authentically manifesting its traces outwardly. A simple reflection where one did not expect it was enough. Is the self that has passed over into the machine nothing but evanescent? The sign—the general law relegating well-established law to nothingness—detached from the content it offers seems itself to be naturally the truth it pronounces. Where is the self in all this? I cease to be grounded in truth because I no longer hear myself in any true sign. The phonograph has killed the truth of the subject.

Sex, violence, identity: these are also the three poles of the phonographic mechanism for Leiris. It is worth our while to retrace briefly the different stages of extremely perceptive unravelling the author engages in.[24] *The phonograph is a word instrument;* this is the first thing one learns, the one from which all the rest derive. It is also an active physical figure, a symbolic living thing one cannot escape: it possesses you as soon as you possess it. That is the principle.

This device bears—by homophony, of course—a name, borrowed from the little creature called the "earwig" (*perce-oreille:* "ear-piercer"):[25] Persephone, queen of the underworld. Something intrudes, enters. Something that comes from beneath, inside, below, that comes "negatively." Something that comes back, intrudes, forcible and violent. Sound is not a sound, but an act—an index—in iron:

A spur..., the coil of a ram's horn, all this, I believe I find in Persephone's name, in a state of potential and waiting only for an imperceptible click to be set off like the steel band tightly wound about itself at the middle of a clockwork mechanism or the coil spring in the box with closed top from which the bristly-bearded devil has not yet popped out. (RJ1, p. 86)

A device, a name, a form—here seeing is implied in hearing—uttering *all together* what Leiris calls a "second-degree enigma":

All the more reason why, when the source of the song, rather than being a human mouth (that is, an organ that we more or less know), will be a mechanical contrivance adding to what strangeness already exists in musical language the surprise of reproduction, we shall find ourselves face to face with a mystery in an almost pure state. (RJ1, p. 90)

Triple depth of the machine adjusted in my language, by its form, to my ear; triple application to the "deep region of hearing." The received sound hollows the ear; the noise creates "anfractuosities" or "cavities" inside me and penetrates by successive dull, fragile cracklings—so many failures, so many successes! It is a mineral voice that comes to me: it resounds and, in so doing, materializes. Materialized, it becomes denatured—of a subject that everything indicates as having been turned into matter and its own metal: "bronze!" Now, an unavoidable complication of the textual reality we are examining: this device, which Leiris places in his childhood, is twofold. It is first a "graphophone" with cylinders, exclusive property of his father, a contrivance at once perfected and capable—I am following the description closely—of recording and reproducing (which means that it possesses two appearances relating to the two functions it is supposed to fulfill, the one male and the other one irresistibly female); then it is a "phonograph," a simple model, deprived of its recording mechanism, reserved for the child. The entire family is thus on the table in the perfect forms of the objects with which it surrounds itself. There is a striking description of the father's genital equipment through the interposed "graphophone": what fascinates Leiris the boy is, of course, its "prowess"—he hears "faun" (satyr) in "phone," hears it twice in fact. Edison outdoes Pathé, "father" is "untouchable" and "cannot be analyzed," sex jr. must content himself with "manipulations" of his own equipment. A minute description—we never do see enough!—of paternal recording and reproduction by interposed loudspeaker—how feminine!—equipped with its uvula. The effect of the song of copulation is evidently that of rejection when under a spell: reproduction—I am never it, never in it; I see it from without as at the theater, from high above, from the worst possible vantage, from "heaven."

But Leiris, at the end of the journey, takes pains to deny this construction, this unfolding through the words of the machine:

Charles Grivel

"Persephone, might you be only a metaphor?" But this doubt—that's what it is—will be effaced, in the work that follows, by two key episodes: the vegetations operation (recounted in *L'Age d'homme*, 1946)[26]—the operation is ascribed to a ruse on the part of his parents, and the aggression of which the child imagines himself the victim introduces him to the sensations of anguish and of being trapped—and the tracheotomy undergone by the author himself many years later, which changed his voice.[27]

A device plus a double operation—violence received, with transference, in the same place. A device that operates—for it is the device that commands sense and applies it. I hear that it reproduces, and it is taken away from me. Ablation, of self, but through the mouth. The surgical scraping, the aim of which was clearly to rid the person of parasitic growths, fulfills the mechanical message: I find myself in complete lack of self. From a distance of years, in either direction, from the phonograph to the operating table or vice versa, a destiny becomes entwined with the throat (or with the ear, depending): I hear a voice that is not a voice, I speak a voice that is not a voice. Selfless self like *Nightless nights*. Such is the lesson of the horn—the lesson of the faunlike ram, the surgical knife, the phonograph, the example of the bull: how to be where the bull thrusts his horns?[28]

This identifies, but it comes from nowhere. And if it comes, it cuts or tears apart. The voice one has is a voice restored, but what has been restored to me is not at all my own.[29] Anyway, when it's there, it doesn't come out anymore: I come out dumb from the surgeon's office, and in the bathroom, from the exertion of excretion, accordion, or piping, what I am is a wreck.[30] As Leiris says, "I have broken I don't know what sound barrier"—my voice has been lost. I pull myself up, "like an alpinist," with no more truth than these words, to make my companion come out from there.

6. Phonographic torture. Jarry. The machine represents the irruption of sense—two principles in one, male as well as female—as well as its intolerability. The machine speaks to me in my head (speakers in the past used to be affixed to one's ears), it resonates in my bones with a violence the text of which no song can diminish. It's no accident, of course, that the first word ever given birth, ever expectorated by the phonographic method—Cros' method, in the years prior to the submission of his patent in 1877—was "*Merde!*"[31] One cannot close oneself to the phonograph's insistence. That device penetrates whosoever uses it: can one close one's ears to something that murmurs, mechanically, immediately, without end, beyond intention? can one fail to succumb to what produces, by simple repetition, memory itself? Rape, violence, femininization of the person: sense catches me, the voice it assumes forces me and empties me, impels me and inhales me. Chasm and void—of a subject ousted by a machine; a subject penetrated, lost, by his voice, which he hears. The device takes possession of its user—sex to sex, the text says it, the stage shows it, the head thinks it. Of a subject dispossessed, liquidated, substituted by his language as his voice returns it to him. The classic torment that Père Ubu inflicts on his victims includes, in succession and entirely in keeping with the logic of demonstration, "twisting the nose and teeth," "extracting the tongue," and "cramming little sticks of wood in the ears."[32] Someone will thus be captured, emptied, and crammed. Emptying by

Charles Grivel

way of occupation. By an Ubu machine mainly concerned with that; by an Ubu phonograph strong enough to sing the death-dealing motion into one's ear.

Leiris and Jarry: the machine is a sexual organ. What it plays before us and in us is a copulation, with the female principle on the one hand, contained in the horn, and the male principle on the other, in its play of rollers, needle, and head speakers. The machine is twofold: "it has claws everywhere";[33] it grasps, bites, penetrates and enters, but it's a machine-skin—it has its diaphragm, its mucus membrane, and skin. Phallic and flaccid—if you will. Put in motion, it "loves," embraces its lover—the machine's user—cracks him open and empties him:

The mineral siren holds her beloved by the head, like a steel dress-clip gripping a dress. . . . She slaps her lame hands abruptly to the right and left of her temporary lover's head, but does not injure him in the least. . . . her single finger . . . grafts her wiry erection onto the tragi of the listener. . . . And the two black leeches hang from the listener's ears. . . . The mandible lowers and rises like a piano key. . . . The song of the old sirens paralyzed by crystallization, bursts forth and catches flame like a bit of powder upon contact with the two gas-carbons burning the listener's eardrums with luminous notes. The lifeless cold warms up and becomes mobile again upon contact with the warm brain, through ears pierced with nails. Now words thaw through the airs of the north sea. . . . Rise and fall, mandible. . . . Sing, copper stalactites. . . . Sing forever, so that he who listens to you shall not turn away.

The madness of the phonographic fantasy: the machine is these two, which I am not, two in one, simultaneously loving me within the voice. Killing on the one hand, but pleasure on the other. I exist only in absence. "Inverse coitus," precisely. I only have pleasure without self. Finally rid of being, and aware of it (she tells it to me, she does it to me)—through the representation of what I see there; through the vocal influx that blazes a trail through my ears; by the metal embrace; by the woman clutching me. Selfless self, in short: "Sometimes strange vibrations are heard in this pipes: it is legitimate to think that it is Truth that is singing."[34]

Jarry's position in the text-lever that we read is not critical: he doesn't condemn anything, he uses. The phonograph helps him, visibly, to deliver an otherwise unutterable, and certainly sexual, message that thought, psychological or otherwise, is unsuited to discover: the machine enables me to think something I am unable to think. As though its representation in me broke the line of suppression. As though the word it directs at me, however deformed it may be, or precisely for this reason, became, in its repetition, by the mechanical aspect it possesses, finally audible. As though, from a latent conception, the machine alone was able to create an awareness. The machine-mirror reflects the *unheard-of*—we must dare to look in it—even the unimaginable, the hidden within, the possible within.

The Jarryan phonograph effects an emptying, it substitutes the subject for the subject: it is *modern* (more than). It makes so that *nothing* replaces *nothing*, removes *nothing* from *nothing*; it immediately appropriates the person listening to it, by a gentle violation. The device's voice, the murmur it whispers to me, blank, which has lost its character to the point that I have difficulty recognizing it, this soulless breath, this material, unaccented, cold, neutral sound, pure sound of an organ that seizes and condescends, this metallism—all this the machine conveys to me or inserts in me as my own. The machine does not only have the degenerative function that has always been recognized in it; it does not reveal only the abolition of the subject; it affirms itself, in the subject itself, as its being—its unthought, its unthinkable: I am this single string it man-

Charles Grivel

ages to make vibrate. It is therefore no accident that Jarry, in his theater, imposes a *monotony* of diction on his marionettes and himself—to speak in the very voice that the phonograph sends back to me, to achieve this lack of expression, to unoriginalize myself, to depersonalize myself, to become it (machine), to become it in it (mechanized flesh), to give myself to it, but also to attract it into myself. The machine is a violent act of apprehension of the subject by the subject. Medium of cellular shrillness, *reality* arises where nothing (little and under control) indicated it would. Whether it arises falsely, truly, or imaginarily, doesn't matter.

NOTES

1. André Breton, *Les Pas perdus* (1924; reprint, Paris: Gallimard, 1949), p. 105.

2. M. Le Bot, *Peinture et machinisme* (Paris: Klinksieck, 1973), p. 76.

3. Since we're talking about symptoms, let us remember that the word *phonograph* was launched, in the late 1870s, in *La Semaine du clergé,* a right-minded publication, by a certain abbot Lenoir who signed his name Leblanc (cf. E. H. Weiss, Phonographes et musique mécanique (Hachette, 1930), p. 27).

4. Manual Alvarez Bravo, *Ladder of Ladders.* Photograph in *Minotaure* 12–13 (1939), p. 34. Reprinted in E. Jaguer, *Les*

Mystères de la chambre noire: Le surréalisme et la photographie (Paris: Flammarion, 1982), p. 80.

5. André Breton, "Souvenir du Mexique," *Minotaure* 12–13 (1939), p. 35. Text reprinted in *La Clé des champs* (Paris: Pauvert, 1967), p. 36.

6. Ibid., p. 36.

7. Rémy de Gourmont, *Sixtine* 10–18 (Paris: Union générale d'éditions, 1982), p. 234.

8. Marcel Bealu, *Mémoires de l'ombre* (1944; reprint, Verviers, Belgium: Marabout, 1972), p. 116.

9. This is the subject of Bealu's preface to *Dormeur debout* (ibid., p. 189).

10. In the framework of theoretical research on intertexts, cf. "Serien textueller Perzeption," in *Dialog der Texte: Hamburger Kolloquium zur Intertextualität,* ed. von Wolf Schmid und Wolf-Dieter Stempel, (Vienna: Wiener Slawistischer Almanach, 1983), pp. 53–83.

11. Charles Cros, "Procédé d'enregistrement et de reproduction des phénomènes perçus par l'ouïe" and "Note au sujet du phonographe de M. Edison," in *Oeuvres complètes* (Bibliothèque de la Pléiade, 1970), 579–582.

12. Villiers de l'Isle-Adam, *L'Eve Future* (Pauvert, 1950).

13. Marcel Schwob, "La Machine à parler," *Le Roi au masque d'or* (1892; reprint, Paris: Union générale d'éditions, 1979), pp. 10–18, 112–117.

14. Maurice Renard, "La Mort et le coquillage," in *L'Invitation à la peur* (Paris: Belfond, 1970), pp. 67–72.

15. Michel Leiris, "Perséphone: Gorge coupée, in *La Règle du jeu: Biffures* (1948; reprint, Paris: Gallimard, 1977), 77–138.

16. Alfred Jarry, "Phonographe," in *Oeuvres complètes,* vol. 1 (Bibliothèque de la Pléiade, 1973), 185–187.

17. For more details, cf. "Serien textueller Perzeption,"

18. Giovanni Battista della Porta, *Baptistae Portae Neapolitani Magiae naturalis libri viginti* (Batavorum: Apud Petrum Leffen, 1651), book 16, chapter 12.

19. Johann Joachim Becher, *Narrische Weissheit* (Frankfurt: J. P. Zubrod, 1683), No. 18.

20. Felix Nader, *Quand j'étais photographe* (New York: Arno Press, 1979), p. 252.

21. Villiers de l'Isle-Adam, *L'Eve future,* 220–221. The "eternal words" in question were recorded by the too human woman with whom the hero is in love—unbeknown to her. A complementary cylinder contains, "in relief," her walk and demeanor. Hadaly is thus the stuff of echoes.

22. Schwob, *La machine à parler,* 114–115.

23. Ibid., 115–116.

24. Michel Leiris' work will be indicated by these symbols: *Biffures* = RJ1; *L'Age d'homme* = AH. RJ3 refers to *La Règle du jeu: Fibrille* (Gallimard, 1966); RJ4 to *La Règle du jeu: Frêle bruit* (Gallimard, 1976).

25. Translator's note: The logic of the argument here plays on the French name of the earwig, *perce-oreille* ("ear–piercer"), and on the false etymology (and homophony) of the name *Perséphone.*

26. Leiris, "Perséphone: Gorge coupée," 118–120.

27. RJ3.

28. AH, pp. 10, 12.

29. It's the "fibula," a device for closing, opening, and writing (RJ3, p. 292).

30. RJ3, p. 120.

31. Weiss, *Phonographes et musique mécanique*, p. 26.

32. *Tout Ubu* (Le Livre de Poche, 1985).

33. Ibid, p. 117.

34. Alfred Jarry, *La Chandelle verte* (1969), p. 303.

THE LAMENTATIONS OF EDISON
FROM *L'EVE FUTURE* (1886)

Villiers de l'Isle-Adam

translated from the French by Robert Martin Adams

All grief is but a diminution of self

Spinoza

He was murmuring to himself in an undertone:

——————————————— What a latecomer I am in the ranks of humanity! Why
wasn't I one of the first-born of the species? . . . .

. . . .
. . . .
. . . . Plenty of great words would be recorded
now, *ne varietur* —(sic)—word for word, that is, on the
surface of my cylinders, since the prodigious development
of the machine now allows us to receive, at the present
moment, sound waves reaching us from a vast distance.
And these words would be engraved on my cylinders,
with the tone, the phrasing, the manner of delivery, and
even the mannerisms of pronunciation that the speakers
possessed.

We needn't pretend to that life-creating cliché, *Fiat lux!*, a
phrase coined approximately seventy-two centuries ago
(and which besides, according to immemorial tradition—
perhaps invented, perhaps not—could never have been
picked up by any recording machine). Still, I might have
been able to record—for example, just a little after the
death of Lilith, while Adam was still a widower and I
would have been lurking behind some secret thicket in
Eden—first of all that sublime soliloquy,

"It is not good for man to live alone!,"
and then
"Ye shall be as gods!,"
then
"Increase and multiply!,"
and lastly the gloomy jest of the Almighty,
"Here is Adam become as one of us!"
—and all the rest.

Later, when the secret of my vibrating diaphragm was well known, wouldn't it have been pleasant for my successors to record during the great days of paganism, for example, the famous
"To the most beautiful!,"
the angry
"Quos ego!," the oracles of Dodona, the chants of the Sybils—and all the rest? All the important speeches of men and gods, down through the ages, would have been indelibly engraved in the sonorous archives of copper, so that by now no doubt would have been in any way possible concerning their authenticity.

Even among the noises of the past, how many mysterious sounds were known to our predecessors, which for lack of a convenient machine to record them have now fallen forever into the abyss? . . . .
. . . .
. . . .
. . . .
. . . .
. . . .
. . . .
. . . .
. . . .

. . . .

. . . . Who nowadays could form, for example, a proper notion of the sound of the trumpets of
Jericho? Of the bellow of Phalaris' bull? Of the laughter of
the augurs? Or the morning melody of Memnon? And all
the rest?

Dead voices, lost sounds, forgotten noises, vibrations lock-
stepping into the abyss, and now too distant ever to be
recaptured! . . . .

. . . .

. . . .

. . . . What sort of arrows would be able to
transfix such birds?

Edison touched with a casual finger a button of porcelain set in the wall beside his chair. A blinding blue
jet leaped from an electric condenser just a few feet away—a jet capable of striking dead a certain
number of elephants. It blazed like lightning through a block of crystal, then disappeared in the same
hundred-thousandth of a second.

——————————————— Yes, said the great engineer, continuing his meditation, I
have this little spark . . . .

. . . .

. . . .

. . . . which is to sound what the greyhound
is to the tortoise. It could give the sounds a start of fifty
centuries and yet chase them down in the gulfs of out
space, ancient refugees from the earth! But on what wire,
along what trail, could I send it? How teach it to bring the
sounds back, once it has tracked them down? How redi-
rect them to the ear of the investigator? This time, at least,
the problem seems insoluble.

Sadly, Edison tapped off the end of his cigar with a little finger. After a silence, he rose with a half-smile and began to walk up and down in his laboratory.

——————————— And to think that after six thousand and some years of painfully doing without my phonograph, he murmured again, humans were so still so insensitive that all they could do was make jokes when my first venture came forth. "A childish toy!" most people grumbled. Of course, I understand that when people are taken by surprise, some stock phrases are necessary to ease the adjustment. . . . .
. . . .
. . . .
. . . . Still, in that situation I would have tried to develop a few phrases superior to those crude jests that the public struggled to crack over my project.

For example, I would have complained that while the phonograph was reproducing sounds, it was unable to represent the sound, say, of the fall of the Roman Empire. It can't record an eloquent silence, or the sound of rumors. In fact, as far as voices go, it is helpless to represent the voice of conscience. Can it record the voice of the blood? Or all those splendid sayings that are attributed to great men? It's helpless before the swan song, before unspoken innuendos; can it record the song of the Milky Way? No? Ah, I go too far. —In any case, I see clearly that to satisfy my peers I must invent a machine that replies before one has even addressed it—or which, if the experiment says to it,
"Good morning, how are you?"
will answer
"Thank you, just fine, and yourself?"
Or, if someone in the audience sneezes, it will cry out,
"Gesundheit!"

Villiers de l'Isle-Adam

—
or
"God bless you!"
—something of that sort.

——————————————— Men are amazing.

I agree that the voice of my first phonograph sounded a bit like the voice of conscience talking with the crafty Pulcinello; but you might have expected that before men made merry with it, they might have waited till progress had improved it, as it did the first plates of Nicephore Niepce or Daguerre, ancestors of modern photography.

——————————————— Well, since there's no overcoming the craze for skepticism regarding my work, until things change I'll just have to keep secret the amazing, the ultimate development of my research . . . . which I have, right here, underground. And Edison tapped lightly on the floor with his foot. —I'd hardly let it go for less than five or six million old phonographs; and since everyone wants a good laugh, well, I'll have the last one.

He paused a few seconds, then shrugged his shoulders:

——————————————— Bah, he concluded, there's always something good at the root of human folly. Let's dispense with the empty jokes from now on.

Suddenly a soft whisper, the voice of a young woman murmuring very gently, was heard close by:

——————————————— Edison?

The Lamentations of Edison

DOUGLAS KAHN

The reanimated dead that populate Raymond Roussel's *Locus Solus* (1914) extend far beyond the pages of this one novel to haunt every aspect of his writing. For instance, reanimation accompanies his famed writing method—in which wordplay, puns, and isomorphic sentences form the basis for the construction of images and stories. He revealed this method in a posthumously published book, *How I Wrote Certain of My Books,* after committing suicide.[1] The book's disclosure reanimated the corpus of his writings, vitalized what might have been lost to obscurity, brought the writings into a second, literary life, and furthermore operated, according to Foucault, in its very *posthumousness* to textualize his life and make it methodical as well.[2] It would be very risky to speculate on whether Roussel brought any tactical sense to his death and resurrection—the dead can only say so much—but it is not unreasonable to notice how Foucault's own concerns were influenced by the very project of critical resurrection in and of itself. Foucault simply started at the end, at the Rousselian second sentence, at the fortuitous meeting of method and posthumous revelation, and thereupon conveyed the trappings of this juncture—language (especially writing) and death—to find them lurking behind Roussel's every line. Despite what has been noted as Foucault's antivisualism, he does not demonstrate any heightened sense of aurality: for him Roussel is text, that is, mute.[3] Yet Foucault could have just as easily perceived Roussel's posthumous statement as a writing *and* a voice from the grave; whatever lurked behind every line could have produced at least a rustle, a word caught in the throat. That is why, when I listen for Roussel's voice playing backward through his life, I hear a phonograph.

Phonography represents, as its needle scratches out its jagged line, an amalgam of writing and speech, joining writing through graphic inscription and speech through audibility. It thus carries a fuller complement of language and can better embrace the range of machinations in Rousselian wordplay than can the operations of language alone. The mechanics involved can fuse, in an economy of parts and movement, procedures of repetition and imitation with his technophilia and penchants for the popular arts, such as ventriloquy and vocal imitation. The phonograph can fix the ephemerality of sound into the concentrated form of objecthood, handing it over to Rousselian fetishism, and simultaneously can grind the transience of sound to a halt as effectively as any death motif. Furthermore, for the fifty years straddling 1900, it was the machine of choice for repopulating the world by reanimating the dead, especially by returning celebrities, despots, and loved ones to that desperately exaggerated degree of vitality: glory. Consequently, Roussel can be resurrected in a profusion of other individuals just as glorious, fulfilling his own deep desire to be recognized among the greats of literature. But recording is indiscriminate, it picks up background noise as faithfully as it records the golden throat in the foreground, it captures individuals not so glorious, aspirations unrealized, claims lacking legitimacy, and the type of noise that rattled throughout the nineteenth century, the historical machine shop of Roussel's own reanimations. When this background is played back, an interesting thing occurs: Roussel's writings cease sounding so peculiar.

But why listen to a Roussel novel? There are few works as sundrenched. His writing has been repeatedly described in glowing terms: "a poetry at high noon, in which objects cast no shadow around them";[4] Foucault talks of Roussel's linguistic "solar void" while Robbe-Grillet believes that sight may indeed be

"Roussel's favorite sense."[5] And it is true as far as it goes. Light paints the skin of objects in his novels while the surface of the writing itself teems with scenes nested among the minutia of other scenes. Nowhere are enigmas left unexplained; nothing is left dark and mysterious: even the moon in *Locus Solus* is bright enough to usher the parade of spectacles undiminished deep into the night. The novel's preoccupation with death could be traced to the death of Roussel's mother at the time of the writing of the novel, but throughout the novel the manner in which he successfully resists dwelling on a failing light or a claustrophobic mourning is mirrored in the window he installed upon the lid of his mother's coffin.

Roussel, moreover, understood his adult life as one long attempt to return to an early illumination, the ecstasy he experienced for several months at age nineteen while writing *La Doublure* (1897). As he told the psychiatrist Dr. Pierre Janet,

Everything I wrote was surrounded in rays of light; I would close the curtains for fear the shining rays that were emanating from my pen would escape through the smallest chink; I wanted to throw back the screen and suddenly light up the world. To leave these papers lying about would have sent out rays of light as far as China and the desperate crowd would have flung themselves upon my house. But I did indeed have to take precautions, rays of light were streaming from me and penetrating the walls, the sun was within me and I could do nothing to prevent the incredible glare.... I was more alive at that moment than at any other time of my whole existence.[6]

This euphoric light etched Roussel a third eye of sorts: he finds himself basking in the glory of "those who feel burning on their forehead...the resplendent star which they carry there,"[7] a figure he apparently borrowed from Camille Flammarion, the prolific popularizer of astronomy, the paranormal, and especially life after death, whom Roussel avidly admired.

Roussel did not die within the luminosity he sought. But what he did achieve was audible: "The only kind of success I have ever really experienced derived from singing to my own piano accompaniment and above all my numerous impersonations of actors and ordinary folk. But there at least my success was enormous and complete."[8] These talents were embodied in the four-year-old Bob Bucharessas, in the 1910 novel *Impressions of Africa,* who "began a series of imitations which he accompanied with expressive gestures; the different sounds of a train getting up speed, the cries of domestic animals, a saw grating on a free-stone, the sharp pop of a champagne cork, the gurgling of liquid as it is poured out of a bottle, the fanfare of hunting horns, a violin solo and the plaintive notes of a 'cello, all these comprised an astounding repertoire which, to anyone who shut his eyes for a moment, afforded a complete illusion of reality."[9]

We need go no further than his two main novels to hear Roussel demonstrate his own skills, the fantastic sound technologies and the remarkable sounds produced.[10] It is also obvious how sound, working inward and outward from the surfaces of his texts, operates to supply an environmental and corporeal volume that vivifies and gives dimension to his scenes. It becomes difficult, in fact, when confronted with these sonic achievements of Roussel, to place him so confidently behind the eye alone; instead, one must acknowledge a tenaciously persistent aurality in an otherwise visualist universe. This persistence, which can be found at every level of his writing, is exemplified by his writing method, which is actually several devices with a common homophonic operation: "This method is ...related to rhyme. In both cases there is unforeseen creation due to phonic combinations."[11] Unlike conventional rhyme, however, Roussel's homophonics have no mnemonic function and do not link divergent elements to a shared meaning; they instead unleash highly divergent meanings from minor phonic alteration. It is then the role of the long, labored detailings used to construct certain images or entire stories to unify what phonics split apart. Language rushes in to restore an acoustic equilibrium and to defuse disjunctures brought about by puns and other wordplay. The investment of language in this gap, the labor replacing the play, operates as the same vivification.

Douglas Kahn

Sound reverberates between both poles and underscores every moment, yet whenever sound occurs in Roussel's works, it is never far from visuality. A visual germ is contained within some instances of the method; a slight variation in sound is often paralleled by an equally slight graphic variation, and they work in tandem to explode into divergent meanings. The example most commonly referred to is a delicate plosive difference generated by the shift of the stem of a *b* down to form a *p*.[12] The descent of the stem of the *b*— the pen comes down upon the paper and the stylus drops down upon its surface—relates aurality to visuality within the phonemics of writing and the inscriptive basis of phonography, which itself was preceded by the nineteenth-century developments of visible sound and visible speech and provoked speculations about the possibilities of a fully technologized alphabet of all sounds. The phonographic capacity to store time itself was prefigured in popular practices of astronomy, in seeing how starlight reaching the earth contained the years of its travel and was thus a recording mechanism, bracketed by the seemingly instantaneous perception of the star and some idea of the light's actual age. An instaneous perception of earth from the heavens could itself travel recursively, its own light beam hitting the earth like a stylus, sparking recall of all the events of years past. Like the phonograph, Roussel too was prefigured by astronomy and the speed of light, by the glorious individuals who bore a star on the forehead and by the astronomy and spiritualism of Camille Flammarion.

THE SOUND OF OLD STARLIGHT

That time could run backward and raise the dead from the vantage of starlight was demonstrated in Flammarion's story *Lumen*.[13] The story consists of a dialogue between the Inquirer and the spirit of a recently deceased friend, Lumen. In one scene Lumen describes his travels far into space where he joins a group of spirits from other worlds who look back instantaneously upon Earth and witness France, 1793. The

Death in Light of the Phonograph

spirits ask, "Have they enacted a law of death, these creatures tainted with human blood? And what mean these scaffolds erected every morning, whence drop the heads of men and women, children and gray-beards?..." (p. 19). Lumen realizes that by traveling through space and moving through (protocinematic) planes, he can observe any past event as it unfolds, or in reverse. After witnessing the battle of Waterloo in reverse, he is reminded of a poem:

> *The drum sounds strange,*
> *Its echoes beat the skies;*
> *In their trenches, come to life,*
> *The dead old soldiers rise. (p. 74)*

The existence here of percussion jerking back into a sharp sucking sound and echoes transformed into utterances leads to a description of the words of General Cambronne running backward in time that contains the type of homophony found in Roussel's method:

LUMEN:

It is evident that if we moved in the air with a speed greater than that of sound, we should hear inversely sounds proceeding from the lips of an interlocutor. If, for instance, he recites an Alexandrine, an auditor, retiring with the speech above stated, starting from the moment in which he heard the last foot, would successively encounter the eleven other feet which had gone before, and hear the Alexandrine backwards.

INQUIRER:

Hence, to return to the battle of Waterloo,

you would have heard ...

LUMEN:

If what happens in the order of light happens also in the order of sound, I should have heard a shapeless jumble of syllables like this:

Pas-rend-se-ne-et-meurt-de-gar-la
[the inverse of La garde meurt et ne se rend pas.]
which would have been incomprehensible to me. I should have
sought different meanings in these syllables.

INQUIRER:

Perhaps you would have thought, logically modifying the sounds,
that Cambronne, answering the summons of the English officer,
told him to go to the home of shades, thus:

Pars en ce lieu, et meurs! De guerre las...
[Hence to that place, and die! Tired of war...] (p. 81)

For Flammarion, light and sound were merely sepa-
rated by degrees of speed. Light, however, required an astronomical
position for the comprehension of its speed while sound was within
the reach of terrestrial experience. Lumen was required to look at
earthlight from a great distance, as though it were old starlight, to
witness history in reverse, yet he could imagine sound slowing down
while on earth's *terra firma* to the point where

*men could not speak while walking. Two friends are talking together, one is a
step, two steps, in advance,—metre ahead, say; and as sound occupies several
seconds in traversing this metre, it would follow that instead of hearing the
sequel of the phrase uttered by his friend, the pedestrian would hear over
again, in inverse order, the constituent sounds of the first phrases. Hence, it
follows that we could not talk while walking, and that three-fourths of men
could not understand one another. (p. 82)*

Light here is a state, too regular, pervasive, and fast
to be traced to an action or to evidence duration. Sound, on the
other hand, is experientially connected with an action and utterance
(people produce sounds with their bodies, but they cannot produce
light), generating a space between action and sound (exception: hearing one's own voice). The distance between these two poles could be

Death in Light of the Phonograph

traversed without much recourse to concept. It thus seems that the story's scientific proposition—"The physical law of the *successive transmission of light* into space is one of the *fundamental elements of the condition of eternal life*. Under this law every event is imperishable, and the past is always present" (p. 161)—would be better experienced through sound.

EDISONIAN AFTERLIFE

The phonograph was the old starlight of earth on earth, a self-perception stored in time and relayed instantaneously from a great distance. To the extent that it spoke, it appeared already old at its birth, as if its grooves were the wrinkles of both infancy and old age with speech folded in a furrowed brow. Perhaps this perception of generations collapsing into one another arose because of the phonographic capacity for perfect memory, or because the simplicity in materials and design suggested that its birth was long overdue. A more likely reason was its instant mastery of adult speech, which is already precociousness enough, but this brought some individuals to entertain the idea of a maturation process that could develop another realm of communication altogether, that of backward speech: "An attempt has been made to obtain speech from the phonograph by taking the words registered inversely to their true direction. In this way the sounds obtained were necessarily quite unlike the words uttered; yet Messrs. Fleeming Jenkin and Ewing have observed that not only are the vowels unchanged by this inverse action, but consonants, syllables, and even whole words may be reproduced with the accent they would have if spoken backward."[14]

Just as from the stellar vantage point in Flammarion's story, backward phonographic speech was accompanied by a replaying of the past and the resurrection of the dead.[15] It is no surprise, therefore, to find Lumen-like spirits at the root of Edison's own eschatology and cosmology of recording. After all, Edison developed his philosophy and his status as an expert on the afterlife only after his body had techno-melded with the mediational properties of the phonograph, becoming a quasi-body which could better commune with ghosts—his famed halo effect actually began with the invention of the phonograph, after which he was named the Wizard of Menlo Park. People expected to hear dead voices played back through this half-man, half-phonograph, this machine that could die, a man that contained voices of the past. Does the recently deceased William James have anything else to say? And what about the final fates of those already killed in the Great War? As one appeal went, "Mothers, sisters, wives and sweethearts who have lost their beloved in the war, find their souls hungering for them....You, it becomes known, are investigating the problem, the question whether personality persists after so-called 'body-death'.... People everywhere are anxiously awaiting word from you."[16]

As his dying body drew closer to the spirit realm, it promised an especially high fidelity; thus millions of people were at his deathbed, huddling close to hear his dying words: "It is very beautiful over there."[17] Another technobody, Henry Ford, had already by this time been transported by Edison's proclamations: "The greatest thing that has occurred in the last 50 years is Mr. Edison's conclusion that there is a future life for all of us."[18] Consequently, the phonograph also prefigured Edison's designs for a device to communicate with the dead; his lengthy reasoning for this device even kept skipping at a certain point: the number 50,000.

Edison's spirit physics took place in the brain, where "life units" used the Broca's fold, the third convolution at the left frontal lobe held to be the cortical locus of speech, as a respite from their dispersion in the ether. When "life units" swarmed, things were created or changed. "Swarms do it all. The daisy has been the same for, say, 50,000 years. Then comes a variation. Perhaps the daisy becomes blue."[19] He was sure that, while constituting a human, they congregated inside the head because "eighty-two remarkable operations upon the brain have definitely proven that the meat of our personality lies in that part of the brain known as the fold of Broca."[20]

Death in Light of the Phonograph

The life units, personified as "little people," were tiny creatures of recording, concentrating their mnemonic functions in a high-density cortical medium: "Everything we call memory goes on in a little strip not much more than a quarter of an inch long. That is where the little people live who keep our records for us."[21] The precision of this phonographic workmanship threw Edison into a state of reverie because it so thoroughly outstripped his prior vision of putting "the 50,000 words...of one of Dickens's novels" onto a disc the size of a dinner plate.[22]

There was a chance that the life unit swarms did not scatter immediately after the body died, so Edison planned a device to detect any attempts that a swarm might make at communication. He would provide the dead with an extremely delicate instrument, an open mike, as delicate as the tasimeter, which measured starlight with an accuracy of 1/50,000 degree Fahrenheit,[23] or as powerful as his carbon microphone, which could amplify objects and events to magnitudes of total transformation: "The passage of a delicate camel's hair brush was magnified to the roar of a mighty wind. The footfalls of a tiny gnat sound like the tramp of Rome's cohorts. The ticking of a watch could be heard over a hundred miles."[24] Edison's "spirit catcher" would be something of a valve against which the "slightest conceivable effort is made to exert many times its initial power for indicative purposes. It is similar to a modern power house, where man, with his relatively puny one-eighth horse-power, turns a valve which starts a 50,000-horse-power steam turbine."[25] Lest he be accused of "barnumizing" vaporware, he assured people that "I have been working out the details for some time; indeed, a collaborator in this work died only the other day. In that he knew exactly what I am after in this work, I believe he ought to be the first to use it if he is able to do so."[26]

The figure of Edison paralleled and made incursions into *Locus Solus* in many ways. The novel, which takes its name from the estate of the brilliant and wealthy inventor Martial Canterel, consists entirely of a tour of the fantastic relics and inventions found upon the site and is thus modeled on Menlo Park and its proprietor. In Janet's essay, Roussel uses the petty fiction of the pseudonym "Martial" and consequently identifies with Edison, perhaps under the auspices of his literary inventions. Canterel and Edison were well known for the tours of their estates, and Roussel for his touring, and they all commanded seemingly unlimited wealth and inventiveness. The list goes on.[27]

REANIMATION IN LOCUS SOLUS

There are two scenes of reanimation, among many others in *Locus Solus,* to which phonography is central. Both represent the nexus where reanimation and an accumulated repopulation, historical glory, and archived immortality congeal in the phonograph and thereby provide a good occasion to call forth some history and voices from the dead to accompany Roussel in his solitary place. The two scenes are (1) the reanimation of Danton's deboned head, and (2) the attempt by Lucius Egroizard to write phonographically his dead daughter's voice.

SCENE 1: THE REANIMATION OF
DANTON'S DEBONED HEAD

The narrator was among a small group of visitors on a tour of the estate conducted by Canterel. Near the beginning of the tour the group came to an enormous, jewel-like glass vat filled with a very special lustrous, highly oxygenated liquid of metallic and electric properties capable of freely sustaining terrestrial creatures immersed within its depths; this water was known as *aqua micans.* Among the fantastic entities inhabiting the tank was a hairless Siamese cat and the deboned head of Danton. The cat was very intelligent and well rehearsed in carrying out tasks within the vat: when it was first submerged into the tank, its already electrifiable short hair reacted to the aqua micans by conveying the sound of "a feeble and confused hum" (p. 66) and by becoming even more electrified, which caused

Canterel pain in its handling. Because the cat's electrified fur would interfere in a special demonstration involving Danton's deboned head that required the cat's assistance, the fur was removed and the once-white cat became pink. Danton's pickled head was in the possession of Canterel after having been passed down through several generations, from an initial behest of Danton himself. Because of an amateur embalming job, however, the head had lost all its skin, hair, and flesh, and only the muscles, nerves, and brain remained. Canterel removed the encumbrance of the skull and suspended the flaccid mask by threads to maintain a semblance of its original proportions.

In the demonstration, Canterel fed the hairless cat a bright red pill made from a substance he had discovered while researching animal magnetism. This pill "temporarily changed the cat's entire body into an extremely powerful electric battery" (p. 59). The cat swam toward a metal cone that had several holes in it, placed his muzzle into the cone, and then proceeded to make contact with the cortical surface of Danton's brain, passing along a charge through the cone.

It seemed as though life once more inhabited this recently immobile remnant of facies. Certain muscles appeared to make the absent eyes turn in all directions, while others periodically went into action as if to raise, lower, screw up or relax the area of the eyebrows and forehead; but those of the lips in particular moved with wild agility, undoubtedly due to the amazing gift of oratory that Danton once possessed.

...Earlier, in the course of similar experiments, Canterel had accustomed his eyes to interpret the movements of the buccal muscles, and now as the words appeared, passing over the remains of the great orator's lips, he revealed them to us. They were disjointed fragments of speech, full of vibrant patriotism. Stirring periods, once publicly uttered, surged pell-mell from the pigeon-holes of memory to be reproduced automatically on the lower part of the ruined mask. The intense twitching of the other facial muscles, likewise originating in the manifold recollections sent up from the depths of the past by certain climactic hours full of parliamentary activity, showed how

Douglas Kahn

expressive Danton's hideous snout must have been on the platform.
(pp. 59–60)

SCENE 2: LUCIUS EGROIZARD'S ATTEMPTS TO WRITE HIS DEAD DAUGHTER'S VOICE PHONOGRAPHICALLY

Lucius, an expert craftsman and devotee to the legacy of Leonardo da Vinci, went mad upon witnessing his one-year-old daughter, Gillette, viciously murdered by a dozen bandits who trampled her while dancing a jig. His first reaction at the end of this ritual was to "burst out laughing, imitating the gait of the odious dancers as he raved" (p. 198). He continued his imitations by repeatedly reenacting the same macabre scene using finely crafted constructions, products of a unity of art and science characteristic of Leonardo, whom Lucius, in his delirium, thought himself to be. After a series of unsuccessful stints at asylums, Lucius was taken in by Canterel for both therapy and public display. The therapy was founded upon giving full rein to Lucius' imitative urges so that his lament might find its fullest expression and mourning could run its course.[28]

The most promising course of therapeutic action was Lucius' attempts to recreate Gillette's voice phonographically. If anything would bring her back, it was this invocation, for her voice would infer her body, her presence, her very being. He would draw her closer with his endeavors to speak phonographically, empathizing with her own struggles to speak, both when she was still alive and as she attempted to speak from the dead. Taking notice of the spectators on the tour, Lucius barked out the single command, "Sing." Prompted by Canterel, a female member of the tour started to sing a phrase from an opera that began, "*O Rebecca....*" "Lucius briskly interrupted her and made her endlessly repeat the same fragment, paying particular attention to the very pure vibrations of the last note" (p. 192). With this tune fresh in his mind, he conducted a complex procedure using a number of implements set out before him upon a table. First he took a piece of fatty bacon that had been constructed into a miniature fathom, with slivers of red meat forming the measurement lines, that retained its proportions when compressed or stretched, and used it to register small points upon a green wax tablet with a golden needle. "Finally the green tablet showed a short, thin, straight line composed of short pricks resembling those on phonograph cylinders when a voice has been recorded on them" (p. 193). He then lit a lamp that flashed brightly at three-second intervals, feeding the flashes through a faceted red garnet cradled at the center of a white card. Focusing a varying number of flashes (from one to fifteen) through different facets of the garnet upon the indentations already inscribed on the wax tablet, he thus formed the flashes almost imperceptibly, with subtle variations in the warmth of the red light and green wax, as subphonemic elements in "the future quality of the embryonic sounds" (p. 194). After carefully modeling each indentation separately, he ran a hand-held phonograph over the resultant line on the tablet, and we heard a close simulation of the original "*O Rebecca...*" just as the phrase had initially been sung by the tour member. "It appeared that the madman artificially created all sorts of human voices by the process submitted to our eyes. In an effort to recover the voice of his daughter in her first attempts to talk, he multiplied the trials, hoping to discover by chance some timbre which might guide him towards success by approaching his ideal" (p. 195). He concentrated on the last vowel *a* and with another attempt created a "long, merry syllable which,... recalling the smiling first efforts of very young children eager to talk" (pp. 203–204), paralleled, with other attempts at the simulation of her speech, the initial attempts of the child to produce her first words, the first letter of the alphabet. Finally, his efforts bore fruit: "Her voice.... It's her voice... my daughter's voice!... It's you, my Gillette.... They haven't killed you. ... You're here ... beside me.... Speak, my darling" (p. 204).

These two scenes are separated by a chapter devoted entirely to tableaux of resurrected individuals who reenact what appear at first to be entirely enigmatic rituals, but with inspection they are revealed to be powerfully emblematic scenes from their lives. Encouraged by his success with Danton's head, Canterel decides he could formulate a chemical procedure applicable to a greater number of deceased. The process begins with the injection of the red substance of resurrectine into the cranium of the deceased where it hardens to encase the brain. A second substance, vitalium, is then introduced in the form of a rod to any point on the surface of the resurrectine. The reaction between the two substances produces a vitalization of the corpse, which then automatically performs a scene from its life, over and over again until the rod of vitalium is withdrawn. The interaction of a rod that bears down upon a surface, resulting in activity and life, is modeled on the phonograph, with its stylus bearing down upon the recording surface. We can hear the phonograph clearly when Foucault writes, "[The rod of vitalium] comes from the outside and brings to the secret shell the vivacity of the moment...with it the moment starts and the past returns."[29]

Usually in the process of dying, which moves in a forward direction, people have their *entire* lives flash before their eyes. In reanimation by resurrectine and vitalium, when the process reverses and a person becomes undead, only *one* scene of singular importance is replayed, and replayed again. The same is true of other reanimations: Lucius sought out Gillette's momentous entry into speech, and when the funnel on the cat's muzzle phonographically bore down upon the grooves of the brain, it was Danton's oratory of historical import that was redelivered, rather than a profusion of everyday speech. Selection comes into play when confronting the expanse of a life or the historical stockpile of lives, resulting respectively in exemplary moments or individuals basking in glory. The stockpiling of lives and their moments was accelerated by the fact if not by the function of the phonograph, by the repopulation that attends the repeatability of voices and by the recuperation of eons of unrecorded sound. The mechanical simplicity of the phonograph itself led many to question why it hadn't been invented long before;

they then wondered only about the voices and sounds of distinguished people and events; for example, Edison wanted most to hear Napoleon's voice, many more wanted to hear the Word.[30] In this din, light attracts light. Roussel is drawn to Dante, Shakespeare, the famous table turner Victor Hugo, Wagner, and Napoleon, all those with a resplendent star burning on their forehead.

The proximity of the phonograph enabled Lucius Egroizard to resurrect Leonardo da Vinci into his own body—Lucius had been a member of a "cult of Leonardo" and then in his delirium thought himself to be Leonardo—thus forming another link in the novel's complex of imitation and repetition. Joining Edison, Canterel, and Roussel, Lucius and Leonardo are revealed as inventors who displayed themselves as they displayed their inventions. Lucius's phonographic writing can be derived from a combination of Leonardo's predilection toward prosthesis, specifically the speech synthesis implied by the laryngeal flute, and his enigmatic script, thought by some to be demonic. An even closer connection may exist, with respect to his handwriting, through an image with the following description: "Leonardo da Vinci giving thanks to God for having escaped from Murderers with only one of his hands dislocated. One of the Criminals is beheaded and another is seen at a Distance."[31] Leonardo's injury to his right hand, and adapation to a left-handed script, occurred, in other words, as a result of the same type of confrontation with bandits experienced by Lucius and his family.

THE FIRST SCRAWL OF SPEECH

Lucius' delirious attempt to resurrect his dead daughter phonographically through her voice demonstrates one of Roussel's clearest connections with nineteenth-century technology. In this instance, Roussel generates many of the aspects of the story by filtering the century's aspirations and actualities through key moments of his writing method and, most interestingly, through the technology of his own ecstatic delirium. Roussel, moreover, looks back into the past century, as if into his own past, for the enthusiasm accompanying the birth of a world of mechanical wonder that might regenerate the momentous vitality, the unlimited possibility, of his youthful ecstasy. In other words, he searches the death that is the past, for a vivification machine. This machine is the phonograph, releasing its voice at the intersection of three powerful discursive and technological trajectories, in the same way that Gillette's voice is released as a result of the skilled deployment of a number of technologies. The three areas are visible sound/speech (Chladni plates, Wheatstone's kaleidophone, singing flames, phonautograph), speech synthesis and automata in general,[32] and universal languages and alphabets.[33] Their intersection immediately produced ideas and actual attempts to read and write phonographically, but even by the time that Edison's phonograph etched its surface with "dots and dashes, like the marks on the fillet of a Morse instrument,"[34] there was already speculation that a phonographic alphabet was possible where *all* sounds would be writable and readable.

All these influences, the protophonographic trends leading to the birth of the phonographic voice, the writing technologies embodied in the resurrection or animation of youth—Gillette on the cusp of speech, the first machine words, Roussel's return to ecstasy—were manifested in the experiences of Edison's main competitor, Alexander Graham Bell. After accompanying his father, Melville, to Charles Wheatstone's demonstration of Baron von Kempelen's eighteenth-century speech automaton, the young Alexander set out with his brother to construct a speaking machine. The brothers' speaking machine was cast from a human skull and fitted in part with rubber cheeks, rubber lips stuffed with cotton batting, and a wooden tongue controlled by levers from a keyboard. During a related experiment they were party to killing a neighborhood cat, "an animal that produced sounds greatly resembling the human voice, especially at night," in order to study its larynx, and they also enlisted the family dog in their projects: while the dog produced a steady growl, the brothers manipulated its jowls to say, at the

Death in Light of the Phonograph

height of articulation, "How are you, grandmamma?"[35] Their father, like so many others in the family an elocutionist and teacher of the deaf, devised a system of Universal Alphabetics, a graphic prosthesis, based upon the positioning of the speech organs. Alexander assisted the demonstration of this system in which, after he was sent out of the lecture hall

the members of the audience were invited to make any sorts of sound they desired, to be symbolized by my father. It was just as easy for him to spell the sound of a cough, or a sneeze, or a click to a horse as a sound that formed an element of human speech.

Volunteers were called to the platform, where they uttered the most weird and uncanny noises, while my father studied their mouths and attempted to express in symbols the actions of the vocal organs he had observed.

I was then called in, and the symbols were presented to me to interpret; and I could read in each symbol a direction to do something with my mouth.

I remember upon one occasion the attempt to follow directions resulted in a curious rasping noise that was utterly unintelligible to me. The audience, however, at once responded with loud applause. They recognized it as an imitation of the noise of sawing wood, which had been given by an amateur ventriloquist as a test.[36]

The young Alexander soon matured from the type of imitative skills displayed by Roussel's prodigal Bob Bucharessas to full-grown phonography; he just matured a little too late. While teaching his father's Universal Alphabetics, he developed a range of modifications on the phonautograph. Later, he lamented his mistake of trying to develop a stylus modeled on a "pencil of air" instead of a metallic stylus; otherwise he was certain he could have invented the phonograph before Edison. In a letter to his father-in-law written only a few months after Edison's patent, Bell wrote, "It is an astonishing thing to me that I could possibly have let this invention slip through

Douglas Kahn

my fingers when I consider how my thoughts have been directed to this subject for so many years."[37]

During demonstrations of Universal Alphabetics, Melville Bell "symbolized" and animated his son's jowls, without touching him, without wires, just as effectively as Alexander and his brother had done in a less mediated form with the family dog. This generational descent of speech—reminiscent of the scene in Roussel's *Impressions of Africa* where Stephen Alcott echoes speech off his sons' chests, beginning with a shout against the oldest son and ending with a whisper off the youngest—is repeated in Lucius' attempt to write his dead daughter's voice. Prior to her death she had been in the process of learning to speak, thus, when Lucius labors to recreate her voice phonographically, he is also pedagogically teasing speech out of his less mechanized offspring. We find the same parent-teacher association with Edison, who was also involved in a project to write speech. His first recorded word, "Halloo!" (on embossed paraffined paper) showed him that "mechanically speaking the letters of the Alphabet" was plausible.[38] "Halloo!" as if someone were there, ready to respond. Apparently there was someone there, for Edison and his assistant, according to one biographer, "had heard the first strangled cries of the infant talking machine."[39] As if to allay these cries, Edison sang "Mary had a little lamb" as his first words to the phonograph, making it the first baby in history to sing its own lullaby.

The design of Lucius' two-tiered technology recapitulated the birth of the phonograph in the way it is split between phonautographic and phonographic technologies: the hog bristle and lampblack of the phonautograph and the phonographic sapphire stylus on wax are repeated in his dual inscriptive process using needle, (sputtering) lamp illumination, and precious stone (garnet) on wax tablet. Lucius' process of writing is also an expression of Roussel's own writing technology during the instant genius of his neuropathic episode. The demented Lucius' deft light-ray melting of the fine points etched into the wax tablet contains Roussel's ecstatic fear that

Death in Light of the Phonograph

"the shining rays that were emanating from my pen would escape through the smallest chink."[40] The resurrection of Roussel's youthful illumination, the first moment that his glory had shone through, the cusp into immortal speech, was thereby repeated in the phonographic simulation of Gillette's first stammerings and in the nineteenth-century stammerings of mechanized speech as it struggled to move past transcription and reproduction to utterance.

Roussel also supplied Lucius with a writing method similar to his own. In the structure of Roussel's method slight homophonic differences splay one sentence into two highly divergent ones, or as Foucault says, the "isomorphic sentence whose strange images create a void toward which the language rushes."[41] The same type of homophonic relation exists within Lucius' method between the processes of vocal reproduction and simulation, the transcription of the opera singer and the approximation of Gillette's voice, respectively. The first stage involved the phonographic writing of a phoneme from the opera singer's "O Rebecca..." only after she endlessly repeated the same phrase, that is, only after she engaged in phonographic playback. The reproduction process was then enacted in a reverse of the biological gender relations, with the opera singer providing the germ and Lucius being responsible for the period of gestation. The germ was contained among the select vibrations from one of the many repetitions of the last "aaaaaa" in "O Rebecca..." The distance between this "aaaaaa" and Gillette's smiling "aaaaaa" was covered by a process of simulation; in other words, there was already a goal in mind toward which to write, a Rousselian second sentence, one already heard in the opera singer's very first utterance. Instead of language rushing into the gap between this homophonic difference, in rushed a long story of technology, from birth to death and vice versa. The main difference, however, between their respective methods was that one used it from posterity, the other from parentage, to resurrect the dead. But, of course, they were the same person talking.

Douglas Kahn

Whereas Lucius' phonographic written voice occurred at the meeting of nineteenth-century technological trends of writing and machines, Danton's head was the product of neurotechnological activities of the same period, specifically, the search for the voice, a search that in many ways the phonograph solved and complicated, lodging it in a machine where it could faithfully be found and repeated while at the same time removing it from the body where it had been kept from contamination by sociality. This search, preceding and concurrent with phonography, was elaborated by a set of fundamental questions: Where might the voice reside? What was its attachment to the soul, and where might the soul itself be located? When and where did the voice become detached from the soul? Where in the body was the voice, and what relationship might it have to the body, brain, and mind? When and where did the voice become detached from the body? What happens when it is located outside the body? What happens to the body then? What happens to the soul, has it atrophied? The neurotechnological strategy toward these problems did employ, however, tactics from the same class of scriptural techniques used by Lucius: the surface of the brain had to be exposed and read; styluses prodded and traced the cortical folds to find the voice and flush it out. These techniques were accompanied by various violences—the data derived from combat and self-inflicted wounds, vivisection—whatever was required to remove the skull, exposing the slate of the brain, while the subject was still alive and free to talk. In the figure of Danton, Roussel makes a connection between the sabre and the phonographic stylus, with their respective violences, decapitation, and the voice wrenched from the throat. In addition, as the cat jockeys the funnel/stylus to the specific spot on Danton's cerebrum, animating the lips into famous oratory, speech in Roussel is also located. Roussel's poem "My Soul," written at age seventeen and renamed after his ecstatic encounter as "The Soul of Victor Hugo," contains a self-observation of his own disembodied brain: "Licked by the sublime flame/Arising from my brain."

Foucault finds Roussel's soul—"My soul is a strange root where fire and water struggle"—best represented by Canterel's vat of *aqua micans* and Danton's severed head.[42] In this way, the observation of Danton's deboned head by the *Locus Solus* tour is also the observation of Roussel's soul and brain, for psychotechnics naturally begs self-consciousness.

The speech of the historical Danton was severely dislocated by a sabre-induced Cartesian split, his head coming to rest in the basket/vat of Descartes' own *aqua micans*, the ethereal "subtle matter" that phosphoresces when agitated. Danton rehearsed the deliverance of his head by parceling out parts of his body: "If I left my balls to Robespierre and my legs to Couthon the Committee of Public Safety could last a bit longer."[43] He received some assistance from Vadier who said, "That fat stuffed turbot, we'll gut him too," to which Danton replied that he would cannibalize Vadier, eat his brains and shit in his skull.[44] Just before the fateful moment, in his famous last words Danton made an observance of his own disembodied head, "Above all, don't forget to show my head to the people: it's worth seeing."[45] In the novel, Canterel came into possession of Danton's decapitated head because it was a family heirloom; his great-great-grandfather, who was a close childhood friend of Danton, had been entrusted with the head. With such generational descent ending in the first spasmodic cries of speech, the *aqua micans* could very well have been amniotic, if it weren't for the impossibility of a breech birth. Roussel himself happened to be in a curiously homophonic descent from the historical Danton's protégé: Rousselin de Saint-Albin. Rousselin, known as a primary anecdotal source on Danton's life, leaves the storytelling mantle to Roussel and Canterel, who become responsible for generating the anecdotal record of Danton's afterlife.

The period of Danton's decapitation was the historical pivot from which earlier attempts to locate the soul physiologically (e.g., Swedenborg's scalpel) were transformed into nineteenth-century attempts to locate speech on the cerebral cortex,

Douglas Kahn

a transformation characterized by speech being set askew from its prior singular, symmetrical, and central position in the psyche and ousted from its cohabitation with the soul.[46] A crucial moment came in 1839 when Jean Baptiste Bouillaud finally found an appropriate patient to provide him with empirical proof for his speculations on the cortical localization of speech. The patient had shot off the front part of his skull, disclosing his frontal lobes and supplying Bouillaud with the type of deboning necessary to make visual and manual contact with the lair of speech. "Curious to know what effect it would have on speech if the brain were compressed, we applied to the exposed part a large spatula pressing from above downwards and a little from front to back. With moderate pressure, speech seemed to die on his lips; pressing harder and more sharply, speech not only failed but a few words were cut off suddenly."[47] The area that the spatula prodded would soon be known, after Paul Broca, as the Broca's area or Broca's fold, the very same spot so important in Edison's cosmology of recording. The patient responsible for Broca's discovery was a severely aphasic patient named Leborgne, who was known as Tan, the word he used in Morse-code/table-rapping fashion to communicate. Instead of waiting for a fortuitous self-surgical accident, the physician Paul Broca had to wait for Leborgne to die. The degeneracy of his speech, the absence of his words, could then be read, once the skull was removed, in the hole in his brain, which is exactly what hundreds of people have since done because his brain, like the head of Danton, was pickled and put in a glass jar. The gouged inscription is the recording of his recorded silences, and his brain on display, his posthumous glory.[48] In the next decade, the German physicians Gustav Theodor Fritsch and Eduard Hitzig successfully electrostimulated the brains of soldiers with fortuitous head wounds and, against the protests of antivivisectionists, the opened skulls of dogs and cats (Roussel reverses the role of the cat), yielding the Dantonesque jerky movements of, among other bodily parts, the face, tongue, throat, and lips. Parallel to these developments were corresponding speech acts in Mesmerism and spirituality in general.[49] It was not until nearly

Death in Light of the Phonograph

two decades after *Locus Solus* that electrostimulation of the cortex caught up with the cortical tweaking of Danton's memory when, during Wilder Penfield's neurological operation upon a fourteen-year-old epileptic female, a stray electrode brought forth memories of a traumatic event; in some circles the story she recalled is just as historically significant as any French political oration. The formidable phonographic memories of both the historical Danton and Roussel, however, needed only hair-trigger voltage: Rousselin tells the story of Danton having memorized the entire *Encyclopedia*,[50] while Roussel supposedly could recite verbatim the entirety of *Locus Solus*.[51]

Ventriloquy, like neurology and spiritualism, anticipated the phonograph's dislocation and control of speech, for its dislocated voice came not from the throat but from the stomach (ancient oracle attendants were known as belly prophets); it was released not from the mouth but thrown from the body (or the bowels of the earth). In one remarkable instance in 1878, however, ventriloquy's base in popular culture and legerdemain came into direct conflict with the scientific presumptions of neurology, at the site of the phonograph and involving the person of Jean Baptiste Bouillaud, no less. Bouillaud, who had managed to control remotely the speech of another person without moving his own lips, was unwilling to accept the fact that speech could be elicited without the aid of ventriloquy by a meatless, lipless machine—as Edison said, "It is funny after all. You have to pucker, to whistle, but the phonograph doesn't."[52] The incident occurred at the demonstration of Edison's phonograph to the Académie des Sciences in Paris. It was well under way when it was interrupted by Bouillaud. "Wretch! We are not to be made dupes of by a ventriloquist!"[53] Six months later Bouillaud appeared before a similar body and declared after close investigation of the apparatus "that it was impossible to admit that mere vile metal could perform the work of human phonation."[54] An 1899 account of this incident by Flammarion connects ventriloquy, phonography, and neurology with spirituality; he said Bouillaud's actions should stand as a warning of the dangers of dogmatic scientific incredulity and how

Douglas Kahn

such dogmatism can obstruct discussions of spiritualist phenomena.

The true threat of phonography came not from its ability to displace a voice but its ability to displace a person's *own* voice—*"The metal plate is talked to.... It talks back to you what you said to it"*—as one early account emphasized.[55] What did control of other people's voices mean when compared to the frightening experience of having an imposter quote you verbatim while other people, despite your protests, noticed no difference? The phonographed voice had lost its loyalty; it no longer evaporated in the moment of expressivity but lived on to plague one's absence, and it had no respect for the dead. As Edison said, "This tongueless, toothless instrument, without larynx or pharynx, dumb, voiceless matter, nevertheless utters your words, and centuries after you have crumbled to dust will repeat again and again to a generation that will never know you, every idle thought, every fond fancy, every vain word that you choose to whisper against this thin iron diaphragm."[56]

Edison used to bite the horn of the phonograph, as though in hapless revenge for the theft of the voice, in order to conduct the sound through his skull and compensate for his deafness. Hearing one's own voice takes place in large degree through bone conduction; it is generated in the throat and carried via the bones in the head to the inner ear, whereas the phonographed voice returns to its parent through air conduction, that is, without the bones. The phonographed selfsame voice is deboned.[57] Nineteenth-century skull-removal practices culminate, therefore, in a violent rupture with the body where the voice, wrenched out of the throat and lodged into the phonograph, takes the skull with it, establishing in a profound way, moreover, the first time in human history that the voice had been returned—unlike the myriad reflections that had always responded to one's own gaze. Phonographic deboning is, therefore, a machine-critique of Western metaphysics a century before Derrida's critique of Husserl,[58] for it uproots an experiential centerpiece for sustaining notions of the presence of the voice—hearing oneself speak—and moves the selfsame voice from its sacrosanct location into

Death in Light of the Phonograph

the contaminating realms of writing, society, and afterlife. Thus Danton's head, deboned by the phantasmagorical torque of the turntable, is the perfect emblem for the trajectory of nineteenth-century skull removal and for the phonographic reproduction of the selfsame voice with its violent corporeal and philosophical rupture.

For Roussel's purposes the phonographic voices of Lucius and Danton are the best voices of light, for light can hit the voice only on the surfaces of objects and environs. Western symbologies have generally located the workings of the voice above the clavicle yet they remain submerged in the body, whereas Danton's voice surfaced at his cerebral cortex, at his wagging lip muscles, and on a face that lacked any depth. Gillette's voice was first stamped out of her body, then synthesized through a process of writing with light. In both instances light exposed a raw surface, a raw voice, *skinned,* close to death, but light also illuminated a vivification, coming back from death, a giving of life where there should be none. The damaged figures involved—the delirious Lucius, the dishrag that was Danton—represent this odd purgatory that can go either way, as well as the metaphysical violence experienced during the historical moment signaled by the phonograph. Recording has since progressed to become submerged once again in the body, in genetics, where it can grow instead of engineer new voices and bodies, no doubt equally peculiar.

NOTES

1. Raymond Roussel, *How I Wrote Certain of My Books*, trans. by Trevor Winkfield (New York: SUN, 1977). Referred to hereafter as *How I Wrote*. The most familiar form of the method consists of creating a sentence (A) predisposed to mutations by punning, then making a very slight change in this sentence, completely mutating the sentence and creating a second sentence (B) with a very different meaning. A story is then constructed that links (A), in its role as the first sentence of the story, with (B), the last sentence. The story must go to wits' end to make ends meet; its contrivance is thereby generated out of the predictability of its conclusion, its waywardness generated out of its resolve, and the profusion of its detailing out of the identity that produced the story's frame. Most important, the story has ended before it has begun.

2. Michel Foucault, *Death and the Labyrinth*, trans. by Charles Ruas (New York: Doubleday, 1986).

3. See Martin Jay, "In the Empire of the Gaze: Foucault and the Denigration of Vision in 20th Century French Thought," in *ICA Documents 4*, ed. Lisa Appignanesi (London: Institute of Contemporary Art, 1986).

4. See Michel Leiris, "Conception and Reality in the Work of Raymond Roussel," in *Raymond Roussel: Life, Death and Works*, ed. Alastair Brotchie, Malcolm Green, and Antony Melville, as *Atlas Anthology No. 4* (London: Atlas Press, 1987), p. 74. This anthology is henceforth referred to as *Atlas*.

5. Alain Robbe-Grillet, "Riddles and Transparencies in Raymond Roussel," in *Atlas*, p. 104.

6. Pierre Janet, "The Psychological Characteristics of Ecstasy," in *Atlas*, pp. 40–41.

7. Janet, *Atlas*, p. 39.

8. Roussel, *How I Wrote*, p. 19

9. Raymond Roussel, *Impressions of Africa*, trans. by Lindy Foord and Rayner Heppenstall (New York: Riverrun Press, 1983), pp. 32–33.

10. For example, in *Impressions of Africa* alone we find, among other things, a limbless one-man band, a candle whose sputter imitates the sound of thunder, a man playing a flute carved from his own tibia, the pitched wheels of twelve chariots performing "a variety of popular airs," an orchestrion replete with gramophone fueled by the expansion and contraction of a thermally sensitive metal, a hiccupping mollusk, a talking horse, a man who can simultaneously sing four different parts from four different areas of his enormous

mouth, and rodent hair that produces two distinct notes per strand when bowed. In one scene, which takes place out on a field "suitable for certain experiments with long-distance acoustics," Stephen Alcott carefully arranges his six emaciated sons in a zigzag pattern with the oldest son closest to him descending back in age to the youngest (p. 84). The sons stand flexed, hollowing out their thoracic cavities into acoustic mirrors, off of which the father bounces a series of vocal pyrotechnics, the initial loudness on the eldest son's chest echoing into a whisper off the youngest son's chest. In another scene, a zither player teaches a huge, docile, and musically entranced worm, the inhabitant of a spring with water of unusually dense viscosity, how to play the zither. The worm rests in a mica trough filled with the heavy water. Touching the worm's body at certain points releases a drop onto the strings of the zither. The worm immediately remembers the sequence of touches and can soon play back/secrete musical pieces of the most complex "polyphonic acrobatics normally excluded from [the zither player's] own repertory" (p. 273).

11. Roussel, *How I Wrote*, p. 11.

12. This example was the genesis of the story "Among the Blacks" and is described in *How I Wrote*, p. 3:

I chose two almost identical words (reminiscent of metagrams). For example billard *[billiard table] and* pillard *[plunderer]. To these I added similar words capable of two different meanings,*

thus obtaining two almost identical phrases. In the case of billard *and* pillard *the two phrases I obtained were:*

1. Les lettres du blanc sur les bandes du vieux billard...
   [The white letters on the cushions of the old billiard table...]
2. Les lettres du blanc sur les bandes du vieux pillard...
   [The white man's letters on the hordes of the old plunderer...]

In the first, "lettres" was taken in the sense of lettering, "blanc" in the sense of a cube of chalk, and "bandes" as in cushions.

In the second, "lettres" was taken in the sense of missives, "blanc" as in white man, and "bandes" as in hordes.

The two phrases found, it was a case of writing a story which could begin with the first and end with the second.

13. Camille Flammarion, "Lumen," in *Stories of Infinity* (Boston: Roberts Brothers, 1873). Albert Michelson's determination of the velocity of light occurred at nearly the same time as the invention of the phonograph, but this was only the best determination. That light had velocity was known at least since Galileo, who thought it could be measured by two individuals well rehearsed in quickly uncovering lanterns and noting the difference. Flammarion's fascination with it was common for its time.

14. Count du Moncel, *The Telephone, The Microphone and the Phonograph* (New York: Harper and Brothers, 1879), p. 244.

15. Two examples. "In April 1889 Gouraud had recorded the voice of Robert Browning and the following year, after the poet's death, a small number of his friends were invited to the Colonel's home.... Browning began to recite his own poem, "How they brought the Good News from Ghent to Aix."

I sprang to the stirrup, and Joris, and he;
I galloped, Dirck galloped, we galloped all
three.

Then he faltered. 'I forget it,' he said. He was prompted, continued for a few more lines, then said: 'I am exceedingly sorry that I can't remember my own verses: but one thing that I shall remember all my life is the astonishing sensation produced by your wonderful machine.'" (From Ronald W. Clark, *Edison: The Man Who Made the Future* [New York: G. P. Putnam's Sons, 1977], p. 164.) An early *Scientific American* editorial (22 December 1877) heralded "the startling possibility of the voices of the dead being reheard through this device ...the voices of such singers as Parepa and Titiens will not die with them, but will remain as long as the metal in which they may be embodied will last." (Francis Jehl, *Menlo Park Reminiscences* [Dearborn, Michigan: Edison Institute, 1937], p. 168.)

16. A. D. Rothman, "Mr. Edison's 'Life Units': Hundred Trillion in Human Body May Scatter After Death—Machine to Register Them," *New York Times*, 23 January 1921, sec. 7.

17. Wyn Wachhorst, *Thomas Alva Edison:*
An American Myth (Cambridge, MA: The MIT Press, 1981), p. 140.

18. Wachhorst, *Thomas Alva Edison*, p. 140. This was the same Edison who in 1878 attended several meetings with Madame Blavatsky, and later, under the influence of a parapsychologist introduced to him by Henry Ford, attempted to engineer a telepathic device by "winding electric coils about his own and three other persons' heads." (Robert Conot, *Thomas A. Edison: A Streak of Luck* [New York: Da Capo Press, 1979], p. 428.

19. Thomas A. Edison, *The Diary and Sundry Observations of Thomas A. Edison*, ed. Dagobert D. Runes (New York: Philosophical Library, 1948), p. 226.

20. Shaw Desmond, "Edison 'Spirit Finder' Seeks Great Secret: Electric Wizard Discusses Life Beyond," *San Francisco Chronicle*, 27 August 1922, sec. F.

21. Ibid.

22. Clark, *Edison*, p. 78.

23. The temperature of the star Arcturus was used by Edison to gauge a solar eclipse during the Draper Astronomical Expedition in Rawlins, Wyoming. The tasimeter's sensitivity was discovered by accident when the carbon button, which is the central element of the tasimeter, emitted what Edison called "molecular music" after it was pressured slightly by the movements of the telephone handle into which it was situated. This music played on the same scale as the personified society of life units.

24. Jehl, *Menlo Park Reminiscences,* p. 140.

25. Edison, *The Diary,* p. 240.

26. Ibid., pp. 239–240. In effect he wanted to bring table rapping into the modern age by engineering a high-tech séance. The taps of table rapping had mixed with Morse code, Edison's own point of departure. Samuel Morse had already asked, "What hath God wrought?" and the line between Washington and New York was already operable by the time the spiritist craze was transmitted from the Fox family residence in Rochester, New York.

27. Roussel's technological processing of myth overlaps with the mythologization of Edison and his technologies; for example, commenting on the phonograph, one writer said that Edison was "the first mortal who removed the veil of Isis from one of the innermost shrines of Nature's temple" (Wachhorst, *Thomas Alva Edison,* p. 111). Edison's global ransacking to discover a vegetal filament for the electric light closely approximates the genre of imaginary voyage literature that served as a source of Roussel's writings, and they both possessed an admiration for Jules Verne. Edison's "barnumizing," and the use in his films of actual animals and exotic individuals from Barnum's ranks, followed the spectacle of popular entertainments and public demonstrations of technology that

informs both *Locus Solus* and *Impressions of Africa.* Finally, just as Edison received appeals from the companions of the war dead, Canterel too, after he developed a process for reanimation, "received many letters from frightened families who, out of affection, wished to see one of their loved ones live again before their eyes after the fatal moment" (Raymond Roussel, *Locus Solus,* trans. Rupert Copeland Cunningham [London, John Calder, 1983], p. 119.)

28. One example of the therapy recapitulated both the bandits' jig and the imitation of the dance that had deliriously swept over him. He constructed twelve small sculptural figures out of gold leaf that were suspended on drafts of warm air vented from the tiny holes of a piece of fabric stretched over glowing coals; by wandering over the fabric with his fingers, he could delicately interrupt the streams of air and set the billowy figures, like pneumatic marionettes, into the dance that killed his daughter. Just as the frightful dance had originally swept over his psyche, however, so too this recreation provoked an odd scene that hatched itself on the few remaining hairs upon his bald head; the fierce hallucination raging under his scalp sent single hairs leaping from one pore to another, eventually arranging themselves to dance the jig on his pate, in a pun on the scalp dances of the American Plains Indians, and following Roussel's own obsessive scalp-scorching method to keep grey hairs from inhabiting his head. Lucius could do nothing but suffer under this dance, as his daughter had done, until it subsided of its own accord.

29. Foucault, *Death and the Labyrinth*, p. 55.

30. See Carolyn Marvin, *When Old Technologies Were New* (New York: Oxford University Press, 1988), pp. 202–205.

31. Carlo Pedretti, commentary in *The Literary Works of Leonardo da Vinci*, volume 1 (Berkeley: University of California Press, 1977), pp. 96–97.

32. For a helpful chronology, see Hugh Davies, "A History of Recorded Sound," in *Poésie Sonore Internationale,* ed. Henri Chopin (Paris: Jean-Michel Place Editeur, 1979), pp. 13–40. Christian Gottlieb Kratzenstein, who devised a speaking machine in the late eighteenth century (c. 1780), had already anticipated a general telecommunication prosthesis when he conducted the first investigations of the effects of electricity on the human body (1744): "Sparks leaping from the blood running from the opened vein of an electrified man to a tin dish placed to receive the flow, added to the general conviction that electricity was a material substance of the body." (Park Benjamin, *A History of Electricity* [1898, reprint, New York: Arno Press, 1975], p. 502.) The nineteenth century carried on this tradition and became dominated by attempts at speech synthesis using the strategy of prosthetic design. Josef Faber of Vienna designed an apparatus in 1843 in which "a rubber tongue and lips make the consonants; a little

windmill, turning in its throat, rolls the letter R, and a tube is attached to its nose when it speaks French." (Alfred M. Mayer, "On Edison's Talking-Machine," *Popular Science Monthly* (April 1878), p. 719.)

33. The momentum reached past Roussel to others such as László Moholy-Nagy, who promoted phonographic writing in a 1922 *De Stijl* article, "Production—Reproduction."

An extension of [the phonograph] for productive purposes could be achieved as follows: the grooves are incised by human agency into the wax plate, without any external mechanical means, which then produce sound effects.... The primary condition for such work is laboratory experiments: precise examination of the kinds of grooves (as regards length, width, depth etc.) brought about by the different sounds; examination of the man-made grooves; and finally mechanical-technical experiments for perfecting the groove-manuscript score. (or perhaps the mechanical reduction of large groovescript records.)

(See Krisztina Passuth, *Moholy-Nagy* [New York: Thames and Hudson, 1985], p. 289.) He then applied the same ideas to his no-longer-extant drawn sound film, *The Sound of ABC,* which played graphic figures scratched onto the optical sound track, such as letters, lines, and profiles: "I wonder how your nose will sound?" (See Sibyl Moholy-Nagy, *Moholy-Nagy: Experiment in Totality* [New York: Harper & Brothers, 1950], pp. 68, 97.) Grigori Alexandrov, in debatable collaboration with Sergei Eisenstein, experimented with materially manipulated optical sound in the short film *Romance Sentimentale*. In a 1930 article, the film critic Harry Potamkin reports:

Alexandrov, so he told me, has played with the designs of sound by inscribing it directly on the negative and allowing light to make the final registration.... By studying the inscriptions closely one may come to an exact knowledge of these inscriptions and read them as easily as one reads musical notes for sound. The inscription for speech and that of sound differ only in the composition of the intervals and a close student will come to recognize the peculiarities of the different impressions. Actually sound will be created without being uttered!

(Harry Potamkin, "Playing with Sound," in *The Compound Cinema: The Film Writings of Harry Alan Potamkin* [New York: Teachers College Press, Columbia University, 1977], p. 87.)

34. Mayer, "On Edison's Talking-Machine," pp. 722–723. The year after the invention of the phonograph, Alfred Mayer in fact felt compelled to warn against phonographic writing; it was futile, he said, "to hope to be able to *read* the impressions and traces of phonographs, for these traces will vary, not alone with the quality of the voices, but also with the differently-related times of starting of the harmonics of these voices, and with the different relative intensities of these harmonics." (p. 723)

35. Alexander Graham Bell, "Prehistoric Telephone Days," *The National Geographic Magazine* 41, (March 1922), pp. 223–241.

36. Ibid., p. 228.

37. Cited in Warren Rex Isom, "A Wonderful Invention but not a Breakthrough," *Journal of the Audio Engineering Society* 25 (October/November 1977), p. 657.

38. Matthew Josephson, *Edison* (New York: McGraw-Hill, 1959), p. 160.

39. Ibid., p. 161.

40. Janet, *Atlas,* pp. 40–41.

41. Foucault, *Death and the Labyrinth*, p. 53. The separation in this scene between reproduction and simulation, which cannot be strictly demarcated, also represents the communicative transition from writing proper to phonography, which animates the vocal sounds transcribed by a phonetic alphabet, and the desired transition from a passive, transcriptive phonography to one that utters of its own accord.

42. Foucault, *Death and the Labyrinth,* pp. 68–69. The mesmeric connections are obvious: the etheric fluid, animal magnetism, the automatism, tub filled with metal filings, conducting rod, a group surrounding the tub. The sounds emanating from Canterel's vat—"vague strains of music consisting of a strange sequence of melodic passages, arpeggios and ascending and descending scales, which created a marvellous effect" (p. 51)—had added correspondence in Mesmer's sessions when he played on his glass armonica. (See Henri

Ellenberger, *The Discovery of the Unconscious* [New York: Basic Books, 1970], p. 57ff.) The armonica was also played during Robertson's *Fantasmagorie* to accompany his phantoms. The predecessor of Ben Franklin's armonica was the "glass music" played on a series of wine glasses, or *verrillon*. (See "Musical Glasses" in Sibyl Marcuse, *A Survey of Musical Instruments* [New York: Harper and Row, 1975], pp. 111–114.) The *verrillon* relates the sound emanating from fluid enclosed in glass to the sauterne which, when poured into the *aqua micans*, solidified into a miniature sun. Danton is also connected musically to the large zither-playing worm in *Impressions of Africa*; it too was boneless, dwelled in heavy water, created sounds while in a transparent mica sluice filled with heavy water, and had a great memory. The worm is, however, not a flaccid phonograph like Danton but instead belongs to the phonograph's predecessor, a fleshy, clockwork music. The *aqua micans*, where "fire and water struggle," as though the solution were alchemical in formulation, was also titrated from a long history of popular electrical entertainments, including Bose's instigation "Never can fire jump forth from the water's waves," before he drew a spark from water (J. L. Heilbron, *Electricity in the 17th and 18th Centuries* [Berkeley: University of California Press, 1979], p. 269.); Nollet's electric cats, predating Canterel's own feline dynamo; the "electric boy" of Nollet and others (Benjamin, *History of Electricity*, p. 530.); Marat's reputed restoration of sight to a blind man using electricity; the electric eel

treatment for gout; the shocking of corpses back to life; and the expanded electrical medicine of the nineteenth century (see the chapter entitled "Locating the Body in Electrical Space and Time" in Marvin, *When Old Technologies Were New*). Edison himself was convinced of direct current's therapeutic powers, and he developed technology toward this end. He even formulated a salve, "Edison's Polyform," for restoring electrical balance in the body. "Applied externally to the face, it worked on the theory that mucous membranes excrete an alkaline fluid, and serous membranes produce an acid, thus together producing electricity as a kind of battery." (See David E. Nye, *The Invented Self* [Odense: Odense University Press, 1983], p. 142.) Its direct action on the mucous membranes represented an effective removal of skin from the face.

43. Norman Hampson, *Danton* (New York: Holmes & Meier, 1978), p. 174.

44. Ibid., p. 155.

45. Ibid., p. 174.

46. The unity and centrality of the Cartesian pineal gland gave way to the asymmetry and proliferation of Gall's phrenology. Descartes thought that the pineal gland was the seat of interaction with the soul, positioned at the middle of the brain and hydraulically deploying animal spirits to the open pores in other parts of the brain. Only the pineal gland could be the seat of the soul because the bifurcated nature of the body and the senses always came together in "but one solitary and simple thought of one particular thing at one and the same moment," while everything else in the brain was split (Descartes, *The Passions of the Soul,* in *Descartes: Selections,* ed. Ralph M. Eaton [New York: Charles Scribner's Sons, 1927], p. 373.) The unity of utterance followed the unity of thought because the mouth, like the other organs of expulsion, was not split. Speech was dislocated and the soul was set asymmetrically askew by the phrenology of Franz Joseph Gall. He mapped the scalp symmetrically, but this was disrupted temporally because the different loci did not need to function synchronically, and he effectively replaced one soul with "nearly forty." (Anne Harrington, *Medicine, Mind, and the Double Brain* [Princeton: Princeton University Press, 1987], pp. 9, 15.) Gall's phrenological map sank below the scalp, penetrated the skull, and patterned the cortex for Bouillaud.

47. Francis Schiller, *Paul Broca* (Berkeley: University of California, 1979), p. 173.

48. See Schiller, "A Manner of Not Speaking," chapter 10.

49. The mesmerist Marquis de Puységur ranged a radiophonic, Bouillaud-like influence upon "a twenty-three-year-old peasant named Victor who, when magnetized, could read Puységur's thoughts... thus the magnetizer was able to direct Victor's speech, stop him in mid-sentence

and change his train of thought." (Chistopher McIntosh, *Eliphas Lévi and the French Occult Revival* [London: Rider and Company, 1972], p. 55. A similar radiophonic communication occurred in 1916 with the emplacement of Gurdjieff's voice into the chest of Ouspensky, where it conducted protracted conversations with its host and followed him from a Finnish dacha to the streets of St. Petersburg. (James Webb, *The Harmonious Circle* [Boston: Shambhala Publications, 1987], pp. 147–148.) Spencer Hall, a British practitioner of "phreno-mesmerism," during an 1843 public demonstration of his craft magnetized a local girl to react to a manual stimulation of her phrenological areas. The area of Imitation produced a phonographic, Fritsch-Hitzig effect: "Under the influence of Imitation, if the audience clapped, she clapped, and also imitated several other noises which caused considerable laughter." (Janet Oppenheim, *The Other World* [New York: Cambridge University Press, 1985], pp. 216–217.)

50. Hampson, *Danton,* p. 20.

51. Roussel, *How I Wrote,* p. 33, n. 53.

52. Jehl, *Menlo Park Reminiscences,* p. 170.

53. Camille Flammarion, *The Unknown* (New York: Harper and Brothers Publications, 1900), p. 3. Early demonstrations of the phonograph repeatedly met with charges of ventriloquy and demonstrators were often asked to leave the room during playback. In the scene featuring

Stephen Alcott and his sons in *Impressions of Africa*, witnesses of the spectacle felt it necessary to step close to the sons to make sure that the father's ricocheting voice was not in fact ventriloquistically performed by each of the sons.

54. Ibid., p. 4.

55. Mayer, "On Edison's Talking-Machine," pp. 720–721.

56. Conot, *Thomas A. Edison,* p. 81.

57. Hearing oneself speak combines the physiologically separate organs of hearing and speech into a unique sense organ that speaks one's own hearing (if only in acts of self-editing); that is, it receives as well as transmits. Speech in this sense is a form of otorrhea. Eyes are without this utterative function. In instances of mystical and ecstatic states light is projected from the eyes, but this is a private experience, even though Roussel did close the drapes while writing *La Doublure* to make sure the neighbors wouldn't notice. This inability to transmit hallucinations is why visual memories could not be stimulated from the deboned Danton, even if his eyes had remained intact. This is also why he was a phonograph and not a film projector. The deboned voice does have similarities to the *Fantasmagorie,* however, beginning with one of the favorite subjects: Danton. He was one of the dead celebrities conjured up by magic lantern in Etienne Gaspard Robertson's *Fantasmagorie* beginning in the late eighteenth century. The dissolu-tion of his body and the contortion of his face projected against the rising smoke gave the impression of pained speech. Canterel, acting with Edison and Bell in the culture of the deaf, read such phantasmagorical writhing as one would read writing off the lips of Danton. Also, some people see their Doppelganger in the form of a gelatinous (i.e., deboned) bust with their features projected upon it.

58. See Jacques Derrida, "The Voice That Keeps Silence," in *Speech and Phenomena* (Evanston, Illinois: Northwestern University Press, 1973).

CRAIG ADCOCK

Marcel Duchamp produced very few works of music in the same sense that he produced very few works of sculpture: his two or three musical compositions have had a great deal of influence on subsequent developments in music, just as his two or three dozen readymades have had a great deal of influence on subsequent developments in sculpture.[1] The key to Duchamp's seemingly disproportionate success lies in the fact that he was largely responsible for proving that art can be whatever the artist decides it is. In sculpture, it can be the unnoticed objects of the world—the ordinary things like bicycle wheels and bottle racks—that lie undisclosed in the oblivion of disregard. In music, it can be the noise that lies hidden in the intervals between the notes or the gaps left empty between the sounds.

Music is often posited as a corollary of the visual arts, particularly in regard to the development of formalist criticism during the late nineteenth and the early twentieth centuries. Walter Pater's well-known remark typifies this approach: "All art constantly aspires towards the condition of music."[2] Pater means to imply that much of the strength in a work of art is carried by its formal elements, by such things as its color "tones" and "harmonies." Duchamp's approach is very different; he opposes formal approaches and adamantly expresses his antipathy for "retinal" painting; he wants to place art once again "at the service of the mind."[3] Perhaps the most important way in which he tries to add intellectual content to the art process is by choosing readymades. As George Heard Hamilton put it, "Duchamp had annihilated all that haughty aesthetic talk about empathy, pure painting, significant form, etc. Art is what one decides it shall be. We do not so much find it, or make it, as determine it. Consequently it has no value whatsoever except in so far as it exists in the context of a mental event."[4] With his seemingly uncomplicated mental gestures, Duchamp brings a new set of ideas not only to ordinary objects but also to the entire enterprise of making a work of art. He places his chosen objects within a new arena for observation. He does the same thing for music. Duchamp's avant-garde gestures, although certainly revolutionary, are not necessarily nihilistic. Just as his readymades were not exclusively antiart objects, neither were his works of music. "I'm not anti-music," he explained to Otto Hahn. "But I don't get on with the 'cat-gut' side of it. You see, music is gut against gut: the intestines respond to the cat gut of the violin. There's a sort of intense sensory lament, or sadness and joy, which corresponds to retinal painting, which I can't stand. For me music isn't a superior expression of the individual. I prefer poetry. And even painting, although that's not very interesting either."[5] By isolating the interstices between rhythmic notes and by creating a kind of visual or conceptual music not really intended to be listened to—that operates in the gaps between the sounds—Duchamp opens up the ordinary world of nonmusical noise to the artistic considerations of intentionality.

In order to achieve his philosophical purposes, Duchamp often crosses over from one sensory system to another: he looks at hearing and listens to vision. In one of his notes from the *Box of 1914,* he suggests an apparently impossible task: "Make a painting of frequency."[6] Frequency is something we normally associate with sound, as in the "Frequency Modulation" that gives FM radio its name. Of course, "frequency" can also be used to describe the entire electromagnetic spectrum. In that context, it refers to the number of oscillations that occur each second in an electromagnetic wave. In such terms, frequency is a matter of wavelength, and the radio waves that are translated into sound by a radio are essentially the same as the light waves that are translated into colors by the human visual system. Radio telescopes "see" objects in the universe that are radio bright just as optical telescopes see objects in the visible range of the spectrum.

Duchamp does not specifically discuss, so far as I know, the fundamental equivalence of visible light and other kinds of electromagnetic noise, but many of his notes involve hypothetical ways of connecting (or conflating) aural and visual phenomena. He often puts the ordinarily distinct realms of sound and sight together and mixes up hearing and seeing. In one of his most interesting posthumously published notes, he proposes making a sculpture out of sound. He argues that if the right kind of aural environment were constructed, the listener would be able to hear sculptures in space, although such a system would require considerable training and, apparently, the inheritance of acquired characteristics:

Like ... luminous electric lights which light up successively, a line of identical sounds could turn around the listener in arabesques (on the right, left, over, under).

$$a/b = b/a + b, \text{ Golden Section}$$

Develop: one could, after training the listener's ear, succeed in drawing a resembling and recognizable profile. With more training, [one could] make large sculptures in which the listener would be at the center. For example, an immense Venus de Milo made of sounds around the listener. This probably presupposes an aural training from childhood and for several generations. After the Venus de Milo, there would be an infinity of other transformations more inte————.[7]

Duchamp here conceptualizes sound in terms of its taking the place of light; he discusses hearing in terms of its taking the place of seeing (and throws in a casual reference to the Golden Section). Through a hypothetical sequentially ordered technique (with geometrical overtones), he suggests that not only a Venus de Milo but also "an infinity of other transformations" could be carved with sound, but, as so often happens in his notes, he trails off in midsentence, in midword, and it is unclear what he really means. He leaves us, his interpreters, in the gap between his artistic suggestion and our understanding of it.

Duchamp's first readymade, the *Bicycle Wheel,* was chosen in 1913 at just the moment when he was producing his first musical work, *Erratum Musical.* This latter "musical readymade," as it is often called, describes a way of choosing a musical composition much as one might randomly select a manufactured object.[8] Both categories were involved with chance operations. In a discussion of the *Bicycle Wheel,* Duchamp points out that "at first it wasn't even called a Ready-made":

It still had little to do with the idea of the Ready-made. Rather, it had more to do with the idea of chance. In a way, it was simply letting go by themselves and having a sort of created atmosphere in a studio, an apartment where you live. Probably, to help your ideas come out of your head. To see that wheel turning was very soothing, very comforting, a sort of opening of avenues on other things than material life of every day.[9]

Erratum Musical is generated by drawing notes cut from a scale out of a hat at random. When played, the "composition" generates a very provisional kind of music that is not too far from noise. The *Bicycle Wheel* when spun—and it must be spun in order to fully satisfy its design parameters—produces a faintly musical sound, a soft whispering noise. It can also be played. I think we can all remember making musical sounds on our bicycle wheels after turning our bicycles upside down. We could play the turning spokes by dragging our fingers or a stick across them as they turned. The frequency of sound could be varied by moving whatever plectrum we were using back and forth from near the spinning rim to the hub.

A rotating bicycle wheel can thus be thought of as a sculpture of frequency, if not a painting of frequency, and it may have been intended to suggest the equivalence of the visible and the nonvisible parts of the electromagnetic spectrum in the sense suggested previously. At least it could have been meant to deal with blending from the visible to the invisible. Lawrence Steefel in an early discussion of the *Bicycle Wheel* makes several interesting observations about its visibility:

Craig Adcock

If spun slowly, the object becomes blurred at the outer extension of the spokes, but still retains its object-quality. Pushed harder, the spokes blur into what Moholy-Nagy calls a "virtual volume," transforming the object-quality into a luminous illusion of transparent and dematerialized "spatial motion." The rim, which remains a constant enclosing circle, will also glimmer more radiantly, so that the passage of the distinctly delineated forms into an indistinct shimmer (which is half mirror, half window) integrates and fuses the parts of the object into a new unity and also into what seems to be a new physical condition.[10]

By integrating the visual and aural components of the *Bicycle Wheel*, Duchamp could augment its geometrical overtones. Thus, his purposes in choosing the readymade were probably not simply a matter of producing a work of antiart, as Steefel also suggests:

As a conceptual symbol and as a visual phenomenon, Bicycle Wheel *is not so much a "vicious circle" as a "four-dimensional" object. As a Ready-made,* Bicycle Wheel *does not contradict, but supports the contention that Duchamp's preoccupation with mechanical form (and the beauty of indifference which mechanization allows) is not necessarily restrictive or cynical.*[11]

Duchamp's readymades are open ended, and they can stand for many things; they operate at multiple levels throughout his oeuvre. I have argued in another context that the *Bicycle Wheel* can be read as a reference to a four-dimensionally expanded point of view with the moving spokes taken as metaphors for the multiply contingent lines of sight that such a point of view entails; it is also possible that the moving *Bicycle Wheel* is intended to stand for a four-dimensionally expanded "point of hearing." The turning wheel, when it is conceptualized as a sculptural portrait of an $(n + 1)$-dimensional vision, can be related to the Oculist Witnesses in the *Large Glass*. These last designs, drawn with mirror coating on the surface of the glass, can, in their turn, be related to *To Be Looked (from the Other Side of the Glass) with One Eye, Close to, for Almost an Hour*. This latter work clearly involves shifting from binocular to monocular vision, and as I have argued, it too is likely to have been intended as a metaphorical analysis of how one might "see" the fourth dimension.[12] In a note that is directly concerned with *To Be Looked at...*, Duchamp connects hearing with his geometrical speculations: "One could base a whole series of things to be looked at with a single eye (left or right). One could find a whole series of things to be heard (or listened to) with a single ear."[13]

Duchamp may have felt that shifting from hearing with two ears to hearing with one ear could produce the kinds of dimensional transformations that, he argues, occur in shifting from seeing with two eyes to seeing with one eye.[14] Although actually more complex than Duchamp indicates in his statements (the world does not flatten out completely when you close one eye), vision with a single eye is relatively "two-dimensional" when compared with the fully three-dimensional perception provided by binocular disparity. Perhaps the visual changes that occur when the *Bicycle Wheel* is spun, its becoming transparent, have some aural analogue that takes place when the listener puts one ear up beside it in order to hear the faint noise it makes while turning.[15]

In a related work contemporaneous with the *Bicycle Wheel*, Duchamp depicts a bicyclist riding across a sheet of music paper. In *To Have the Apprentice in the Sun*, as the drawing is titled, the bicycle (a machine equipped with two bicycle wheels) rolls up an incline. Its implied movement was presumably intended as a musical reference. Gavin Bryars, in his article about Duchamp's music, suggests that the line the wheels follow should be read as a drawing of a continuous tone, or a continuously rising tone, and that the drawing can consequently be related to Duchamp's interests in producing sound by means of "precision musical instruments" designed to avoid artistic skill, or "virtuosoism," as he calls it.[16] In a 1913 note included in *A l'infinitif*, Duchamp describes such a project:

Construct one and several musical precision instruments which produce mechanically the continuous *passage of one tone to another in order to be able to record without hearing them sculptured sound forms (against "virtuoso-*

ism," and the physical division of sound which reminds one of the uselessness of physical color theories). [17]

Here too Duchamp makes comparisons between a continuum of sound waves and a continuum of light waves. Punctuating these continua with notes or with specific colors, he seems to imply, runs the risk of making a work of art and falling into virtuosoism.

What these discussions have to do with "having an apprentice in the sun" is unclear, but perhaps the various components of Duchamp's interrelated system—his references to readymades, his desire to produce continuous tones, his disdain for color theories, and his nonsensical titles—are unified in their purpose of flattening out the meaning in a work of art.[18] The drawing was included with fifteen other short notes, which are also difficult to understand, in the *Box of 1914.*[19] The title, *To Have the Apprentice in the Sun,* probably fits within a group of works that Duchamp was producing at this time, all of which were concerned with denying meaning. He explained to Robert Lebel that the drawing was produced at a moment when he was mixing together "bits of different arts (e.g., writing and drawing) with no connection to each other (or at least as little as possible)."[20] During this same period, 1913 to 1916, he was also beginning to add meaningless titles to his readymades, something that added a "literary" dimension to them, as he explains: "One important characteristic was the short sentence which I occasionally inscribed on the 'readymade.' That sentence instead of describing the object like a title was meant to carry the mind of the spectator towards other regions more verbal."[21] These more verbal regions were not concerned with conveying rational meaning but rather with suppressing it.

In October 1915, Duchamp composed his first work in English, a kind of readymade text entitled "The." Each time the definite article appears in this work, it is replaced by an asterisk, a slight gap. The point of the exercise was to produce something that "was not a story," as Duchamp explains:

The meaning in these sentences was a thing I had to avoid.... The construc-
tion was very painful in a way, because the minute I did think of a verb to
add to the subject, I would very often see a meaning and as soon as I saw a
meaning I would cross out the verb and change it, until, working it out for
quite a number of hours, the text finally read without any echo of the physical
world.[22]

The resulting text, which includes such statements as "however, even
it should be smilable to shut [the] hair which [the] water writes
always in [the] plural, they have avoided [the] frequency meaning,
mother in law," has, of course, led to a number of interpretations, as
has a similar text in French entitled "Rendez-vous du Dimanche 6
Février 1916..." written a few months after "The."[23] Despite our
ability to hear suggestive echoes in these texts, they are uninter-
pretable, at least in the sense of reading meaning out of them; they
produce noise rather than meaning, and all the interpreter can do is
to read meaning into them because the words themselves are empty
or hollow.

Duchamp's music is also empty or hollow. It is gap
music, "musique en creux" as he called it, and it does not tell a
story.[24] Neither does it sing a song or play a melody. It is not to be
listened to or performed. Duchamp's music is readymade, and just as
the readymades were his most powerful means of analyzing the workings of art, his musical *errata* were his most effective means of
revealing the conventional nature of music.[25] In a discussion of his
archetypal readymade, the *Bicycle Wheel,* Duchamp explained that
"the wheel serves no purpose, unless it is to rid itself of the conventional appearance of a work of art."[26] His forays into music operated
in equivalent terms. He chooses a system, a score, and a libretto, and
then allows chance operations to determine their final outcome,
much as he places an ordinary object, such as a bicycle wheel, a
comb, or a urinal, in a new context and waits to see what happens.[27]
The art exists not only because of the artist's choice, but also because
of the viewer's choice, and it was this reciprocal nature of the inter-
change between art and its audience that so fundamentally interested

Craig Adcock

Duchamp.[28] The art is created, or at least is finished, in the eyes of the beholder or in the ears of the hearer, in the concretely grasped, readymade-aided epistemological insight and audile awareness of the perceiver.

Erratum Musical was included in the Green Box and is therefore intended to be associated with the Large Glass.[29] In addition to choosing the notes by drawing them out of a hat one at a time, Duchamp determined the words for the song "by chance." They consist of a standard dictionary definition of how to make a print: "To make an imprint mark with lines a figure on a surface impress a seal on wax."[30] As happens with so many aspects of Duchamp's work, this ready-made definition pulled from a French dictionary in 1913 sounds exotic and poetic now, some seventy-five years after it was chosen. It functions like the text of "The" or "Rendez-vous du Dimanche 6 Février 1916..." The words of the song do not quite make sense. The title of Erratum Musical is itself poetic. The Latin term, erratum, can be translated as "error" or "mistake" or "misprint." It is the past participle of the verb errare, which means to wander off or to stray, and that is pretty much what the music and the meaning of the text do. They move about and refuse to remain stationary.

Duchamp also produced a more elaborate version of Erratum Musical, and it was apparently meant to be even more closely associated with the Large Glass than the version included in the Green Box, given its heading: La Mariée mise à nu par ses célibataires, même: Erratum musical. This work also uses chance operations to generate a musical score. Duchamp's instructions read as follows:

Each number indicates a note; an ordinary piano contains about 89 notes; each note is the number in order starting from the left.

Unfinishable; for a designated musical instrument (player piano, mechanical organs or other new instruments for which the virtuoso intermediary is suppressed); the order of succession is (to taste) interchangeable; the time which separates each Roman number will probably be constant (?) but it may vary from one performance to another; a very useless performance in any case.

An apparatus automatically recording fragmented musical periods. Vase containing the 89 notes (or more: 1/4 tone). Figures among number on each ball Opening A letting the balls drop into a series of little wagons B, C, D, E, F, etc. Wagons B, C, D, E, F, going at a variable speed, each one receiving one or several balls when the vase is empty: the period *in 89 notes (so many) wagons is inscribed and can be performed by a designated instrument another vase = another period = these results from the equivalence of the periods and their comparison a kind of new musical alphabet allowing* model descriptions *(to be developed).*[31]

When played, both versions of *Erratum Musical* are musiclike.[32] Or, perhaps more accurately, they can be made to appear musical by an interpreter. The gaps can be filled in, so to say, by either a listener or a performer. As with his visual works, the members of Duchamp's audience were apparently meant to carry the notes of *Erratum Musical* to some sense of resolution. In this way, his compositions foreground our eyes and ears. In a sense, they allow us to see the operation of the musical performance. Particularly in the longer note, in which it does not matter what musical instrument is used, the intellectual side of the production is emphasized, and, as Duchamp says, even if produced, it would be "a very useless performance in any case." The note (with its notes) is more to be looked at than to be listened to.[33]

Duchamp's musical notes (his tonal notations) and his readymades have this in common: they come off a potentially infinite line, either the mathematical line of a sound continuum or the physical continuum or a production line. Ostensibly, the printmaking technique described in the *Green Box* version of *Erratum Musical* could be used to produce an indefinite number of prints (or misprints). The replication of the original emblematic work of art, the autograph image, would result in its being lost amid a welter of examples, and like so many of the reproductive categories that interested Duchamp (including mass-production techniques, casting techniques, and photography), the printmaking technique could be used to produce a continuum of identical examples. In a similar manner, every musical note—like every individual example of a bottle

Craig Adcock

rack, a comb, or a print—is a cut, as in a Dedekind cut, along a continuum.

Bringing up the mathematical entity of a Dedekind cut is, I believe, in keeping with Duchamp's intentions, particularly since he himself discusses the concept of a Dedekind cut in a context that is relevant to the present interpretation.[34] Dedekind cuts are used to define irrational numbers along the continuum of a mathematical number line. They can also be used to define the basic concept of dimensionality. Esprit Pascal Jouffret, one of Duchamp's primary mathematical sources, explains that "space divides the four-dimensional continuum into two infinite regions, which are identical between themselves, which sit on each side of the dividing space, and between which the dividing space forms an *infinitely thin* layer."[35] In the fourth dimension, a cut is a space, and, from a mathematical point of view, it can be conceptualized as being infinitely thin. The idea of defining three-dimensional space as a "couche *infiniment mince*" is almost certainly the source for Duchamp's idea of infra-*mince*, or infrathin.[36] It also explains a great deal about his interest in the gaps between things, including the gaps between musical notes. Indeed, the unusual characteristics of normal space when it is conceptualized from a four-dimensional point of view may help to explain why Duchamp was interested in using glass plates for some of his major works. What better way of suggesting an infinitely thin "three-dimensional" layer than a transparent sheet of glass, especially when that sheet of glass "contains" perspective renderings of three-dimensional objects? Works such as the two-dimensional *Large Glass* (said by Duchamp to be concerned with the fourth dimension) are in between three-dimensional space, and the glass itself becomes an $(n-1)$-dimensional gap (or cut) inside an n-dimensional continuum.[37]

Duchamp's work in general and his readymades in particular are, I believe, made intricate with mathematical concepts in order to strengthen the force of the epistemological questions they raise. In other words, Duchamp's purposes in playing complicated geometrical games are almost certainly intended to put just a little more philosophical punch into his attacks on "retinal" painting. By entailing his readymades and his musical notes with the notion of a continuum, he focuses on their status as copies, as examples, along a potentially infinite continuum of identical readymades and sounds. A musical note (say b flat) can be replicated ad infinitum, ad nauseam. Duchamp apparently thought that replication could be used as a means of examining the meaning structures that operate in the art process. Part of his project involved devaluing the "cult of the original," as he called it. He wanted "to wipe out the idea of the original, which exists neither in music nor in poetry: plenty of manuscripts are sold, but they are unimportant. Even in sculpture the artist only contributes the final millimeter; the casts and the rest of the work are done by his assistants. In painting we still have the cult of the original."[38]

Duchamp's musical compositions are analogous to his more complex readymades such as the *3 Standard Stoppages* (a work that he once called a readymade but "not quite.")[39] Both the music and the *Stoppages* are examples of "canned chance." They also involve isolating discrete moments in moving continua. Many of Duchamp's readymades (and proposed readymades) have iterated elements: the prongs of the *Bottlerack,* the teeth of the *Comb,* the spokes of the *Bicycle Wheel,* the floors of the Woolworth Building (proposed as a readymade), etc.[40] In terms of music, the most important such component is the basic temporal interval. The beat of the music (our choice since Duchamp does not provide a time signature) is a rhythmic equivalent of the repeated elements of the readymades. In the most general terms, the teeth of the *Comb,* the prongs of the *Bottlerack,* and the spokes of the *Bicycle Wheel* can be considered analogous to the repeated elements of a sound wave, and the readymades themselves become sculptures of frequency, as suggested earlier. (I think we can also all remember playing music on the teeth of a comb.) Even at the abstract level of repeated basic elements, these readymades function as concrete representations of the wave oscillations of sound (and also of light).

The readymades can be thought of as portraits of sound, visualizations of pulses prescinded from noise, and, as such, they can be conceptualized as conventionalizations of music. At least this much is true: Duchamp's music is involved with the basic notion of the interval, and it is thus mathematical in a way that parallels the iterative nature of the readymades. In an interview with Arturo Schwarz, Duchamp said that the *Comb* was a "remark about the infinitesimal," and there is no way that he could have used such a term without meaning to index its mathematical content. He intends to associate the readymade with his ideas about the continuum. In addition to mathematics, he also emphasized the commonplace nature of the *Comb* and the spaces between its teeth. "The teeth of the comb are not really a very important item in life. Nobody ever cared to consider the comb from such an angle.... I was struck by this unimportance and so I made it important to me."[41] Schwarz then asked Duchamp about a statement that he found difficult to understand. What was the association in one of the *Green Box* notes between a *Comb* and a rattle? "Well," Duchamp explained, "the rattle is a toy for children that makes noise when you turn it, and the comb becomes a generator of space, space generated by the teeth."[42] Schwarz's initial confusion is explained in part by the somewhat misleading English translation of *crécelle* as "rattle."[43] A *crécelle* is a noisemaker that works by rotating a device equipped with a clapper around a ratchet wheel. The tongue of the clapper strikes the teeth of the ratchet wheel and produces a punctuated interval of sound, a sharp clattering noise. In Duchamp's conception, the regularly spaced teeth of the ratchet wheel in the crécelle are analogous to the regularly spaced teeth of the comb.

Again, Duchamp's concerns about the geometrical properties of a noisemaker, its ability to "generate space," are relevant to the notion of interval and repetition that seems so important to his overall conception of the readymades. He uses his concept of "elementary parallelism" to get an n-dimensional configuration to generate an $(n + 1)$-dimensional configuration.[44] In other words, he conceptualizes the teeth of a comb or a child's noisemaker as whimsical devices for generating not only noise (music) but also space. In one of his posthumously published notes, Duchamp explains what he is after: he points out that a "noisemaker with elementary sectioning capacity" can function in terms of the "application of the principle of elementary parallelism." The sketch that accompanies the note shows a group of parallel lines attached at one end to an axis of rotation. In three-dimensional space, "these lines parallel to each other at a unit distance cut the volume, the plane, or the line, each into its constituent elements."[45] The multiple clicks of the teeth generate space, just as the discrete pulses of sound combine into a continuum of tone. Both are analogous "demultiplications." The sound pulses in the musical sense would parallel the light pulses captured in a chronophotograph, as is pointed out by Duchamp's primary source for his ideas about "elementary parallelism," Etienne-Jules Marey. In *Le Mouvement,* Marey points out, as does Duchamp in his remarks to Schwarz, that lines can generate planes and planes can generate solids: "Such objects are said to be 'engendered' by straight lines or curves, which undergo various displacements. Thus a regular cylindrical surface is engendered by a straight line which moves parallel to another straight line, and yet remains at the same distance from it. The straight line which moves is the 'generator' of the cylinder; that which remains fixed is its axis."[46] Marey goes on to explain that this kind of abstract discussion of geometrical figures can be given concrete visual expression by taking multiple-exposure photographs. When a one-dimensional straight line is rotated around a central axis, it generates the two-dimensional surface of a cylinder. When a half circle is rotated around an axis, it generates a sphere, as shown in Marey's illustrations.

Many of Duchamp's discussions are similar in tone, but they are more speculative. He ends the note quoted previously by suggesting that a "four-dimensional noisemaker might be found." By entailing a hypothetical geometry with sound, Duchamp seems to indicate that translation from one invisible realm to another is possible within a highly speculative metaphysics. In the physical world of three dimensions, a four-dimensional rotation is difficult even to visualize, despite its being a fairly trivial mathematical operation. It requires that an object move around a stationary plane while every element perpendicular to that plane remains perpendicular throughout the entire rotation. Carrying out such an operation in ordinary space is, of course, impossible, something that makes the rotation of a four-dimensional "<u>crécelle</u>" highly complex.[47]

Duchamp did produce one noisemaker that is closer to what one thinks of as a "rattle," his "assisted readymade" *With Hidden Noise*, produced in 1916. This work is related to a note included in the *Green Box* that deals with saving or conserving something. Because of Duchamp's fascination with the multivalenced nature of language, the note contains some potential puns. It is headed by a reference to a *"tirelire (ou conserves),"* a "money box" or a "piggybank." The term *tirelire* in French is also related to a verb, *tire-lirer*, which means "to sing like a lark"—something that may give the readymade a "sound" pun. In English, it can be read as a reference to the bicycle wheel: a "tire lyre." The note's instructions read as follows: "Make a readymade with a box containing something unrecognizable by its sound and solder the box."[48] Sealing an unknown object inside a box would produce a noisemaker whose sound, in some ironic sense, could not be seen. This was also the essential purpose of *With Hidden Noise*. The readymade was constructed by placing a ball of twine between two metal plates held together by long screws. Duchamp's friend and patron, Walter Conrad Arensberg, then placed a small object inside the ball of twine which produced a rattling sound when the readymade was shaken. Duchamp himself never knew what the object was, so that the work involved a sound that could not be "seen," at least in the sense of being fully comprehended. The noise the object produced was hidden from view.

Duchamp's purposes in constructing such open-ended systems are of course in many ways hidden from us, and it is not wholly clear what a "hidden noise" could possibly be. However we take the term's meaning, I believe that such crossovers in Duchamp's oeuvre have important purposes. His works, especially those aspects that are contained in his notes, are filled with impossible projects. Much of his fascination with the fourth dimension was entailed with its fundamental invisibility. Such geometry was irretrievably hidden from view; it was not really even imaginable, and thus it was also hidden from the mind's eye. Nevertheless, Duchamp's discussions of the fourth dimension and other n-dimensional spaces are couched in terms of trying to find physical analogies for them.

    With Hidden Noise is an analogical readymade; it stands for what cannot really be seen. Looked at from within the fourth dimension, any three-dimensional object is grasped by an expanded pont of view; looked at from within the third dimension, a four-dimensional object reverberates outward along the "extra" axes of the fourth dimension. Complicating matters further, from within four-space, the normal height, breadth, and depth of three-space seem to be compressed into a "couche infiniment mince" as suggested in the passage from Jouffret cited earlier. In terms of a four-dimensional space, the dimensional effect can be thought of as resembling the reflections of sound waves in an echo. In one of his notes from *A l'infinitif,* Duchamp includes a sketch of a cube containing a sphere that looks very much like *With Hidden Noise*. The sketch is labeled "Echo. Virtual sound." These words indicate a possible way of interpreting his apparent conflation of a readymade with the geometrical category of a continuum. An echo is a repetition. It is, in a sense, a reproduction or a "mass-production" of a natural phenomenon. The hidden source for the noise inside the ball of twine suggests a "virtual sound," in the sense that it cannot be seen or identified. It is an echo of an object. The hidden source for the sound can be taken as a "point source" and thus can stand for an aspect of what "virtuality" means in terms of images: a virtual image involves a point source being reflected in a mirror. Duchamp wants to talk about a "virtual sound," and he can do so only by analogy. Such a source for noise would be analogous to the image in a mirror, but with differences. The "point source" in *With Hidden Noise* is actually there, but it cannot be seen; the point source of a light reflected in a mirror can be seen, but it is not actually there. This kind of noncommensurability between sight and sound may be why Duchamp says in one of the notes in the *Box of 1914* that "one can look at (see) seeing; one cannot hear hearing."[49]

Throughout his career Duchamp tried to "look at (see) seeing." He spent a good deal of his energy writing notes that speculated about how a four-dimensional visual system might work. In these notes, one of the things he makes clear is that any such vision would not be possible for "ordinary eyes." Only in speculative terms could four-dimensional objects be seen. It was a matter of imagining (insofar as it was possible) a four-dimensional point of view. Such concerns were apparently behind Duchamp's interest in crossing between different sensory systems. The object in *With Hidden Noise* is kept from view; it is secret, invisible, and can thus act as a metaphor in aural terms for the invisible directionality or the invisible virtuality of the fourth dimension. Such a realm can be described in mathematical terms, but it cannot be visualized except in piecemeal fashion or by analogy. Duchamp may have been interested in putting sound together with vision because there is a similarity between the reverberation of an echo in the act of hearing it and the transposition of a three-dimensional object in the act of seeing it from a four-dimensional point of view. The object could be represented, in a sense, as an "echo" along the axes of the fourth dimension, as Duchamp suggests:

From the two-dimensional perspective giving the appearance of the three-dimensional continuum, construct a three-dimensional (or perhaps a two-dimensional perspective) of this four-dimensional continuum. Echo. Virtual sound. Virtuality as fourth dimension. Not the reality in its sensorial appearance, but the virtual representation of a volume (analogous to the reflection in a mirror).[50]

In other words, a hidden echo or a virtual sound in normal space could possibly suggest what a four-dimensional vision would be like just as the image of a three-dimensional object in a mirror—its virtual image—could stand for the virtuality of the fourth dimension, its "thereness" that cannot be specified.

With Hidden Noise and Duchamp's other readymades are metaphorical objects that stand for aspects of a geometry that is invisible but that nonetheless has a speculative kind of presence. The readymades represent what is missing. Inscribed on the upper and lower brass plates of *With Hidden Noise* is a nonsensical message written in French and English. The text has small gaps in it:

P . G— . E C I D E S — D É B A R R A S S É .
L E . — D . S E R T . — F . U R N I S . E N T
— A S — H O W . V . R — C O R . E S P O N D S

. I R . — C A R . É — L O N G S E A ⟶
F . N E , — H E A . , — . O . S Q U E ⟶
T E . U — S . A R P — B A R — A I N . ⟶

Duchamp explained that reading this work was "an exercise in comparative orthography (English-French). The periods must be replaced (with one exception: débarassé[e]) by one of the two letters of the other two lines, but in the same vertical as the period—French and English are mixed and make no 'sense.' The three arrows indicate the continuity of the line from the lower plate to the other [upper] still without meaning."[51] Duchamp's pun on "orthography" suggests not only "correct spelling" but also writing at right angles in the sense of "orthographic projection." Turning *With Hidden Noise* over and over, following its implied spiral while taking periodic ninety-degree turns, puts the viewer (the reader) in a position of looking at hearing, but the object making the noise remains hidden from view, just as the cryptic message of the nonsensical words engraved on the brass plates makes no "sense" and the virtual fourth dimension remains located ninety degrees from everything else.

In order to access the beholder's share, Duchamp removes his own message. Rather than filling his works with symbolism, he removes any specific meaning, or at least leaves the meaning very vague and builds into it a multivalenced system with all kinds of loops and turns. The texts of "The," "Rendez-vous...," and *With Hidden Noise* cannot be read. You cannot take the meaning out of the words; you can only put it into them; you can only lay meaning over the top of what Duchamp intentionally removed. In his works, Duchamp focuses attention on what always happens when viewers interact with a work of art: they, as Duchamp says, complete the work and supply what is missing from it. They create a new thought for the art and hear new sounds emanating from it. The artist alone can never supply everything that is contained in the work of art. The artist struggles to make the work of art but can neither be sure that what was intended has been realized nor recognize all that has been realized, as Duchamp explains:

The result of this struggle is a difference between the intention and its realization, a difference which the artist is not aware of.

Consequently, in the chain of reactions accompanying the creative act, a link is missing. This gap, representing the inability of the artist to express fully his intention, this difference between what he intended to realize and did realize, is the personal "art coefficient" contained in the work.

In other words, the personal "art coefficient" is like an arithmetical relation between the unexpressed but intended and the unintentionally expressed.[52]

Turns of language similar to those associated with Duchamp's ready-mades and ready-made texts also appear in his film *Anémic Cinéma*.[53] The spiraling puns alternating with spiral designs concern themselves with looking at seeing, and also with looking at hearing. They are what Duchamp called, in the four-dimensional jargon of mathematics, "perspectives cavalières." They produce ninety-degree turns, like the moves of the knight (the "cavalière") on a chessboard, up from the second dimension into the third, and by implication, up from the third into the fourth.[54] They also produce a very singsong aural quality even when seen. In other words, you can hardly watch the film without hearing the onomatopoetic quality of the French puns. It is like listening to the *Bicycle Wheel*. The spiral of the film turns on and on, engendering a loop of time. The spirals within the film produce meanings that turn back upon themselves. Such effects, implied by the mirror-reversed, palindromic title, are enfolded in a geometrical system that also turns back upon itself. And just as a rotation through the fourth dimension implies a mirror reversal, watching the film inverts meaning.[55] Like the twists and turns that produce secret sounds in *With Hidden Noise*, the silent film sings a song that can neither be heard nor understood but only looked at from the corner of the eye. As a subtle reiteration of the point Duchamp makes in *Anémic Cinéma*, when he includes many of the puns from the film *Box in a Valise* of 1942, the puns are written (calligraphically) on music paper. Again the viewer is asked to look at rather than listen to the singsong sayings of Rrose Sélavy. The juxtapositioning of the different media serves to counteract direct interpretation and to block direct access to meaning.

Duchamp's approach often involves not only putting together different media—writing and drawing, painting and music, poetry and sculpture—but also different levels of difficulty. He mixes simple operations and objects with demanding intellectual and epistemological categories. In Duchamp's turning readymades such as the *Bicycle Wheel*, the child's *crécelle*, *With Hidden Noise*, and *Anémic Cinéma*, ordinary objects and statements are conflated with complex ideas about four-dimensional rotation and reverberation. His interests in speculative *n*-dimensional geometries are involved with his overall skepticism, and his meaning echoes along *n*-dimensional lines. The mathematics provides him with a way of interlarding additional layers of doubt, additional gaps, within his systematic questioning of the art process.

One of Duchamp's most fascinating notes that pulls the various categories of readymade, interval, mathematical contin-

Craig Adcock

uum, and sound (or music) together discusses "gap music." It deals with both spatial and temporal intervals in terms of taking "cuts" out of a continuum. As a continuum of cuts, the "musical" technique described in the note amounts to a nonphysical analogue for the comb. It is another variation on the basic idea of "elementary parallelism." The recto side of the note reads as follows:

Porte Maillot, 1913. Leave out.

Uniformity of rhythm. An-accentuation. Chance. Race between 2 mobile objects A and B. At each cut of time (i.e. the uniform interval between 2 "measures"). A and B are drawn spatially, i.e., A is decorated with all the accidents of the road; B also is shown in a different state: there is not in this race, any rivalry between A and B. A follows its own way, B likewise, each one meeting other roads.

Conventionally, one takes a minimum time period which separates two successive spatial states of A and B. (1", 1/2", or less, no importance). To differentiate A from B, A for example could be the piano, B, the violin (no importance).

The different notation of the non-A or non-B could be pictured by: magnets + or − of A. In other words: at each moment of the duration A will be drawn or repelled by foreign elements (which will be the notes accompanying the nucleus A at that moment of the duration). A and B are certainly the only kinds of indifference, which as such, are the fodder of the magnets, the subject of discord between all these foreign forces.

The note is accompanied by a sketch showing a straight line running from a point labeled "A" on the left to a point labeled "Y" on the right. This line is labeled the "attraction mean of the mobile object A." Above and below the straight line are two jagged lines labeled "the continuum of the magnetization of A or the repulsion of A." The end point of the straight line, "Y," represents the "fall of A into Y." The verso side of the note reads as follows:

Gap music: from a (chord) group of 32 notes for example on the piano not emotion either, but enumeration through the cold thought of the other 52 missing notes. Add some explanations.[56]

Again, the abstract nature of Duchamp's approach to music is revealed in this note. He uses an uncanny blend of simplicity and complexity. The note suggests the toylike, gamelike quality of his musical compositions and recalls the long version of *Erratum Musical* in particular. Here, a race between two mobile objects (two bicycle wheels?) going up and down slopes is entailed with magnetism, a force that emanates though space in fairly mysterious ways. Duchamp's continuum approach to music involves its interval nature, its sequential nature, and like the infinite series of cuts that can be taken along a number line, music can be divided into an infinite number of infrathin gaps. As it is the viewers who fill in the gaps in his literary texts, or his works of visual art, it is the listeners who fill in the gaps of his music. As he once expressed it, "What art is in reality is this missing link, not the links which exist. It's not what you see that is art, art is the gap. I like this idea and even if it's not true, I accept it as the truth."[57]

Much of Duchamp's art operates in terms of the in-between. It is *en creux,* hollow, and full of gaps. It is about the in-between, the interstices, the infrathin space between one sheet of paper (not two sheets of paper), or between a sheet of glass.[58] Much of the work is invisible.[59] All Duchamp's art, including his music, is a way of accepting as provisional any given principle, which may explain why so many of his notes are open ended and not really understandable. He rarely develops anything fully, and the familiar refrains of "to be developed" or "add some explanations" echo throughout his notes. All these techniques, it seems to me, are ways of getting at what cannot be gotten at: real meaning. He reveals to us that any sense of epistemological surety is illusionary. This point about Duchamp was made a number of years ago by Jean-Paul Sartre in a passage that, because it is less well known than it might be, I will quote here at some length:

The Surrealists took a hearty dislike to that humble certainty on which the stoic based his ethics. It displeased him both by the limits it assigns us and the responsibilities it places upon us. Any means were good for escaping conscious-

ness of self and consequently of one's situation in the world. He adopted psychoanalysis because it presented consciousness as being invaded by parasitical outgrowths whose origin is elsewhere; he rejected "the bourgeois idea" of work because work implies conjectures, hypotheses, and projects, thus, a perpetual recourse to the subjective. Automatic writing was, above all, destruction of subjectivity. When we try our hand at it, we are spasmodically cut through by clots which tear us apart; we are ignorant of their origin; we do not know them before they have taken their place in the world of objects and we must perceive them with foreign eyes. Thus, it was not a matter, as has too often been said, of substituting their unconscious subjectivity for consciousness, but rather of showing the object as a fitful glimmering at the heart of an objective universe. But the Surrealist's second step was to destroy objectivity in turn. It was a matter of exploding the world, and as dynamite was not enough, as, on the other hand, a real destruction of the totality of existants was impossible, because it would simply cause this totality to pass from one real state to another real state, one had to do his best rather to disintegrate particular objects, that is, to do away with the very structure of objectivity in these objects-evidences. Evidently this operation cannot be tried out on real existants which are already given with their indeformable essence. Hence, one will produce imaginary objects, so constructed that their objectivity does away with itself. We are given a first draft of this procedure in the false pieces of sugar which Duchamp actually cut in marble and which suddenly revealed themselves as having an unexpected weight. The visitor who weighed them in his hand, was supposed to feel, in a blazing and instantaneous illumination, the self-destruction of the objective essence of sugar. It was necessary to let him know the deception of all being, the malaise, the off-balance feeling we get, for example, from trick gadgets, when the spoon abruptly melts in the tea-cup, when the sugar (an inverse hoax to the one Duchamp constructed) rises to the surface and floats. It was hoped that by means of this intuition the whole world would be exposed as a radical contradiction. Surrealist painting and sculpture had no other aim than to multiply these local and imaginary explosions which were like holes through which the entire universe would be drained out. The paranoiacally critical method of Dali was only a perfecting and complication of the procedure. It also professed to be an effort "to con-

tribute to the total discredit of the world of reality." Literature also did its best to make language go through the same kind of thing and to destroy it by tele-scoping words. Thus, the sugar refers to the marble and the marble to the sugar; the limp watch contests itself by its limpness; the objective destroys itself and suddenly refers to the subjective, since one disqualifies reality and is pleased to "consider the very images of the external world as unstable and transitory" and to "put them into the service of the reality of our mind." But the subjective then breaks down in its turn and allows a mysterious objectivity to appear behind it.[60]

Few passages in the vast literature on Duchamp describe his project better. What we are left with in Duchamp's art is an abiding sense of doubt, but there is some purposiveness behind it. While his work makes doubt itself palpable, it reveals a mysterious objectivity. As he said about the readymade, it is "une chose que l'on regarde même pas, mais dont on sait qu'il existe, qu'on regarde *en tournant la tête.*"[61]

If one thinks about the history of visual art, one realizes that there are almost no representations of sound or music in painting or sculpture. This lack of images of course makes sense because the forms involve mutually exclusive sensory systems: one cannot see hearing, or hear seeing. The exceptions to this general rule seem to be representations of expressions of pain, such as Edvard Munch's *The Scream.*[62] Here the silence of the picture stands as a mute and powerful analogue for the inexpressibility of pain, its non-translatability into anything but itself. Duchamp's approach to the visual representation of sound is much less expressive and emotional, but far more intellectual. Rather than a scream of agony, he depicts a cry in the wilderness, in a silent universe:

The tuner—Have a piano tuned on the stage E E E E E E E E E E E E E E E E E E E E or make a movie of the tuner tuning and synchronize the tunings on a piano. Or rather synchronize the tuning of a hidden piano— or have a piano tuned on the stage in the dark. Do it technically and avoid all musicianship.[63]

Duchamp's gap music, his hollow sound devoid of all musicianship, is akin to Sartre's Nothingness, as Sartre himself suggests in his discussion of the Surrealists' and Duchamp's project:

It is always by creating, that is, by adding paintings to already existing paintings and books to already published books, that it destroys. Whence, the ambivalence of its works: each of them can pass for the barbaric and magnificent invention of form, of an unknown being, of an extraordinary phrase, and, as such, can become a voluntary contribution to culture; and as each of them is a project for annihilating all the rest by annihilating itself along with it, Nothingness glitters on its surface, a Nothingness which is only the endless fluttering of contradictions.[64]

One source for Duchamp's particular Nothingness was in the imaginary realm of *n*-dimensional geometry. The work that Sartre chooses to discuss, *Why Not Sneeze*, aside from its suggesting a short, explosive noise, is directly related to illustrations for projections of the four-dimensional hypercube. Each little marble cube can be taken as a hypostatized cut, a cellule, in the infinite reverberations of the tesseract. Each cube, each subtle parody of the gaps in classical Cubism, is a reification of what cannot be seen. It represents a dimension not contained within real space, but which echoes along the infinite distances of its virtuality. Duchamp himself explained that, in addition to there being "no connection between the sugar cubes and a sneeze," there was a "dissociational gap between the idea of sneezing and the idea of ... 'Why not sneeze?' because, after all, you don't sneeze at will."[65] By suggesting the voluntary control of an involuntary action, the title poetically indexes what cannot be done just as the references to an invisible geometrical realm index what cannot be seen. The title carries the reader, the listener, the viewer to other regions more cerebral; its purpose was, as Duchamp says, "to add a verbal color."[66] The cage of marble sugar cubes that seemingly contradict gravity is a depiction of what Sartre called the Impossible: "the imaginary point where dream and waking, the real and the fictitious, the objective and the subjective, merge."[67]

In his auditory compositions, his gap music, Duchamp strives to express just this in-betweenness, this hypothetical space between the real and the fictitious, the objective and the subjective, in order to reveal the conventionality of music and thereby to imply the conventionality of art in general. It is the same with his visual works. In his music, he represents the plastic being of a sound; he makes a composite out of music, visual art, and poetry. That he does so in order to deal with meaning is made explicit (if such a term can be used in the context of Duchamp's writing) in one of his most interesting notes:

This plastic being of the word (by literal nominalism) differs from the plastic being of any form whatever (2 drawn lines) in that the grouping of several words without significance, reduced to literal nominalism, is independent of the interpretation, i.e. that: (cheek, amyl, phaedra) for example has no plastic value in the sense of: these 3 words drawn by X are different from the same 3 words drawn by Y.—These same 3 words have no musical value i.e. do not draw their group significance from their order nor from the sound of their letters.—One can thus speak them or write them in any order; at each reproduction, the reproducer presents (like at each musical audition of the same work) once again, without interpretation, the group of words and finally no longer expresses a work of art (poem, painting, or music).[68]

Duchamp wanted to *not* express a work of art in order to reveal the inner workings of the art process. The categories he uses in this enterprise range from virtual sound spheres to ball-of-twine readymades; from four-dimensional hyperspheres to closed but unbounded non-Euclidean spherical surfaces; from echoes to the infinite visual regresses in mirror surfaces; from the infrathin sounds made by velvet trousers to the infinitely subtle folds in space-time between the third and the fourth dimensions; from spinning bicycle wheels to the verbal colors of tumbling marble sugar cubes. Duchamp's project is whimsical and humorous, but seriously intentioned. His poetic writings, his unfinished visual projects, and his chance-generated musical compositions allow us to hear and to see an important aspect of art: much of it takes place in the gaps.

NOTES

My research for this essay was facilitated by a grant from the Institute for Scholarship in the Liberal Arts, University of Notre Dame. I would also like to thank Mme Marcel Duchamp for her help and generous hospitality during its preparation.

1. See Gavin Bryars, "Notes on Marcel Duchamp's Music," *Studio International* 192 (November–December 1976), pp. 274–279; also Carol P. James, "Duchamp's Silent Noise/Music for the Deaf," *Dada/Surrealism* 16 (1987), pp. 106–126.

2. Pater's book was originally published in 1873; for a useful critical edition of the text based on the fourth edition of 1893, see Walter Pater, *The Renaissance: Studies in Art and Poetry*, ed. Donald L. Hill (Berkeley and Los Angeles: University of California Press, 1980). The quotation is from p. 106. For a recent citation in the context of a discussion of modernism, see Howard Risatti, ed., *Postmodern Perspectives: Issues in Contemporary Art* (Englewood Cliffs, NJ: Prentice-Hall, 1990), p. 2.

3. See Duchamp's statement to James Johnson Sweeney in "A Conversation with Marcel Duchamp," NBC television interview, January 1956, reprinted in Marcel Duchamp, *Salt Seller: The Writings of Marcel Duchamp (Marchand du Sel)*, ed. Michel Sanouillet and Elmer Peterson (New York: Oxford University Press, 1973), pp. 135–136: "I considered painting as a means of expression, not an end in itself. One means of expression among others, and not a complete end for life at

all; in the same way I consider that color is only a means of expression in painting and not an end. In other words, painting should not be exclusively retinal or visual; it should have to do with the gray matter, with our urge for understanding." See also his remarks to James Johnson Sweeney in "Eleven Europeans in America," *The Bulletin of the Museum of Modern Art* 13 (1946), pp. 19–21, also reprinted in Duchamp, *Salt Seller*, p. 125: "I was interested in ideas—not merely in visual products. I wanted to put painting once again at the service of the mind. And my painting was, of course, at once regarded as 'intellectual,' 'literary' painting. It was true I was endeavouring to establish myself as far as possible from 'pleasing' and 'attractive' physical paintings. That extreme was seen as literary."

4. George Heard Hamilton, "In Advance of Whose Broken Arm?" *Art and Artists* 1 (July 1966), pp. 30–31.

5. Otto Hahn, interview with Marcel Duchamp, "Passport No. G255300," *Art and Artists* 1 (July 1966), p. 8.

6. See Duchamp, *Salt Seller*, p. 25.

7. Marcel Duchamp, *Notes*, ed. and trans.

Paul Matisse (Paris: Centre National d'Art et de Culture Georges Pompidou, 1980), no. 183.

8. See Arturo Schwarz, *The Complete Works of Marcel Duchamp* (New York: Abrams, 1970), p. 437.

9. Ibid., p. 442.

10. Lawrence D. Steefel, Jr., "The Position of *La Mariée mise à nu par ses célibataires, même* (1915–1923) in the Stylistic and Iconographic Development of the Art of Marcel Duchamp" (Ph.D. diss., Princeton University, 1960), p. 174; this passage from Steefel is quoted in Schwarz, *The Complete Works of Marcel Duchamp*, p. 442. The discussion by László Moholy-Nagy referred to by Steefel occurs in László Moholy-Nagy, *Vision in Motion* (Chicago: Theobald, 1947), p. 237 nn.

11. Steefel, p. 174.

12. See Craig Adcock, "Geometrical Complication in the Art of Marcel Duchamp," *Arts Magazine* 58 (January 1984), pp. 105–109; see also Craig Adcock, *Marcel Duchamp's Notes from the Large Glass: An N-Dimensional Analysis* (Ann Arbor: UMI Research Press, 1983), pp. 131–136.

13. This note was originally published in *A l'infinitif*; see Duchamp, *Salt Seller*, p. 76.

14. See, for example, Duchamp's statements in Pierre Cabanne, *Dialogues with Marcel Duchamp*, trans. Ron Padgett (New York: Viking, 1971), pp. 72–73.

15. Carol James ("Duchamp's Silent Noise," p. 107) points out in passing that it might be "better to put one's ear to the silently turning *Bicycle Wheel* than into a torturous sharpener." I disagree that a turning bicycle wheel is silent, but her point is well taken. She makes her remark after recalling one of Rrose Sélavy's suggestions: "Sharpen hearing (a form of torture)" (Duchamp, *Salt Seller*, p. 113). The original French pun, "Aiguiser l'ouïe (forme de torture)," turns on the similarity of the words "ouïe" (hearing) and "aïe" (ouch), (see James, "Duchamp's Silent Noise," p. 122, n6). She also cites Duchamp's statement to Calvin Tomkins that the *Bicycle Wheel* was "something to have in my room the way you have a fire, or a pencil sharpener, except that there was no usefulness. It was a pleasant gadget, pleasant for the movement it gave" (see Calvin Tomkins, *The Bride and the Bachelors* [New York: Viking, 1968], p. 26).

16. Bryars, "Notes on Marcel Duchamp's Music," pp. 274–275.

17. Duchamp, *Salt Seller*, p. 75.

18. Adding to the sketch's complexity is a statement included in Duchamp's *Notes*, no. 128: "On the slopes of flow: put like a comment illustrating the photo of *Having the Apprentice in the Sun*." With this entry into the *Large Glass*, the interpreter can proceed in a large number of directions.

19. See Duchamp, *Salt Seller,* pp. 22–25.

20. Robert Lebel, *Marcel Duchamp,* trans. George Heard Hamilton (New York: Grove Press, 1959), p. 165; quoted in Schwarz, *The Complete Works of Marcel Duchamp,* p. 457.

21. Marcel Duchamp, "Apropos of 'Readymades,'" talk delivered at the Museum of Modern Art, New York, 19 October 1961; published in *Art and Artists* 1 (July 1966), p. 47; reprinted in Duchamp, *Salt Seller,* p. 141.

22. Duchamp quoted in Schwarz, *The Complete Works of Marcel Duchamp,* p. 457; also p. 584.

23. See Octavio Paz, "* Water Writes Always in * Plural," in *Marcel Duchamp,* ed. Anne d'Harnoncourt and Kynaston McShine (New York: Museum of Modern Art; Philadelphia: Philadelphia Museum of Art, 1973), pp. 143–158; see also Schwarz, *The Complete Works of Marcel Duchamp,* pp. 457–460, 584.

24. See Duchamp, *Notes,* nos. 181, 250, 253, 255.

25. See Craig Adcock, "Conventionalism in Henri Poincaré and Marcel Duchamp," *Art Journal* 44 (Fall 1984), pp. 249–258.

26. Hahn, interview with Duchamp, p. 10.

27. The strategy taken by Duchamp's pseudonymous alter ego Richard Mutt, who signed *Fountain,* is explained in a statement almost certainly written by Duchamp and published as "The Richard Mutt Case," *The Blind Man* (May 1917), pp. 5–6: "He CHOSE it. He took an ordinary article of life, placed it so that its useful significance disappeared under the new title and point of view—created a new thought for that object." For a discussion of *Fountain,* see William Camfield, *Marcel Duchamp/Fountain* (Houston: The Menil Collection, Houston Fine Arts Press, 1989).

28. The most famous of these statements is "The Creative Act," *Art News* 56 (Summer 1957), pp. 28–29; reprinted in Lebel, *Marcel Duchamp,* pp. 77–78.

29. Duchamp, *Salt Seller,* p. 34; Marcel Duchamp, *Duchamp du Signe, Ecrits,* ed. Michel Sanouillet and Elmer Peterson (Paris: Flammarion, 1975), pp. 52–53.

30. See Anne d'Harnoncourt and Kynaston McShine, *Marcel Duchamp,* exhibition catalogue (New York: Museum of Modern Art; Philadelphia: Philadelphia Museum of Art, 1973), p. 264.

31. Ibid., pp. 264–265.

32. Duchamp's music has been recorded by Petr Kotik and the SEM Ensemble, Buffalo, New York, for West German Radio in Cologne and the Galeria Multipla in Milan, Italy, as *The Entire Musical Work of Marcel Duchamp,* 1976. Percussionist Donald Knaack has also recorded Duchamp's music in an album entitled *The Bride Stripped Bare by Her Bachelors, Even, Erratum Musical (1913)* (New York, Finnadar Records, 1977).

33. Gavin Bryars ("Notes on Marcel Duchamp's Music," pp. 278–279, n. 19) agrees with Duchamp's estimation that it would be useless to perform *Erratum Musical*: such a performance would be "as awkward an enterprise as the vogue, early in the days of graphic notation, for taking extant paintings, especially systemic ones, and treating them as musical scores—the obverse of transcribing Bach fugues into multi-colored grids, or making hazy impressions of Sibelius' *Swan of Tuonela*. If, as a cursory glance would seem to confirm, the second *Erratum Musical* is directly concerned with the *Large Glass*, then it is an important element in the body of notes that accompany it and is an integral part of that work; and it makes no more sense to make 'realizations' of this piece than to do the same for the *Large Glass* itself."

34. In one of his notes in *A l'Infinitif*, Duchamp points out that "in the plane, the two-dimensional native is either on one side of an infinite straight line or on the other side. Therefore this line is for him a Dedekind cut (Poincaré) creating two distinct plane fields." This is one of two times Duchamp mentions the mathematician Henri Poincaré by name. In the original French, the German mathematician Richard Dedekind is not named, but the translator, Cleve Gray, was helped by Duchamp, and a "Dedekind cut" is cer-

tainly what the word "coupure" in the original French note refers to. (See Duchamp, *Salt Seller*, p. 94; see also Marcel Duchamp, *Duchamp du Signe*, p. 133.) Duchamp's reference to a "two-dimensional native" recalls a number of turn-of-the-century popularizations of *n*-dimensional geometry (see, for example, [Edwin Abbott Abbott], *Flatland: A Romance of Many Dimensions, with Illustrations by the Author, A Square* [London: Seeley & Co., 1884]).

35. E[sprit Pascal] Jouffret, *Traité élémentaire de géométrie à quatre dimensions et introduction à la géométrie à n dimensions* (Paris: Gauthier-Villars, 1903), p. xxviii. Poincaré, the other mathematician most likely to have been studied by Duchamp, also talks about crossing "cuts," pointing out that the dimensionality of space can be defined in such terms:

[Space] cannot be divided into several parts either by forbidding the passage through certain points or by forbidding the crossing of certain lines; these obstacles could always be circumvented. It will be necessary to forbid the crossing of certain surfaces; that is, certain two-dimensional cuts. And that is why we say that space has three dimensions.

We now know what a continuum of n dimensions is. A continuum has n dimensions when it is possible to divide it into many regions by means of one or more cuts which are themselves continua of n − 1 dimensions. The continuum of n dimensions is thus defined by the continuum of n − 1 dimensions. This is a definition by recurrence.

(See Henri Poincaré, *Mathematics and Science: Last Essays,* trans. John W. Bolduc [New York: Dover, 1963, p. 29]; Henri Poincaré, *Dernières Pensées* [Paris: Flammarion, 1913], pp. 65–67.

36. See Duchamp, *Notes,* nos. 1–46.

37. Duchamp explained his conception of the four-dimensional aspects of the *Large Glass* in a letter to André Breton published in *Medium* (1955), p. 33: "In the Bachelor Machine an erotic desire in motion is 'brought back' to its 'projection' of machined appearance and character. Likewise the Bride or the Pendu femelle is a 'projection' comparable to the projection of an 'imaginary entity' in four dimensions in our world of three dimensions (and also in the case of the flat glass to a reprojection of these three dimensions onto a surface of two dimensions)."

38. Hahn, interview with Duchamp, p. 10.

39. Francis Roberts, interview with Marcel Duchamp, "I Propose to Strain the Laws of Physics," *Art News* 67 (December 1968), pp. 62–63. Asked if he thought the readymades were trivial, Duchamp answered by saying, "No, they're not trivial, for me at least. They look trivial, but they're not. On the contrary, they represent a much higher degree of intellectuality. And the one I love most is not quite … it's a readymade if you wish, but a moving one. By this I mean three meters of thread falling down and changing the shape of the unit of length, the *3 Standard*

Stoppages, I prefer to call them. I was satisfied with the idea of not having been responsible for the form taken by chance."

40. See Adcock, *Marcel Duchamp's Notes from the Large Glass,* pp. 158–166; for a discussion of the mathematical implications of Duchamp's proposal for making a readymade out of the Woolworth Building, see Craig Adcock, "Marcel Duchamp's Approach to New York: 'Find an Inscription for the Woolworth Building as a Readymade,'" *Dada/Surrealism* 14 (1985), pp. 52–65.

41. Duchamp interviewed in Schwarz, *The Complete Works of Marcel Duchamp,* p. 461.

42. Ibid.

43. For Duchamp's *Green Box* note about a "crécelle," see Duchamp, *Salt Seller,* p. 71; Duchamp, *Duchamp du Signe,* pp. 101–102.

44. For one of Duchamp's own explanations of "elementary parallelism," see interview with Cabanne, *Dialogues with Marcel Duchamp,* pp. 48–49; see also his *A l'Infinitif* note in Duchamp, *Salt Seller,* p. 92.

45. Duchamp, *Notes,* no. 166.

46. E. J. Marey, *Le Mouvement* (Paris: G. Masson, Editeur, 1894), p. 24; the translation is from E. J. Marey, *Movement,* trans. Eric Pritchard (New York: D. Appleton and Company, 1895), p. 24.

47. Jouffret explains the difficulty of carrying out a four-dimensional rotation in his *Traité*, p. 38 (my translation): "Two-dimensional geometry knows only a single rotation, that *around* a point, which is called the *center of rotation;* in the geometry of three-dimensional space, there is also only a single rotation, that around a straight line, which is called the *instantaneous or permanent axis of rotation.* In the four dimensional continuum, rotation around a plane is the simplest movement after that of pure translation."

48. Duchamp, *Salt Seller*, p. 32; Duchamp, *Duchamp du Signe*, p. 49.

49. Duchamp, *Salt Seller*, p. 23; Duchamp, *Duchamp du Signe*, p. 37.

50. Duchamp, *Salt Seller*, pp. 98–99; Duchamp, *Duchamp du Signe*, pp. 138–140.

51. Duchamp quoted in Schwarz, *The Complete Works of Marcel Duchamp*, p. 462.

52. Duchamp, "The Creative Act," in Lebel, *Marcel Duchamp*, p. 78.

53. For discussions of *Anémic Cinéma*, see Toby Mussman, "Marcel Duchamp's *Anémic Cinéma*," in *The New American Cinema: A Critical Anthology*, ed. Gregory Battcock (New York: Dutton, 1967), pp. 147–155; Annette Michelson, "'*Anémic Cinéma*': Reflections on an Emblematic Work," *Artforum* 12 (October 1973), pp. 64–69; Katrina Martin, "Marcel Duchamp's 'Anémic Cinéma,'" *Studio International* 189 (January–February 1975), pp. 53–60; Dalia Judovitz, "Anemic Vision in Duchamp: Cinema as Readymade," *Dada/Surrealism*, 15 (1986), pp. 46–57.

54. Duchamp interviewed in Cabanne, *Dialogues with Marcel Duchamp*, pp. 72–73:

At the time, I felt a small attraction toward the optical. Without really ever calling it that. I made a thing that turned, that visually gave a corkscrew effect, and this attracted me; it was amusing. At first I made it with spirals... not even spirals—they were off-center circles which, inscribed one inside the other, formed a spiral, but not in the geometric sense; rather in the visual effect. I was busy with that from 1921 to 1925.

Later, using the same procedure, I found a way of getting objects in relief. Thanks to a [perspective cavalière], that is, as seen from below or from the ceiling, you got a thing which, in concentric circles, forms the image of a real object, like a soft-boiled egg, like a fish turning around in a fishbowl, you see the fishbowl in three dimensions. What interested me most was that it was a scientific phenomenon which existed in another way than when I had found it. I saw an optician at that time who told me, "That thing is used to restore sight to one-eyed people, or at least the impression of the third dimension." Because, it seems, they lose it.

Ron Padgett translates Duchamp's expression *perspective cavalière* as "offhand perspective," which does not accurately render its geometrical meaning. The term is used by Duchamp's mathematical sources, particularly by Jouffret, to describe a four-dimensional coordinate system.

55. For a discussion of four-dimensional mirror reversal, see Craig Adcock, "Duchamp's Eroticism: A Mathematical Analysis," *Dada/Surrealism* 16 (1987), pp. 149–167.

56. Duchamp, *Notes*, no. 181; see also Duchamp, *Notes*, no. 253: "Exercises of gap music for the deaf. Given a conventional agreed number of music notes 'hear' only the group of those that are not played. Agree on a fixed group of music notes and 'hear' only the notes of the group that are not played."

57. Duchamp quoted in Schwarz, *The Complete Works of Marcel Duchamp*, p. 197.

58. Duchamp, *Notes*, no. 15: "Painting on glass seen from the unpainted side gives an infra thin"; Duchamp, *Notes*, no. 17: "Hollow paper [*papier creux*] (infra-thin space and yet without there being 2 sheets)."

59. Jonathan Crary makes a similar point about Duchamp's paintings: *Nude Descending a Staircase* and *Passage from Virgin to Bride* are about "what is not seen." See Jonathan Crary, "Marcel Duchamp's 'The Passage from Virgin to Bride,'" *Arts Magazine* 51 (January 1977), pp. 96–99.

60. Jean-Paul Sartre, *What Is Literature?* trans. Bernard Frechtman (New York: Philosophical Library, 1949), pp. 175–177; my attention was drawn to Sartre's remarks by an article by Anthony Hill, "The Spectacle of Duchamp," *Studio International* 189 (January–February 1975), p. 22.

61. Interview with Duchamp in Alain Jouffroy, *Une Révolution du regard: A propos de quelques peintres et sculpteurs contemporains* (Paris: Gallimard, 1964), p. 119.

62. See David Loshak, "Space, Time and Edvard Munch," *Burlington Magazine* 131 (April 1989), pp. 273–282; also Elaine Scarry, *The Body in Pain: The Making and Unmaking of the World* (New York: Oxford Unversity Press, 1985), pp. 51–52:

Even prolonged, agonized human screams, which press on the hearer's consciousness in something of the same way pain presses on the consciousness of the person hurt, convey only a limited dimension of the sufferer's experience. It may be for this reason that images of the human scream recur fairly often in the visual arts, which for the most part avoid depictions of auditory experience. The very failure to convey the sound makes these representations arresting and accurate; the open mouth with no sound reaching anyone in the sketches, paintings, or film stills of Grünewald, Stanzione, Munch, Bacon, Bergman, or Eisenstein, a human being so utterly consumed in the act of making a sound that cannot be heard, coincides with the way in which pain engulfs the one in pain but remains unsensed by anyone else.

63. Duchamp, *Notes*, no. 199.

64. Sartre, *What Is Literature?* p. 178.

65. Jean-Marie Drot, "Jeu d'échecs avec Marcel Duchamp," interview with Marcel Duchamp (soundtrack of an ORTF film, 1963), quoted in Schwarz, *The Complete Works of Marcel Duchamp*, p. 487.

66. Duchamp quoted in Schwarz, *The Complete Works of Marcel Duchamp*, p. 456.

67. Sartre, *What Is Literature?* p. 178.

68. Duchamp, *Notes*, no. 186.

CHRISTOPHER SCHIFF

BANGING ON THE WINDOWPANE
SOUND IN EARLY SURREALISM

Surrealism was acutely aware of its history and prehistory. Even with its first codi-fication in the *Manifesto of Surrealism* (1924), the Surrealist movement displayed an awareness of and concern for the past which clearly set it apart from such predecessors as Futurism and Dada. Over the long course of their movement, the Surrealists acted as archeologists of the intellect, unearthing and revitalizing theories and ideas that had long since been forgotten or discarded but that still held the potential for significant revolution.

Such was the case with Surrealist sound theory. Sound played an important part in the initial moment of Surrealism, when the word was used almost exclusively within theatrical produc-tions and was still considered the intellectual property of Apollinaire.[1] After the death of Apollinaire, Surrealism moved away from the the-atrical and into the theoretical and personal, but sound did not lose any of its importance. Reacting to the excesses of Paris Dada, the Surrealist movement turned to ideas voiced by Giorgio de Chirico and his brother Alberto Savinio shortly before the First World War. These became the basis for most Surrealist music theory, the two best-known pronouncements of which were Paul Nougé's *Music Is Dangerous* and an excerpt from André Breton's *Surrealism and Painting*. On the personal level, sound became the primary focus of the Surrealist movement, for the Surrealists made it their purpose to give concrete form to internal sound—sound, they would argue, that might only be heard in silence.

PARADE

It is well known that the term *surréalisme* was created by Guillaume Apollinaire for a program note to the ballet *Parade*.[2] Although Apollinaire only briefly describes the ballet, and even more briefly describes what he means by *surréalisme*, he makes it clear that the word refers to a multidimensionality which seemed to pervade the work. *Parade* succeeded in amalgamating several disciplines—music, ballet, painting, costuming, and literature—into an aesthetically focused whole. It also succeeded in amalgamating styles together, giving Picasso a venue for both his Cubist and realist styles of art, Satie a venue for both his classical and vaudeville styles of music, and Cocteau a venue for two styles of nonverbal literature: noise and expressive movement.[3]

But as with all amalgamations, there was no permanent bonding of these disciplines or styles. With the possible exception of Cocteau, who had always planned that the work be a multimedia extravaganza, each individual creator thought of *Parade* in terms of his own discipline. Thus most of the points of contact among the various media came in the form of compromises: Satie appended an introduction and a postlude to his work when he found that music was required for the viewing of Picasso's hand-painted drop curtain; Cocteau was forced to abandon his vocal text when it was decided that it interfered with the dance and the music; the dancers were to execute intricate dance steps and to make sounds while they danced, but their contribution was all but obliterated when they were clothed in Picasso's costumes.[4] These compromises resulted in a ballet that was significantly different from Cocteau's original vision.

Of all the elements of the ballet, the sonic elements were the most compromised. Indeed, though Apollinaire saw it as a quintessentially French work,[5] *Parade* was a compromise of French theatrical music with Italian Futurist noise, and the result was at least as much Futurist as it was Surrealist. In 1914, about three years before the premiere of Satie's ballet, Diaghilev had proposed to Stravinsky that they collaborate on a stage presentation of the Russian Orthodox liturgy. Failing to win the composer's approval, the impresario decided to present a balletic *Liturgie* with absolute silence accompanying the dance.[6] While rehearsing this version of the piece, however, it was discovered that there was and could be no such thing as absolute silence in a theatrical setting. Ambient noise was always present in some form or another. Rather than accept this as a fact of nature and present the work with whatever environmental noise might occur, Diaghilev sought the advice of F. T. Marinetti, who arranged for the impresario to hear the orchestra of *intonarumori*, the "noise instruments" developed by Luigi Russolo.[7] Thus Diaghilev was persuaded to substitute loud, intentional noise for soft—yet more obtrusive—unintentional noise. *Liturgie* was rehearsed in this form but was never presented before an audience.[8]

Meanwhile, Jean Cocteau had reinvented the Futurist *parole in libertá* when he joined the ambulance corps at the beginning of World War I. According to André Gide, Cocteau came home on leave from the front and assailed his Parisian friends with a barrage of vocal sound effects in imitation of the war and of the personages he had encountered in the field.[9] When *Parade* was first conceived, it was to have included a spoken text of such vocal pyrotechnics. As the project progressed, though, suggestions for reworking the piece came from several sources, with Cocteau's text being the primary target for revision. It even appeared for a time that the librettist's contribution might be deleted from the work completely. Still, it was undeniable that the concept of *Parade* was Cocteau's, and his exclusion from the ballet could have killed it. Rather than risk this, Diaghilev invited him to Rome, hoping that the change in scenery might inspire better ideas. It was there that Cocteau was introduced to Futurism, including the Futurist theories of noise music. Their influence was precisely what Diaghilev had hoped it might be. Recognizing in Futurism a better-stated version of some of his own ideas, Cocteau readily replaced his whole verbal text with mechanical noises.

Banging on the Windowpane

Although this pleased Diaghilev, since it fulfilled his vision of a noise ballet, Satie was not nearly so enthusiastic. He felt that the noise detracted from his music and even insulted it by reiterating things that had been made perfectly clear in the score. This point became the basis for a long-standing argument between the composer and librettist: Satie sarcastically dismissed his own contribution to *Parade* as a mere background for a few incidental noises; Cocteau responded condescendingly that Satie was exaggerating his insignificance.[10] The noises were also resisted by the orchestral conductors and musicians who were obliged to execute them. Whenever Cocteau was not present to assure the integrity of the work, the noise might be completely deleted or reorganized into meaningless nonsense.[11]

The sound innovations of *Parade* remained experiments. They were never allowed to reach the heightened level of an aesthetic. Cocteau had borrowed the idea for noise music and had not had time to assimilate it into his own notion of art before he was forced to reconcile it with Satie's notion of music. Without the proper foundation the noises were weak, and they grew weaker each time they were compromised. In the end the result was not an enlightened unification of music and noise but rather a mediocre mixture that was obvious in its lack of achievement. Apollinaire, the great proponent of the New Spirit and early supporter of the Futurists, praised Picasso's embellished Cubism and Satie's vaudevillian classicism but had absolutely nothing to say about Cocteau's borrowed Futurism.[12] Noise might have been considered more radical than music in a timbral sense, but it was not necessarily a surreal sonic event because of this. In Surrealism, the purpose in making a sound was as important as the sound itself, and Satie's well-executed (if passé) music may well have been more radical in its purpose than Cocteau's poorly executed attempt at bruitism.

LES MAMELLES DE TIRÉSIAS

Apollinaire certainly considered Satie's contribution

to *Parade* more noteworthy than Cocteau's, and perhaps closer to his vision of the surreal. When he tried his own hand at writing and producing a work that he called "Surrealist," his play *Les Mamelles de Tirésias*, Apollinaire sought Satie's collaboration, and though he was notorious for never writing two pieces in the same style, the composer did at least entertain the idea of producing a second Surrealist score. According to Georges Auric, however, Satie was disappointed by Apollinaire's play and declined to compose music for it, choosing instead to write and score his own dramatic work, *Socrate*.[13]

Meanwhile, a new generation of poets and artists was looking to Apollinaire for direction. Before the war he had been the principal French theorist of modernism, and with an end to the war near, many hoped that he could provide similar insight in the postwar period. Thus his program note for *Parade* was given more attention than such a work usually received. He prophesied that Surrealism would be the "point of departure for a whole series of manifestations of the *New Spirit*."[14] Jacques Vaché would organize the first of these manifestations at the premiere of *Les Mamelles*, but it would have little to do with Apollinaire's Surrealist play.

Like *Parade*, *Les Mamelles* included two separate scores—one of music, and the other of noise. Since Satie would not compose music for the production, Apollinaire chose Germaine Albert-Birot, the wife of the poet Pierre Albert-Birot, to compose it. Apollinaire himself wrote the noise score. Unlike *Parade*, *Les Mamelles* was well suited to the inclusion of noise. In the ballet there had been a few caesuras that allowed the dancers to stamp their feet audibly in the absence of music, but all other noises were sounded simultaneously with the music, blending with and being obliterated by it. In *Les Mamelles* the noise was not in competition with the music, since the latter was sounded only during breaks in the play, whereas the former was treated as part of the text of the work. By avoiding such simultaneity, Apollinaire emphasized the noise and gave it a clear, nonsymphonic meaning.

Apollinaire uses both vocal and instrumental sound

in *Les Mamelles,* but whereas the former is used universally among the characters, the latter is restricted to a single character, the enigmatic "People of Zanzibar." This one-person Greek chorus acts as character, commentator, and generator of sound effects. As occasions arise the People uses a revolver, musette, bass drum, accordion, snare drum, thunder, sleigh bells, castanets, toy trumpet, and breaking dishes to color certain already colored words—"war" with a thunder sheet; "love" with a musette; the husband's request for lard with the sound of breaking dishes. Because of its ability to create both music and sound effects (e.g., glissandi and tone clusters), the most frequently played instrument of the group is the accordion. Its use is quite similar to that of an organ in a silent movie theatre, whereas its physical presence is in keeping with the intentional poverty of Apollinaire's setting. Its portability also allows it to act as a visual prop. Apollinaire shows considerable flair in using this type of sound—but in ways that are not particularly unique.

Apollinaire's use of sound effects can also be quite innovative: sometimes purposefully ironic—using a thunder sheet to portray the singing of the newborn reporter—sometimes inexplicable—the toy trumpet flourish that follows the introduction of Arthur, the curdled milk tycoon. But as informative as the sound of sound is within the play, it is only half of the sonic component, for in *Les Mamelles* sound becomes both an aural and a visual event. Its production is no longer limited to the orchestra pit or to offstage areas but intrudes into the dramatic milieu of the play. Thus when Presto and Lacouf fight a duel with fake guns, the People of Zanzibar is seen firing the actual shots that are heard, making it ambiguous whether the duel has taken place or whether the People has simply taken it into his own hands to settle the argument.

Along with instrumental effects, Apollinaire uses vocal effects such as sneezes, cackles, and the imitation of the sound of trains scattered throughout his play. Even more pervasive is the use of specific accents in the delivery of standard dialogue. Although the overt plot of the work is one of sexual ambiguity, ambiguities of setting, nationality, and even of race become equally important subplots. Thus understanding whether or not an accent accurately denotes the nationality of a character is essential when trying to understand the work as a whole. Prior to the transformation of Thérèse/Tirésias, the husband speaks with a Belgian accent, but this accent appears to be a factor of his wife's sexuality, not of his nationality. When Thérèse loses her breasts, her husband loses his accent. Likewise, the adult Reporter speaks *without* an accent, since it might betray too soon the fact that he is from Paris—a town in America—and not from Paris, France. Yet the lack of an accent does not mean the lack of a characteristic vocal sound. For instance, when the Reporter laughs, he uses the four vowels *a, e, i,* and *o*—rather than just *a*—thus uttering all four two-letter words beginning with *h* in the English language: *ha, he, hi,* and *ho.*

Such vocal quirks are not meant simply to mystify, for elsewhere in the play they are used as a means of generating poetry. In act 1, scene 7, the following untranslatable dialogue occurs:

HUSBAND
Ma femme est un homme-madame
Elle a emporté le piano le violon l'assiette au beurre
Elle est soldat ministre merdecin

POLICEMAN
Mère des seins

HUSBAND
Ils ont fait explosion mais elle est plutôt merdecine

POLICEMAN
Elle est mère des cygnes
Ah! combien chantant qui vont périr
Écoutez [Musette, air triste][15]

Of course one of the predecessors of this dialogue is Père Ubu's famous simultaneous desanctification of motherhood and sanitization of excrement: "Merdre." Yet Apollinaire has gone several steps further than Jarry.

Beneath the created words *merdecin* and *merdecine* (an awkward translation might be shit-doctor) and their rhymes *mère des seins* and *mère des cygnes* lie the theories of assonant language proposed by Jean-Pierre Brisset, a nineteenth-century philosopher who is cited by both André Breton and Marcel Duchamp as an important predecessor to twentieth-century art, particularly Surrealism. Brisset boils his philosophical theories down into a succinct law:

There exist in the spoken word numerous Laws, unknown until today, of which the most important is that a sound or a group of identical sounds, intelligible and clear, can express different things, through a modification in the manner of writing or of understanding these names or these words. All ideas enunciated with similar sounds have a single origin and all relate, in their principle, to the same object.[16]

If this law might sound plausible for a moment, Brisset's application of it dispels any pretension of logicality. First, it must be understood that Brisset considered his linguistic laws universal and cross-cultural. In other words, he believed that all human utterance was one single language, inflected with myriad dialects. Structuralists such as Noam Chomsky have proposed similar ideas, but these theorists are satisfied to discuss language in evolutionary or ethnological terms. Brisset, the philosopher, has a much grander purpose to his studies: he proposes to use pronunciation to answer the most basic ontological questions. For instance, he is able to determine linguistically that sex is the "origin of all living speech" by creating a new word, *exe,* and subjecting it to a series of self-answering assonant questions, such as, "Ce exe, sais que ce? Sexe. Sais que c'est?" followed by a series of declarative transformations: "Ce exe est. Sexe est. Ce excès. Ce excès, c'est le sexe."[17] Likewise when Apollinaire creates a word *merdecin* and applies it to Tirésias, the mere utterance of the word serves to characterize her entire nature, including her initial incarnation as the *mère des seins*—the "mother of breasts," which blew up in the first scene—and as the *mère des cygnes*—the "mother of swans," whose voices rise sadly from the musette.

Elsewhere in *Les Mamelles*, a chamber pot and a urinal are misidentified as, respectively, a piano and a violin. While it might seem that this is simply a bawdy visual joke, since the toilet articles are not made to function as musical instruments, the explanation of the confusion can again be found in the transformative language of Brisset: the French term for violin, *violon,* has the assonant counterpart *viole-on*—"does one violate?" In Brisset's system, all similar sounds have at their root the same object, thus a urinal, which invites one to violate it, and a violin are one and the same. By enabling the sound of this pun to alter the objects themselves physically, Apollinaire has achieved a level of correlation between sound and object that goes beyond coincidence to absolute interdependence. In Apollinaire's theatrical scheme, the sound of the work and its physical properties are inevitable consequences. The compromises and amalgamations that held *Parade* together are almost completely transcended.

In *Les Mamelles*, the most common sound effect is the change in timbre achieved by the use of a megaphone. Again this is an effect that Cocteau had planned to use in *Parade*, but again his idea for using it was less profound than he thought. For Cocteau, the megaphone was simply a means of amplification—an adjunct to the carnival, and ultimately to self-promotion. For Apollinaire, the megaphone was a transformative tool that not only amplified sound but that identified the level of thought from which the sound issued. Indeed, Apollinaire's megaphone does not even appear as such, rather a *cornet acoustique*—"ear trumpet"—is hidden inside a *cornet à dés*— "dice cup"—so that the actors speak into something that is not overtly an instrument of amplification.[18] Again, the verbal identification of an object is used to transform its physical nature. In this case, however, the dice cup does function as a megaphone. Whenever Apollinaire intends that the actors differentiate between verbalized and internal speech, he directs them to step up to the cup and scream their lines, creating a heightened presence of sound similar to the "selective" sound used to indicate heightened awareness and internal speech in sound film. Thus Apollinaire differentiates between the timbres of words that are to be understood as having been uttered and those that are to be understood as not having been uttered—a significant advance in theatrical soliloquy. If this technique has become rather cliché in the last seventy years, it is only because film-makers have tempered it to the point where it can indicate virtually any abstraction: death, thought, retrospection, the passage of time, etc. Apollinaire's version, like most of *Les Mamelles de Tirésias,* bears a mark of the true innovator: complete intemperance.

AUDIENCE THEATER

French theater had often involved some form of audience participation, confined, for the most part, to singing along with operatic arias in a participatory manner, or—in the rare instance—to expressing vocally one's opinion of the action on stage. In either case, the audience response was usually as carefully orchestrated as the presentation itself. Apollinaire used bawdy humor as a means of provoking a violent, prudish reaction to *Les Mamelles.* At the same time, though, he maintained a conservative presentational style which ensured that this reaction would never cross the proscenium—would never bring the audience into direct conflict or participation with the actors.

Still, the premiere of *Les Mamelles* was the occasion for a spontaneous unveiling of a new form of theater, which did promise to break down the barriers between the audience and the stage. Having viewed the first half of Apollinaire's play, a young soldier, Jacques Vaché, produced a gun and threatened to kill his fellow audience members by firing directly into the crowd. Vaché was not suffering delayed battle stress, as many of his potential victims must have thought, but was rather acting in his own special production. Throughout his life, Vaché reversed the roles of the performer and audience member so that he was passive when a social situation

Christopher Schiff

required him to be active and active when a social situation required him to be passive. He refused an active role as a struggling bohemian, choosing instead boredom, drug addiction, and work as a stevedore. Yet even in his pursuit of boredom, he did not allow himself to fall into the patterns of society at large, for the theatrical audience, the very image of bourgeois passivity and boredom, became the center of furious activity for Vaché. He did not accept the notion of a separation between the realities of the theater and audience or, for that matter, between the realities of wartime barbarism and polite entertainments.

During evening outings, Vaché might attend a few moments of several movies, never bothering to find out what he was entering and never staying long enough to determine the plot. At other times he might stay but would carry on as though he were not in a theater at all. With André Breton he would "settle down in the orchestra, opening cans, slicing bread, uncorking bottles, and talking in ordinary tones, as if around a table, to the great amazement of the spectators, who dared not say a word."[19] In these instances, Vaché's primary tool was sound. Silence was the rule in the audience, so giving the audience a voice—particularly one that was completely independent of the stage presentation—was a revolutionary act. Thus although Breton describes Vaché's threat to fire into the audience at *Les Mamelles* as being due to excitement over the scandal of the play,[20] it must be admitted that it was only a slightly more radical version of Vaché's normal behavior in theaters. The entire audience expressed its opinion of Apollinaire's play loudly and freely, thus the ultimate revolutionary act would have been to impose a permanent silence on some—if not all—of that audience.

To understand the sonic import of Vaché's act, it is necessary to compare it with the noises that Cocteau and Apollinaire had inserted, respectively, into *Parade* and *Les Mamelles de Tirésias*. Both of these had gunshots included in their libretti, Cocteau's signifying a robbery that was being mimed on stage and Apollinaire's signifying the previously described duel. Still, these gunshots were merely symbolic. They had no real import for the performers, other than as cues for an imitation of action. Neither did they have any import for the audience, except as a reminder of the sound of events that were being imitated but that were not actually occurring. No one tried to restrain the person firing the shots, nor did anyone rush to the defence of the performers. In contrast, Vaché recognized that sound and consequence could not be divorced. By transforming a violent act into an entertaining theatrical sound, Cocteau and Apollinaire were glorifying passivity in the face of mortal danger. By confirming, in the same theatrical setting, the violence of a violent act, Vaché did away with symbols and glorified both his own free will and the collective action that the audience no doubt took to prevent him from exercising that free will.[21]

In the history of Surrealism this was a critical moment, for when a Surrealist movement was in the process of development, André Breton would utilize Vaché's idea for one of the key definitions of Surrealism: "The simplest surrealist act consists of going out into the street, revolver in hand, and firing at random into the crowd, as often as possible."[22] Furthermore, Breton would state in *Surrealism and Painting* that it was the responsibility of artists within the Surrealist movement to "make use of their particular means of expression to prevent the domination by the symbol of the thing signified."[23] Vaché's medium was gunshots, Apollinaire's play the symbol, and the audience the thing signified. The gunshots forced the audience out of its symbol-induced passivity and into a clear, active awareness of its own reality. Ultimately this would become the goal of all Surrealist disciplines, including the sonic arts.

PARIS DADA

TRISTAN TZARA

Paris Dada made its debut on 23 January 1920 in the form of a soirée: a series of poetry readings, a lecture on symbolism by André Salmon, music by Satie and *Les Six*,[24] and finally an unan-

Christopher Schiff

nounced presentation by Tristan Tzara.[25] This last presentation was radically different from the rest of the show. After being lulled to sleep by numerous unmemorable works, the audience was forced to confront a work of pure sound art: the simultaneous reading. Unlike most simultaneous readings, this did not involve the speaking of multiple texts nor any sort of polyglot. Instead the work consisted of Tzara reading a speech by the protofascist parliamentarian Léon Daudet—Tzara's poetry had been read earlier in the program by Louis Aragon—only to be grotesquely overbalanced by the ringing of two electric bells. The whole point was to frustrate the passive audition of expected sounds by the performance of unexpected and unusually aggressive sounds. The audience response was not much different from that which simultaneous readings had received in Zurich. Most of the auditors were annoyed—as were some participants, none of whom had been informed of the *geste* beforehand. Some complained vocally, and all left when it became clear that the rest of the program would not be nearly as annoying as Tzara's reading had been.[26]

This became the archetype for most of the events of Paris Dada: a brief event, rooted in the traditional arts, is made scandalous by the skewing of some element. In this case it was the environmental noise that overtook the spoken word—the traditional focus of a speech. In Tzara's plays it is a compounding of skewed elements: phonetic poetry; actors hidden in paper bags or dressed as free-floating body parts, each with its own voice and will; non sequitur piled upon non sequitur. Very often, musical techniques were either used as the focus of a geste or as operators that might alter the form of some other element of a performance. In Tzara's *Vaseline symphonique*, a work whose title is more scandalous than its content, twenty people sing ascending scales first on the syllable *cra*, followed by ascending scales one third higher on the syllable *cri* ... et cetera ad infinitum.[27] There are two elements at work here: the poetic and the musical. Tzara places his boring and repetitive phonetic poetry into the most boring and repetitive musical format that he can. For every change in the text, for every new vowel, there is a change of one musical element, the tonality.[28] The result was nothing more than a backstage choral warm-up, displaced and purposefully executed before an audience—a grandfather to Kagel, Berio, Stockhausen, and the Swingle Singers.

This last piece was particularly telling in terms of Surrealism and sound, for André Breton's reaction to it was extremely negative. Though the program forbade movement during the performance of *Vaseline symphonique,* Breton stormed out of the theater and waited in another room until it was over, grinding his teeth. Sanouillet suggests that Breton's reaction was due to his dislike of music,[29] but this is putting the cart before the horse. It was just such wanton musicality that made Breton despise the discipline. He did not hate music until Dada showed him the fallacy of attempting to revitalize it.

Strangely enough, Tzara himself professed to be against the creation of art. When the Dadaists tried to disrupt a concert of bruitist music given by Marinetti and Russolo in June 1921, they claimed that they did so because of hostility toward "the false endeavors of a modernist art."[30] The reasons for the disruption were, however, more complicated. Marinetti and Cocteau were viewed by the Dadaists as opportunists who were trying to capitalize on the infamy of Dada by denigrating and plagiarizing it simultaneously. The concert that was disrupted was part of a series presented by Jacques Hébertot at the Théâtre des Champs-Elysées which was to include the *Salon dada,* as well as the premiere of Cocteau's *Les Mariés de la Tour Eiffel.* Yet the Dadaists objected strongly to the implication that their works were in any way equivalent to those of Cocteau or Marinetti, and they decided that they had to distance themselves publicly from the other presenters.[31]

At the concert, Tzara stood up and began to insult both the Futurists and their supporters; however, Marinetti, a professional troublemaker himself, was prepared. Hébertot was sent to ask Tzara to be quiet and then to leave. Failing on both counts, he

Christopher Schiff

brought a policeman who ejected the leader of the Dadaists. Meanwhile, Hébertot announced that he would cancel the *Salon dada* as a means of retribution against the "infantile" Dadaists.[32] Having thus played his final card, though, he ensured that the Dada protest would continue, and the other Dadaists took up where Tzara had left off. When Marinetti tried to intervene by requesting that the audience show respect for the war heros who played in the orchestra, the Dadaists responded with the indictment, "All the more reason to boo them, poor things....who asked them to make war!"[33]

This particular incident played an important role in the demise of Paris Dada, for it became a public display of the Dadaists' reliance on the bourgeoisie and their vulnerability to its whims. As a group dedicated to the perpetration of *scandales,* the Dadaists were absolutely dependent on a conservative audience upon which to visit insults. Stripped of the opportunity to present their *Salon dada,* they were also stripped of that audience and hence rendered unable to act. Momentarily, the Dadaists thought to sue Hébertot over the cancellation of the *Salon dada,* but facing certain defeat, they decided to forego any action. Thus their attempt at undermining the representatives of modern art became instead a tacit admission of their own inability to confront modern art with anything but hollow theatrical threats.

RIBEMONT-DESSAIGNES AND DISSONANCE

George Ribemont-Dessaignes is one of the Paris Dadaists who remained absolutely true to the movement, never espousing Surrealism. Even Tzara, despite his arguments with Breton, was eventually completely coopted into the Surrealist movement. Ribemont-Dessaignes' contributions to the Dada soirées were often musical compositions, the most famous of which were two piano solos: *Le Pas de la chicorée frisée* and *Le Nombril interlope,* performed at the soirées of 27 March and 26 May 1920, respectively. The format of these works was the same in both instances: a tonal composition was thoroughly composed, only then to be subjected to chance operations. The result was a piece that could be both traditionally serious and outlandish, since it was cast in the form of a standard romantic work with humorous dissonances built in. The audience, unaware of similar experiments in chance and gratuitous dissonance by Mozart, Marcel Duchamp, and even their own Satie, was disturbed by the works. According to the composer, the performance was drowned in "an incredible riot, composed of the music of frightfully little consonance, of the continuing murmur in the hall, of its shouts, of its whistling, which united into a crash of broken glass of rather curious effect."[34] Despite the delightful racket, the end result was no advance in either music or sound art, however.

The problem was that Ribemont-Dessaignes accepted both the traditional idea of music and the traditional idea of unmusicality that that brought with it. Thus he considered it sufficiently radical to compose works with the added punch of dissonance. Unfortunately, dissonance is not an absolute entity. It is a segregation of tones based on an arbitrary identification of what is harmonious and what is inharmonious. In fact, the history of common-practice harmony was the history of harsher and harsher dissonances being adopted by composers, until finally, around 1910, many quit trying to differentiate the consonant from the dissonant altogether—or at least quit resolving dissonance into consonance. Music theorists were slow to accept this, however. As late as the 1960s, dissonance was the safe ground onto which they would retreat when discussing Surrealism, since to some extent, the word provided the only common terminology between Surrealism and music.[35]

Surrealist arts relied heavily on the use of incongruity. Yet while dissonance may be a combining of two incongruous elements that have a mentally bestowed affinity, it is not necessarily surreal, for all harmonic music would then be surreal, since it all relies on some dissonant tension to give it direction. Musical harmony was the very precedent that Apollinaire chose to explain Surrealism in his program note for *Parade*, but it was discussed only as an analogue to the more important combination of disciplines and styles that has already been discussed. Musical harmony itself was of little concern to him.

Complicating the analytical consideration of dissonance as a genus is the more subjective consideration of dissonance as humor. This aspect is clearly of French origin. Germans such as Schönberg and Strauss exploited dissonance unashamedly, but they very seldom used it for comic effect. As anti-Wagnerian music took hold in France, one of its main features was a lack of dissonance, since this subverted the Wagnerian concept of tension and release. Satie's early works are some of the most famous of this genre: short modal piano pieces that do not even use the primary dissonance of the leading tone of the dominant chord. A similar modality is heard in the incidental music written for Jarry's *Père Ubu* by Claude Terrasse. In this case modality is intended to create the atmosphere of the medieval puppet theatre, as well as depicting the semiexotic location of Poland.[36]

Satie, some twenty years after the premiere of *Père Ubu,* was the composer who gave the Parisian audience a taste for dissonance as humor. The piano music that he wrote just prior to World War I often contained subtle instances of discord that were dictated by the literary script serving as directions to the pianist. It was his avowed wish that these scripts not be shared with the audience, however, so the mistakes and jokes were heard as abstractions rather than as bits of programmed slapstick. As Satie's music grew in popularity, his use of such humor became less subtle. His *Cinq grimaces,* for instance, forego the fleeting gestures of his piano pieces, opting instead for the blatant mock pomposity of the circus band. This ostentatious use of humor was continued in *Parade.*

Thus by the time of the premiere of *Les Mamelles de Tirésias,* dissonance had become a recognizable trait of the music of the Parisian avant-garde. This posed an interesting problem for composers, for though the essence of dissonance is surprise and disturbance, it was suddenly being expected by audiences and even praised by critics for its light-hearted quality. Paul Souday writes of the score to *Les Mamelles,* "Mme. Birot's music, appropriately eccentric and dissonant, helped towards the audience's enjoyment."[37] Certainly, then, when Ribemont-Dessaignes wrote his Dada piano compositions, dissonance was something other than the expression of romantic tension. In writing his music of "frightfully little consonance," he was only giving the audience what it expected.

MARGUERITTE BUFFET

The most common assessment of Dada performers is that they were amateurs who were unusually gifted at inciting riot. To a certain extent, this image is a matter of convenience for art historians, who tend to portray Dada as a "boys' club." Although it is true that the more famous participants in the movement were untrained as actors or musicians, many of the less-known Dadaists were professional performers, and several of these were women. On the program of the first Dada soirée, for instance, one finds the names of Margueritte Buffet, a professional pianist, Hania Routchine, a well-known vaudeville singer, and Musidora, a film actress who was extremely famous at the time.[38] Of these, Margueritte Buffet was the most active and dedicated Dadaist.

The cousin of Gabrielle Buffet, Margueritte Buffet is deserving of much greater recognition for her part in Paris Dada. She performed several works at each of the soirées, executing piano music by Ribemont-Dessaignes and Picabia as well as acting in Tzara's *Second Celestial Adventure of Mr. Antipyrene* and testifying for the prosecution at the *Trial of Maurice Barrès by Dada.* Even taken by itself, this last role should confirm her importance within Paris Dada. One reason for Buffet's omnipresence was her ability to give Dada an air of legitimacy. The Dadaists wished to expose bourgeois institutions by revealing them in their most solemn guise, and sometimes this called for a presentational style somewhat at odds with the content of the work being presented. A case in point is *Le Pas de la chicorée frisée,* a lampoon of the sort of performances that could be seen daily in the numerous predominantly female salons of Paris. In order to make the salon reference clear, *Le Pas* had to be performed with the utmost decorum. Furthermore, it had to be performed by a woman, since women provided most of the salon entertainment. It was not beyond the realm of possibility for Ribemont-Dessaignes to perform the work himself in drag,[39] but that would have allowed the audience to ignore the music in favor of the performance. Margueritte Buffet was able to realize the work perfectly, both in terms of technique and atmosphere. Thus the performance was unimpeachable, and all attention was focused on the sound itself. No other Dadaist could have achieved such an effect.

At the first Dada soirée, Buffet performed *Le Pas de la chicorée frisée,* then immediately returned to the stage with André Breton to perform Picabia's *Cannibal manifesto.* Like the previous piece, this was an attack on a salon tradition, the inspirational lecture. Also like the previous piece, the "manifesto" was executed with impeccable technique, the rousing pseudopatriotic invective of Breton's speech accompanied by an aggressive piano score. In this case the music required none of the modernisms of Ribemont-Dessaignes's works, since the whole point was to emphasize the words without distracting attention from them. It was, nonetheless, absolutely necessary, since music tied the performance directly to an identifiable bourgeois activity. It made the work patriotic, and without it Breton's exhortation of the crowd to stand as though it were hearing the *Marseillaise* would have been at best a bit of conceptual poetry. Instead the music was used to heighten the emotional intensity of the piece just as it would have been used to heighten the emotional intensity of a genuine patriotic speech. Thus without the contribution of Margueritte Buffet, *Cannibal manifesto* would have been no more than another incendiary reading among many.[40]

Several works intervened at this point in the program, including Tzara's *First Celestial Adventure of Mr. Antipyrene,* a play/manifesto that involved phonetic poetry and invective sonically punctuated by a klaxon and three echoes—not unlike his previously described reading of Daudet. The final work of the evening was a manifesto to be sung by Mlle Hania Routchine who, for all her professionalism and renown, was not willing to participate in the spirit of the performance that had gone on before her. In all fairness, the Dadaists themselves claimed that she had been asked to perform a piece that would soothe the spirits of the audience, and the work that was to be sung—Henri Duparc's *Claire de Lune*—would seem to confirm this. At any rate, she made the mistake of prefacing her song with the statement, "I hope that you will do me the honor of listening to me." This as much as anything sealed her fate, for after being regaled with insults for hours, it is doubtful that the audience was willing to do anyone any honor. After listening to Tzara's play fairly calmly, the audience rioted during Routchine's attempt to sing a song that was the epitome of bourgeois sensitivity. She was booed off the stage and did not complete the work.[41] The only way that the Dadaists could have enticed the bourgeoisie to attack its own sacred institutions was to confuse it to the point where it wasn't sure whether a performance was intended to be soothing or simply another grotesque joke. This was the major achievement of Margueritte Buffet as a Dadaist performance artist. Willing and able to perform in either a traditional manner or an ultramodern manner, she made the audience mistrust its ears, leaving it guessing as to which style it was currently hearing.

ERIK SATIE

Satie is the one established composer whose personal aesthetics corresponded with those of the Dadaists. His *musique d'ameublement* (furniture music), for instance, was premiered shortly after the first manifestations of Paris Dada. The point of the piece was to provide a sonic experience that was functional only when dysfunctional: "It hopes to contribute to life the way that a casual conversation does, or a picture in a gallery, or a chair in which one is not seated."[42] Compare this to Tzara's account of his reading of Daudet: "An attempt was made to give a futuristic interpretation to this act, but all that I wanted to convey was simply that my presence on stage, the sight of my face and my movements, ought to satisfy people's curiosity and that anything I might have said really had no importance."[43] Tzara might have remained silent and achieved this effect, but like Satie's music, his speech had to exist before it could be properly ignored. Both pieces provided information but then stripped it of all but decorative value. In Tzara's piece the information was denuded by electric bells; in Satie's, by a polite reprimand to those attempting to listen to the music. The latter method was less irritating, but the pieces were clearly rooted in the same aesthetic.

As a critic, Satie often attacked the music of other composers, and at times his disapprobation took on overtones that would eventually be associated with Surrealism. In 1920, he wrote a response to his own question, "Which do you prefer, music or pork butchery?": "In many places, excellent and sweet silence has been replaced by bad music....The remedy? Formidable taxes; terrible punishments; severe repressions. Torture, even."[44] Elsewhere, he makes it clear that he considers "bad" music to be Wagnerian. Satie came to personify French artistic independence and the hopes of those who wished to fortify Parisian theaters and salons against the infiltration of Germanic aesthetics. Ribemont-Dessaignes, for instance, called him the "eternal resting place of the head of French music."[45] It was in this capacity that he toured Europe after the war, performing *Socrate:* meeting and influencing many young Dadaists.[46]

The musical participation of Satie and *Les Six* in Dada soirées was sporadic. The latter, younger composers had been formed into a nominal school by Cocteau, who from the very beginning had been on bad terms with the Dadaists. When Cocteau began his own pseudo-Dada manifestations, *Les Six* concentrated their musical talents there. Satie was always his own man, though, and Cocteau's proprietary attitude toward him was enough to drive him directly into the Dadaists' camp—not so much as an artist but as an *agent provocateur*. In fact, when one reads the numerous memoirs of those who claimed to be influenced by Satie, few cite his music as their inspiration. It was Satie himself, the last bohemian *flâneur,* who impressed the Dadaists.

Still, his renown as a composer was undeniable, and it caused his actions within the Dada movement to be viewed as though they were official actions taken on behalf of the entire musical discipline. Thus when Paris Dada began to factionalize, his political position became, in effect, the position of music with regard to Dada. When Dada split into an absurdist group that followed Tzara and a more serious-minded group that followed Breton, Satie became an active partisan of Tzara's faction. As a young man he had been one of the chief bureaucrats of the Rosicrucian Society, but a sudden reversal of thought had left him a lifelong absurdist. In a rebuke to the Rosicrucians, he formed his own church, commanding for all time the "removal from My presence of sadness, silence and dolorous meditation."[47]

When Breton announced a Congress of Paris dedicated to the "defense of the modernist spirit," he seemed to be touching on the very sort of "dolorous meditation" that Satie had banished from his presence thirty years earlier. Together with Tzara, the composer wrote a letter that denounced the organizers of the Congress as "willing the annihilation of all that is living."[48] Ribemont-Dessaignes and Paul Eluard likewise signed the declaration. Thus of the four men leading the attack on the Congress of Paris, three had been associated closely with Dada musical activities. Of the four, Breton was upset only by the attitude of Satie, for he had promoted him frequently in *Littérature,* and he believed that Satie could have aided and benefitted from the Congress.[49] It is perhaps for this reason that Breton was so unrelenting in his attitude toward music, for at the very time when musicians could have played a significant role in his designs for a new movement—eventually designated Surrealism—he was betrayed by the one composer whose opinion he valued.

The immediate results of the argument over the Congress of Paris are well known. Tzara's group began to publish attacks on Breton, including Satie's *Office de la domesticité,* aphoristic variations on a theme of Breton's subservience to purist theorist Amadée Ozenfant.[50] At first Breton did not confront Satie directly, confining his retribution to more prominent members of Paris Dada. In the following years, however, Satie became a target of the soon-to-be Surrealists. In fact, one of the first group activities of the Surrealist movement was a disruption of Satie's ballet *Mercure*, instigated by Georges Auric and executed by Breton and Aragon: The two latter began to applaud vociferously the sets of Picasso. When admonished by Milhaud for ignoring the work of Satie, Aragon began to cry, "A bas Satie!" and then as he was being forcibly ejected from the ballet, "A bas les flics!"[51] Henceforth Satie was connected, in the minds of the Surrealists, with the oppressive establishment.[52]

Having thus permanently alienated themselves from Satie—the embodiment of French music—the Surrealists turned to the composer who had conspired with them against Satie. Georges Auric is the only musician named in the *Manifesto of Surrealism* as being welcome at Breton's still-lamented—and by then (1924) nearly mythical—Congress.[53] Auric's attentions were divided at best, though, and his relations with Cocteau proved to be stronger than his relations with the Surrealists. Had this not cost him their respect, his eventual acceptance of the Legion of Honor most certainly would have.[54] Auric's vacillation was the final straw. The Surrealist movement ended up following a course proposed by Ribemont-Dessaignes in 1919: "If, for the purposes of political morale, one might consider regulating the usage of the Arts and the life of artists, here is what one ought to do to begin: forbid music and hang the musicians."[55]

DE CHIRICO AND SAVINIO

NO MUSIC

Nursing, at this point, a decided hatred of the musical, the Surrealists looked for confirmation of their attitudes in the writings of earlier artists whom they respected. By far the most famous statement to this effect was Giorgio de Chirico's *No Music*:

Music cannot express the essence of sensation. One never knows what music is about, and after all, having heard any piece of music, whether by Beethoven, Wagner, Rossini, or Monsieur Saint-Saëns, every listener has the right to say, and can say, what does this mean? In a profound painting, on the contrary, this is impossible; one must fall silent when one has penetrated it in all its profundity, when one turns the corner of all its walls, and not of its walls alone. Then light and shade, lines and angles begin to talk, and music too begins to be heard, that hidden music that one does not hear. What I listen to is worthless: there is only what I see with my eyes open—and even better closed. There is no mystery in music; that is precisely why it is the art people enjoy most, for they always discover in it more sensations. I felt this last night; yes, I felt it in a profound and silent fashion, in a fashion filled with terror. Should I perhaps call such an experience a truth?

But such truths do not talk, they have no voice; still less do they sing; but sometimes they look at one, and at their glance one is forced to bow one's head and say, yes that is true. What results—a picture, for example, always has a music of its own; that is inevitable, that is the mysterious destiny of all things to have a thousand souls, a thousand aspects.

I felt this yesterday at evening: painting, painting: In my picture: the end of the meal or the music of shattered light, this sensation beyond music is written in letters of fire. Music remains confined, something one takes before the meal or after, but which is not the meal itself. Here is an enigma which I do not advise imaginative minds to dwell upon too long, for in spite of its afternoon warmth, it is icy. But what joy, great God, what joy you give me when I understand. Is this life, or its opposite, or is it neither one nor the other? Yet it makes me happy, I would not desire it to be otherwise, although who knows, perhaps it is otherwise, and perhaps also....[56]

This document was written in 1913 but remained controversial in the 1920s when it was rediscovered by Paul Eluard. In retrospect, it is neither very clear nor very informative, but in a way this is the aspect of the work that most attracted the Surrealists. De Chirico's stream-of-consciousness writing style approximated the

Christopher Schiff

automatism with which Breton and Soupault began to experiment in 1919. Yet when Breton himself chose to paraphrase *No Music* in his famous treatise *Surrealism and Painting,* he stripped away much of the imagistic, ecstatic confusion that characterizes De Chirico's work:

To these varying degrees of sensation correspond spiritual realizations suffi-ciently precise and distinct to allow me to grant to plastic expression a value that on the other hand I shall never cease to grant to musical expression, the most deeply confusing of all forms. Auditive images, in fact, are inferior to visual images not only in clarity but also in strictness, and, with all due respect to a few megalomaniacs, they are not destined to strengthen the idea of human greatness. So may night continue to descend upon the orchestra, and may I, who am still searching for something in this world, be left with open eyes, or with closed eyes in broad daylight, to my silent contemplation.[57]

The main problem with *No Music* is that its specificity narrows its scope unnecessarily. De Chirico's criticism of long-dead composers is moot, for their aesthetics had been dead longer than they. At no point does he attack modern music, nor even the late romantics. In fact, in the very document from which these three paragraphs are excerpted, he praises Henri Rabaud's *Daughter of Roland,* "above all...the melody, '*Mariez joyeuse avec des Duvandel.*' It is something beautiful, terrible and profound."[58] As time went by, De Chirico seemed to find more and more music that was "beautiful, terrible and profound." For instance, just as his writing was having its greatest effect on the Surrealist movement, he himself was collaborating on a ballet with Diaghilev and the Italian composer Vittorio Rieti.[59]

De Chirico's change of heart with regard to music was mostly due to the modernization of musical aesthetics. When he wrote *No Music,* his understanding of musical style was limited to romanticism and impressionism: movements wherein composers tried to duplicate the sound of nature. Yet as a substitute, he could only propose structuralism: "The truly profound work will be drawn up by the artist from the innermost depths of being. There is no murmur of brooks, no song of birds, no rustle of leaves... in their stead appear measurements, lines, forms of eternity and infinity."[60] Musical neoclassicism, which was heavily dependent on a linear style, seems to have fulfilled De Chirico's search for eternal forms. It may have been what he found attractive in Henri Rabaud's work, as well as Rieti's. It is assuredly what he found attractive in the work of Stravinsky, with whom he became lifelong friends.[61]

Had common-practice orchestral music been the entire subject of *No Music,* De Chirico's contribution to Surrealist sonic practice would have been minimal. Yet this manifesto is unique in its discussion of two different musics: traditional classical music and music as a mystical experience. De Chirico proposes that the objective and the symbolic be discarded and that the auditor be drawn inside a work, where some essential "truth," "mystery," or "enigma" might be found. Thus the power and meaning of an artwork is directly relative to a person's own transcendent experience of it—the experience that De Chirico calls "sensation."[62] He had himself discovered this relativity as a result of convalescence from an intestinal illness that had left him in a "nearly morbid state of sensitivity." Sitting in a bare Florentine plaza, he hallucinated that his personal mental state was a universal state: "The whole world, down to the marble of the buildings and the fountains seemed to me to be convalescent."[63]

While recognizing that sound, as well as matter, could become a vehicle for such revelations, De Chirico suggests that his own transcendent auditory experiences are usually triggered by vision: "lines and angles begin to talk"; "a picture always has a music of its own"; "in my picture... the music of shattered light." This is more than synesthesia, it is sonic animism. Sound is not produced and diffused in De Chirico's universe but is rather concentrated within substance, waiting to be released by the artist. The duty of this latter is then to create a set of vocal cords out of form and light that will allow the artwork to speak to the viewer with its own unique voice—the sound that De Chirico associates with his visual "enigmas." In other words, the artist does not create or organize the "hidden music that one does not hear" but only enables it.

For De Chirico, there is no sonic corollary that would either mimic or induce the aural "sensation" induced by his metaphysical painting style. This is not due to an ignorance of the musical arts, since the painter was sufficiently knowledgeable about music to translate the dialogue between his brother, Alberto Savinio, and his brother's composition teacher during their lessons.[64] According to De Chirico, it was a reaction to the lack of "mystery" in music. Yet in stating this, the painter states also that music has no clear meaning, delineating a separation between mystery (i.e., inscrutability) and meaninglessness that may or may not exist, "meaning" being very much subject to the whims of the auditor. To confound matters all the more, De Chirico begins interchanging the term *music* with the terms *mystery* and *enigma,* implying that *music* is the very thing that he finds lacking in music as a discipline. He was not alone in confusing disciplines and intangible sensations. Most Surrealists used the term *poetry* to designate the same enigmas that De Chirico designated *music.* Poetry was for the Surrealists an absolute measure of the emotive and affective force of any given aspect of existence, not simply a rhythmic concatenation of words. Similarly, *music* must be understood to signify for them something other than a rhythmic concatenation of tones.

NEW MUSIC

De Chirico's own brother, the aforementioned Alberto Savinio, was one of the Surrealists-to-be who first began to use the term *poetry* to describe the intangibles in his art. In an article published in *291* in 1915, *Give Me the Anathema, Lascivious Thing,* Savinio describes a "New Music"[65] that is centered around poetry:

The creative artist is a political man. He enjoys the law of inviolability which preserves the person of a constitutional monarch.

The formidable and architectural poetry which drives the artwork *is no more than* poetic penchant: *it is no more than* poetic poetry.

Nonsense holds itself in prodigious equilibrium. It is the expression of natural and superior sentiment—true everywhere—which has roots in the earth and which rises beyond to the seventh heaven.

It is there that music floats.

An entirely new creation is set into motion now, everything is a singer.[66]

The first words—"The creative artist is a political man"—describe the very basis of the Surrealist movement: the recognition that art was at all times a political tool, and that any attempt to subdue the political impact of an artwork through absurdism, functionalism, or purism was a denial of the artist's transcendent social vision.

The splicing of Dantesque images into a structure imitating Nietzsche's *Also Sprach Zarathustra* lends this statement a grandiose character that might lead one to believe that Savinio was a musical mystic. This is far from the case. His compositions were more akin to the works of Bartok than to those of such mystics as Scriabin or Satie,[67] and his manner of performance was in direct conflict with mystical notions of a perfectly ordered universe. In the spring of 1914 he played salon concerts under the auspices of *Les Soirées de Paris*, advertised by Apollinaire thus: "Those who have the honor and the privilege of attending this first concert of new music will be astonished to see how roughly the young musician treats his instrument. This is an indication of the tremendous energy that propels our artist. To see him play the piano is an experience. There he sits in shirt-sleeves, a monocle in his eye, screaming and throwing himself about while his instrument struggles to attain his own pitch of enthusiasm."[68] Savinio's performance techniques included smashing the piano with his fists and dragging a board up and down the keys. The results were predictable but exciting. After one concert André Billy recalls hearing Apollinaire exclaim: "He broke the piano! Now that's what I call a musician!"[69] In a written review of the same concert, Apollinaire goes further: "I believe that within two years he will

Christopher Schiff

have broken all the pianos existing in Paris, after which he might leave to traverse the world and break all the pianos existing in the universe. This will perhaps be a good riddance."[70]

For a short time following these concerts, Savinio became one of the most celebrated composers in Paris. Fokine, trying to develop a repertoire that might compete with that of the Ballets Russes, commissioned him to write two new ballets, effectively placing the young composer in direct competition with Stravinsky.[71] Unfortunately, this collaboration was planned for political reasons and ignored the important aesthetic differences between Fokine and Savinio. Fokine conceived modern ballet to be a fabric unified by interdisciplinary referencing. His experiments in artistic interdependence started with *The Firebird* and were repeated over and over in the productions of the Ballets Russes—even those he did not choreograph, such as *Parade*. Savinio, on the other hand, tried to expose the artificiality of such interdependence as early as 1914, proposing as a substitute a theatrical music that came directly from the performance context, ignoring the traditional dictates of plot almost entirely. In "Drama and Music," published in *Les Soirées de Paris,* he suggests that multi-media works be compounded by chance:

It is by no means the business of music to translate into its particular language either literary thoughts, or impressions, or yet states of the soul; and it is even less its business to represent phenomena, actions or movements.

Music is an exceptional art which does not tolerate fashioning, and which insists on being employed as it is. One degenerates the art if one wishes to apply to it—as has always been done—the expression of dramaticity and of human psychology, because it possesses, itself, a dramaticity and a psychology (so to speak) which is inherent to it.

So then, when presenting, in the ensemble of a work, the element of concert music with the element of drama—as I have proposed it— one ought not perceive in this association anything but a completely disinterested setting side-by-side, since the musical element depends little on the dramatic element, and the latter is equally independent of the former.

It will do, in the end, to make the independent musical element participate in the drama with the same value and the same liberty that this element possesses when it appears accidentally amidst the continuous dramas of life. There are, moreover, typical and gross examples: in considering traffic on a street as a dramatic action, one could find a musical element, if not in the cries and voices of the same street, in the sound of the piano coming from a nearby house; or better yet in wishing to place the dramatic element in the interior of a room, one could there make a horn sound participate like a musical element, rising from the street to traverse the open window; workers who accomplish their manual labors by accompanying themselves with songs constitute, without a doubt, the essence of drama in music.[72]

The disjuncture of sound from action is, of course, one of the many techniques that Apollinaire used in *Les Mamelles de Tirésias*.[73] Savinio is much more of a naturalist than Apollinaire, however. Where the latter organizes sound into a performable text, Savinio accepts sound as an a priori condition of the performance situation. Sound will either be encouraged into the frame of the performance, or it will intrude of its own volition. The essential thing is that it not be *restricted* from the performance. To this end, Savinio suggests two potential settings for his new drama: a crowded street, where "music" could enter the scene from a myriad of unpredictable sources or a salon with intentionally opened windows.[74]

In both cases, the context dictates which sounds will and will not be considered music. The musical element within the street scene is the sound of a piano drifting from a house that is outside the designated set. Conversely, the musical element within the salon is the traffic noise that drifts through the purposefully opened window. Thus in these instances music is sound that is exotic to the performance situation but that at the same time defines the performance situation. It is the element that crosses between two different spheres of influence meaningfully, uniting two separate theaters—the theater of the salon and the theater of the street—into a single metatheater. The meaning of the music arises from its composite role: the sound of the piano in the first instance might have been intended to be lighthearted and entertaining in the salon, but it could easily take on a tragic tone when heard in combination with events on the street; the horn sounded in the street might be intended to express anger or impatience but could become ironic or comic when heard in the salon.

These metatheatrical elements explain, to an extent, what Savinio meant when he identified the artist as a "political man." The artist is a facilitator of a political dialectic, literally leaving the door open to the transmission of ideas. For Savinio, theater was no longer dictatorial. Though the oft-cited "fourth wall" was still in place between the performers and the audience, a window was opened so that the performers might themselves become an audience for the outside world.

AUTOMATIC SOUND

Savinio's theater was in mood (though not in time) transitional between the public spectacle of the first Surrealist theatrical works and the hermeticism of the first surrealist experiments with automatism. In *Les Mamelles de Tirésias*, the primary issue was the universal ambiguity of identity, and one of the techniques used to express that ambiguity was a change in vocal character or accent. Savinio's drama focused on the ambiguity of the theatrical situation, particularly on that of the performer who becomes auditor of the exotic world beyond the window. Breton's experiments with automatism were spurred by a recognition of the ambiguity of his own identity, split as it was into the conscious and the unconscious, the latter differentiated from the former, once again, by vocal character or accent:

Therefore, one evening, before sleep, I perceived, clearly articulated to the point that it was impossible to change a word of it, but yet devoid of any vocal timbre, *a rather bizarre phrase which reached me without carrying a trace of the events in which, by consent of my conscious, I found myself embroiled at that moment, a phrase which appeared to me insistent, a phrase I will venture to say* which banged on the windowpane.[75]

The first message that Breton could recall having received from this source—"There is a man cut in two by the window"[76]—metaphorically described the very bifurcation of personality that he was beginning to explore within himself. As Apollinaire's word *violon* was integrated with the object that it represented, so Breton's verbal image is sonically integrated with the message that it wishes to convey. Since the communication concerns a window, the internal sound must first enter the conscious through a *mental window* and then assert itself by banging on the mental windowpane to assure that it is not ignored by the logical faculties.

Breton was later to recognize that in heeding these internal voices, he was actually establishing a new form of theater: "Spoken as if by an actor offstage, they were quite distinct and, to what is aptly called the interior ear, constituted a remarkably autonomous group."[77] The voices entered his conscious from his unconscious in precisely the manner that Savinio proposed sound be allowed to enter the salon—from "offstage," and/or through a "window." Furthermore, whether the windows through which they arrived were architectural or mental, the sounds were treated as though they had a common origin, for if Savinio intended to encourage the sound of the extraneous and exotic into the frame of his theatrical performance, so Breton intended to encourage the sound of the *internal exotic* into the frame of his consciousness.

Yet where Savinio allowed sound to flow in either direction—from the street to the salon or from the salon to the street—Breton was adamant that the sound of the conscious not become entangled with the sound of the unconscious. In fact, to clear the way for unconscious sounds, he began to strive for a mental environment unpolluted by the conscious—or at least by things perceived by the conscious. In the previously quoted excerpt from *Surrealism and Painting*, he—echoing De Chirico's *No Music*—praises the precision of images received with eyes closed, but does so in a way that reveals not so much a real preference for vision over audition as a frustration with the lack of a physical mechanism by which the ears might be adumbrated, leaving the "interior ear" uncompromised and free to hear precisely. This was the primary reason for Breton's championing of silence. The only natural way to limit sound perceived by the conscious was to limit sound generated by the "outside world":

It sufficed to forget the existence of the outside world and thus, during two months, they reached us in ever greater numbers and soon followed each other unceasingly, so swiftly that we had to use abbreviations to be able to write them down... whenever we lent an ear, even a malicious one, to another voice than that of our unconscious, we ran the risk of jeopardizing in its essence a self-sufficient murmur, and I think that is what happened. Never again, when we called forth that murmur and collected it, later on, for precise ends, did it lead us very far. And yet it is such that I still await no further revelation but from it. I never ceased to be convinced that nothing that is said or done has any value except when obeying this magical dictation. [78]

Of course, Breton was not satisfied simply to observe the phenomenon of internal sound, but attempted, as a poet, to put it to use. As stated above, however, literary premeditation or imperious exploitation of the unconscious by the conscious led to dubious results. According to Breton, this was because of the tendency of syntactically arranged words to "re-create the world each instant upon its old model ... as though a concrete reality existed outside the individual ... as if such reality were immutable."[79] Since the conscious—and hence the aesthetic—preferred mimicry of the known over acknowledgement and exploration of the unknown, poetry was enslaved by what the poet perceived of the outside world. Thus, as had De Chirico, Breton deplored the imitative: "Language can and should be torn from this servitude. No more descriptions from nature, no more sociological studies. Silence, so that I may pass where no one has ever passed! Silence! After you, my beautiful language!"[80]

The avoidance of premeditation did not, however, free the Surrealist movement from method. Along with such terminology as "the conscious" and "the unconscious," the Surrealists borrowed from the then-novel field of psychiatry methods of scientific observation that they substituted for aesthetics. Chief among these was automatism, taken not from Freud but from pre-Freudian French Dynamic Psychiatry.[81] Although the Surrealists would eventually employ methods of interrogation similar to Freudian "free association," more frequently they resorted to self-analysis as proposed by such early French psychiatrists as Janet.[82]

The difference was that in Freudian psychiatry, the patient acted as a mouthpiece or translator of the unconscious, either wittingly or unwittingly making interior speech intelligible so that it might be transcribed and appraised by the analyst, while in French dynamic psychiatry, the patient *personally* transcribed and appraised interior speech, foregoing either the need for its mimicry or its translation into a language that is understandable to anyone but the patient—avoiding, as Breton preferred, both the imposition of syntax and imitation. In the latter method, the patient is turned into a stenographer[83] of internal sound or—in the words that Breton would usurp from French psychiatrist Emmanuel Régis—into a "simple recording instrument";[84] an automaton whose sole purpose is the evaluation and insurance of its own efficient functioning.

As Jennifer Gibson points out, this equation of self-analysis with the mechanical is deeply rooted. The word used by Régis and Breton, *enregistreur* (recorder), came from the sonic discipline of telegraphy, the recipient of a telegraphic message being referred to by this title.[85] With the advent of radiotelegraphic technology, Breton refined the concept of mental technology as well: "Wireless telegraphy, wireless telephony, wireless imagination, they say. Induction is facile, but in my opinion it is also permissible."[86] The term *wireless imagination,* which comes from Italian Futurism,[87] was adopted by Breton because the lack of wires corresponded more closely to a total separation between conscious and unconscious—for him undesirable but nevertheless a fact—than did a closed-circuit system, connected by wires and hence less susceptible to interference.

Although the Surrealists usually treated automatic messages as though they came from an internal source, there were exceptions. Breton read Hegel literally, taking dialectic materialism to be a constant, perceivable (though probably not audible per se) chatter among inanimate objects. In the *Introduction to the Discourse on the Paucity of Reality* he describes an incident in a castle where the illumination of the vestibule seems to engender a conversation or "Colloquy of the Suits of Armor."[88] This of course brings to mind De Chirico's discovery of sound within an artwork—"lines and angles begin to talk." Breton also shared with De Chirico an appreciation for the feeling of universality that could be concentrated within persons or matter. De Chirico was satisfied to identify the source of this feeling as enigmatic, but Breton saw it as the result of having absorbed the essence of automatic speech:

There lies the secret that certain beings exercise, interesting solely because they became one day the echo of what we are tempted to consider as universal conscience, or again, because they caught, without strictly penetrating their meaning, a few words that fell from the "mouth of darkness."[89]

Thus, despite his calculated polemic statement "auditive images, in fact are inferior to visual images not only in clarity but also in strictness, and...are not destined to strengthen the idea of human greatness,"[90] Breton remained infinitely more in awe of and susceptible to the auditive than the visual. Indeed, in the thirties he stated,

It has always seemed to me that in poetry verbo–auditive automatism creates for the reading some of the most exalting visual images; never has verbo–visual automatism seemed to me to create for the reading visual images which might, at a distance, be comparable to them. *Suffice it to say that today, as ten years ago, I am completely taken (with it), I continue to believe blindly (blind ... with a blindness that covers visible things for all time) in the triumph,* by the auditive, *over the unverifiable visual.*[91]

Banging on the Windowpane

The writings of De Chirico and Savinio had an unsurpassed influence on Surrealism as a conscious political entity. In fact, Breton referred to the brothers as the originators of "the entirety of the modern myth."[92] Coming out of the annoyingly uncritical Paris Dada, it was not surprising that the Surrealists found their writings fresh and direct. De Chirico's simple phrase *No Music* provided the Surrealist movement with a forceful statement of purpose regarding the sonic arts, while Savinio's writings provided a basis for more detailed, theoretical speculations on sound.

Savinio's discussion of the ambivalence of sound in *Drama and Music*—intended as a positive basis for new uses of sound in the theater—was inverted by the Belgian surrealist Paul Nougé into a justification for the avoidance of music. Citing numerous instances in which benign sound has had some dire consequence when taken out of its original context, Nougé delivered his famous lecture *Music Is Dangerous* (1928), wherein he describes sound as an intelligent and malicious force:

It would reach us in its most pervasive forms; the song rising from the lips of those about us, of such and such a stranger, perhaps in the most haunting circumstances; that mechanical music which floats our way from the background of deserted places; and most sly and dangerous of all, the voice that suddenly materializes from some forgotten corner of our memory.... We cannot escape music.[93]

Of course the one most dangerous sound that Nougé identifies, the mental voice, is the very sound that Breton considered the source of Surrealism itself. It is a mistake to think that because Nougé defines music as being "dangerous," though, that he is at the same time prescribing a bourgeois conservatism to combat it, for in fact the Surrealists were more apt to court danger than to avoid it, since danger held the potential for greater rewards than did safety:

Among all the forces capable of bewitching spirit—forces which it must both

submit to and revolt against—poetry, painting, spectacles, war, misery,
debauchery, revolution, life with its inseparable companion, death—is it possi-
ble to refuse music a place among them, perhaps a very important place?
Whence the specific hopes and fears which it unceasingly calls upon us.
Spirit proceeds by disruptive inventions.
Let no one think in terms of strictly intellectual inventions.
Other areas are open to us.
It is time we realized that we are capable, also, of inventing feelings—perhaps
fundamental feelings—of a power comparable to those of love and hatred.
Spirit is nourished by our risks and our defeats, no less than by our victories.[94]

Despite the eloquence of this statement, Nougé was
at a loss to describe the sonic mechanism—or any other mechanism
for that matter—that might bring about a Surrealist art of feelings.
Interestingly, the professional musicians within the movement were at
a similar loss to describe a Surrealist sonic practice. The Belgian
Surrealists E.L.T. Mesens and André Souris, both trained musicians,
resorted to leading double lives, renouncing music in their Surrealist
activities and then going about their musical careers as though there
were no contradiction—a course that was also followed by the
numerous Surrealists who objected to the hermetic, intellectual cast
that avoidance of music brought to their daily lives.[95]

Yet if they did not achieve an active sonic practice,
members of the Surrealist movement did succeed in *portraying* an
active sonic practice within the context of other arts. Such artists as
Man Ray, Max Ernst, Dali, Magritte, and Remedios Varo cultivated a
rich musical iconography in their visual art, but none was more adept
than Luis Buñuel at using music either visually or verbally.[96] Buñuel
was a professed Wagnerian whose first published poem,
Instrumentation (1922), included the definition "Cymbals—shattered
light."[97] Since he was almost certainly ignorant of *No Music* when this
was written, his inadvertent quotation of De Chirico carries the
added import of displaying the collective vision of sound shared
by disparate Surrealist artists before Surrealism was ever codified.

Buñuel's use of sound in his films merits an entire study of its own, but because it begins around 1930, it is out of the scope of this paper.

Not only did the Surrealists borrow their music theory from De Chirico and Savinio, they borrowed an enthusiasm for violent, Savinio-like performances from Apollinaire. When rumors began circulating that a young American pianist was playing "mechanical" music throughout Europe, and that he threatened his audiences with a gun—Vaché once again comes to mind—to maintain order during concerts, the Surrealists' curiosity must certainly have been piqued. Thus it was that George Antheil became the musician of Surrealism—in spirit only. Although his technique was every bit as violent as that of Savinio, and although his compositions were based on dreams which were by his own assessment De Chirican,[98] Antheil's music was more a response to prewar Stravinsky than to the avant-garde speculations on sound. Still the Surrealists—particularly expatriate Americans such as Man Ray—attended his concerts religiously, assaulting anyone who expressed displeasure with the performance.[99]

Outside the concert hall, Antheil led a life of inspired debauchery, which was also conducive to good relations with the Surrealists. He frequented the same cafés that they frequented—an important sign of one's political and artistic predilections in Paris during the twenties—and engaged in outlandish behavior which rivaled that of Philippe Soupault.[100] He became friends with Louis Aragon, and their casual relations led in 1929 to collaboration on a Surrealist opera, with libretto by Aragon and Breton and music by Antheil. Antheil describes the opera, *Faust III*, thus:

It was to be in five long acts, but when we arrived at the fourth, the Surrealist movement split into two factions, Aragon leading one party and Breton the other. They willed me the ruins of the manuscript, which I then took to a bookbinder to keep as a memento of a lost ideal. The bookbinder, an ancient Russian, falling in with the spirit of the thing, bound the book backwards, starting with the last page and ending with the first. I accepted his unasked-

for editorial comment without arching my eyebrow, paid my bill, and the book now reposes on my bookshelf. I figured I had gotten out of the whole Faust III *lightly.* [101]

It was not by accident that this fleeting attempt to create a Surreal opera coincided with the schism between Breton and Aragon. The concept of Surrealism had originally been developed to explain the structural workings of large multimedia productions such as opera and ballet. Yet when Breton broke with Paris Dada and founded a Surrealist movement based on "pure psychic automatism," he took Surrealism out of the realm of public spectacle. The fact that Antheil and Aragon could even consider returning it there was an indication that the movement was in danger of becoming—as had Dada—a mere vehicle for entertainment.

For its own survival, it was essential that the Surrealist movement avoid this trap. Dependence on an audience, and hence dependence on the whims of promoters like Hébertot, had put an end to Paris Dada. With the rise of fascism in the thirties—heralded by the indictment of Aragon over the sentiments expressed in his poem *Red Front,* the trial of George Sadoul and Jean Caupenne for their infamous letter to the Saint-Cyr Military Academy, and the right-wing terrorist attack on a showing of Buñuel's *L'Age d'or*—public taste proved to be considerably more dangerous for the Surrealist movement than it ever was for Surrealism's immediate predecessors. Surrealist speculation into music and theater, fields that left the movement vulnerable to the violence of public taste, were therefore rightly curtailed in favor of the more overtly political speculations of the movement's middle years.

NOTES

1. The most common chronology of Surrealism as a movement—that is, as a philosophy understood and practiced similarly by several individuals—begins in 1919 with Breton and Soupault's *Les Champs magnétiques*. For the purposes of this paper, the decade beginning with this publication and ending with the schism between Surrealist factions led by Breton and Aragon will constitute the "early" part of the Surrealist *movement*. However, with regard to sound art, it is necessary to concentrate also on such precedents as the brief episode of Surrealist theater that occurred at the end of World War I, concurrences such as Paris Dada, and later developments such as the ex post facto Surrealist adoption of sound theories proposed by Brisset, Savinio, De Chirico, and others.

2. Guillaume Apollinaire, *"Parade,"* *Apollinaire on Art: Essays and Reviews 1902–1918,* trans. Susan Suleiman, ed. Leroy C. Breunig (New York: Viking Press, 1972), p. 452.

3. The word *surréalisme* is as caught up in its immediate prehistory as is the movement itself. On one hand it can be said to refer to a transcendent Cubism, for many of the Cubist theorists claimed their painting style to be, above all else, an accurate portrayal of "reality." It may have also been an attempt to slight Cocteau, who had termed the work *"ballet réaliste,"* the impli-

cation being that if Cocteau's contribution was *"réaliste,"* then surely Picasso's and Satie's contributions were *"sur-réaliste."* The third—and most likely—possibility is that the term was invented without much forethought, only achieving significance after Apollinaire had had a chance to understand it himself. According to Pierre Albert-Birot, the word was first uttered as an alternative to the more connotatively colored *surnaturalisme:* "When Apollinaire and I, in 1917, searched for a term to describe *Les Mamelles de Tirésias,* Apollinaire suggested *'surnaturaliste',* and I cried out, No! No!, *'surnaturalisme'* is something entirely different. In principle, the *'surnaturel'* is a miracle. Immediately Apollinaire replied, 'That's right—let's put in then *drame surréaliste.'"* (Quoted in Annabelle Melzer, *Latest Rage the Big Drum: Dada and Surrealist Performance* [Ann Arbor: UMI Research Press, 1980], p. 126.)

4. Jean Cocteau, "Cock and Harlequin," *A Call to Order,* trans. by Rollo H. Meyers (London: Faber and Gwyer, 1926), p. 52.

5. "It is a scenic poem transposed by the innovative musician Erik Satie into astonishingly expressive music, so clear and simple that it seems to reflect the marvelously lucid spirit of France." (Apollinaire, *"Parade,"* p. 452.)

6. The influence of Dalcroze's Eurythmics on the Ballets Russes has often been noted. Less frequently noted are the possible influences of other dance pioneers. The silent aspect of the *Liturgie* project is strikingly similar to experiments being performed at the same time by Wigman and Laban.

7. "After 32 rehearsals for *Liturgie*, we have concluded that absolute silence is Death, and that there is and can be no absolute silence in any air space. Thus the action must have some accompaniment, not musical accompaniment but, rather, sounds. The source of the sounds must not be revealed, and the passage from one to another must not be noticeable to the ear, i.e., they must flow into each other. No rhythm should exist at all, because the beginning and end of sound should be imperceptible. The proposed instruments are: *guzli* (psalteries), bells with tongues wrapped in felt, aeolian harps, sirens, tops, and so on. Of course, this all has to be worked over. Marinetti urges us to plan a meeting in Milan, if just for a day, in order to discuss matters with the orchestra's representatives and to examine all of their instruments." (Letter from Diaghilev to Stravinsky of 8 March 1914, quoted in Igor Stravinsky, *Selected Correspondence*, II, edited and with commentaries by Robert Craft [New York: Alfred A. Knopf, 1984], p. 19.)

8. Boris Kochno, *Diaghilev and the Ballets Russes*, trans. by Adrienne Foulke (New York: Harper and Row, 1970), p. 101.

9. See Gide's account of one such perfor-

mance in Francis Steegmuller, *Cocteau: A Biography* (Boston: Little, Brown and Company, 1970), p. 123.

10. Cocteau both confirms and denies that he considered Satie's contribution to *Parade* as little more than a background for his noises. (See Cocteau, "Cock and Harlequin," pp. 23, 54.) Satie was most intractable and most vulnerable in arguments with friends. He was clearly more hurt by such statements than Cocteau believed.

11. Kochno, Diaghilev and the Ballets Russes, p. 120. The conductor Ansermet speaks of replacing the typewriter with "woodwinds and brasses." Such a substitution is hardly satisfactory, for in the libretto the typewriter sound is used to indicate secretarial duties—duties that seldom include the playing of either woodwinds or brasses.

12. Apollinaire, "*Parade*," p. 452.

13. Roger Shattuck, *The Banquet Years: The Origins of the Avant-Garde in France, 1885 to World War I*, rev. ed. (New York: Vintage Books, 1968), p. 294.

14. Apollinaire, "*Parade*," p. 452.

15. Guillaume Apollinaire, *Oeuvres Poétiques*, ed. Marcel Adéma and Michel Decaudin (Paris: Gallimard, 1956), p. 894.

16. Jean-Pierre Brisset, "La Grande Loi ou la clef de la parole," in *Anthologie de l'humour noir*, ed. André Breton (Paris:

Jean-Jacques Pauvert, 1972), p. 223. My translation.

17. Brisset, "La Formation du sexe," in *Anthologie*, ed. André Breton, p. 225.

18. Furthermore, the dice cup is intended to remind the audience of the dice game "Zanzibar," thus establishing the setting of the play through a visual/verbal pun.

19. André Breton, *What Is Surrealism? Selected Writings*, edited and introduced by Franklin Rosemont (New York: Monad, 1978), pp. 10–11a.

20. Maurice Nadeau, *The History of Surrealism*, trans. Richard Howard, intro. Roger Shattuck (New York: Collier Books, 1965), p. 54.

21. Although Vaché did not carry through with his threat at this time, it was not because of any moral conviction against murder—even murder of the innocent. He killed himself with an overdose of opium a few months after the incident at the premiere of *Les Mamelles*. But having once written that "it's too boring to die alone," he first administered another lethal dose to a novice who had asked to be introduced to use of the drug. (Breton, *What Is Surrealism?* p. 11a.)

22. Ibid.

23. André Breton, *Surrealism and Painting* (New York: Brentano's, 1972), p. 8.

24. Georges Auric, Louis Durey, Arthur Honegger, Darius Milhaud, Francis Poulenc, and Germaine Tailleferre—a group of young composers who were primarily allied through their close association with Cocteau and their more tenuous association with Satie.

25. Melzer, *Latest Rage the Big Drum*, p. 208. The idea for such a soirée was Tzara's. Whereas the soirée was perhaps the ideal format for Paris Dada, since the Parisians were already accustomed to such entertainment, it was also the ideal format to set it at odds with Surrealism. The ideas of Tzara's detractors amongst the Zurich Dadaists were much more closely in line with Parisian Surrealism. Huelsenbeck, for instance, made the statement that one should "make literature with a gun in his hand"—a point of view remarkably similar to Breton's and Vaché's.

26. Ibid., p. 5. Melzer suggests that Tzara's speech was covered in order to hide his Romanian accent, since wartime xenophobia still held sway in Paris in the years after the war. To reach this conclusion, Melzer dismisses Tzara's own account of the incident as having been written with "almost precious naïveté." In support of her argument, she cites Sanouillet. For numerous reasons, however, Sanouillet does not say that this particular work was tailored to accommodate French xenophobia. First, Tzara had a reputation in Paris long before his debut. The Parisians were not being presented with an unknown entity, and the very name of Tzara was enough to stun the audience. (Michel

Sanouillet, *Dada à Paris* [Paris: Jean-Jacques Pauvert, 1965], p. 147.) Second—and Melzer discusses this—it was common practice in Zurich Dada for the entire performance to be accompanied and covered by the sound of Richard Huelsenbeck beating the bass drum. Tzara's bells were only an updating and amplification of this same technique. Finally, and most important, foreign accents were not the only means of provoking French xenophobia. Accents were included in a long list of things considered *boche,* including foreign-sounding names such as Tzara and Picasso. More provocative than either name or accent was modern art, for the whole field was presumed to be a German plot. Even *Parade,* the ballet of the quintessentially French Satie, was labeled boche because of the sets of Picasso—who had been in Paris well over a decade—and the production company, the almost exclusively Parisian Ballets Russes. If the presenters had wanted to hide Tzara's accent, they could have picked a thousand ways of doing so. Instead, they chose the one manner of presenting the poet that was more provocative than his Romanian accent would have been.

27. Sanouillet, *Dada à Paris,* p. 175n.

28. It is interesting that Tzara would choose boredom as one of his primary aesthetic tools, since he had originally conceived of the soirée as a means of alleviating his own boredom. (Melzer, *Latest Rage the Big Drum,* p. 4.)

29. Sanouillet, *Dada à Paris,* p. 175n.

30. The Futurists were, by this time, no longer perceived as being on the cutting edge of the avant-garde, but rather they were considered classicists, falling well within the established traditions of Western music. One reviewer wrote of the concert: "All these instruments ... made the pathetic noise of a water-driven mill in the mountains, provoking neither stupor, nor fear, nor scandal.... Indeed, the Bruitists claimed quite seriously to create new artistic sensations. The musicians of Luigi Russolo weren't a bunch of cacophonists, but excellent performers who interpreted a classical symphony, the new mechanism of noise not intervening except to superimpose itself on conventional instruments." Ibid., p. 284n. My translation.

31. Ibid., p. 277.

32. Ibid., p. 284.

33. Georges Ribemont-Dessaignes, "Déjà jadis," quoted in Melzer, *Latest Rage the Big Drum,* p. 53.

34. Sanouillet, *Dada à Paris,* p. 165.

35. See, for instance, Nicolas Slonimsky, "Music and Surrealism," *Artforum* 1, (September 1966), pp. 80–85. Slonimsky seems to find Surrealism lurking behind virtually every composition written since 1920. His own concoction "Surrealistically Dodecaphonic Birthday Greetings" is particularly telling in the context of dissonance and Surrealism. Lacking any better connection between the two, Slonimsky resorts to confusing "surreal music" with "serial (dodecaphonic) music." He was neither the first nor the last to make this mistake.

36. Alfred Jarry, *Oeuvres Complètes,* vol. 8 (Monte-Carlo: Editions du Livre, 1948), pp. 121–148.

37. Marcel Adéma, *Apollinaire,* trans. Denise Folliot (London: William Heinemann Ltd.), p. 251.

38. Much has been made of the Dadaists' spurious advertisement of an appearance by Charlie Chaplin on this program. (Melzer, *Latest Rage the Big Drum,* p. 141.) At the time, however, Musidora was nearly as famous as Chaplin. She, second only to Louise Brooks, became the archetype of the woman of the twenties with her role as the femme fatale of the French serial *Les Vampires.* So powerful was her performance that the term *vamp* became a synonym for any dark, designing woman. (Sanouillet, *Dada à Paris,* p. 72.)

39. At the second Dada soirée, Ribemont-Dessaignes was called upon to replace Breton and Soupault's *Vous m'oublierez,* which he did by appearing in a ballet tutu. (Sanouillet, *Dada à Paris,* p. 174.)

40. On the second Dada soirée Buffet performed another work of Picabia's *La Nourrice américaine,* which was billed in the program as an example of "sodomist music." This score involved no spoken text. Rather it consisted of three notes repeated monotonously on the piano. (Maria Lluïsa Borràs, *Picabia* [New York: Rizzoli, 1985], p. 204.) The connections—beside those of lasciviousness and blatant provocation—between an "American wet-nurse," sodomy, and repetitive notes are not clear.

41. Sanouillet, *Dada à Paris,* pp. 167–168.

42. Shattuck, *The Banquet Years,* pp. 168–169. Fernand Léger describes an explanation of musique d'ameublement that Satie once gave after a noisy dinner: "There ought to be a furniture music, that is to say a music which will take advantage of ambient noise, which will take it into account. I imagine it to be melodious, it will soften the noise of knives and forks without dominating them, without imposing itself. It will fill the heavy silences that sometimes fall between guests. It will spare them the current banalities. It will at the same time neutralize the noises of the street that enter the parlor without discretion." ("Satie inconnu," *La Revue Musicale* 214 [June 1952], p. 137. My translation.) This definition of furniture music is in direct conflict with Alberto Savinio's renovation of drama, wherein the indiscretion of sounds entering the parlor is essential.

43. Tristan Tzara, "Memoirs of Dadaism," printed as an addendum in Edmund Wilson, *Axel's Castle: A Study of the*

Imaginative Literature of 1879–1930 (New York: Charles Scribner's Sons, 1943), p. 304.

44. Erik Satie, *Ecrits,* ed. Ornella Volta (Paris: Editions Champ Libre, 1981), pp. 24–25.

45. Georges Ribemont-Dessaignes, "Musique eventail et le serin crocodile," *391* 10 (1919), p. 3.

46. In this regard, see the numerous memoirs of Satie in *La Revue musicale* 214 (June 1952). Of particular interest are those of Valentine (Gross) Hugo and E. L. T. Mesens. Satie was Hugo's mentor, and she carried much of his spirit directly into her active role as a Surrealist in the 1930s. Mesens, a Belgian Dadaist (and later Surrealist) was a composer whose works included *Garage,* a song on a text of Philippe Soupault, which is one of very few Dadaist musical works to survive. See the score in Marcel Mariën, *L'Activité Surréaliste en Belgique, 1924–1950* (Bruxelles: Editions Lebeer-Hossmann, 1979), pp. 114–115. Satie's influence was quite broad. Man Ray credits the composer with assisting him in the manufacture of *Le Cadeau,* the flat-iron with the tacks glued to the bottom. (Man Ray, *Self Portrait* [Boston: Little, Brown, and Company, 1963], p. 115.)

47. Shattuck, *The Banquet Years,* p. 123.

48. Sanouillet, *Dada à Paris,* p. 333.

49. Ibid., p. 515.

50. Satie, *Ecrits,* p. 52.

51. "Presentation et commentaires de José Pierre," *Tracts surréalistes et declarations collectives, 1922–1969, Tome I,* (Paris: Le Terrain vague, 1982), p. 369. Also see Satie, *Ecrits,* p. 260.

52. If Apollinaire's death assured his place in Surrealism, since it came before his nationalist rhetoric completely alienated Breton, Satie's death assured his eternal conflict with the Surrealists. Shortly before his death Satie had premiered *Relâche,* and the publicity had included a direct invitation for the Surrealists to attack the work: "Messieurs the ex-Dadas are asked to come to manifest and above all to cry: 'Down with Satie! Down with Picabia! Long live *La Nouvelle Revue Française!*'." (*391* 19 (1924), p. 4.) Unfortunately, Satie didn't live long enough to be reintegrated into Surrealist prehistory as were Tzara and several others who had opposed Breton in the Congress of Paris. It is interesting that Louis Aragon, in the mid-seventies, admitted his affinity for Satie's music: "Breton detested all music. Not me. And notably the humoristic songs of Erik Satie whom I knew, and who had been a free-mason before entering the communist party." (Satie, *Ecrits,* p. 249.)

53. André Breton, "Premier Manifeste du Surréalisme," in *Les Manifestes du Surréalisme, suivis de prolégomènes à un troisième manifeste du Surréalisme ou non* (Paris: Éditions du Sagittaire, 1946), p. 33.

54. The negative influence that Cocteau had on Surrealist sonic practices should not be underestimated. Breton states that Surrealist antipathy to music was "accentuated by the fact that in Paris the cause of modern music acknowledged as its champion a notorious fake poet" (Breton, "Silence Is Golden," in *What Is Surrealism?* p. 266b. The term "fake poet" was used by the Surrealists when referring to Cocteau because in "Cock and Harlequin," his treatise on music, he states "A dreamer is always a bad poet." (Cocteau, "Cock and Harlequin," p. 12.)

55. Ribemont-Dessaignes, *Musique eventail,* p. 3.

56. Printed in James Thrall Soby, *Giorgio de Chirico* (New York: Museum of Modern Art, 1955), pp. 245–246.

57. Breton, *Surrealism and Painting,* pp. 1–2.

58. Soby, *Giorgio de Chirico,* p. 245. Henri Rabaud was a main-stream operatic composer who was an avid antimodernist. The opera mentioned was written in an academic style that corresponded somewhat to De Chirico's own neoclassicism.

59. Kochno, *Diaghilev and the Ballets Russes,* p. 270. The Belgian surrealist Paul Nougé makes note of De Chirico's backsliding with regard to music in his famous lecture *Music Is Dangerous:* "'Not interested in music,' wrote a great painter who, later on, went to pot. This phrase of De Chirico's coming in a sense that was unexpected to say the least, and which

doubtless surprised its author as much as anyone, enjoyed, under favor of the shock it provoked, a singular success." (Paul Nougé, "Music Is Dangerous," *View* 7 [Dec. 1946], p. 15.)

60. Soby, *Giorgio de Chirico,* p. 245.

61. In a conversation with the author, Robert Craft recalled De Chirico and his brother Alberto Savinio as the only two Surrealists with whom Stravinsky associated. In 1922, Francis Picabia sent Stravinsky a scenario for a ballet entitled *Les Yeux chauds,* in which the Russian composer may have been interested, but which was never realized. (Stravinsky, *Selected Correspondence,* pp. 193–194.) Stravinsky and Edgar Varèse were, incidentally, listed among the 360 presidents of Dada. Satie was not.

62. The reason for the Surrealist adoption of *No Music* over other antimusical writings—for instance the previously quoted ones of Satie and Ribemont-Dessaignes—was this emphasis of experience over aesthetics.

63. Soby, *Giorgio de Chirico,* p. 34. De Chirico treated these revelations as epiphanies, but later Surrealists found that they could just as easily be experimentally induced. In the twenties and thirties, for instance, Breton and Eluard created literature while in various states of self-imposed mental illness. Whether achieved by happenstance or by design, the shift in mental perspective resulted in the same heightening of sensation, and this heightening cast an aura over the artist's experience that (it was thought) was transferred directly into the resultant artwork.

64. Ibid., p. 16. Association with Savinio's teacher, the German organist Max Reger, may have had a strong negative effect on both brothers, for they seem to have had simultaneous and equally violent reactions to the music of the immediate past and present—particularly the post-Wagnerian romanticism that Reger represented. One of the songs from Savinio's *Album 1914*, "La mort de M. Sacerdote," consists of the characteristically bilingual text: "Voici la maison où est mort mon professeur Monsieur Sacerdote ... Imbecilli! Imbecilli!" (Alberto Savinio, *Album 1914*, ed. L. Rognoni and A. Ballista [Milano: Edizioni Suvini Zerboni, 1981], pp. 20–22.] It should be noted, however, that Reger did not die until two years after the song was written.

65. Savinio may have written this as a direct response to his brother's *No Music*, although it is difficult to say which essay came first. Before World War I, De Chirico seems to have followed his brother around Europe, which has led to speculation that the painter gained his fame—not to mention many of his best artistic ideas—by exploiting his relationship with Savinio. De Chirico is said to have first discovered the works of Böcklin—whose painting style so influenced his own—while in Reger's salon. Beyond this secondary influence, Savinio's *Chants de la mi-mort* had a more direct influence.

Critics, and Savinio, have identified the mannequins that De Chirico painted as a visual manifestation of the protagonist of these songs, who has neither voice, nor eyes, nor face. (Soby, *Giorgio de Chirico*, p. 97.)

66. Alberto Savinio, "Dammi l'anatema, cosa lasciva," in *Scatola sonora*, intro. Luigi Rognoni (Torino: Giulio Einaudi, 1977), p. 429. My translation.

67. Savinio's most famous works were his song cycles. Rather than write songs wherein the melody closely paralleled the text and wherein the accompaniment provided harmonic impetus and movement, Savinio "disharmonized" his music: fragmentary texts were scattered throughout the composition, with little or no consideration for musical concerns. Furthermore, the texts were often written for multiple voices singing in multiple languages to indicate the disjuncture of dialogue into its component disinterested monologues. At other times texts were simply disjunct syllables or exclamations such as "Mama mia!" The music was similarly constructed on the principle of disinterested simultaneity and fragmentation. It consisted mostly of furiously repeated motifs, played in parallel major sevenths, minor ninths, or any other interval which stressed that the notes were not related by triadic harmony.

68. Apollinaire, "New Music," in *Apollinaire on Art*, p. 391.

69. Louise Faure-Favrier, "Guillaume Apollinaire et la Musique," in *Guillaume Apollinaire: souvenirs et témoignages inédits de Louis de Gonzague Frick—Louise Faure Favier—Roche Grey— Jeanne-Yves Blanc— Pierre Varenne—Jean Mollet—Pierre Albert-Biro—Albert Gleizes—Jean Metzinger— Lépold Survage réunis et présentés par Marcel Adema* (Paris: Editions de la tête noire, 1946), p. 15. My translation.

70. Quoted in Savinio, *Scatola sonora*, p. 436. My translation.

71. Apollinaire, "New Music," p. 392. Had artistic and international politics not intervened, these ballets might have become the first works of Surrealist theater. They were known to Apollinaire, who found Savinio to be a more innovative composer, even, than Satie. The competition between Stravinsky, Satie, and Savinio was a critical fabrication, however. In later years Savinio became an active apologist for both of the composers with whom he was supposedly in contention.

72. Alberto Savinio, "Le Drame et la musique," in *Scatola sonora*, p. 426. My translation.

73. There is a strong possibility either that Apollinaire may have been influenced by Savinio or vice versa. In 1914, the year in which he was most closely associated with Apollinaire, Savinio composed a series of songs including one entitled "Tirésias est mort" and another "Les helmes dorées offrande" which has as its sole lyric the chant "ha hé hou ha hi ha"—remarkably similar to the laughter of the reporter in *Les Mamelles de Tirésias*. Furthermore, this reporter is to have no facial features save a mouth, a quality perhaps borrowed, like De Chirico's mannequins, from the protagonist of Savinio's *Chants de la mi-mort*. (See note 65.) Although *Les Mamelles* was not completed until 1917, it was begun in 1903, but lacking the manuscripts, it is difficult to say whether it influenced or was influenced by Savinio's work.

74. It should be noted that Savinio uses the term *music* in its broadest sense, including words, cries, and noises, but that he does so in a way that avoids the Futurist glorification of the mechanical and melodramatic. Whereas the Futurists heard music in the machines of industry, Savinio hears it in the voices of the common, distinctly passéist street vendors and laborers who run the machines.

75. Breton, "Premier Manifeste," p. 38, my emphasis.

76. Ibid., p. 39.

77. André Breton, "The Automatic Message," in *What is Surrealism?* p. 97b.

78. André Breton, "Enter the Mediums," quoted in *The Autobiography of Surrealism*, p. 101.

79. André Breton, "Introduction to the Discourse on the Paucity of Reality," in *What is Surrealism?* p. 24b.

80. Ibid., p. 25b.

81. See Jennifer Gibson, "Surrealism Before Freud: Dynamic Psychiatry's 'Simple Recording Instrument,'" *Art Journal* 46 (Spring 1987), pp. 56–60.

82. Ibid., p. 56.

83. This explains Breton's reference to dictation and abbreviated writing in *Introduction to the Discourse on the Paucity of Reality* and later in the *Manifesto of Surrealism*, where he states, "It seemed to me, and seems to me again,...that the speed of thought is not superior to that of speech, and that it does not defy the tongue perforce, nor even the pen which [cuts] short." (Breton, "Premier Manifeste," p. 41. My translation.)

84. Gibson, "Surrealism Before Freud," p. 57. In the *Manifesto of Surrealism*, Breton states, "We, who are not given up to any act of filtration, who make ourselves in our works into deaf receptacles for so many echoes, modest *recording instruments* who do not hypnotize themselves with the design which they trace, perhaps we serve again a more noble cause." (Breton, "Premier Manifeste," p. 48. My translation.)

85. Gibson, "Surrealism Before Freud," p. 58.

86. André Breton, "Introduction au discours sur le peu de réalité," in *Point du jour* (Paris: Editions Gallimard, 1970), p. 7. My translation.

87. The term is found in F. T. Marinetti's 1912 "Technical Manifesto of Futurist Literature" (see F. T. Marinetti, *Selected Writings,* trans. by R. W. Flint and Arthur A. Coppotelli, ed. R. W. Flint [New York: Farrar, Straus and Giroux, 1971] and expanded in his 1913 manifesto "Destruction of Syntax—Wireless Imagination—Words in Freedom" (see Richard J. Pioli, *Stung by Salt and War: Creative Texts of the Italian Avant-Gardist F. T. Marinetti* [New York: Peter Lang, 1987]).

88. Breton, "Introduction to the Discourse on the Paucity of Reality," in *What is Surrealism?* p. 18b.

89. Breton, "Enter the Mediums," p. 101.

90. Breton, *Surrealism and Painting,* pp. 1–2.

91. André Breton, "Le Message automatique," in *Point du Jour,* p. 186.

92. Breton, *Anthologie,* p. 341.

93. Paul Nougé, "Music Is Dangerous," *View* 7 (March 1947), p. 23.

94. Ibid., p. 28.

95. Man Ray recalls that one Surrealist poet became "attached" to listening to the radio, immediately shutting it off when other Surrealists came to visit, on the pretence that he listened only to news. (Ray, *Self Portrait,* p. 175.)

96. The frequency with which Surrealists used musical imagery might seem unremarkable in that they lived in an environment where musical images were omnipresent, but it should be remembered that Surrealist iconography was rigidly controlled by the group at large and that artists who used unapproved icons in their works were subject to expulsion from the movement. Dali was, for instance, expelled from Surrealism for including Hitler in his iconography and in his theoretical writings. Although he truly believed that his thoughts on Hitler were justified in their context, it was decided that certain ideas or images could have absolutely no redeeming qualities. Musical imagery was not treated nearly as harshly. Thus the Surrealists put themselves in the curious position of making the visual element of musical performance acceptable while making the sound itself unacceptable.

97. Francisco Aranda, *Luis Buñuel: A Critical Biography*, trans. David Robinson (New York: Da Capo, 1976), p. 252.

98. From George Antheil, *Bad Boy of Music* (Garden City, NY: Doubleday, Doran & Company, Inc., 1945), p. 20:

Lovely streamlined buildings were built into the hillsides and upon the flat plains; the houses were beautiful, each with its swimming pool, its tennis court, its sheltered garden. Some of the houses were large, others small; but all were handsome. Children running about in the nearby parks, well clothed, well fed, well educated.

The scene had the atmosphere of Chirico, without the atmosphere of ruins, factories, or wars. Except for the music of children's voices, everything was strangely quiet.

I found myself walking along a pathway of small residential buildings. Out of each of them, as I passed it, came the music of a symphony orchestra playing—my music!

99. See for instance the account of Antheil's Paris debut in Antheil, *Bad Boy of Music*, pp. 3–8, 300. Although Antheil later admitted that the disturbance was partially staged in order to shoot a scene for a movie starring Georgette LeBlanc (p. 136), the rioting at his concerts was probably no more staged than any other Surrealist activity.

100. Antheil's autobiography abounds with anecdotes that both intentionally and unintentionally confirm his clear understanding and espousal of Surrealism. Sylvia Beach was impressed by the fact that Antheil would climb the front of her bookstore and enter his second-story apartment through the window. (Sylvia Beach, *Shakespeare and Company* [New York: Harcourt, Brace and Company, 1959], p. 122. Also see the photograph in Hugh Ford, *Four Lives in Paris* [San Francisco, North Point Press, 1987], p. 52.) Beach also displayed a Man Ray photo of Antheil—taken after one of the pianist's Berlin concerts—sporting a Louise Brooks haircut. While this might not seem remarkable now, the image of a male wearing a hairstyle that had been developed for women who wished to appear androgynous was almost as shocking in its time as was either the star that Duchamp had shaved on his head or Dali's mohawk.

101. Antheil, *Bad Bays of Music*, p. 300. Concerning *Faust III* André Thirion states, "The title might ultimately have tempted Breton, but he could never forget the miserable *Treasure of the Jesuits*. The thought of collaborating once again with Aragon didn't excite him, and he was even less enthusiastic about becoming a librettist. All that remains of the project are some preliminary fragments sketched by Aragon, which leave little room for regret." (André Thirion, *Revolutionaries Without Revolution,* trans. Joachim Neugroschel [New York: Macmillan Publishing Co., Inc., 1975], p. 255.)

GIVE ME THE ANATHEMA, LASCIVIOUS THING (1915)

Alberto Savinio

translated from the French by

Christopher Schiff

NEW MUSIC

The creative artist is a political man.

He enjoys the law of inviolability which

preserves the person of a constitutional monarch.

The formidable and architectural poetry which drives the *artwork* is no more than

poetic penchant: it is no more than *poetic poetry.*

Nonsense holds itself in prodigious equilibrium.

It is the expression of natural and superior sentiment—true everywhere—

which has roots in the earth and which rises beyond to the seventh heaven.

It is there that music floats.

An entirely new creation is set into motion now,

everything is a singer.

[This is] the,

without a doubt charming,

but terrible and thrilling reality.

MORS STUPEBIT ET NATURA.

More sweet lies,

more pink steam baths,

more saunas of forgetfulness,

more blue mists; more dreams,

more sugared poison, more aqua-teffana.

The curtain of the Ballets Russes

    has finally fallen before the multicolored stage lights,

    and has recovered that obscene bric-a-brac.

    One can say no more.

    Requiescat in pace, amen.

    Machines, enormous and black—wheels and pistons—prodigious and fatal,

    sing with the continuity of the eternal stroke:

"They are poor! they are poor! they are poor!"

(heartrending lamentations)

Dionysus, messieurs, has stolen the siren from a fire engine.

    He is even more *terrible*.

    It truly distressed one to listen to the dolorous grinding of those poor little chairs of the Avenue des Champs-Elysées, which hop around on their overly fine and nervous legs.

        A sixth-class burial passes at the end of the street.

        In music the song is beautiful as it *is*. Beautiful and atrocious.

        In a previous article, I banished song from my music.

        I considered song in the manner that it has always been treated by composers: sung words.

The song *without thought,* the *strange* song, the *true* song,

        is pure and flamboyant like the scarlet banner.

Do you not hear the song in the execution of General Ramorino?

    (*Chants de la Mi-Mort,* dramatic scenes of the *Risorgimento*) ... "*All was sweetness and light in the citadel of Turin—May 22, 1849—The sky of pearl-grey silk. The banner of the Hotel Lutetia slapped like a tongue which savors Benedictine. Ah, my friends, é terribile! é terribile! é terribile!*"

Fie! far from me the charming dilettantism upon which the today's art drifts.

> Why is it that art is thought of—in France above all—as an amiable thing, and not as an atrocious suffering—a six-foot-long jack-knife planted in the kidneys, or a spray of buckshot discharged full in the face?

See how the modern artists of Paris, having forsaken their atavistic logic, attack the non-

> sense of things. Henceforth nonsense will be a domain open to all forms of idiocy. I console myself: there remain some walls where certain men may yet never enter.

Giuseppe Verdi: sweet and terrible mannequin, inlaid with polychrome strips. Animal of

> strange fidelity. His lungs of living red paper broke off from the thorax like the fins of a flying fish, —they are displayed in a shop window on the Boulevard Saint-Germain.

>> —Heart and entrails were multiflorous.

>> These same organs sang terrible emotions; gentle lightning.

>>> *... the lightning of your smile*

>> Troubadour, nostalgic adventurer,
>> clash of white armor, *parade de sixte,*
>> heroism and freedom, enigma of a man:

>>> *... deserted on the earth ...*

>>>> *and by every D major.*

How long before the annihilation of anthropomorphism?

> Kill the monster.

> Stretch the noose to animism so that it may hang itself.

> Release *the water-spirit which runs to the Zulus.* Women, learn to faint at the spasmodic cry of a steam whistle. Men, learn to flagellate yourselves at the sight of target-men in the field of fire, dancing reflected flashes.

Give Me the Anathema, Lascivious Thing

Music is a registered prostitute: she has undergone humiliation *at the hands of morals,* even as the human spirit (has been humiliated) through the influence of Christianity, and above all of neo-Christianity. She ceased to be *that which ought to be.* She ceased to act with her proper force. *Moralized music!* She locked up everything terrible and problematic, stifled it with her thick blanket of idealism. And that was long ago. Moreover, I believe that never, at any time, has music existed *for itself,* according to its *own value.* Music is an enslaved art; it would be futile for one to seek a music *without morals.*

I tell you again that she is a registered prostitute!

The race of musicians: they have scaly eyes, pale and sweaty fingers, generally dirty fingernails; their love affairs are most squalid; as to the flesh of their faces, it is horrible to see—their faces are made with the flesh of feet.

My music runs without stopping, and with a vertiginous speed.

Tranquility is an illusion. All is mystery now, all is movement. In this way, death will no longer be considered to be inert, since it is a slight mystery, and since the slightest mystery requires *prestissimo* movement.

Alberto Savinio

Contemporary music is nothing but a vague drone.
A true music achieves the outburst of a spiritual detonation.

Intermittence restores to music all its vivacity; frees it (wherever it may lie, restrained as a
        result of its moralization) from the *method of equalization.*

Note: by itself, music is an incomplete means of expression;
        one mates it with drama, but in an accidental way.

The style of old Italian melodrama—magnificent and discredited, crude and sincere—
seems to me much better than the system of continuity which weakens contemporary
music. In melodrama, the different pieces are distinguished from one another, they
become isolated within the whole, because there the *recitatives* only act as unifying features without musical significance.

To have reduced music to its current homogeneity,
        the responsible composers reduced music to the rank of an inferior art,
        insignificant, sensorial, and pleasant.

Music is the emanation of a real metaphysic.

I said: the creative artist is a politician.

Art penetrates into vast domains: politics, finance, industry, science; among doctors,
        dentists, chiropodists; among railroad engineers and those of Bridges
        and Dykes; among soldiers, tacticians, strategists, etc., etc ....

Trecento. Henceforth the creative artist is a political man, frock coated, immortalized in
stone << *dice Mario Filefo che l'altissimo Poeta sostenna in nome de' Fiorentini quattordici
ambascerie* >> (*Storia de la Letteratura Italiana, del cav. Giuseppe Maffei, cappellano
aulice di S. A. Massimiliano Ducha di Baviera*).

MEL GORDON

SONGS FROM THE MUSEUM OF THE FUTURE
RUSSIAN SOUND CREATION (1910-1930)

NOISE AND SOUND CREATION IN THE NINETEENTH CENTURY_____

The concept of noise was a by-product of the Industrial Revolution. Throughout the jerry-built and already shabby proletarian living quarters and workplaces of Europe in the 1840s and 1850s, there was a constant din of construction and pounding, of the shrieking of metal sheets being cut and the endless thump of press machinery, of ear-splitting blasts from huge steam whistles, sirens, and electric bells that beckoned and dismissed shifts of first-generation urbanized laborers from their unending and repetitive days. The normal sounds of rural life—the bleating of domesticated animals, the chirping of birds and insects, the ping of hand-held tools shaping wood and stone—whether pleasant or not, were all recognizable. Here, however, the cacophony of sounds in the nineteenth-century street, factory shop, and mine—seemingly random and meaningless—could not be easily isolated and identified. They became novel and potentially dangerous intrusions on the overworked human mind.

European artists of the late 1800s quickly discovered "noise" as one more weapon in their burgeoning artistic arsenal. In previous eras, the deliberate production of dissonant and percussive sounds (together with nonsense syllablization) were associated with traditional children's activities and rhyming games, with the prattle of madmen, and religious glossolalia. Now the very idea of abstract sounds divorced from normative meaning and traditional rhythms became another inspirational tool of the avant-garde. Writers, composers, and graphic artists explored this new city aesthetic according to their specialized means. Starting from a scientific or occult base—although both attitudes freely intermingled—creators of early phonetic poetry and atonal music invented complicated phoneme alphabets, internal octave scales, chromatic music, universal sonant vocabularies, and electrified instruments that correlated colors, scents, shapes, and gesture with invented languages and mechanical sound.

SPIRITUAL RUSSIA

Locked into a rigid, if overlapping, economic and political structure, nineteenth-century Russia proved to be much less fertile ground for the modernizing roll of the Industrial Revolution. Only after many painful fits and starts did large-scale industrialization take place in the years around 1880. Almost as recalcitrant as the Czar's bureaucrats were to Western-style progress, Russian artists and composers of the realist, neoromantic, and symbolist schools resisted the possibilities of abstract vocalization and music already popular in Paris and Berlin. The use of nonrepresentational speech developed relatively late in Russian culture, beginning in the decade just before the First World War. Yet between the linguistic investigations of Russian mystics around 1905 and the avant-garde filmmakers and radio directors of the early thirties, some of the most radical and adventuresome experimentation ever in utopian and abstract sound appeared. Curiously, the spiritual and the mechanical tendencies in Russian Sound Creation coexisted equally through both the Czarist and early Soviet periods. The divine flapping of angels' wings held as much interest to Russian listeners as the revolutionary melodies that wailed from Baku factory whistles.

The twilight years of the Russian Empire easily invoke the hazy and overheated imagery of an Indian-summer night. The First World War and a smoldering social unrest combined to create a special atmosphere of uncertainty and excitement among Russia's aristocracy and upper classes. While Rasputin held court in Petrograd, advising the Czarina and her family on their daily regimen, a new interest in the occult, seances, and sexual magic overcame Moscow's high society. Demonstrations of yogic spiritualism and astrology were attended by frenzied crowds, often reaching more than a thousand at a single lecture. In addition, the period of 1900 to 1916 was a heyday for secret spiritualist organizations across imperial Russia, especially those linked to such Western European imports as Rosicrucianism, Madame Helena Blavatsky's theosophy, and Rudolf Steiner's anthroposophical science.

GURDJIEFF, GURU OF THE NEW AGE

Carpet seller, stage hypnotist, possible Czarist spy, and New Age prophet, George Ivanovich Gurdjieff (1872–1949) became one of the most intriguing personalities of Nikolai II's Russia and the postrevolutionary emigration that followed. Born in a Caucasian village and of Armenian and Greek parentage, Gurdjieff claimed that he was descended from a long line of ancient Armenian bards. At the turn of the century, he visited several dozen esoteric Christian and Lamaist brotherhoods, shamanistic retreats, dervish centers, and nearly inaccessible but still functioning academies of hidden wisdom in central and East Asia. An enterprising master of psychological manipulation and physical disguise, Gurdjieff even managed to show up at the court of the Dalai Lama as the "living God's" personal tutor. The man who resembled an Armenian version of Rasputin was nothing if not an indefatigible seeker of "the miraculous."

What distinguished Gurdjieff from the common variety religious charlatan or itinerant showman was his ability to transform his striking (and often contradictory) occult beliefs into modern scientific language and concrete artistic practice. Despite his mesmerizing appearance—he looked like a Balkan, six-a-day carnival clairvoyant—and tyrannical demeanor, Gurdjieff attracted rather impressive groups of middle-aged intellectuals, enervated but often well-known artists, and masochistic society women. Where Gurdjieff received his sophisticated background in astronomy, non-Euclidian mathematics, and advanced physics is not recorded, but it is likely he picked it up during his studies in medicine at the University of Kars. Gurdjieff's special knowledge of music and dance, on the other hand, appear to be self-taught and the product of his wide travels, especially those in Islamic Asia and Tibet.

When Gurdjieff came to Moscow at the end of 1912, he had already gained access to Russia's highest political chambers by marrying one of the Czarina's ladies-in-waiting. But it was through his "Objective" art that he hoped to ensnare true believers and life-long devotees. Pyotr Demianovich Ouspensky, a European-educated philosopher and orientalist, was one of the most celebrated and influential examples of Gurdjieff's initial Muscovite flock. When reading *The Voice of Moscow* in the spring of 1915, Ouspensky noticed a short item describing the production of an esoteric ballet, *The Struggle of the Magicians.* Composed by a "Hindu," the pantomime, it announced, would reveal the "true mystery" of India. Although at first skeptical about Gurdjieff's grandiose claims, Ouspensky, like so many who came in contact with the "dark magician," soon joined a small study circle led by the master. To his budding disciples, Gurdjieff expounded on the "inner octaves" in the musical scale that correspond to organs in the body and planets in the solar system and on breathing techniques whose rhythms mathematically correlate to occult patterns on Persian and Bukharan carpets or the lives of near-eastern saints.

Objective Music, Gurdjieff told his Russian pupils, was based on universal inner octaves. Therefore it possessed certain psychological and psychophysical powers. In fact, the first myths and legends of all nations referred symbolically (or actually) to the primary efficacy of this seven-note scale. Orpheus imparted knowledge with his lyre. Jericho's walls were shattered by Joshua's trumpet. "Plain music," the kind created for solipsistic self-expression or simple amusement, had no ability to influence the body's three centers.

Mel Gordon

According to Gurdjieff, sacred central Asian and Sufi dervish melodies still retained much of the potency of primordial Objective Music. In a pilgrimage to a Christian monastery, Gurdjieff had observed a seed fully germinate to maturity in thirty minutes as the monks played "ancient Hebrew music." Another contemporary, although adulterated, manifestation could be found in the hypnotic flute music of Indian street entertainers: "Snake charmer's music in the East is an approach to Objective Music, of course, very primitive. Very often it is simply one note which is long drawn out, rising and falling only very little; but in this single note "inner octaves" are going on all the time and melodies of "inner octaves" which are inaudible to the ears but felt by the emotional center. And the snake hears the music or, more strictly speaking, he feels it, and he obeys it. The same music, only a little more complicated, and men would obey it."[1]

G. I. Gurdjieff's "Inner Octaves"

Musical Note	Universal Meaning	Cosmic Symbol
C	Level of Result	—
D	Level of Actualization	Moon
E	Level of Preparation	Earth
F	Level of Small Details	Planets
G	Level of Specifics	Sun
A	Level of the Particular	Milky Way
B	Level of All Possibilities	Universe
C	Level of Absolute	—

Source: P. D. Ouspensky, *In Search of the Miraculous* (New York: Harcourt, Brace, 1949), p. 297.

Fleeing the Bolshevik coup d'etat in 1918—which Ouspensky called the "rule of the criminal classes"—Gurdjieff and his party left Moscow and the northern Caucasus for Tiflis, the capital of the Menshevik-controlled Georgian Republic. Once established, Gurdjieff cajoled the provisional government into providing him with a space for his Institute for the Harmonious Development of Man. Immediately, Gurdjieff wired for Thomas de Hartmann and his wife, Olga.

Thomas De Hartmann (1886–1956), a well-known Russian composer of theatrical and occult themes, slavishly followed Gurdjieff's teachings and commands, even at great personal risk. Brought to Gurdjieff's institute, the De Hartmanns were quickly introduced to Gurdjieff's adaptations of dervish and Tibetan devotional dances. At first, Gurdjieff taught De Hartmann the esoteric songs by tapping on the piano with one finger while whistling out the melody. De Hartmann supplied the harmony. They were perfect accompaniments to one another in Tiflis and remained so for the next thirty years. While De Hartmann labored over an old upright piano, Gurdjieff initiated his students into the Movement Work, consisting of abstract "sacred gymnastics" ("The Thirty Gestures") and "sacred dances."[2] Yet when rehearsals for the epic *Struggle of the Magicians* reached their final stages in Tiflis, the ever-devious guru bizarrely jettisoned the entire production, smashing the costumes and sets. Soon after, Gurdjieff and his acolytes escaped to Turkey in the footsteps of the retreating British army, which once promised to defend the anti-Bolshevik republic.

During his various exiles in Constantinople, Paris, and New York, Gurdjieff's interest and activity in dance and Objective Music increased. Performances of the sacred dances and De Hartmann's mystic concerts were frequently presented between 1920 and 1924 and once again proved to be strong public attractions. After a near-fatal automobile accident in 1924, however, Gurdjieff abandoned much of the Movement Work and concentrated on writing and publication. Reportedly, Gurdjieff also composed hundreds of Objective songs in an unintelligible notation style during the thirties and forties. In the last years of his life, Gurdjieff sometimes brought students to his Parisian flat and played mournful improvisations on Muslim and Greek Orthodox religious themes, keening like a broken-hearted mendicant with his specially built harmonium.

Mel Gordon

Primarily known for his early pioneering work in abstract painting and theosophical investigations into the relationships between color and shape, Wassily Kandinsky (1866–1944) also exhibited a constant fascination with pure sound and "independent music." Once in Munich during a concert of *Lohengrin,* Kandinsky actually saw, in a synesthetic hallucination, each note as a color. In 1909, Kandinsky began an experiment to find the linkage among color, music, and human movement. In his Munich studio, he collaborated with de Hartmann and the modern Russian dancer Aleksandr Sakharov. Selecting one of Kandinsky's watercolor paintings, De Hartmann promptly composed a theme for it. De Hartmann's piano composition was then played to Sakharov, who, after creating an improvisation, attempted to guess which painting inspired the music.

In his influential journal, *The Blue Rider Almanac* (Munich 1912), Kandinsky promoted the dissonant, "anti-geometrical, anti-logical" harmonic experiments of Arnold Schoenberg, Aleksandr Scriabin, and De Hartmann. In fact, Kandinsky engaged De Hartmann in 1909 to compose a radically antidiatonic, polychromatic score for his minimalist fantasy-opera, *The Yellow Sound.* Despite De Hartmann's extensive involvement, Kandinsky's *The Yellow Sound* was never mounted in their lifetimes. Still the script and Kandinsky's introduction, "On Stage Composition," published in the *Almanac,* were widely read and discussed in many artistic and spiritualist circles.[3]

Applying his mystic-scientific analysis to the performing arts, Kandinsky declared, in "On Stage Composition," that the function of art was to stimulate certain "vibrations" in the spectator's soul. Traditional theater, ballet, and opera, even Wagnerian opera-drama, normally use overlapping musical and scenic elements to reinforce the identical "vibration." For instance, in a typical opera production, when the heroine sings, "Yes!" all the orchestral instruments, brightening lights, elaborate set pieces, and expressive behavior of the singer duplicate the "Yes vibration" according to their own means. Kandinsky suggested another approach.

Unlike Richard Wagner's nineteenth-century notion of the *Gesamtkunstwerk*, which called for the superheated forging of every artistic form into unified points within the opera-drama spectrum, Kandinsky's theory of total theater spoke to a different and more modernistic sensibility. Each scenic "vibration" in Kandinsky's design had an isolated and independent existence. Colors, movements, and sound could appear on stage individually in a structured fashion without parallel references to one another. A dancer's falling arm gesture expressing sorrow, for example, could be challenged by a cheerful C note or an overhead flashing green light.

Dissonance, the newest technique of music composers, Kandinsky proclaimed, deepens the theatrical experience. The predictable and redundant designs of realism and romanticism could finally give way to a purer and more potent form of stage art. Kandinsky identified three external and separate characteristics of performance that internally "touch" the spectator: music, movement (of humans or objects), and color. To music, Kandinsky added the human voice, freed of intelligible word sounds. In this theater of abstract elements and symbols, not the cold mind but the "strings" of the spectator's soul could be tugged and gently vibrated.

Kandinsky returned to Russia at the start of World War I. After the revolution, he took part in the organization of the prestigious Moscow Inkhuk school and the Russian Academy of Artistic Sciences. Lecturing on the scientific and intuitive basis of artistic creation, Kandinsky often recalled his music-movement-color experiments in Munich. Disillusioned with the Soviet cultural program in 1921, however, Kandinsky emigrated once again to Germany, where he taught at the Weimar Bauhaus and continued his examinations in color and form. In 1933, he was forced out of Germany by the Nazis and left for France. He died in Paris in 1944.

Nikolai Kublin (1868–1917) occupied a special place in the cross fire of avant-garde movements in prerevolutionary Russia. A professor at the St. Petersburg Military Academy and a doctor to the Russian general staff with civilian rank equivalent to a major general, Kublin taught himself painting and writing relatively late in life. Beginning in 1908, the forty-year-old Kublin enthusiastically became involved with various post-Symbolist and Futurist splinter groups, organizing major art exhibitions and funding several important publications. His generosity to Russian artists was legendary. In fact, Kublin had an irritating habit of considering practically any member of an avant-garde group an absolute genius. In January 1914, Kublin warmly welcomed F. T. Marinetti, the megalomaniacal leader of the Italian Futurists, to Moscow while Kublin's younger compatriots were somewhat less than gracious to their Western European counterpart. In addition to his experimental graphic and poetic activities, Kublin, with Nikolai Evreinov, founded the infamous Stray Dog cabaret, the chief haunt of Moscow's Bohemian set.

Kublin's promotion of microtonic music and abstract sound manifested itself at every turn in his artistic career. As early as 1910, Kublin militated for the abolition of staves—to be replaced by "colored music" notation and quarter tones. Like Kandinsky, he was under the influence of the St. Petersburg theosophist, Aleksandra Unkovskaya. Music, as he later wrote in *The Blue Rider Almanac,* had its own independent power and should remain as "free" as the everyday sounds in nature.[4] If permitted, this new, "anarchistic" music, floating outside the standard reaches of the five-line scale, could greatly enlarge the composer's vocabulary. Moreover, Kublin called for musical compositions that utilized quarter and eighth tones. Although no contemporary instruments could easily play quarter tones, and eighth tones were nearly inaudible to the human ear,

Kublin praised their qualities as carriers of dissonant tunes and as lyrical "strings" to the listener's soul. Kublin even suggested the construction of new instrument boards in the piano, doubling the string and keyboard sections while reducing the number of octaves, and the creation of homemade xylophones.

A tireless supporter of Futurism, Kublin wrote a word-sound manifesto, "What Is the Word?"[5] in which he borrowed from the French symbolists and the theosophists to devise the beginnings of his own synesthesic alphabet. While declaring that every vowel has its own special pitch, he assigned colors to the hard consonants. Previously, Kublin had lectured on the relationships between thought patterns (or universal symbols), graphic images, odors, and tastes. (Like many theosophists, he had a special affinity for the triangle.) But the "Word" manifesto signaled a high point in Kublin's career. Between 1915 and 1917, as Russian Futurism dissolved into bickering factions, Kublin, in his final years, suffered frequent ridicule and sardonic abuse from his former poet-colleagues.

Nikolai Kublin's Sound-Color Symbology		
Phoneme	Color	Theosophical Color Meaning
G	Yellow-Black	Selfishness
K	Black	Hate
Kh	Gray	Fear
R	Red	Sensuality
S	Blue	Spirit
Z	Green	Transformation
Zh	Yellow	Intelligence

Source: Compiled from the 1914 manifesto by Nikolai Kublin, "What Is the Word?" in *Charters and Declarations of Russian Futurists;* and C. W. Leadbeater, *Man: Visible and Invisible* (London: Theosophic Society Press, 1902).

SCRIABIN, VISIONARY AND SCRIBE OF THE WORLD'S END

The preeminent Russian composer of the early twentieth century, Aleksandr Scriabin (1872–1915) and his works were long associated with occult symbolism and theosophical art. A brilliant pianist who was strongly influenced by the works of Chopin, Liszt, and Wagner, Scriabin began creating complex and lyrical keyboard compositions in the 1890s. His early Nietzschean idealism, however, by the time of the 1905 revolution, gave way to Madame Blavatsky's pan-Aryan "Timeless Wisdom" and the apocalyptic Slavic prophecies of Vladimir Soloviev. To be sure, Scriabin's fragile mental health and childish temperament were more suited to the pessimistic end-of-the-world preachings of the Nikolai II era than the philosophy-based neoromanticism movement that inspired central European artists.

After the turn of the century, Scriabin left Russia for a total of six years in search of new musical venues and freedom from his nominal family responsibilities. There were other reasons as well. His growing egocentricity began to manifest itself in pronounced and disturbing ways: Scriabin not only referred to himself in the third person, like a member of royalty, but he also started to think of himself as the primal man incarnate and then as the primal creator—God. In Brussels, just before 1905, Scriabin discovered the writings of Madame Blavatsky, the founder and central figure of the international Theosophical Society, which quickly became the major influence in his personal and artistic life.

Theosophy was the first and most lasting nineteenth-century attempt to bridge esoteric Western and Eastern religious teachings into a single doctrine. The invention of Helena Petrovna Blavatsky (or H. P. B.), a remarkable conwoman from a mixed Russian and British background, theosophy grew into a full-fledged occult religion by the 1880s. Although poorly educated, Blavatsky managed to carefully weave neo-Platonic texts and indigenous American spiritualism to a tapestry of traditional Hindu and Buddhist beliefs. Many important Western artists and writers, such as Maurice Maeterlinck and William Butler Yeats, found themselves attracted to theosophy's ritual use of universal symbology and homeopathic magic in their ceremonies and writings. In addition, synesthesia, the invisible attachment of one physiological sensation with another, H. P. B. proclaimed, was divinely ordained. At centers in Madras, New York, London, and Paris, theosophists actively investigated hidden relationships between the seven bodily senses and their corresponding astral planes.

For Scriabin, theosophy magically resolved the most pressing and personal dilemmas in his conflicted life. Before 1905, Scriabin felt that he could write any kind of music, but the motivation was always purely artistic. Now his modernistic, difficult compositions could generate something other than praise or mad controversy. Scriabin would be the revealer, the vehicle, the supreme commander for a great superhuman enterprise: *The Mysterium,* an initiation rite of hallucinatory music that would instantly transform humanity. It was the ultimate theosophical dream.

Despite a total obsession with the project, long stretches of time passed before Scriabin began actual work on *The Mysterium.* In 1908, he completed his *Poem of Ecstasy,* a lushly harmonious "tone poem" that found wide approval among aficionados in New York, where it premiered, and more feverish enthusiasm in Moscow and St. Petersburg. (When the Soviet cosmonaut, Yuri Gagarin, was catapulted into space in 1961, the *Poem of Ecstasy* became the first earthly music ever broadcast from outer space.)

Completed in 1910, Scriabin's fourth symphony, *Prometheus: A Poem of Fire,* brought him closer still to the theosophical world of *Prometheus.* A product of a synesthesic fusion of the senses, *Prometheus* was written to be accompanied with a "light keyboard," that projected colored images according to Scriabin's intuitive music-color code. Even the music was otherworldly. The symphony began with a variant of Scriabin's idiomatic "Mystic Chord," a chord that consisted of superposed fourths and that allowed him to dissolve any normative time sense. Although the first *Prometheus* concert in Moscow was performed without the colored projections in 1911, the symphony soon became totally identified with the patented color organ. Constructed by Aleksandr Mozer, the simple apparatus unveiled only one or two colors at a time, and these changed very slowly, usually fixed to *Prometheus'* pitch or double-horn line, rather than to the individual notes in the total orchestra.

Scriabin's Music-Color Symbology for
Prometheus and the "Prefatory Action" of *The Mysterium*

Musical note	Color	Feeling/Image
C	Red	Human Will
C#	Violet	Will of Creative Spirit
D	Yellow	Joy
D#	Steel	Mankind
E	Frost to Moon-color	Dreams
F	Dark Red	Differentiation of Will
F#	Navy Blue	Creativity
G	Orange-Pink	Play
G#	Purple	Descent of Spirit into Matter
A	Green	Materialism
A#	Steel	Ravishment
B	Sky Blue	Dreams

Source: Compiled from Leonid Sabaneiev's chart in *Musik* (January 1911), p. 199, as cited in Wassily Kandinsky and Franz Marc, eds., *The Blaue Reiter Almanac,* ed. Klaus Lankheit (1912; reprint, New York: Viking Press, 1974), p. 131; and from Fabin Bowers, *Scriabin,* vol. 2 (Tokyo: Kodansha International Limited, 1969), p. 205.

     Scriabin's ultimate project, *The Mysterium,* was never finished although some twelve years were invested in it. The extant sketches, called the "Prefatory Action," and private notebook entries, mostly written in 1914 and 1915, give some notion of Scriabin's grandiose and expansive intentions. Every occult musical idea from the ancient Eleusinian Rites to Meister Eckhart to Blavatsky's Secret Doctrine somehow found a place in *The Mysterium.* Like Kandinsky, Scriabin experimented with the correspondences among human movement, color, and sound. While he completed a choral text in simple Russian, he dreamed of incorporating Sanskrit words, unintelligible shouts and cries, as well as the sounds of yogic aspiration.

Songs from the Museum of the Future

Suspended from clouds high over the Himalayas, Russian bells would beckon spectators from the world over to *The Mysterium*. After six days and twelve hours of prophetic art, including poetic dialogues, fire festivities, supernatural music, rhythmic dancing (performed by the orchestral members), nonmatrixed mime (where the actors do not assume characters), perfume and incense burning, tactile displays, color and light fountains, and audience participation, Scriabin would declare that a new race of men would be propagated. (Earlier, Scriabin prophesied the entire world would come to an end through "physical shocks of sound power.") Standing at the altar of his universal temple, shaped like a globe with twelve columns (all reflected in a semicircular pool), Scriabin the musician, the conductor, the high priest would transform man and nature, male and female, brother and brother into an ectoplasmic unity. A kind of death experience would blend all mankind into a single mass illuminated by the "ecstatic abyss of sunshine." Seared of their earthly garments and almost dematerialized, the spectators would rediscover their innate "sonhood" as their father, Scriabin, would lead them into an ineffable understanding of ultimate life and death.

In 1914, Scriabin welcomed the world war as a physical manifestation of his cataclysmic beliefs. Yet, suffering from the rapid devastation of a septic carbuncle, Scriabin himself was the one to be spiritually transported to another astral plane. On 27 April 1915, after months of musical work on his "Prefatory Action," interrupted by a series of medical operations, Scriabin, the visionary composer, died.

RUSSIAN FUTURISM

Similar to its Italian namesake in creed and artistic bravado, Russian Futurism challenged its culture's proscribed entertainment structures, conventionalized grammar, and accepted modes of language and music. Yet, unlike the Western European Marinetti-dominated movement, Futurism's history in Russia bobbed to the many vitriolic and competing claims of its literary circles and individuals. But even as they attacked one another, each of the four major Russian Futurist groups promoted a collective poetic agenda. Dislocated syntax, lullaby trills, nonsensical word making, children's rhymes, weirdly "drawn" poems with doodlelike graphics, startling imagistic juxtapositions, paper collage texts, mirrored lettering, and concrete poetry were among their many common linguistic innovations.

Formally inaugurated in 1912 with the manifesto "A Slap in the Face of Public Taste," Russian Futurism managed to outrage critics and arbitrators of artistic fashion as it quickly attracted the attention of sensation-seeking journalists and a curious public. Signed by the major literary figures of Cubo-Futurism (the Hylaeas), David Burliuk, Velimir Khlebnikov, Alexei Kruchenykh, and Mayakovsky, "A Slap" called for "word novelty," or neologistic invention, as the primary means to enlarge the poet's vocabulary. In still another untitled manifesto of theirs that appeared in the almanac *A Trap for Judges 2* a few months later, the Hylaea group declared that words should be endowed with meaning according to their "phonic characteristics" and that vowels should be understood as carriers of time and space; consonants as "color, sound, and smell."[6] Two members of the Cubo-Futurists, in particular, were celebrated for their radical experiments with Sound Creation. These were Alexei Kruchenykh (1886–1968) and Velimir Khlebnikov (1885–1922). Together they promulgated the theory of zaum, or transrational speech.

THE LAWS OF ZAUM

Alexei Kruchenykh

Trained as an artist in Odessa, Kruchenykh became involved with the Russian Cubo-Futurists in 1911, appearing in virtually all of their manifestos and exhibitions. After his poetry and Futurist opera, *Victory Over the Sun*, Kruchenykh's most lasting contribution was his invention of *zaum*, a rubric that embraced the private languages of schizophrenics, folk incantations, baby talk, glossolalia, random onomatopoetic verse, and Futurist neologisms. Called zaum from the prefix "za" (beyond) and the root "um" (mind), Kruchenykh's concept originated in the natural dissociation between thought and speech in the highly charged brain. Once in a truly inspired state, the primitive man (clinically insane person or poet) must express his emotions in novel pronouncements and rhythms, far from everyday "frozen" language with its conventional attachments that link precise meaning with articulation. According to Kruchenykh, the Futurist poet has at his disposal this other form of vocalization, one rich with private associations and new sound ideas: zaum. The secret of primordial creation, that is, transrational language, could lead the artist far beyond the restraints of socially sanctioned patterns and the vise of national vocabularies.

Citing the divinely dictated, ecstastic (and meaningless) language of the contemporary religious flagellant V. Shishkov—"nosoktos lesontos futr lis natrufuntru kreserefire"[7]—Kruchenykh revealed one of the natural sources for his exalted, absurd speech. His earliest attempts at zaum, however, more closely resembled Marinetti's *parole in libertà* (words-in-freedom) than the self-revelatory "speaking in tongues" of Russia's wandering mystics. Emphasizing the universality of vowel sounds and eliminating all grammatical genders but the masculine, Kruchenykh produced this zaum poem in 1913:

> *i*
>
> *che*
>
> *de*
>
> *mali*
>
> *gr*
>
> *iu*
>
> *iukh*

Mel Gordon

d d d

d d d

se

v

m'

In the same manifesto, "Explodity,"[8] in which the poem above appeared, Kruchenykh declared that "on April 27th, at 3 o'clock in the afternoon, I instantaneously mastered to perfection all languages.... I am here reporting my verses in Japanese, Spanish, and Hebrew:

ike mina ni

sinu ksi

iamakh alik

zel

Later still, in *Secret Vices of the Academicians* (Moscow, 1915), Kruchenykh wrote that a typical Russian laundry bill had superior sound qualities to any line in Aleksandr Pushkin's *Eugene Onegin*. But better than either was Kruchenykh's own zaum poem:[9]

kvab

tarad

pin

pur

kvara

kuaba

vabakr

trbrk

brkt

Such provocative statements (and poetry) probably should have led to overwhelming ridicule and condemnation, but Kruchenykh's basic ideas on the relationship of ecstatic states to language creation proved to fascinate as well as intrigue. After all, similar investigations were taking place in the West, such as Sir James Frazer's *The Golden Bough*. And although Kruchenykh had a tiresome habit of constantly quoting himself and recycling his nonsense poetry in various booklets, zaum quickly invigorated the receding fortunes of Russian Futurism. Finally, in his "Declaration of Transrational Language," published as a leaflet in Baku in 1921, Kruchenykh summarized all of zaum's central characteristics and foundations. He stated that artists use transrational language under the following conditions: (1) when general "rhythmic-musical excitement" causes them to resort to "protosound"; (2) when they only want to hint at, rather than define, an image or object; (3) when they become overcome by an emotional state, like jealousy; and (4) when love or religious ardor clouds their ability to reason.

Long after after the revolution, Kruchenykh had supporters, especially among Mayakovsky's LEF group. Yet the novelty of Kruchenykh's theories slowly faded by the mid- and late twenties. The aging Kruchenykh retreated into literary obscurity, producing occasional Futurist bibliographies and anthologies. In addition, zaum soon became more associated with Kruchenykh's more radical cocreator.

Velimir Khlebnikov

Born near Astrakhan, Khlebnikov led the life of an itinerant visionary, searching always for the temporal relationships between historical upheaval, human evolution, and numbers. Having studied mathematics, biology, and philology at the universities of Kazan and St. Petersburg, Khlebnikov delved into literature. At first influenced by the Russian symbolists and the Pan-Slavic nationalists,

Khlebnikov began to experiment with neologistic poetry, exploring the ancient Slavonic roots and partitive forms of contemporary words. But sharing few values with the effete and basically apolitical symbolists, Khlebnikov gravitated toward an avant-garde group centered around Mikhail Matyushin, a violinist, and his wife, the writer Elena Guro (said by some to be the real inventor of zaum notation).

Khlebnikov's literary notoriety started with the publication of "Incantation by Laughter" in Kublin's 1910 anthology, *The Studio of Impressionists*. A morphological drill, relating all the possible (and unlikely) phonetic derivations on the word laughter, "Incantation by Laughter" launched Khlebnikov's career and remained his best-known poem. Soon joined by Kruchenykh in Moscow, Khlebnikov became the most consistently extreme innovator among the Cubo-Futurists—a kind of "point man" of Futurism. In addition, beginning in 1912 Khlebnikov charted out the hidden and mathematical connections between whole integrals, calendar dates, major scientific discoveries, and the decisive battles in world history. Curiously, he correctly predicted the outbreak of the First World War and the Bolshevik Revolution, which later appeared in the pamphlet "A New Theory of War, Battles 1915–1917" (St. Petersburg, 1914). The calculations from Khlebnikov's "Tables of Destiny" fueled his own Futuristic manifestos and theatrical sketches.

Like Kruchenykh and his disciples, Khlebnikov heralded zaum as the ultimate poetic language. Yet Khlebnikov related zaum more to his utopic fantasies than to "holy ghost" visitations or the babble of infants. For Khlebnikov, zaum was a future language, an emotional Esperanto, "the alphabet of the stars." Scientifically, one could find in zaum the sounds of man's deepest linguistic impulses. Although based on his study of rudimentary Slavonic phonemes, zaum, according to Khlebnikov, spoke universally and subconsciously to all mankind.

Khlebnikov's Universal Alphabet

Phoneme	Characteristic	Color
A	Causes negation	—
B	Collision, magnification	Red, flame
Ch	Covering, chamber-like	—
D	Movement away from its source	—
E	Causes decay	—
G	Insufficiency, height	Yellow
H	Emptiness	—
I	Causes unity	—
K	Stasis, tranquility, death	Sky blue
Kh	Protection (man-made)	—
L	Lengthening, cessation of falling	White, ivory
M	Smallness, division, disintegration	Dark blue
N	Philosophic loss, nothingness	Light red
O	Causes increase in size	—
P	Explosion, release of pressure	Black outlined in red
R	Unruly movement, ripping, insubordination	—
S	Returning, multiplication, radiation	—
Sh	Reduction, merging	—
Shch	Separation, cracking	—
T	Arrested motion, dark, unnatural	—
Ts	Penetration	—
U	Causes submission	—
V	Subtraction, threat, turning	—
Z	Reflection	Gold
Zh	Independent movement, combustion	—

Source: Compiled and edited from Khlebnikov's manifestos and notebook entries, 1913–1921, in Velimir Khlebnikov, *Collected Works,* Volume One, trans. Paul Schmidt, ed. Charlotte Douglas (Cambridge, MA: Harvard University Press, 1987).

One of the most striking uses of zaum appears in Khlebnikov's science fantasy play, *Zangezi: A Supersaga in Twenty Planes,* printed shortly before his death from malnutrition in 1922 and staged by the constructivist artist Vladimir Tatlin the next year. Khlebnikov's superhero, Zangezi—"the speech-maker" and human interpreter of the birds, insects, gods, and stars—attempts to explain transrational language to the gathered masses. Before the eternal

Nietzschean figure, Zangezi, appears, the god Eros speaks in zaum language:[10]

EROS

Mara-roma

Beebah-bool

Oook, kooks, ell!

Rededeedee dee-dee-dee!

Peeree, pepee, pa-papee!

Chogi goona, geni-gan

Ahl, Ell, Eeell!

Ahlee, Ellee, Eelee!

Ek, ak, oook!

Gamch, gemch, ee-o!

rr-pee! rrr-pee!

MUSICAL FUTURISM

As in Italy, Futurism in Russia provoked a series of radical innovations in music. Mikhail Matyushin (1861–1934), one of the founders and most active members of the Hylaea group, was a violinist in the imperial court orchestra for almost thirty years before turning to Futurism. A writer, painter, sculptor, and theoretician as well as a composer, Matyushin used his enormous wealth to publish the writings of his wife Elena Guro, Khlebnikov, and Kruchenykh. After organizing "The First Pan-Russian Congress of the Seekers of the Future" on his Finnish estate in June 1913, Matyushin completed the score for Kruchenykh's opera, *Victory over the Sun*. It would be his most significant musical contribution to Cubo-Futurism.

Staged on 3 and 5 December 1913 with Mayakovsky's ironic monodrama *Vladimir Mayakovsky, A Tragedy* at the Luna Park Theatre in St. Petersburg, *Victory over the Sun* was the product of Russian Futurism's greatest talents. Kazimir Malevich designed the abstract sets and costumes, and the practically invisible and taciturn Khlebnikov wrote the prologue. (Oddly, zaumlike speech appeared in Kruchenykh's dialogue only when characters indicated fright.) Although the performers had difficulty with Kruchenykh's weird direction—each syllable was to be evenly spaced and accented—everyone, with the exception of Mayakovsky, praised Matyushin's music, a wicked and dissonant parody of Verdi. Played on an out-of-tune, upright piano, Matyushin's quarter-tone arias and four-part simultaneous recitatives propelled the opera forward even as the plot unravelled. At one rehearsal, Kruchenykh shouted the ultimate Futurist compliment to Matyushin, "That certainly isn't Tchaikovsky!" *Victory's* two performances resulted in a huge scandal and Russian Futurism's finest hour. Over the years, Matyushin and the other participants would frequently return to their personal memories of it.

Primarily known as a teacher and painter of Futurist and Suprematist themes, Matyushin organized several important art studios in the early days after the Revolution. Working with Kandinsky and Malevich at their own schools, as well as in his private studio shop, Matyushin conducted many scientific experiments on the relationship of color to form, including some that measured color perception as a function of sound interference. Drawing on the theories of French Cubism as well as Ouspensky's Gurdjieffian speculations, Matyushin wedded cogent scholarship with intuitive leaps of the imagination. Surprisingly, the empirical results of his color-shape work were diametrically opposed to Kandinsky's theosophical pronouncements.

Matyushin's final discoveries, brought to Germany by Malevich in 1927 and later published in *The Natural Law of Changeability in Color Combinations* (Moscow-Petrograd, 1932), were the result of nine years of precise laboratory work. According to Matyushin, noise levels and the intensity of different colors influence one another. When either a monochord or pure color dominates, the other will appear weaker than it would normally to human receptors.

If both are equally strong, then the noise will cause the color to be more visually "active." High, sharp sounds lead to a lightening—that is, to a "cooling, or blueing"—of the color. Conversely, low, rough notes have a tendency to "redden," darken, and condense the color in the eye of the spectator. After Matyushin's death in 1934, such studies on abstract sound and color disappeared from the studios and laboratories of Soviet universities.

MONUMENTAL PROLETARIAN MUSIC

During the first weeks of the Russian Revolution, a striking, unreal, and even theatrical feeling permeated the air. The significance of the political and social events taking place in the cities and countryside emotionally overwhelmed their participants and spectators. Could the world's history truly be shifting before our eyes, in our own streets? people wondered. By 1918 the Bolshevik Revolution settled over the Russian people like a dream. And even after the maelstrom seemed to die down, the Bolshevik leaders understood the emotive and intellectual appeal of the revolution to peasants and workers.

Following the artistic regimen of the French Revolution, the new Soviet elite created its own cultural bureaucracy to promulgate revolutionary and statist values. Political allegiance to the workers' republic took the form of large-scale processions and symbolic outdoor spectacles. A left-wing theatricalism would soon replace the visceral thirst for age-old religious ritual and ceremony, promised the followers of Lenin, and the commissars of education and culture found that their announced mission was not difficult at all. In fact, hundreds of thousands of ordinary Russians rallied to participate in the street festivities and arranged mass spectacles to celebrate the various seasonal anniversaries of the Soviet victory. A theatrical mania would overtake Russia for more than a decade.

The vast majority of celebrations were primarily visual, laced with threads of symphonic music, but Arseni Avraamov (c. 1890–c. 1943) directed at least four unique monumental sound concerts between 1918 and 1923 that commemorated the October Revolution. Avraamov was inspired by a primitive nighttime spectacle in Petrograd that celebrated the Soviet Union's first May Day in 1918 with the blazing of factory and ship sirens. All in all, it was little more than a sound accompaniment to a military fireworks display. For the 7 November festivities in Nizhny Novogorod, however, Avraamov repeated the Petrograd experiment but along a more sophisticated and "politically correct" theoretical line. The Austrian specialist on Russian culture, René Fulop-Miller, claimed that Avraamov's factory sirens were selected as the instrument of choice because "its tone could be heard by whole quarters and remind the proletariat of its real home, the factory."[11]

In Petrograd for the 1920 ceremonies, Avraamov began to develop Futurist-like outdoor musical equipment and complicated signaling devices for his sound choruses and mechanical technicians. At the Rostov Conservatory the following year, Avraamov experimented with a "forty-eight step" octave system that could refine the sound design of mass spectacles. If outdoor proletarian music had a future, it was with Avraamov.

Avraamov's best-known creation appeared in the Caspian port of Baku for the Fifth Anniversary of the Soviet Republic on 7 November 1922. This bruitist spectacular, called the *Symphony of Factory Sirens,* used the services of a huge cast of choirs (joined by spectators), the foghorns of the entire Caspian flotilla, two batteries of artillery guns, a number of full infantry regiments (including a machine-gun division), hydroplanes, and all the factory sirens of Baku. "Conductors" posted on specially built towers signaled various sound units with colored flags and pistol shots. A central "steam-whistle machine" pounded out "The Internationale" and "La Marseillaise" as noisy "autotransports" (half-tracks) raced across Baku for a gigantic sound finale in the festival square. Villages far beyond the walls of Baku could hear the revolutionary melodies of Avraamov's percussive concert. *The Symphony of Factory Sirens* immediately entered the annals of avant-garde entertainments.

One year later, Avraamov took his instructional manuals and assistants to Moscow. Backed by sixty members of the Metal Workers Union, Avraamov directed another *Symphony of Factory Sirens* on 7 November 1923. Playing the standard Soviet compositions, including "The Young Guards' March," "Varshavyanka," and "The Workers' Funeral March," posed many more difficulties in Moscow than in the open port space of Baku. Distances between the sirens and other sound units were so great that it became impossible to maintain a uniform acoustical impression. Even the well-known "Internationale" sounded unintelligible to the assembled spectators. Soviet technology could not keep pace with Avraamov's vision. Russian Sound Creation returned to the enclosed spaces of the theater auditorium and concert hall.

CONSTRUCTIVIST ENTERTAINMENTS

The constructivist movement was an aesthetically rich if short-lived episode in the history of the Soviet theatre, lasting some four years beginning in 1921. Graphically, Russian constructivist scenic design, with its signature scaffolding sets and ubiquitous bare stairs and ladders, became internationally known and influential for decades after its heyday in the twenties. The stage as a functional machine captured the imagination of designers everywhere. Less understood was the constructivist machine ethic as applied to acting and theatrical sound design. And even among constructivist directors of the time, theoretical debate over the function of sound, music, and voice in the theater filled their trade papers and manifestos.

FOREGGER AND THE NOISE ORCHESTRA

A Ukrainian intellectual with an unerring talent for theatrical novelty and satire, Nikolai Foregger (1892–1939) inaugurated his MASTFOR studio in Moscow at the onset of Lenin's New Economic Policy in the fall of 1921. MASTFOR (an acronym for Workshop of Foregger) attracted many gifted young artists, such as

the twenty-two-year-old designer Sergei Eisenstein and the re-
nowned "hot music" composer Yuri Miliutin. There was a jazz-age
exuberance and devil-may-care attitude in Foregger's spicy music-hall
routines and theatrical parodies. MASTFOR's wicked debunking of
Meyerhold and Tairov's large-scale productions appealed to leftist
critics and spectators alike. Some maintained that the MASTFOR
imitations were superior—and certainly more entertaining—examples of the constructivist ethos than the grandiose originals.

By October 1922, when the MASTFOR established
a permanent theater in the Arbat district, Foregger added to his
already successful repertoire a whole series of innovative techniques
that would transform the Soviet avant-garde. Wooden contraptions
with pulleys and ropes, for example, reportedly taught audience
members how to act (in the MASTFOR style) during the intermis-
sions. Most significant was Foregger's Machine Dance—a human
display of motor parts that demonstrated the workings of conveyor
belts, pistons, flywheels, transmission bands, and pumps as they
reassembled into complete dynamic mechanisms.

Altogether some eighty different Machine Dances
were presented at the MASTFOR. For a sound accompaniment,
Foregger invented the Noise Orchestra, an eccentric band that created all the crushing, sucking, and metallic sounds needed to produce
the machinelike illusion. The instruments consisted of boxes of broken bottles, old packing cases, strips of metal sheets, cheap whistles,
paper horns, a gong, wooden and copper sticks, and a reed pipe. In
November 1923, Walter Duranty described the efficacy of the Noise
Orchestra in a *New York Times* review entitled "Dance Machine
Delights Moscow": "Arms wave, bodies are flung to and fro in regular oscillation, like machines in a factory. Rumbling, rattling, buzzing,
and whirring noises off-stage aid the illusion, and, after the spectator's
first astonishment is past, one does begin to see the effectiveness of
the mimicry."[12]

Suffering from a devastating fire and adverse opinions from local censorship boards, MASTFOR disappeared in the summer of 1924. Yet Foregger's Machine Dances and Noise Orchestra became something of a rage among Russian agitprop and nonprofessional factory theaters in the middle and late twenties. The huge amateur Blue Blouse movement (1923–1928), in particular, adapted Foregger's techniques as a means of proselytizing for the New Russia. Although many Blue Blouse directors and theoreticians favored popular dance or folk melodies to set the tone for their comic-propaganda sketches and civic parades, others hewed closely to MASTFOR's futuristic vision. Writing in the *Blue Blouse* journal in 1925, one director, A. Lubimov, protested against the use of old-fashioned "home-brewed music." To these pseudopeasant compositions, Lubimov juxtaposed A. Sergeev's orchestral workshop that invented MASTFOR-like instruments capable of imitating the "humming of a tractor, the screeching of wheels, the chugging of trains, the whistles of factories and steamers."[13]

In all parts of Soviet Russia, culturally enfranchised workers and their families sat transfixed as they viewed the human imitation and mastery of machine sound and rhythm. The torrential racket of the workplace was finally captured by enthusiastic young performers and aesthetically transformed into the popular music of the clubhouse. Fulop-Miller described one such "noise orgy" staged by a group called the Engineerists in the auditorium of the Moscow Trade Union Palace: "The first public divine service of these "machine-worshippers" began with a noise orchestra composed of a crowd of motors, turbines, sirens, hooters, and similar instruments of din; the choir master stood on a balustrade and "conducted" the din with the aid of a complicated signalling apparatus. After the noise overture had raged long enough to deafen the audience completely,... reckless gymnastics were zealously performed with choppy movements mechanized as far as possible, on all kinds of gymnastic apparatus, under, in, on, between, before, and beside various machine structures."[14]

Foregger had many rivals in Moscow. Whereas he was recognized as the "High Priest of the Machine God," other directors utilized different sound designs for their constructivist entertainments. Boris Ferdinandov (1889–1959), the founder of the Heroic-Experimental Theatre, developed an actor-training technique called Metro-Rhythm. Defining human existence as the complex alteration of stressed and unstressed rhythmic activities, Ferdinandov declared his Metro-Rhythmic demonstrations to be a scenic form of "concentrated life." A heavily accented sound followed by two weaker ones, for instance, represented "an obvious trend toward death and immobility."[15]

Classic and "heroic" plays at the Heroic-Experimental Theatre, such as Sophocles' *Oedipus Rex* and Aleksandr Ostrovsky's *The Storm,* were reworked into mechanically programmed performances that unfolded according to precise Metro-Rhythmic schemes. Moving and speaking like a "walking metronome," each Ferdinandov actor responded individually and automatically to the backstage stimuli of blaring sirens and horns. Critics found themselves totally confused by this austere robotic mise-en-scène, but many Muscovites were fascinated by Ferdinandov's "scientific" theories of theatrical rhythm. When the Heroic-Experimental Theatre was forcibly closed in January 1923, after four seasons of productive work, government officials blamed it on Ferdinandov's arrogant character and overt homosexuality.

The Factory of the Eccentric Actor [FEX], launched in December 1921 in Petrograd, mostly concerned itself with grotesque movement and comic gesture. This was in part related to influence of the Russian circus and Western silent film comedians, especially Charlie Chaplin and Max Linder. Accordingly, human movement was to replace the word, which they related to boring realism and nineteenth-century drama. But following the lead of the Western European-traveling intellectuals Osip Brik and Vladimir Parnakh, who introduced their versions of Berlin and Parisian jazz to constructivist theatres in Moscow, FEX later celebrated the "hot music" of America's cities. They even claimed that in the United States, workers manipulated machinery all day so they could dance to the mechanized rhythms of jazz at night. In his declamatory FEX manifesto "AB!" Georgi Kozintsov called for new Eccentric speech and sound: "The word equals a music-hall song, Pinkerton, an auctioneer's hawking, street cursing.... The Eccentric music is blaring horns, shots, typewriters, whistles, sirens. The tap dance is the beginning of the new rhythm."[16]

RADLOV'S LABORATORY OF THEATRICAL RESEARCH

For two years beginning in January 1920, Sergei Radlov (1892–1958) directed a series of wildly paced melodramas and contemporary farces that mixed circus antics with Soviet propaganda in unequal proportions at his Petrograd Theatre of Popular Comedy. Most of the productions charmed audiences and critics alike. Yet in the fall of 1921, Radlov, under pressure from his codirectors, returned to an old, prerevolutionary format of historical revivals of Molière, Shakespeare, and Spanish Renaissance plays. Calibrating the actors' speech and movement to the "internal rhythms" of the text created only spectator confusion. Each recreation was more disastrously received than the last.

At the end of the traumatic 1921 season, Radlov decided to start over. Typically, he began with a manifesto, "The Electrification of the Theatre." In it Radlov clarified his intentions. Instead of looking to the past, he was determined to invent "entertainments for the future." In February 1922, Radlov disbanded the once-successful Theatre of Popular Comedy.

The Laboratory of Theatrical Research, Radlov's new theater studio, opened in December 1922. It was dedicated to the "pure mathematical essence" of drama and theater. Prefiguring Oskar Schlemmer's Bauhaus dance-movement pieces, the Laboratory unveiled a series of completely abstract sketches. The first experiments, entitled *Opus #1* and *Opus #2,* were severely attacked by the

Songs from the Museum of the Future

Petrograd press, who saw nothing more than displays of meaningless body movement and weird vocalization. Not only were the Laboratory actors' gestures and poses "geometrized," but their voices also articulated the linear shapes and pure forms of constructivist art. Reviewers contemptuously referred to Radlov's scenic compositions as "theatrical Suprematism," an appellation with which both Radlov and Malevich must have concurred.

In "On the Pure Elements of the Actors' Art," another Radlov manifesto of the period, the Laboratory's artistic director traced the efficacy of Sound Creation from the biblical Joshua and mythic figure of Orpheus to the French symbolists and Russian Futurists. Praising Kruchenykh's most recent vocal discoveries, published in a booklet entitled *Phonetics of the Theatre* (Leningrad–Moscow, 1923), Radlov wrote, "As for the voice, it is the bearer of pure forms of sound. Freed of words—for the actor is not obliged to utter one semantic word!—the actor will give us richly articulated, now high, now low, now slowed, now accelerated pure sound. In this wordless speech of his, the actor sounds freely, like a bird."[17] Here Radlov differentiated himself from the absolutist standards of Kruchenykh and other Futurist poets by allowing for improvisation by his actors in their word-sound performances. Exactly how Radlov's actors were trained at his Laboratory remains a mystery. His experimental studio soon folded. Sensing a social and political change in the Soviet theater, Radlov returned to the staging of classical dramas and socialist realist plays.

MUSIC OF THE FUTURE

The Bolshevik Revolution unleashed a torrent of innovative and modernistic trends in New Music. Revolutionary themes, especially those involving industrialization and the call for a massive socialist reconstruction, inspired many young composers of the post-Scriabin and dissonant schools. Such agitprop compositions as Leonid Polovinkin's "Electrification" (scored for piano), M. A. Korchmarev's

"Song of the Sowing Machines" (which incorporated the appropriate threshing sounds), and G. Smetanin's "The Factory" (orchestrated for a full-scale noise band), although now forgotten, were mainstays of a popular twenties repertoire. One composer commonly associated with early twenties machine worship was Vladimir Deshevov. His three-minute piano piece, "Railroad" was praised by the Leningrad Association for Contemporary Music as musically better for Russian workers than "the pessimism of Tchaikovsky and false heroics of Beethoven."[18] In 1924 Deshevov started to write for the ballet and opera stage. Although labeled decadent and absurdly primitive by Soviet critics, Deshevov's constructivist ballet, *The Red Hurricane* (1924), and comic football operetta, *The Friendly Hill* (1928), were well received by local audiences. Ironically, it was Deshevov's mildly socialist realist opera, *Ice and Steel* (1930), which dramatized the story of the 1921 anti-Soviet Kronstadt rebellion, that brought him the most fame. The modernist trend in Soviet music belonged to two less compromising figures: Nikolai Roslavetz and Aleksandr Mosolov.

REVOLUTION ACROSS THE MUSICAL SCALE

Nikolai Roslavetz

Nikolai Roslavetz (1880–1944) devoted himself to the destruction of tonality in classical Russian music as early as 1913. In the middle and late teens, Roslavetz associated himself with the boisterous activities of the Russian Futurists, but his songs and cantatas at that time revealed a closer affinity to French Impressionism. Two years before the revolution, Roslavetz completed his dodecaphonic system of harmonics and polyrhythms—as well as a weird-looking notation to record it—that foreshadowed Western European serialism.

An avowed Marxist, Roslavetz claimed that his tonic inventions, including the "synthetic chord" technique and "mirror symmetry," were structural reflections of the revolution itself. Although he became involved with Soviet propaganda music, composing marches for physical culture clubs in 1919 and 1920,

Roslavetz rebelled against superficial "Proletkultism" by 1924. For Roslavetz, pure music was created directly in the subconscious, not to be manufactured on request. Attacked for his bourgeois writings and atonal compositions, Roslavetz, quickly tagged the "Russian Schoenberg," went into a forced exile to Tashkent in 1930, where he composed the first Uzbek opera and was excised from the Soviet musical world. Roslavetz died in 1944, having spent the latter part of life studying indigenous Uzbek folk music.

Aleksandr Mosolov

Aleksandr Mosolov (1900–1973) a disciple of Scriabin and a decorated Civil War hero, was considered one of the most original and controversial Russian composers of the postrevolutionary era. Mosolov represented the New Objectivity in Soviet music, devoting himself to industrial themes that utilized mechanical-sounding instruments. Said to be the leading representative of musical constructivism, Mosolov's compositions were often criticized as being "antipsychological" and harsh. His subject matter too, which included newspaper advertisements and children's street games, also amazed and startled conservative audiences. Mosolov's international fame rested on a single cacophonic Machine-Age paean, entitled "The Iron Foundry" (also called "Iron Foundry, Music of Machines," "The Spirit of the Factory," "Steel Foundry," or simply "Foundry").

Originally a three-minute section from the ballet *Steel,* written to honor the Soviet Union's tenth anniversary in 1927, "The Iron Foundry" took on a life all its own as Western conductors and choreographers from Toscanini to Adolph Bolm jockeyed to gain local performance rights. Scored primarily for violas and dissonant, almost scratchy-sounding brass instruments (with a trademarked metal sheet standing in the orchestra), "Iron Foundry" captured the feverish rhythms of the smelting process and blast furnace as it was stoked and restoked through the superhuman and machinelike activities of the new worker. Yet in spite of his acceptance as world-class composer, Mosolov's reputation in the Soviet Union diminished steadily through the thirties. In 1936, he was expelled from the Union of Soviet Composers for alcoholism and engaging in "drunken brawls." Certainly, Mosolov's affinity for vodka may have explained how suitcases of his earliest manuscripts became lost forever during his travels. Like Roslavetz, Mosolov retreated into the kingdom of folk song and patriotic music. Between 1944 and 1969, he composed dozens of folkloric choral arrangements, celebrating the Red Army, the work of collective farmers, and the Russian countryside.

RUSSIAN SOUND CREATION IN EXILE

Hundreds of thousands of émigré Russians flooded the capitals of central and Western Europe beginning in 1915. For eight years, as world war, revolution, government-sponsored appropriations, and civil war shattered the paper-thin tranquility of Czarist society, refugees streamed west and south out of Mother Russia. Although the majority, from the former moneyed or propertied classes, identified with the various counterrevolutionary White armies, all shades on the political spectrum were represented in Russian European and Chinese exile, including rabid supporters of the Bolshevik regime. Intellectually and artistically, Berlin and Paris, in particular, found themselves greatly enriched by the innovative Russian immigrants, especially in the fields of avant-garde music and Sound Creation.

BARNOFF-ROSSINÉ, INVENTOR OF THE COLOR-MUSIC SHOW

Scriabin and Kulbin's experiments relating sound to music and light were carried on after the revolution by Vladimir Barnoff-Rossiné (1888–1944), a sometime Russian expatriate and protégé of Parisian artists Robert and Sonia Delaunay. In 1915, Apollinaire praised the metallic sculpture of this "French Futurist." When Barnoff-Rossiné returned to the new Soviet Republic in 1918, he organized an art workshop in Petrograd and, two years later, at Kandinsky's Moscow school, the Vkhutemas. It was there that

Barnoff-Rossiné perfected his celebrated "Phono-Optic Piano" machine, a Rube Goldberg-like contraption consisting of weighted prisms, swing mirrors, colored filters, and transparent disks that were linked by levers and cogwheels to the keys of a tiny electric piano.

First exhibited on 6 April 1923 at Meyerhold's Theater as the centerpiece of a "Color-Vision Concert," the Phono-Optic Piano projected onto a large screen sets of overlapping, abstract images emanating from painted disks rotating in opposite directions. On the piano keys of his color-light box, Barnoff-Rossiné and his wife played music from Beethoven, Edvard Grieg, and Wagner. How Barnoff-Rossiné mechanized and structured the relationships between his dynamic, Futurist-inspired, painted compositions and the traditional nineteenth-century music is not clear, but an encore performance was given at the Bolshoi Theater the following year.

Eventually with the help and urging of his old Parisian friends, Barnoff-Rossiné left the Soviet Union in 1925. At the Second Aesthetic Congress in Berlin that year, he once again successfully demonstrated his sound-color machinery, gathering still more fans. And at his haunting grounds in Paris, Barnoff-Rossiné developed several variations on the Phono-Optic Piano, including a similar-looking device used to measure precious stones. In 1943, Barnoff-Rossiné, the Russian-born progenitor of the Fillmore light-and-sound show, was arrested by the Gestapo and sent to Germany, where he died one year later.

RUSSIAN FUTURISM IN THE WEST

Yefim Golyshef

Yefim Golyshef (1897–1970), a legendary figure in the history of Berlin Dada, was considered a musical *wunderkind* and an accomplished painter at twenty-two. Born in a Ukrainian town, where his father befriended Kandinsky, but educated in Germany, Golyshef had developed an atonal twelve-tone scale, based on the principles of the "duration complex," independently of Schoenberg and Roslavetz. He returned to Moscow at the start of the First World

War, but by 1919 he was once again back in his beloved Berlin, carrying with him the pronouncements and aesthetic ideas of Khlebnikov and Matyushin. Golyshef's youthful enthusiasm and Russian Futurism's novelty reinvigorated the Berlin Dada crowd, who, having exhausted their negativist ethic, were now in constant search for new performance techniques.

Raoul Hausmann was entranced with Golyshef's untitled abstract ink drawings and Assemblages of jelly jars, hair, glass, and paper lace. On 30 April 1919, Golyshef appeared at the Graphisches Kabinett for a soirée entitled "DADA-Machinel." Hausmann, with his "eidophonique memory," recorded Golyshef's delivery in remarkable detail years later:

Golyshef entered with a young woman dressed in white. I can still see this scene today as if nothing had changed. With a feeble smile, Golyshef turned toward the grand piano and, making a tiny gesture of an innocent, white angel with his hand, sat down. He said in the voice of an electronic puppet: "A performance of

The Antisymphony in Three Parts (The Circular Guillotine).

a) The Provocative Injection.

b) The Chaotic Oral Cavity.

c) The Piable Super-FA.

Well, well, Herr Johann Sebastian Bach, your well-tempered trash will experience the clashing of the dodecahedral Antisymphony! Out and away with the fine pedantries of the, ach, so splendid, established traditions! Dada will triumph in sound as well! Ladies and gentlemen, do your rust-encrusted ears resound? Then, let the musical circular-saw cut right through them! Douche away the dregs of your voice from the chaotic oral cavities with Golyshef!"[19]

With the assistance of a kitchen utensil–playing orchestra and an imitative Dalcroze dancer, Golyshef performed his atonal *Antisymphony*. For Hausmann, the jumbled noise of found objects was a revelation: "His arhythm, his transparent notes, his mix of tones … which no longer want to be harmonies, is simply

Songs from the Museum of the Future

DADA."[20] Then after signing a few Dada manifestos, Golyshef gravitated toward Berlin's more traditional avant-garde music scene. He became friendly with Ferruccio Busoni, Kurt Weil's master teacher, and composed two experimental operas and the symphonic poem "The Iron Song." Mostly, Golyshef created scores for silent and early sound film. In 1931, Vsevolod Pudovkin, the pivotal Soviet filmmaker, commissioned Golyshef to write the musical accompaniment for his motion picture *Igbenbu, the Great Hunter.*

"A degenerate artist with Bolshevik tendencies," Golyshef knew enough to depart Berlin quickly after the Nazi coup in 1932. The thirties found him, like so many other Jewish intellectuals, circulating across Portuguese, Spanish, and French borders. Caught in the Vichy zone during the Nazi occupation of France, Golyshef worked as a "German" chemist for the Axis war effort. In 1956 he emigrated to Brazil, where he was engaged as a director of a university art museum in São Paulo. Golyshef returned to Paris in 1966 to prepare a Dada exhibition and died there four years later.

Artur Vincent Lourié

Another Russian composer associated with Futurism was Artur Vincent Lourié (1892–1966), who achieved a measure of fame in Paris and Los Angeles. A protégé of Kublin, who, needless to say, heralded him as an "absolute genius," Lourié was a thoroughly annoying, foppish character, always appearing with a monstrous black bow tie beneath a sarcastic, pasted-on smile, and introducing himself with a surfeit of bizarre patronymics that included, in addition to "Vincent" (from Van Gogh), "Percy Bysshe," in honor of Shelley. A superb pianist with an eccentric style, he put into practice Kublin's 1910 plea for independent music utilizing quarter and eighth tones. At the beginning of 1914, Lourié collaborated with the Georgian painter Georgi Yakulov and Futurist writer Benedikt Livshits to produce the first counter–Western European manifesto, "We and the West." It was as much an attack on Marinetti as on the tradition-bound artists of France and Germany.

During the First World War, Lourié easily floated from antibourgeois Futurist polemics to revolutionary politics. A polychromatic piece of his accompanied Mayakovsky's pro-Soviet 1918 poem, "Our March." That same year, Lourié had himself appointed head of the Music Section of the Soviet Education Ministry. Wielding immense power for the first time, Lourié attempted to promote quarter-tone and dissonant music, but negative responses from members of the musicians' union were so uniform and vociferous that Lourié had to consider resigning. In 1922, Lourié did more than that—he emigrated to Berlin, where he joined with Busoni. Two years later, Lourié moved to Paris, this time befriending Stravinsky. In France, Lourié produced many symphonic compositions with Russian themes and a opera based on the bubonic plague in medieval England. Following Stravinsky's lead, Lourié came to the United States in 1941 and continued to teach and work until his death in 1966.

Iliazd

The son of a Georgian French instructor, Ilya Zdanevich (1894–1975), or Iliazd, as he was later known, discovered Futurism in 1911 when he read the works of Marinetti. Over the next five years, while ostensibly studying law in St. Petersburg, Iliazd participated in various Futurist activities of the Centrifuge group. (Iliazd thought the Hylaeas, except for Kruchenykh and Khlebnikov, were completely out of date.) Defying the censors who banned its publication even though all the dialogue appeared in pseudo-Albanian, Iliazd's first play, *Yanko, the King of Albania,* was staged privately in a Petrograd studio space in 1916. A parody in the style of Alfred Jarry's *Ubu Roi, Yanko* resembled something on the order of an absurd, medieval Ukrainian folk play, with a ridiculous narrator, defecating groans, and an unfolding slapstick plot. In 1917, Iliazd returned with the poets Igor Terentiev and Kruchenykh to his native Tiflis. There he launched his own Futurist unit, 41°, complete with cabaret and publishing imprint. Between 1917 and 1922, he finished a cycle of five zaum plays.

A natural linguist and the only non-Russian zaum writer, Iliazd invented a transrational language that owed little to Slavic roots or the anti-Westernizing attitudes of Khlebnikov. For Iliazd, zaum was indeed a personal if universally expressive language with inventive scatological and humorous spoken thoughts. Like children's nonsensical rhymes, an exciting sense of almost-decipherable meanings and near intelligibility floated over each his poetic neologisms. Moreover, Iliazd's plays (called *dras*), although printed in a wild, idiosyncratic typographical style, anticipating Surrealist design, were dramatically more stageworthy than *Victory Over the Sun* or *Zangezi.* In his *Le-Dantyu as a Beacon,* the fifth number in the series, each of the characters, including those based on real people, articulates with a phonetic quality that matches personality to a zaumatic directive: the Holy Ghost character uses strange and breathless words formed only from consonants to denote firmness; in an earlier play, *Donkey for Hire,* the vocabulary of the nymphomaniac figure, Zokhna, centers around the labial and "female erotic" sounds of *b*, *m*, and *p*.

Sent to Paris in 1922 as a curator of a Russian modern art exhibit, which was cancelled by the Soviet government when he arrived, Iliazd remained in France in protest or as a matter of artistic choice. After joining the Paris Dadas, the ever-resourceful Iliazd quickly staged *Le-Dantyu as a Beacon* and published the text in a small but overly elaborate edition. Emigré avant-garde artists, such as Hausmann, Hans Arp, Max Ernst, and Picasso, with whom he formed a long and successful collaboration, were totally fascinated with Iliazd's zaum writings. Iliazd's curiosity was limitless. He worked in ballet, travel and science literature, book design, poetry, and historical scholarship, producing several studies of ficticious biographies and a volume on Byzantine culture. After marrying a Nigerian princess in 1943, Iliazd's writings took on a somewhat conservative bent, leaving it to others in Paris to document the Georgian's earlier zaum period. Still active in literature in 1975, he died at age eighty-nine.

CREATORS OF ELECTRONIC MUSIC

Lev Termin

In October 1921, an acoustical engineer, Lev Termin (1896–1980), played Glinka's "Lark" on his electronic musical oscillator, the Aetherophon, before a fascinated Lenin. This opened the doors for Russia's participation in synthesized electronic music. In fact, Russians would soon dominate the field in Europe and North America. Although similar signal generators existed elsewhere, Termin's invention, later called the theremin, or thereminvox (to match the Soviet physicist's new francophied name, "Dr. Leon Thérémin"), was the first high-frequency electronic instrument to gain fame and widespread acceptance. The music-organ module consisted of a vertical antenna and a circular wire affixed to a beat-frequency audio box. The theremin emitted a single tone whose pitch and volume was controlled by the motion and proximity of the performer's hands over and around the two protrusions. Because of difficulties of transversing pitches manually, a fingerboard was later added. Still, the theremin produced near-miraculous sounds. Some predicted that it would replace the modern orchestra completely.

In 1923, Thérémin's machine was successfully exhibited in Berlin. An even greater sensation was created the next year when the first full-scale electronic music concert was given in Leningrad. Written for a full orchestra and a theremin, which was expertly manipulated by its inventor, Andrei Pashchenko's "Symphonic Mystery" was presented to an amazed crowd. Other Soviet composers, such as Vladimir Sokolov, based their entire repertory on the electric synthesizer. Traveling to the United States in 1927 with an improved design, Thérémin gave several solo performances in Germany and France. In New York, after a spectacular demonstration that was broadcast on radio, he applied for an American patent.

Songs from the Museum of the Future

Within days, RCA brought the manufacturing rights to the theremin, making the Russian Thérémin and RCA considerably wealthier.

Concerts that relied on the new sounds of the theremin marveled Western audiences from Paris to Los Angeles. Hollywood, in particular, as it reorganized for the revolution in talking pictures, understood the commercial value of the electrically generated device. Composers could approximate the true sounds of a large orchestra (as well as added filmic sound effects) in their bungalows or in rehearsal halls as they correlated their music to the directors' rough cuts. By the time Thérémin returned to the Soviet Union for the life of a senior engineer in 1938, all the major American film studios possessed several versions of the RCA music machine and worked them repeatedly. Nearly every electronic synthesizer invented since then owes it origins to Dr. Thérémin's "ether-wave" box.

Joseph Schillinger

The most successful composer for the theremin was Joseph Schillinger (1895–1943), a legendary émigré and mentor to George Gershwin. Born in Kharkhov to a middle-class Jewish family, Schillinger manifested, from the earliest age, contrasting musical traits of strict, traditional classicism and impulsive experimentation. Shortly before the revolution, he graduated from St. Petersburg Imperial Conservatory of Music with high distinction. Within a year, however, Schillinger published a Futurist-like treatise, "The Electrification of Music," calling for known orchestral instrumentation to be abolished and replaced by electronic and mechanical sound paraphernalia. A natural teacher and linguist as well as designer and mathematician, he held a series of important cultural posts in Ukrainian academies and administrations between 1918 and 1922, when Kharkov changed hands politically fourteen times. In 1922, Schillinger moved to Petrograd, where he received a professorship in musicology at the State Institute of Musical Education and a senior lecturer position at the Art History University. In addition, he served on the Board of Education there and in Moscow.

During the twenties, Schillinger gained recognition as a foremost Soviet composer. A modernistic keyboard variation on "The Internationale," called *Sonata Rhapsody* (1924) brought him carefully voiced accolades from many quarters, including, curiously enough, members of the GPU, the feared secret police. Lifelong studies in ethnographic music informed Schillinger's next orchestral work, *The March of the Orient* (1924), which was performed by the Persimfans, the experimental "conductorless" orchestra of Moscow. In 1927, Schillinger was awarded highest honors for his *October, a Symphonic Rhapsody,* a work that celebrated the Soviet Union's first decade and that was favorably compared to Beethoven's revolutionary opus. A duel interest in the music of primitive Caucasian tribes and American jazz brought Schillinger to the attention of John Dewey, who invited him to the United States.

In America, Schillinger collaborated with Thérémin to produce several electronic music performances, including Schillinger's *First Airphonic Suite* (1929) in Cleveland and two programs of modern music at Carnegie Hall with an ensemble of fourteen theremins. For three years, Schillinger promoted Thérémin's invention, assisting his *landsman* from Leningrad by writing theremin manuals and developing second- and third-generation models of the instrument. Schillinger's schoolboy prophecy of 1918 was slowly coming true: "music plus electricity equals the sound of the twentieth century."

From 1930 to his death in 1943, Schillinger revolutionized the teaching of composition in America. At music departments in East coast universities and among private studios, the Schillinger System, based on absolute mathematical principles, became the dominant theory for commercial and popular music. It was said that Schillinger could cover a two-year course of harmonics in three short sessions. Professional composers and musicians such as Oscar Levant, Vernon Duke, Benny Goodman, and Glenn Miller flocked to study with the Russian master. George Gershwin credited him with his dazzling orchestrations for *Porgy and Bess*. Most of all,

Hollywood adapted Schillinger's ideas, which were published in *Schillinger's System of Musical Composition* (New York, 1941) and in the posthumous *Mathematical Basis of the Arts* (New York, 1948).

In the years 1927 and 1928, Soviet public interest in experimental theater and music plunged dramatically. While the government was gearing up for a grand and tumultuous campaign at the beginning of the thirties, attacking the avant-garde in the name of Socialist realism, the novelty of revolutionary and anti-nineteenth-century techniques had worn remarkably thin. The majority of Russian people wanted simple, bourgeois entertainment. The established leftist theaters did not go out of business, but their productions generally took on a less radical, more literary bent. Melodramatic action and cinematic decor replaced abstract language and sound. Of course, there were notable exceptions.

TERENTIEV, THE LAST FUTURIST

The former 41° poet and "grammarian" of zaum, Igor Terentiev (c. 1895–1941) opened his own studio theater in the Leningrad journalists' club in 1928. Supported by the students of Pavel Filonov, the Russian painter whose work most resembled that of the French Surrealists, Terentiev redesigned the house and staging area in a riotous display of transparent-skinned animals, plants, and humans. Each of his four productions, staged over a two-year period, employed ingenious sound and speech devices that sonically echoed the disturbingly piercing drawings. Words in the mouths of bored characters decelerated to meaningless phonemes or zaum; backstage city noises overlapped musically with the slang of hooligans and prostitutes; internal thoughts and stage directions were recited by actors in a manner anticipating Brecht's alienation theories. Critics and spectators had little sympathy for Terentiev's comic experiment, however. The Theater of the House of the Press closed in 1929.

MIKHAIL CHEKHOV'S ANTHROPOSOPHICAL
SPEECH FORMATION

Mikhail Chekhov (1891–1955), the nephew of the writer Anton Chekhov, became one of the most popular and acclaimed actors in Moscow during the teens and twenties. He was also the most important theatrical practitioner to emigrate to the West. In his exile, Chekhov attempted to form a series of studios and dramatic workshops that would totally transform the crass, commercial theater world of Europe and America into spiritual vehicles and showcases for great art. Yet, for completely different reasons, the material problems that Chekhov encountered in atheistic Soviet Russia were recapitulated in the capitalist West. In Paris, New York, and Hollywood—but long before that, in Moscow—Chekhov utilized one of the most intricate systems of abstract phoneme alphabets for the modern stage.

Famous for his emotionally striking characters and grotesque patterns of gesture, Chekhov received glowing praises from both the traditionally minded Moscow Art Theater and the avant-garde followers of Vsevolod Meyerhold and the constructivists. Beginning in 1917, however, Chekhov exhibited signs of nervous fatigue and alcoholic-induced depression. Strange fits of uncontrollable laughter and stammering plagued his early acting career. Offstage, the morose Chekhov even claimed to be able to "hear" and "see" faraway conversations. His director and mentor, Konstantin Stanislavsky, hired a team of psychoanalysts to cure Chekhov of his self-destructive behavior and acute paranoia. They failed utterly, as did a pair of hypnotists that followed. Yet books on Hinduism and yoga seemed to assuage the spiritually starved artist. Chekhov's fascination with reincarnation and other aspects of the occult quickly developed. After the revolution, he discovered Rudolf Steiner's spiritual science, called anthroposophy.

An apostate theosophist, Rudolf Steiner had established his own religious centers in Germany and Switzerland during the teens that, among other esoteric activities, investigated the correspondences among color, movement, sound, and thought. (Anthroposophists demonstrated equal interest in architecture and agriculture.) Movement recitals and enactments of Steiner's Mystery Dramas proved to be ideal forums for anthroposophical belief. To accommodate these artistic rites, Steiner and his colleagues invented Eurhythmy, "the science of visible speech," and Speech Formation. These were separate theatrical tools that borrowed from secret but universal movement-and-sound vocabularies.

In Moscow, Chekhov witnessed demonstrations of Eurhythmy and Speech Formation as presented by small groups of Steiner's Russian disciples. Immediately, Chekhov adapted these anthroposophical teachings to aspects of Stanislavsky's actor training. In 1919, he opened his own independent studio, where he tried to blend the theatrical truth of Stanislavsky's system with the spiritual and aesthetic qualities of Steiner's occult science. Financial and psychological conditions militated against the success of such an antimaterialist project until 1924, when Stanislavsky gave Chekhov an entire theater studio complex, the Second Moscow Art Theater, to carry out his experiments.

Finally, Chekhov was able to train young professional actors in the ineffable work of Steiner. Eurhythmy and Speech Formation giddily came out of the Soviet closet. In the spirit of synesthesia, performers were asked to convert the sounds of words into pure movement and color, forgetting their so-called meanings. Shakespeare, Chekhov maintained, could only be magically understood in accordance with his abstract use of language. For rehearsals of *Hamlet,* Chekhov substituted the throwing of balls for the normative interaction of dialogue. Against all predictions, Chekhov's anthroposophical *Hamlet* (1924) achieved its lofty goals. It was one of the sensations of the interwar Soviet theater. Other productions of the Second Moscow Art Theater, starring Chekhov, were almost as well received, but Chekhov's actors began to doubt the efficacy or social health of the Eurhythmy and Speech Formation regimen. In

1927, a full-fledged rebellion against Chekhov was reported in the Moscow newspapers. "Sick mystic" and "decadent" were among the appellations hurled at the director-actor. To save his life and career, Chekhov prepared to go into exile.

Rudolf Steiner's Speech Formation as Taught by Mikhail Chekhov

Phoneme	Feeling/ Image	Pose- Movement	Color
Ah	Wonder	Arms raised over head	Red
Aa	Protection	Arms crossed over chest	Pale red
B	Shelter	Arms wrapped around chest	Blue
Ch	Change	Arms flexed upward	Dark violet
D	Gravity	Arms bent and down	Lilac
E	Power	Right arm raised in salute	Yellow-orange
F	Release	Elbows and wrists bent	Reddish
G	Move against	Left arm bent over head, right arm pointing down	Blue
H	Delight	Arms around chest with left arm above	Blueish
K	Aggression	Right hand in oath	Vermillion
L	Creative force	Arms by side and down	Orange
M	Agreement	Arms crossed with left over right	Violet
N	Contempt	Right arm up and bent with palm cupped	Lilac
O	Sympathy	Arms in a ring	Blue
P	Sharpness	Arms raised and bent at elbow and wrist	Green-blue
R	Transformation	Upper torso bent back, wrists out and bent	Green
S	Potency	Arms down with right hand pointing at left	Black
Sh	Disappearance	—	—
T	Union	Arms bent over head	Green
Ts	Excitability	—	—
U	Penetration	Arms out and parallel	Lilac
V	Expansion	Arms out and bent away at wrists	Red
Y	Change	—	—

Compiled from Rudolf Steiner, *Über Eurythmische Kunst* (Cologne: DuMont Verlag, 1983), *passim;* Gordon, *Program of the Minor Leftists in the Soviet Theatre,* pp. 122–125; and transcriptions in the Michael Chekhov archive in New York. Note: Eurhythmists affixed three different colors (internal, veil, and robe) to each phoneme and movement. For purposes of this chart, I have included only the "internal" color.

In Berlin, Vienna, Paris, and Riga, Chekhov's plans to establish new theaters and studios ultimately failed. An esoteric production of *The Castle Awakens* was mounted in 1931 by one of Chekhov's Parisian workshops using a Steinerian Speech Formation language, but local reviewers and émigré Russians thought little of it—mostly for reasons of language. In 1936, Chekhov began his last journey, teaching and acting in the English-speaking world, first in Britain and then in the United States. Chekhov continued to employ teachers of Speech Formation at his studios, but resistance to occult beliefs in any form was powerful on Broadway and in Hollywood. At the time of his death in 1955, Chekhov had already been nominated for an Academy Award and praised as a master coach for film actors. Marilyn Monroe called him the greatest influence on her life, except for Abraham Lincoln.

SOVIET RADIO

The dramatic use of radio entered Russian life around 1929. Radio had captured the imaginations of Russian Futurists and constructivists from Khlebnikov to Sergei Tretyakov in the early twenties, but little resulted from it. Meyerhold and Tairov directed innovative theatrical pieces on radio in the thirties; yet again these were isolated incidences.[21] Only in the early sixties—possibly related to Thérémin's 1961 appearance on Radio Moscow—did Russian Sound Creation find its way to Soviet radio.

NOTES

1. P. D. Ouspensky, *In Search of the Miraculous* (New York: Harcourt Brace, 1949), p. 297.

2. Mel Gordon, "Gurdjieff's Movement Demonstrations," *The Drama Review* 22 (1978), pp. 32–44.

3. Wassily Kandinsky and Franz Marc, eds., *The Blaue Reiter Almanac*, trans. Henning Falkenstein, ed. Klaus Lankheit (1912; reprint, New York: Viking Press, 1974). This translation contains both *The Yellow Sound* and "On Stage Composition."

4. Nikolai Kublin, "Free Music," in *The Blaue Reiter Almanac*, pp. 141–146.

5. Included in a privately printed anthology, Nikolai Kublin, *Charters and Declarations of Russian Futurists* (Moscow, 1914.)

6. Anna Lawton and Herbert Eagle, eds., *Russian Futurism through Its Manifestoes, 1912–1928* (Ithaca: Cornell University Press, 1988), pp. 53–54.

7. Quoted in Lawton and Eagle, *Russian Futurism*, p. 65.

8. Ibid., pp. 65–66.

9. Ibid., pp. 93–94.

10. Velimir Khlebnikov, *The King of Time*, trans. Paul Schmidt, ed. Charlotte Douglas (Cambridge, MA: Harvard University Press), pp. 193–194.

11. René Fulop-Miller, *The Mind and Face of Bolshevism*, trans. by F. S. Flint and D. F. Tait (New York: Alfred Knopf, 1928), p. 262.

12. Walter Duranty, "'Machine Dance' Delights Moscow," *The New York Times*, 30 November 1923, p. 26.

13. Quoted in Richard Stourac and Kathleen McCreery, *Theatre as a Weapon* (London: Routledge & Kegan Paul, 1986), p. 53.

14. Fulop-Miller, *The Mind and Face of Bolshevism*, p. 261.

15. Quoted in Gordon, "Program of the Minor Leftists in the Soviet Theatre, 1919–1924" (Ph. D. diss., New York University, 1981), p. 189.

16. FEX Group, "Eccentric Manifesto," trans. Lynn Ball, *The Drama Review* 19 (1975), pp. 95–109.

17. Sergei Radlov, "On the Pure Elements of the Actors' Art," trans. Lynn Ball, *The Drama Review* 19, p. 123.

18. Quoted in Boris Schwartz, *Music and Musical Life in Soviet Russia 1917–1970* (London: Barrie & Jenkins, Ltd., 1972), p. 53.

19. Quoted in Mel Gordon, "Berlin Dada: A History of Performance," *The Drama Review* 18, (1974), pp. 114–124.

20. Raoul Hausmann, *Am Anfang war Dada* (Giessen: Anabas-Verlag, 1971), p. 106.

21. For a complete history, see Aleksandr Sherel, *Rampa u Mikrofona* (Moscow: Iskusstvo, 1985).

THE SYMPHONY OF SIRENS (1923)

Arseni Avraamov

translated from the Russian by Mel Gordon _____

When the morning whistles roar

In the outlying districts

It is not the call of slavery

It is the song of the future.

A. Gastev

Of all the arts, music possesses the greatest power for social organization. The oldest myths show mankind's awareness of this. Orpheus tamed wild beasts with his lyre. Joshua smashed Jericho's stronghold with a mere trumpet. Amphion's flute conjured up majestic cathedrals in Thebes. Pythagoras heard the music of the spheres in the structure of the cosmos and in the very movements of celestial bodies.

In myth and history, music and community singing were the common features of mankind's social life and, in religious and secular rites, its most festive moments. Collective labor (from serfs to soldiers) is inconceivable without songs and music. One would have thought that the high organizational level of factory labor under capitalism would have created a worthy form of musical embodiment. It needed the October Revolution, however, to bring to life the concept of the *Symphony of Sirens*. The capitalist system creates anarchistic tendencies, but fear of workers rallying in solidarity prevented their own music from shaping itself freely. Every morning, a chaotic industrial roar beckoned the people for bondage.

Then the revolution came. Once, at night—an unforgettable night—Red Petersburg sounded with a many-thousand mighty chorus of horns, whistles, and sirens. And in response, thousands of trucks rushed to the outposts throughout the city bristling with bayonets. The Red Guard rushed to encounter Kornilov's vanguards. In this formidable moment, the shrieking chaos had to be tied together with one single will in order to substitute the cries of alarm for the victorious hymn of "The Internationale." The Great October Revolution! Again sirens scream all across Russia and the cannons roar but still there is no unified organizational voice.

Nineteen nineteen. The Volga. Lower Novgorod. We see echelons of Red soldiers leave to oppose Kolchak in Kazan. The entire fleet's whistles sound until the great smoke disappears. This is the first organized attempt. It is difficult—unable to succeed because there are too many sirens—but the contours of "The Internationale" can nevertheless be distinguished.

The year 1922. Baku. Navigation opens. Twenty-six ships of the oil fleet leave for Ashtrakham. The entire fleet roars, including the docks and shipworks. A grandiose orchestra. It's decided: it will harmoniously play on the Fifth Anniversary of the Revolution. And it did.

For the Sixth Anniversary, we want every town with at least ten boilers to organize a well-deserved "accompaniment" for the revolutionary festivities, and here we present a manual for organizing the "Symphony of Sirens" applicable to various local conditions.

THE STEAM-WHISTLE MACHINE

One of the most important conditions of a successful performance is a preliminary construction of the steam-whistle machine. The machine is mounted either on a conveniently situated factory boiler or on a portable steam engine or a ship steamer. In Baku, it was put on the destroyer *Dostoyny*. Advantages of the mobile machine are evident: it can be moved to one or another part of town at different moments of a holiday and displayed independently outside town.

The steam-whistle machine's equipment is not very complicated: from twenty to fifty whistles are screwed into a larger pipe. The pipe can be any shape, depending on the site of the installation: straight, semicircular, or with two (to three) bends. It's all the same concerning the sound. It is important to arrange the steam supply in the center since, at the ends, faucets or valves are mounted to draw off water before performing.

Otherwise water will pour through the sirens' valves and the rhythmical accuracy of performance will suffer.

The sirens are tuned by shortening the air column in a supplementary cylinder by any means, either by using a piston or just by hammering a wooden log in and fixing it at a particular depth. The least hydroscopic wood should be selected; otherwise its swelling under the influence of the steam will spoil the accuracy of pitch even after two or three rehearsals. Cylinder-shaped sirens can be retuned (only in the range of one tone, and at most one-third) by putting in washers and removing the bottom from a steam spout. A considerable change of height will spoil a timbre and tone power. If available sirens lack the ability to produce higher tones, one can change that by fixing the steam outlets in the cylinder. Also, one can achieve an overtone sounding (an octave, one fifth, or a double octave higher) through an eccentric mounting. However, such sirens require caution and constant checking—they may "deceive" at the moment of performance due to the slightest change of pressure.

Generally, it's necessary to find a pressure norm and keep it constant through both tuning and performing. One hundred–120 pounds will provide good effect (the furnace should be constantly restoked). The steam-whistle machine's installation should be sufficiently high in place not to deafen the performers with the roar. It's quite natural that after the completion the structure should be tested for stability of steam or water pressure, otherwise the performers take risk of getting burnt. The entire machine must be warmly wrapped so that the siren's valves will avoid frequent steam cooling and water concentration in the valves. The machine's expenses are relatively small and in return it can be utilized for permanent factory use.

The number of tones is minimal (for one melody of "The Internationale" twelve: E, F, Fis, G, Gis, A, H, C, D, E, F, G). With seventeen tones, it already becomes possible to harmonize the melody. More tone pipes untie the musician's hands, allowing him to give his own interpretation, freely harmonize the anthem, and, in general, write a genuine symphony. An increase in tones follows the chromatic scale from two and a half to four (if possible) octaves.

One can manage without a steam-whistle machine only if there is a sufficient number of the mobile boilers (steam engines, ships) and if it's possible to concentrate them in one place (railroad station, pier). But even in this case, a steam-whistle machine helps create the impression of a unified "musical instrument." When there are many immobile sirens (from factories, plants, steam mills, docks, depots, etc.), they can be spaced, developing the feeling of a musical picture. Thus, for example, in Baku (see the following instructions) the picture of alarm and battle was created. Since there was a great distance between implacements, performers were signaled by gun shots. Groups played in compact harmony and provided a background for the principal collective and the steam-whistle machine.

It is necessary to take into account sound distances from the signal gun to the group and from the group to the festival square for precise sequences. Too distant groups cannot take part in performing "The Internationale" because the gun, for the time being, plays the role of a "big drum" in the song and cannot be used as a signal. But the mobile steam-whistle machine can be temporarily moved to enforce one or another group if it is returned to its position by the finale.

SIRENS, AUTOMOTIVE TRANSPORT, BELLS, AND AIRPLANES_____

Fleet and plant sirens make up a specific group of instruments although they do not take part in harmonic evolution of a musical work. They sound off independently at particular episodes, either one at a time or in unison on a signal. Bass horns with rifle and machine gun volleys are the best means of soundwriting and signaling. With "good performers" one can attempt to give them harmonic or melodic assignments though it is hardly applicable in the ordinary tone music structure. "Differential" music of sirens belongs completely to the future, whereas today we are scarcely able to feel specific rules of its harmony and melody.

Automobile transport located close to the place of celebration (in one of the neighboring streets) is valuable mainly for its noise effects. But we can make up a special timbre and tone group provided the transport has a sufficient variety of tone signals. Engine noise, especially of trucks, as well as that of low flying hydroplanes, creates strong effects of overwhelming impression.

Chimes of alarm, sorrow, of cheerful festivity are used for adequate episodes without harmonic consideration. Or, the entire structure of the symphony can be selected beforehand with regard to available bells. (In Baku, the whole "Internationale" performance was accompanied with melodic chime of fleet bells.)

ARTILLERY

If the sirens are scattered around a large area, it is necessary to have at least one heavy cannon for signaling and to fire an artillery shell (buckshot will not do, since explosion in the air is dangerous and gives a secondary report which may fool the performers). A field gun can pass for the "big drum" effect. Experienced machine gunners (in case they use real ammunition) can not only imitate drumming but can do complicated rhythmical figures. Blank shots and continuous volley fire are for soundwriting moments.

TOWER

To conduct a symphony, a tower must be erected on an elevated spot close to the center of the performance. The simplest construction consists of a few telegraph poles connected with their ends in a "Swedish mast." A platform with a compartment is topped with holes for flagstaffs or a device to hoist them. A tower should be designed with respect to the performers' field of vision set against a clear sky. Brightly colored flags should be chosen (like those used for sea signaling) to be seen from a distance. Performers from the fleet, steam engines, army batteries, machine gunners, and autotransport take their positions near the tower to see the signals precisely. A field telephone must be installed on the tower connected with the battery, festival square, shooting range, and the most important groups. It is useful to have a megaphone and live communication with the steam-whistle machine. The leader should conduct with the right hand while he signals to the artillery with his left. The battery should be one or two hundred meters closer to the square of celebration than the tower to avoid fire delay.

[Editors' note: Notes to the performance text of "The Internationale" have here been deleted.]

On 6 November, last year, in issues of *Baku's Worker*, *Labor*, and *Communist* (published in the Turkish language), the following appeared:

For the 5th Anniversary of the October Revolution.
Instructions for "The Symphony of Sirens"

On the morning of the Fifth Anniversary on 7 November, all vessels of Gocasp, Voenflot, and Uzbekcasp, including smaller ships and boats, concentrate near the railroad pier by seven o'clock am. Every vessel will receive written instructions and a group of musicians. Then each will take a designated place by the customs pier area. The destroyer Dostoyny with the steam-whistle machine and small vessels will be anchored ahead opposite the tower.

By $9{:}00$ the entire fleet should be in place. All available shuttle engines, local and armored trains, and repaired steam engines will arrive at the same time. Cadets of the Fourth Armavir courses of the higher party school, students of Azgoconservatory, and all professional musicians should be at the pier no later than $8{:}30$.

At $10{:}00$ troops, artillery, machine guns, armored cars, and autotransport will take their positions according to the garrison's order. Airplanes and hydroplanes should be ready as well.

At no later than $10{:}30$, the signalers take their place at regional and rail terminals.

The noon cannon is cancelled.
The fireworks volley will signal Zykh, Bely Gorod, Bibi, Abot, and Baylon to head off toward the road roaring.

The fifth gun signals the 1st and 2nd district of the Black Town.

The tenth gun—sirens of trade offices, Azneft, and docks.

The fifteenth gun—town districts, airplanes take off. Chimes.

The eighteenth gun—sirens of the depot and steamengines left there. (At the same time, the first company of the Armavir courses headed by joint brass orchestra and "Varashavanka" marches off the square toward the piers.)

An alarm reaches its climax and terminates by the twenty-fifth cannon.

Pause.

The triple chord of the sirens "Hurrah" from the piers

Termination signal from the steam-whistle machine.

"The Internationale" (four times).
On the half verse, a joint brass orchestra sounds and the automobile chorus with the "Marseillaise."

At the second repetition, the whole square joins in the singing.

At the end of the fourth verse, cadets and the infantry return from the square
where they are met with a "Hurrah."

At the end, there is a universal festive chorus of all sirens and horns
for three minutes accompanied by the bells.

Termination signal from the steam-whistle machine.

Ceremonial march. Artillery, fleet, autotransport, and machine guns receive their signals directly from the conductor's tower.
Red and white flag is used for the battery;
blue and yellow for the sirens;
a four-colored flag for machine guns,
and a red flag for solo ships, steam engines, and automobile chorus.

The Symphony of Sirens

On the battery's signal, "The Internationale" repeats two more times during the final procession.

Stoking of the furnaces is obligatory wherever there is a signaling siren.

All the above is for the leadership and irrevocable execution under the responsibility of the leading establishments: military authorities, Azneft, Gocasp, and related educational institutions. Every performer must have his Instructions on him during the celebrations.

The Chairman of TSOK is M. Chagin.

Symphony of Sirens organizer is Mrs. Avraamov.

As seen from the instructions, the symphony symbolized in sound the image of unrest, of ongoing battle, and then the victory of "The Internationale" army.

Any program can be created. Everything depends on the orchestra's power and district's location. "The Internationale" music alone can be a minimum performance. Also a mourning march, if the procession passes the graves of the revolution's martyrs. After all, any musical work can be performed provided it fits with the number of invented tones and artistic means of a town. A medley of revolutionary melodies is possible. For example, in Baku, as can be seen in the Instructions, the combination of "The Internationale" with the "Marseillaise" was played.

If the steam-whistle machine is kept untouched after the performance, it can be used again, even for signaling the beginning and end of the work day. It would be much better to create a machine with a keyboard to be played by only one or two players, but the problem of this construction (with electromagnetic mechanisms) is in its prohibitive cost of thousands of gold rubles.

GREGORY WHITEHEAD

OUT OF THE DARK
NOTES ON THE NOBODIES OF RADIO ART

The lightning flashes through my skull; mine eye-balls ache and ache; my

whole beaten brain seems as beheaded, and rolling on some stunning

ground. Oh, oh! Yet blindfold, yet will I walk to thee. Light though thou be,

thou leapest out of darkness; but I am darkness leaping out of thee!

Captain Ahab

For most of the wireless age, artists have found themselves vacated (or have vacated themselves) from radiophonic space; thus, the history of radio art is, in this most literal sense, largely a history of nobodies. Periodic visitations have remained isolated occasions; in the context of radio's more entrenched commercial and military identities, such fleeting interference decays quickly.

The nobodies of radio art have been diminished even further by the numbing absence of critical discourse. Such silence can only feed upon itself, eventually making even the thought of radio as cultural space seem remote, farfetched, improbable. By consequence, when radio has appeared under the name of art, it is most often under the degraded guise of industrial artifact, with its commercialized cacophony providing one sound source among others. In this reduced state, radio is no longer an autonomous public space but merely an acoustic readymade to be recontextualized, switched on, and played.[1] Alternately, the investigation of radio has disappeared into the investigation of *sound,* the wireless body stripped and redressed to provide a broadcast identity for the nebulous permutations of diverse *ars acustica.*[2] In this variation, radio art is defined as simply whatever any artist from any medium happens to represent, acoustically, on air.

Radio's gradual drift into such a flatly pedestrian state of mind contrasts sharply with the high-flying and exuberant aspirations first triggered by Marconi's twitching finger: promises of communication with alien beings, the establishment of a universal language, instantaneous travel through collapsing space, and the achievement of a lasting global peace. "It would be almost like dreamland and ghostland, not the ghostland cultivated by a heated imagination, but a real communication from a distance based on true physical laws."[3] However breathless in formulation, this author's coupling of "dreamland and ghostland" roots radio in a vibrant double infinity, the dreamland infinity of the human nervous system oscillating with (and against) the vast ghostland of deep space.

If the dreamland/ghostland is the natural habitat for the wireless imagination, then the material of radio art is not just sound. Radio *happens* in sound, but sound is not really what matters about radio. What does matter is the bisected heart of the infinite dreamland/ghostland, a heart that beats through a series of highly pulsed and frictive oppositions: the radio signal as intimate but untouchable, sensually charged but technically remote, reaching deep inside but from way out there, seductive in its invitation but possibly lethal in its effects. Shaping the play of these frictions, the radio artist must then enact a kind of sacrificial autoelectrocution, performed in order to go straight out of one mind and (who's there?) then diffuse, in search of a place to settle. Mostly, this involves staging an intricate game of position, a game that unfolds among far-flung bodies, for the most part unknown to each other.

Radio art does have something of a *pre*history in the variously electrified adventures recorded in nineteenth-century literature, one conspicuous example provided by Poe's M. Valdemar: a mesmerized Recording Angel. Less obviously, why not rewind Melville's narrative of the Nantucket whaling vessel *Pequod* as an early journey into charged ghostland air? However improbable such a reading may appear at first glance, it is hard to resist including *Moby Dick* within such a discussion because Ahab so persuasively prefigures at least one

Gregory Whitehead

persona for the twisted, schizoid nature of wireless telegraphy. Mad Captain Ahab, himself split from the head down by a "rod-like mark, lividly whitish," resembles, in Ishmael's awe-struck description, "that perpendicular seam sometimes made in the straight, lofty trunk of a great tree, when the upper lightning tearingly darts down it, leaving the tree still greenly alive, but branded."[4] Indeed, Ahab's split body is so unseemly to Ishmael's narrative eye that he almost fails to notice "the barbaric white leg" which for the duration of the voyage will telegraph, through coded tappings across the wooden quarterdeck, the slow unwinding of the captain's mind.

Binding Melville's story to its foregone conclusion and *Pequod*'s crew to his doomed hunt for the White Whale, Ahab's brand haunts *Moby Dick*. The most stunning demonstration of its unearthly spell occurs late in *Pequod*'s ill-fated voyage, when the ship is illuminated by an eerie outburst of corposants in the midst of a violent squall. Her three masts "silently burning in that sulphorous air, like three gigantic wax tapers before an altar," the *Pequod* falls dead silent, her crew transfixed by the spectacle of "God's burning finger."[5] Overruling Starbuck's pleas for mercy, Ahab sets the authority of his own electrocuted body against the lightning that cuts its wild course through the moral fiber of his crew, proclaiming, "Oh, thou clear spirit, of thy fire thou madest me, and like a true child of fire, I breathe it back to thee."

When Ahab's harpoon, fired by his own hand to spear the scarred blubber of Moby Dick, is momentarily transformed into a lightning rod, the crew panics, pushed by the uncanny fireworks display to the brink of mutiny. Without missing a step, Ahab snatches the torched harpoon, waves it among the terrified whalers, and pronounces his single most piercing ultimatum: " 'All your oaths to hunt the White Whale are as binding as mine; and by heart, soul, and body, lungs and life, old Ahab is bound. And that you may know to what tune this heart beats; look ye here; thus I blow out the last fear!' And with one blast of his breath he extinguished the flame." Inflicted by some nameless confrontation with nature, Ahab's brand, doubled by the steel transmitter of his inflamed harpoon, names the *Pequod*'s destiny. The old navel of the *Pequod* (the gold doubloon, nailed to the mainmast as a reward for the first seaman to lay eyes on the White Whale) is displaced by the flare of Ahab's wireless signature or, perhaps closer to the mark, by his *call sign*. So many agitated and authoritarian wands wagging about must invite catastrophe, and *Pequod* herself is soon punctured by Moby's battering brow. Fittingly enough, Ishmael saves himself by seizing upon a floating book jacket: the coffin crafted by Queequeg to store his own dead body-book, inscribed with the intricate cosmogony of his native tribe by a needle-driven recording device: the tattoo.

Though killed by a whale in a novel that predates the first transatlantic transmission by almost exactly half a century, Ahab still stands as one chilling prototype for the wireless persona: suspended between life and death, between redemptive dissemination and lethal degeneracy, *what is it made of and what does it want?* With its scorched skin, aching eyeballs, prosthetic limbs, shocking tail, brain on fire, and blasted breath, should we follow to eternity or stage a mutiny, cut the mindless thing off, tune it out? Is the twitching finger of the telegraph an invitation to electromagnetic pleasure or is it pulling a trigger, pushing a button?

The radiobody cannot give a straight answer, but it challenges the audience to cross and recross the obscure boundaries that separate radio dreamland from radio ghostland, living from dead, utopia from oblivion. Just beneath the promise of a lightning connection to a world of dreamy invisible things lurks a darker potential for spotlessly violent electrocution, for going up in smoke, or going down with the ship. Begin in a radio dreamland, end in a radio war.

II

Incorporating the promise of universal communication bound together with the more immediate prospect of irreversible decay, the radiobody is a composite of opposites: speaking to everyone abstractly and to no one in particular; ubiquitous but fading without a trace; forever crossing boundaries but with uncertain destination; capable of the most intimate communion and the most sudden destruction. Radio is a medium voiced by multiple personalities, perfect for pillow talk, useful as an antidepressant, but also deployable as guiding beam for missile systems. Over the course of the twentieth century, the radio ghostland has come very fully into its own. No surprise, then, that the most notable artist proposals for radio should air on frequencies populated by so many zombie bodies, limbo dancing, inside out.

1. In 1921, Velimir Khlebnikov's Futurist brand of brain fever produced a proposal for radio as "the spiritual sun of the country," built to sing the strange unearthly songs of "lightning birds."[6] Pushing buttons at master controls, the Great Sorcerer of Radio, Khlebnikov would have the power and means to mesmerize the minds of the entire nation, both healing the sick via long-distance hypnotic suggestion and increasing labor productivity through the seasonal transmission of prescribed notes, "for it is a known fact that certain notes like 'la' and 'ti' are able to increase muscle capacity." Depending on the ornithographic predispositions of the wizard-in-the-main-station, human bodies might well be recast as passive receptacles for bird droppings.

Once radio waves have fused with the nation's mental life, the slightest interruption of broadcast projection would provoke "a mental blackout over the entire country, a temporary loss of consciousness." Given the constant threat of blackout, massive brain damage, and collective death, the critical feeders in the main aviary of the Great Sorcerer must be protected, insulated, fortified; fantastic radio projections require protective signage equal to their high-security voltage and are represented in Khlebnikov's vision by the universal

Danger icon of skull and crossbones. Though Futurist artist-engineers would not be permitted the opportunity to orchestrate the polyphony of the Russian Revolution, the design of Radio Khlebnikov's control station anticipates the telecommunications bunkers that would monitor and control the next world war, as the intermingled modulation of birdlike radiowaves with the rattle of human bones certainly provides the wireless imagination with another chilling call sign. Indeed, one of the most accomplished Radio Sorcerers (and bone producers) of all time would spend the last days of his own spellbinding dissemination in just such a "stronghold of steel," searching frantically for the magical "la" or "ti" that might restore muscle power to the atrophied protoplasm of the Thousand Year Reich.

2.   A dozen years later, F. T. Marinetti and Pino Masnata undoubtedly woke up with grave headaches after building the foundation of *La Radia* into their piles of assorted corpses:[7] the corpse of theater, "because radio killed a theater already defeated by sound cinema"; the corpse of cinema, deceased from a variety of "agonizing" wounds, including "reflected illumination inferior to the self-illumination of radio-television"; the corpse of the book, "strangled, suffocated, fossilized"; and the corpse of the The Public, "always retrograde." *La Radia* also mounts an explicit bombing raid on Marinetti's own Variety Theatre, singled out for its crippling dependence on the physical constraints of the earthbound per-forming body. There is also the sinister (though rarely cited) threat of *future* corpse production, in "warning the Semites to identify themselves with their dif-ferent countries if they don't wish to disappear."

Amid the general carnage, who is left to animate *La Radia*? In contrast to Khlebnikov's Grand Sorcerer, whose mission is to conjure up enchanting sensations for airborne delivery to enthralled masses, the Marinetti/Masnata *radiasta* is the engineer of pure emanation, charged with the "detection, amplification and transfiguration of vibrations emitted from dead and living beings." Disdaining the illusionist fantasies of lightning birds and other synesthetic projections, the task of the *radiasta* is nothing less than the realization of an entirely new electromagnetic being, a "pure organism of radiophonic sensations." In sum, the artist-engineer *radiasta* represents the personification of a long-standing Futurist aspiration, underscored by Marinetti/Masnata in *La Radia* as "the overcoming of death with a metallization of the body."[8]

3. In the postwar period, the feverish condition of the ghosted radiobody explodes through Antonin Artaud's blistering *To Have Done with the Judgment of God*. Artaud's urgent address to the People of France, which at some moments seems almost to consume him, was cancelled at the last minute by the director of French national radio, who solemnly intoned the usual litany of objections: obscenity, sacrilege, and anti-Americanism.[9] After listening to a tape of the broadcast, the sense of a deeper fear hangs in the air, the fear of just what might *happen* should the unprepared public be exposed to such an enraged and afflicted persona. The threatening power of this address resides not only in its pure acoustic projection of Artaud's psychic condition, but in his instinctive grasp of radiophonic space, the space of the two infinities. Modulating among the diverse vocal/linguistic frequencies of news report (bulletin: sperm donation a condition

of enrollment in American public schools), hallucination, incantation, talk show (his furious self-interview), glossolallic ejaculation, death rattle, and political tirade, Artaud's performance mirrors the perpetually slipped and mutating demi-dead dreamland/ghostland of radio itself. Dispersed, self-cancelled, splintered, intoxicated, unprecedented, and out of its mind, the hybrid, polyphonous body of *To Have Done with the Judgment of God* is tailor-made for postwar air.

III

With Artaud in mind, let us now return for a moment to the deck of the *Pequod* on the third and final day of Ahab's quest. Locked into Moby Dick's (yes, and *Moby Dick*'s) "infallible wake" and addressing nobody in particular, Ahab casts out yet another remarkable series of ruminations, first professing that *his* body is a *hot* medium: "Ahab never thinks; he only feels, feels; *that's* tingling enough for mortal man! ... Thinking is, or ought to be, a coolness and a calmness; and our poor hearts throb, and our poor brains beat too much for that."[10]

Ahab next tunes his tingling to the invisible wind, which has consistently interfered with the wail of his obsession. At once praised and despised, the wind stands for everything Ahab cannot get his hands on: "Would now the wind but had a body; but all the things that most exasperate and outrage mortal man, all these things are bodiless, but only bodiless as objects, not as agents. There's a most special, a most cunning, oh, a most malicious difference!" Within a matter of hours, Ahab is finally yanked to his death "voicelessly as Turkish mutes bowstring their victim" by the line of his own harpoon.

In the concluding section of *To Have Done with the Judgment of God,* Artaud announces and puts on display his Last Will and Testament, fresh from the autopsy table of the production studio at *Radiodiffusion française.* Here at last is a theatrical bequest designed to explore, explode, and exploit that most special, cunning, and malicious difference that throbs between object and agency—*a body without organs*. For Artaud, only such a body could be free from the maddening god-itch, free from the plague of human desires and from "microbial noxiousness," free to "dance inside out," delirious but also purified, dead to the world but living on air. Like Ahab, Artaud had ample experience of lightning flashed through his skull, though conducted by means rather more earthbound than God's burning finger. But through the exasperated and outraged agency of his radiophony, he could at last find relief from the "infinitesimal inside" of his tortured flesh. Staged within this most charged scenario, technically primitive but conceptually so electric, Artaud's shocked and shocking body could at last find its real place.

Evidently, inhabiting such an infallible wake is not without concurrent risk. As Artaud himself had already written a few months before, "The magic of electric shock drains a death rattle, it plunges the shocked one into that death rattle with which one leaves life."[11] Enter the territory of Bardo, a Tibetan concept designating the limbo region between living and dead but for Artaud also recalling the limbo region of electroshock, the suspended sentence of Artaud's own corporeal nightmare. For Artaud, it was this most special, cunning, and malicious difference that marked the destiny for a body without organs, rolling on some stunning ground: "The world, but it's no longer me, and what do you care, says Bardo, it's me."

IV

Yes, the circuit from Ahab to Artaud is a circuit powered by magnetic death drives and the sick hunger for signal omniscience: but so beats the pulse of twentieth-century broadcast. The alternative potential for casting conceptual, linguistic, and acoustic commotion into an entirely fresh radiophonic dreamland has hardly been tapped: the wild and lively festival of polyphonous radiobodies still remains to be heard.[12] *Out of the Dark:* Voices in every conceivable incarnation, heating up the airwaves, interrupting the flow of everyday information, breaking wind and chilling out, releasing a powerful resuscitation of the playful, libidinal, and liberating radiodream from the *danse macabre* of the ghostland boneyard.

A revitalized tradition of radio art languishes in cultural limbo because today's wireless imagination applies itself exclusively—fervently!—to questions of intensified commodity circulation and precision weapons systems. So far, all "real" radio has to show for itself is a ceaseless cacophony of agitated sales pitches, pop-song patter, and several mountainous piles of corpses. If the idea of radiophony as the autonomous, electrified play of bodies unknown to each other (the unabashed aspiration of radio art) sounds at times like it has been irretrievably lost, it is most likely because the air has already become too thick with the buzz of commerce and war, too overrun by radar beams, burning harpoons, wagging fingers, body brands, and traffic reports to think of anything else. "Light though thou be, thou leapest out of darkness; but I am darkness leaping out at thee!"

NOTES

1. Possibly the best-known deployment of radio as industrial artifact is performed by John Cage in works such as *Speech* and *Radio Music.*

2. These are *musique concrète,* noise art, sound poetry, soundscapes, and the like. The equation of radio art with the simple act of broadcasting such diverse audio productions has been particularly true in Europe, where many state broadcasting systems have established experimental units from time to time. Since these units operate without any pressure to establish a vital relationship to an audience, it is not surprising that thinking through the *prob-*

Gregory Whitehead

lem of the listener has for the most part remained well outside the province of such experiments.

3. P. T. McGrath, "Authoritative Account of Marconi's Work in Wireless Telegraphy," *Century Magazine* 63 (March 1902), pp. 779–780. I borrow this example from Susan J. Douglas's discussion, "Amateur Operators and American Broadcasting: Shaping the Future of Radio," in *Imagining Tomorrow*, ed. Joseph J. Corn (Cambridge, MA: MIT Press, 1987), pp. 35–57.

4. Ishmael's description of Ahab is located in chapter 28 of Herman Melville, *Moby Dick* (New York: New American Library, 1961), pp. 128–131. The picture of Ahab as a firebody is given even stronger emphasis: "He looked like a man cut away from the stake, when the fire has over-runningly wasted all the limbs without consuming them."

5. These quotes, as well as those that follow, are from Melville, *Moby Dick*, chap. 119. The typhoon scene begins on a light-hearted note provided by Stubb, who sings gamely against the gale: "Such a funny, sporty, gamy, jesty joky, hoky-poky lad, in the Ocean, oh!"

6. From Velimir Khlebnikov, "The Radio of the Future," in *The King of Time* (Harvard University Press, 1985), pp. 155–159.

7. All quoted excerpts are from F. T. Marinetti and Pino Masnata, *La Radia,* trans. Stephen Sartarelli, this volume.

8. The tank battles of World War II would soon provide ample testing grounds for the metallized body, beginning with the Italian invasion of Ethiopia.

9. I am indebted to Allen Weiss for helping me to hear Artaud's performance in the broader context of his physical/psychic condition in the period following his release from Rodez. In addition to the essay included in this volume, see Allen Weiss, "Psychopompomania," in *The Aesthetics of Excess* (Albany, SUNY Press, 1989), pp.113–134. All excerpts from Artaud are quoted from the Eshleman translation in this volume.

10. The story of the third day, and Ahab's airborn soliloquy, are both in Melville, *Moby Dick*, chap. 135.

11. Both this statement and the Bardo quote below are from Antonin Artaud, "Artaud le mômo," in *Conductors of the Pit*, trans. Clayton Eshleman (New York: Paragon House, 1988), pp. 179–183.

12. Not to say the airways are entirely dead—isolated bursts of activity have continued to cast out against the current. In the United States, for example, radio art programs such as *New American Radio, Soundings,* and *The Territory of Art* have all helped sustain the potential for future practice.

LA RADIA (1933)

F. T. Marinetti and Pino Masnata

translated from the Italian

by Stephen Sartarelli

Futurism has radically transformed literature with words in freedom aeropoetry and the speedy simultaneous freeword style emptied the theater of boredom through alogical surprise synthesis and dramas of objects immensified the plastic arts with antirealism plastic dynamism and aeropainting created the geometric splendor of a dynamic architecture that uses lyrically and without decoration the new construction materials abstract cinematography and abstract photography   In its second National Congress Futurism decided that the following have been overcome

Overcome the love for woman "by a more intense love for woman as opposed to the erotico sentimental deviations of many foreign avant-gardes whose artistic expressions have failed in fragmentarism and nihilism"

Overcome patriotism "with a more fervent patriotism thus transformed into authentic religion of the Fatherland warning to Semites that they should identify with their various fatherlands if they do not wish to disappear"

Overcome the machine "with an identification of man with the very machine destined to free him from muscular labor and immensify his spirit"

Overcome the Sant'Elia architecture "today triumphant with a Sant'Elia architecture even more explosive with lyric color and originality of discovery"

Overcome painting "with an aeropainting more intensely lived and a polymaterial-tactile plastic art"

Overcome the earth "with the intuition of means devised to realize a voyage to the Moon"

Overcome death "with a metallization of the human body and the purification of the life spirit as a machine force"

Overcome war and revolution "with a ten- or twenty-year artistic-literary war and revolution that you can put in your pocket like indispensable revolvers"

Overcome chemistry "with a nutritional chemistry perfected with free vitamins and calories for everyone"

We now possess a television of fifty thousand points for every large image on a large screen   As we await the invention of teletouch telesmell and teletaste we Futurists are perfecting radio broadcasting which is destined to multiply a hundredfold the creative genius of the Italian race to abolish the ancient nostalgic torment of long

distances and to impose words in freedom everywhere as its logical and natural mode of self-expression

La radia, the name that we futurists have given to the great manifestations of the radio is STILL TODAY (a) realistic

(b) enclosed on a stage (c) idiotized by music that instead of developing toward greater originality and

variety has attained a repulsive, gloomy, or languid monotony (d) a too-timid imitation of the Futurist syn-

thetic theater and words in freedom for the writers of the avant-garde

Alfred Goldsmith of Radio City in New York has said "Marinetti has invented the electric theater   Quite different in con-

ception the two theaters have a point of contact in the fact that in order to be realized they cannot do

without a work of integration, an effort of intelligence on the part of the spectators   The electric the-

ater will require an effort of imagination first from the authors, then from the actors, then from the

spectators"

Even French Belgian German theoreticians and actors of avant-garde radio dramas (Paul Reboux   Theo Freischinann

Jacques Rece   Alex Surchaap   Tristan Bernard   F. W. Bischoff   Victor Heinz Fuchs   Friedrich Wolf

Mendelssohn etc.) praise and imitate the Futurist synthetic theater and words in freedom though almost

all are still obsessed with a realism nevertheless quickly overcome

LA RADIA MUST NOT BE _____

1   theater because radio has killed the theater already defeated by sound cinema

2   cinema because cinema is dying (a) from rancid sentimentalism of subject matter (b) from real-

ism that involves even certain simultaneous sytheses (c) from infinite technical complications (d) from

fatal banalizing collaborationism (e) from reflected brilliance inferior to the self-emitted brilliance of

radio-television

3   books because the book which is guilty of having made humanity myopic implies something

heavy strangled stifled fossilized and frozen (only the great freeword tableaux shall live, the only poetry

that needs to be seen)

F. T. Marinetti and Pino Masnata

LA RADIA ABOLISHES

1   the space and stage necessary to theater including Futurist synthetic theater (action unfolding on a fixed and constant stage) and to cinema (actions unfolding on very rapid variable simultaneous and always realistic stages)

2   time

3   unity of action

4   dramatic character

5   the audience as self-appointed judging mass systematically hostile and servile always against the new always retrograde

LA RADIA SHALL BE

1   Freedom from all point of contact with literary and artistic tradition   Any attempt to link la radia with tradition is grotesque

2   A new art that begins where theater cinema and narrative end

3   The immensification of space   No longer visible and framable the stage becomes universal and cosmic

4   The reception amplification and transfiguration of vibrations emitted by living beings living or dead spirits dramas of wordless noise-states

5   The reception amplification and transfiguration of vibrations emitted by matter   Just as today we listen to the song of the forest and the sea so tomorrow shall we be seduced by the vibrations of a diamond or a flower

6   A pure organism of radio sensations

7   An art without time or space without yesterday or tomorrow   The possibility of receiving broadcast stations situated in various time zones and the lack of light will destroy the hours of the day and night   The reception and amplification of the light and the voices of the past with thermoionic valves will destroy time

8   The synthesis of infinite simultaneous actions

9   Human universal and cosmic art as voice with a true psychology-spirituality of the sounds of the voice and of silence

10   The characteristic life of every noise and the infinite variety of concrete/abstract and real/dreamt through the agency of a people of noises

11   Struggles of noises and of various distances, that is, spatial drama joined with temporal drama

12   Words in freedom   The word has gradually developed into a collaborator of mime and gesture   The word must be recharged with all its power hence an essential and totalitarian word which in Futurist theory is called "word-atmosphere"   Words in freedom children of the aesthetics of machines contain an orchestra of noises and noise-chords (realistic and abstract) which alone can aid the colored and plastic word in the lightning-fast representation of what is not seen   If he does not wish to resort to words in freedom the radiast must express himself in that freeword style which is already widespread in avant-garde novels and newspapers that typically swift quick synthetic simultaneous free-word style

13   Isolated word repetitions of verbs in the infinitive

14   Essential art

15   Gastronomic amorous gymnastic etc. music

16   The utilization of noises sounds chords harmonies musical or noise simultaneities of silence all with their gradations of appoggiatura crescendo and decrescendo which will become strange brushes for painting delimiting and coloring the infinite darkness of la radia by giving squareness roundness spheric geometry in short

17   The utilization of interference between stations and of the birth and evanescence of the sounds

18   The delimitation and geometric construction of silence

19   The utilization of the various resonances of a voice or sound in order to give a sense of the size of the place in which the voice is uttered

     The characterization of the silent or semisilent atmosphere that surrounds and oolors a given voice sound or noise

20   The elimination of the concept or the illusion of an audience which has always had even for books a deforming and damaging influence

ALLEN S. WEISS

——————— Nobody in Europe knows how to scream any more.

Antonin Artaud

What does it really mean, "To hear death in his voice?" How can one attain the impossible narrative position established from the point of view of one's own death? In 1933 Antonin Artaud gave a lecture at the Sorbonne entitled "Le Théâtre et la peste" ("The Theater and the Plague"), which was to become a chapter of his masterpiece, *Le Théâtre et son double* (*The Theater and Its Double*). His presentation is described by Anaïs Nin:

> But then, imperceptibly almost, he let go of the thread we were following and began to act out dying by plague. No one quite knew when it began. To illustrate his conference, he was acting out an agony. "La Peste" in French is so much more terrible than "The Plague" in English. But no word could describe what Artaud acted on the platform of the Sorbonne.... His face was contorted with anguish, one could see the perspiration dampening his hair. His eyes dilated, his muscles became cramped, his fingers struggled to retain their flexibility. He made one feel the parched and burning throat, the pains, the fever, the fire in the guts. He was in agony. He was screaming. He was delirious. He was enacting his own death, his own crucifixion.[1]

This extremely disturbing scene may serve as our prolegomenon to a consideration of a later disruption of our aesthetic field, Artaud's *Pour en finir avec le jugement de dieu*, his final work and major radiophonic creation.

Artaud's internment in psychiatric institutions— where he suffered a spiritual, symbolic, metaphysical "death," as he so often claimed—corresponded with the duration of the Second World War. Perhaps the terrible manifestations of war—the shrieks of sirens, screams, shattered and dismembered bodies, the explosions of bombs, innumerable ways to die—already evident in Artaud's theater, were displaced by Artaud once again, expressed in both his subsequent aesthetic mannerisms as well as in the more immediate and morbid symptoms of his illness. His behavior in the asylum was characterized by delusions, auditory hallucinations, repetitive ritualistic acts, coprophilia, glossolalia, uncontrollable violent tantrums, etc. The therapeutic response was equally violent: electroshock therapy and insulin shock therapy. (Electroshock therapy, creating violent convulsions of the body, was developed in Rome in 1938; insulin shock therapy, which puts the body in a comatose state, was developed in Vienna in 1933.) These tortures, in addition to his confinement (under extremely difficult wartime conditions), his total dispossession (all of his personal belongings, including several objects of highly symbolic value, were stolen), and his internal psychic torments, all resulted in his understanding of his situation as an *imitatio Christi,* which was at the very center of his theologically oriented paranoia.

Artaud returned to Paris in 1946 a physically broken man. (This is strikingly apparent in a comparison of photographs of Artaud taken before and during his incarceration.) Finally, his condition was mortally aggravated by a long-undiagnosed terminal rectal cancer. (When this condition was finally discovered, it was too late for treatment, and the diagnosis was withheld from Artaud, as it often was in such cases, due to the vilification and fear of cancer in that epoch. Yet given Artaud's extreme sensitivity to his body, and given the terrible pain caused by this disease, he must have known the gravity of his condition.) The manner in which cancer has been stigmatized in our century is investigated by Susan Sontag in *Illness as Metaphor:*[2] it is ill-omened, abominable, repugnant, desexualizing, corrosive, corrupting, parasitic; it is a revolt of the organs, metaphorized as demonic possession or as demonic pregnancy; cancer is, ultimately, a disease that cannot be aestheticized, and to name it is an incitement to violence. It is thus *a fortiori* a perfect disease for paranoids, where in Artaud's case it would not be too extreme an analogy to liken his cancer to the parasitic God with which he struggled during his confinement in the psychiatric institutions.

Would it be too extravagant to suggest the electric shocks that traversed and convulsed his body were countered with electric "shocks" of his own: a radiophonic transmission? The redemptive quality of such a work cannot be overlooked, nor can its role as psychic overcompensation for his previous isolation, suffering, and position as an outcast: in contrast to the demonic voices that had tormented him, he can now broadcast and thus orally universalize his passions, his art, and his cultural critique. (It would thus be a misconception to read the viciously anti-American opening passages of *Pour en finir avec le jugement de dieu* as a political statement, especially given Artaud's antipolitical rhetoric, articulated as early as in his polemic against the Surrealists.)

The cosmos is a rigged theatre.

Antonin Artaud

In November 1947 Fernand Pouey, director of dramatic and literary broadcasts for French radio, commissioned Antonin Artaud to create a recorded work for his series *La Voix des poètes*, to be broadcast on *Radiodiffusion française*. This was the origin of Artaud's final work, *Pour en finir avec le jugement de Dieu (To Have Done with the Judgment of God)*.[3] In May 1946 Artaud returned to Paris after nine years of incarceration in insane asylums, where during the last sixteen months at Rodez he produced the *Cahiers de Rodez* (XV–XXI), notebooks documenting the deliria of those years, as well as the material, psychological, and spiritual conditions of his confinement. He returned a sort of tragic poet laureate, whose public celebration took place on 13 January 1947 as the famous lecture/poetry reading that he gave at the Théâtre du Vieux-Colombier, attended by many of the most notable figures of the French cultural scene, including Gide, Camus, and Breton. Here he transfixed the audience by reading the poems contained in *Artaud le mômo*, the texts of which were interspersed with his idiosyncratic glossolalic outbursts and incantations. This period also saw the creation of *Van Gogh le suicidé de la société (Van Gogh, the Man Suicided by Society)*, which, as we shall see, evoked Artaud's estimation of his own treatment by society and prefigured his own fate.

Pour en finir avec le jugement de dieu was recorded in the studios of French radio between 22 and 29 November 1947, with the sound effects recorded later and added to the final tape. The broadcast was scheduled for 10:45 P.M. on Monday, 2 February 1948, and was widely announced. But at the last moment, the day before, Wladimir Porché, the director of French radio, prohibited the broadcast. Serving as the conscience of the French public, he rationalized this suppression by arguing that the French people should be spared, or indeed protected from, Artaud's scatological, vicious, and obscene anti-Catholic and anti-American pronouncements.

In immediate response, Pouey organized the selection of a sort of aesthetic jury to consider the issue. Approximately fifty artists, writers, musicians, and journalists met at the offices of *Radiodiffusion française* for a private audition of the tapes on 5 February 1948; among those present were Raymond Queneau, Roger Vitrac, Jean-Louis Barrault, Jean Cocteau, René Clair, Paul Eluard, Jean Paulhan, Maurice Nadeau, Georges Auric, Claude Mauriac, and René Char. The opinion was almost unanimously favorable; Porché nevertheless persisted in his interdiction. Pouey quit his job in protest; the tape was not broadcast, only to be given a private audition at the Théâtre Washington on the evening of 23 February 1947 (to be broadcast on French radio only thirty years later); on 4 March 1948 Artaud died. Artaud's reaction to this crushing blow is documented in a series of letters written to Porché, Pouey, and several friends (XIII, 121–147). In a letter to Porché, Artaud insists that it was he, Artaud, who should be revolted and scandalized by the course of events, and that even if there were violent words and frightening statements in the pieces, it was done "in an atmosphere *so far beyond life* that I do not believe that at this point there remains a public capable of being scandalized by it" (XIII, 132). He wanted to create a "novel work which would connect with certain organic points of life, a work which causes the entire nervous system to feel illuminated as if by a miner's cap, with vibrations and consonances that invite one to corporeally emerge in order to follow, in the sky, this new, unusual and radiant Epiphany" (XIII, 131). And in a letter to René Guilly he further insists that the greater public, those who earn their living with their blood and sweat, eagerly awaited this broadcast, unlike the dung-heap capitalists who opposed it (XIII, 135–136). This debate was pursued publicly in the newspapers, expectedly following the general polarizations of French culture of that epoch.

The description of *Pour en finir avec le jugement de dieu* is extremely difficult, since this work exists in several different states, each highly incompatible with the others. A chronological list follows:

1. The dossier for the preparation of the broadcast (XIII, 231nn) was compiled, in part based on an earlier project for a representation of the Last Judgment. This dossier contains many of the final elements of the work, including texts, poems, glossolalia, indications for sound effects, etc.

2. The recordings themselves. These include readings by Artaud, Maria Casarès, Roger Blin, and Paule Thévenin, as well as sound effects provided by Artaud (drum, xylophone, and gong sounds, and a wide range of vocal effects). We should note that not all of the texts conceived as part of this work were actually edited into the tape: "Le théâtre de la cruauté" ("The Theater of Cruelty") was not recorded due to time limitations, and after the first mixing, Artaud made cuts in both the opening and concluding texts read by himself, and rerecorded the conclusion.

3. The tape was heard only in the two private auditions, and finally broadcast thirty years later. Copies are now available.

4. The published text. A week after the first private audition, *Combat* published "Tutuguri," a part of the recorded text. In March 1948 the review *Nyza 1* published the complete text, including those parts of the introduction and conclusion cut in the final tape. "Le Théâtre de la cruauté" was first published in the review *84* 5–6, 1948, a special issue devoted to Artaud after his death. And in April 1948, *K* published the complete text of *Pour en finir avec le jugement de dieu*, in a book that included a press dossier and a selection of letters pertinent to the events.

Schematically, the tape is divided into the following parts: the introductory text (recited by Artaud); "Tutuguri, le rite du soleil noir" ("Tutuguri, the Rite of the Black Sun"), read by Maria Casarès; "La Recherche de la fécalité" ("The Pursuit of Fecality"), read by Roger Blin; "La Question se pose de…" ("The Question Arises…"), read by Paule Thévenin; the conclusion, read by Artaud. The recited texts are interspersed with percussive music effects, glossolalia, and screams.

The textual complexity of this work is a paradigm of why we must call into question any simply materialist or nominalist model of what constitutes an artistic text. In considering coherent themes developed within disparate texts and media, we will investigate the crucial importance of the differences—phonetic, expressive, and stylistic—between the written and the recorded texts, and in doing so we will chart the effects of the radiophonic work on the body of the artist and his auditors.

"To have done with the judgment of God" may be deemed, literally, the summation of Artaud's lifelong struggle, marking both the origins and the cataclysmic finale of his writings. This is particularly true in regard to the amphibology inherent in the phrasing of the title: it is both a question of God's judgment of Artaud and Artaud's judgment of God. In 1925, Artaud, having just joined the Surrealist movement, was appointed head of the *Bureau de Recherches*

Surréalistes at which time he edited the third number of *La Révolution Surréaliste*, which bore the subtitle *1925: Fin de l'ère chrétienne (1925: End of the Christian Era.)* Among several other short texts by Artaud, this review contained his virulent *Adresse au Pape (Address to the Pope)* (I★★, 41); in good Surrealist fashion, one might have assumed that Artaud would have circumvented the theological problem from the beginning. But as we shall see, this was far from the truth. We should also note here, however, that at the end of his life Artaud chose to begin the definitive edition of his complete works with a new version of the *Adresse au Pape*, written in October 1946.[4] This latter version begins with the diatribe

> 1° *I renounce my baptism.*
>
> 2° *I shit on the christian name.*
>
> 3° *I jerk off on the cross of god (but masturbation, Pius XII, had never been one of my habits, and will never become one of them. Perhaps you will have to begin to understand me).*
>
> 4° *It is I (and not Jesus Christ) who had been crucified at Golgotha, and this occurred so that I could be held up against god and his christ,*
> > *because I am a man*
> > *and because god and his christ are only ideas which bear, moreover, the filthy mark of man's hand; and for me these ideas never existed.*
> > *(I★, 13)*

This revindication of his earlier polemic marks the closure of a life-long trajectory of suffering where the passions of the flesh were rarely dissociated from the spiritual passions of a theological dimension, often bearing cosmic—and markedly paranoid—proportions. To sum up the fundamental theme of these works, and of his deliria, we may cite an early entry in the *Cahiers de Rodez*, dated February 1945: "God is the monomaniac of the unconscious, the erotic of the unconscious, following the effort of conscious work" (XV, 315). In order to delineate this monomania, in order to understand his renunciation of God's judgment, we shall sketch out the salient features of his lifework in order to situate *Pour en finir avec le jugement de dieu* and to consider the efficacy of his own judgment.

Ironically, or perhaps appropriately, Artaud's career began as it ended: with a rejection. In 1923 Artaud had submitted some of his poetry to *La Nouvelle Revue Française (N.R.F.)*, then directed by Jacques Rivière: Rivière's rejection of these works gave rise to the now famous *Une Correspondance,* published in the *N.R.F.* 132 (1924). Rivière rejected these poems on formal grounds but found them interesting enough to wish to meet the author. In the resulting exchange of letters, Artaud outlined for the first time his theory of artistic creativity. Artaud's argument—in opposition to Rivière's insistence on the formal inadequacy of the poems—hinged on the spuriousness of the force/form distinction. Artaud claimed that the authenticity of these works was guaranteed by the suffering and passion invested in them, beyond all formal criteria. For Artaud, the formal turns of phrase characteristic of poetic language, which arise "from the profound incertitude of my thought" (I, 24) are but an exteriorization of the internal passions and torments of the soul. "Thus when *I can grasp a form*, imperfect as it may be, I fix it, for fear of losing all thought" (I★, 24).

This scatteredness of my poems, these defects of form, this constant sagging of my thought, must be attributed not to a lack of practice, a lack of command of the instrument that I employed, a lack of intellectual development; *but to a central collapse of the soul, a sort of erosion, both essential and fleeting, of thought, to the temporary nonpossession of the material benefits of my develop-ment, to the abnormal separation of the elements of thought (the impulse to think, at each of the terminal stratifications of thought, passing through all the states, all the bifurcations, all the localizations of thought and of form). (I★, 28)*

Artaud wrote so as not to go mad; he had the right to speak because he suffered. In a sophisticated use of the intentional fallacy, he explains, "I am a man whose spirit has greatly suffered, and by virtue of this I have the *right* to speak" (I★, 30). This is a "right" that he was often denied. Indeed, owing to the frustrations of rejection, the torments of the soul, and the negative judgments of others, his speech was often transformed into the hyperbolic expression of pain and anger: the scream. The one poem contained in *Une Correspondance* is entitled "Cri" ("Scream" or "Cry"), where we read—in response to his current situation and in anticipation of many future impasses—of the "little celestial poet" in regard to whose work, "silence and night muzzle all impurity" (I*, 31). But it was perhaps this constant struggle—with himself, his peers, his tradition, his god—that motivated him to attempt to express his deepest fears and agonies, manifested throughout his entire work.

By definition, in submitting his works to the *N.R.F.*, he opened himself up to the judgment of others. This judgment was to become a determinant factor in his own self-definition, as well as the axis of his struggle against the world. "To cure me of the judgment of others, I have the entire distance that separates me from myself" (I*, 27), he wrote to Rivière. But he ended the same letter with a curious formula, rather inhabitual in French: "I entrust myself to your judgment" (I*, 30). Whereas he placed these early poetic works before the judgment of one man, the closure of his complete works assumes mythopoetic dimensions as this judgment is raised to a cosmic level; later, it is rather God's judgment that he must be done with, a judgment that will come to define the infinitesimally small space that delineates the self, that divides the self from itself. That space is his unconscious, haunted by God and His demons.

Artaud's role in the Surrealist movement was brief (1925–1927), central, and tragic. His appropriation of Surrealism was certainly nuanced by his already nascent poetics, more than it was influenced by Surrealist dogma. Soon after the publication of Breton's first *Manifesto of Surrealism*, Artaud (as head of the Bureau de Recherches Surréalistes) authored a memo internal to the group, known as the "Déclaration du 27 janvier 1925," which was signed by most of its members, including Breton. This text—a sort of short

"Surrealist manifesto"—closes with a reiteration of Artaud's earlier position on the creative act, in distinct contradiction to Breton's more poetic model. "Surrealism is not poetic form. It is a scream of the spirit which turns back upon itself and which is desperately determined to crush its shackles, if necessary with material hammers" (I**, 30). Other differences became visible: in his report, "L'Activité du bureau de recherches Surréalistes," published in La Révolution Surréaliste 3, Artaud explained that "Surrealism records a certain number of repulsions rather than beliefs" and ends the report by stating that "here a certain Faith is instilled; but let me be heard by coprophiliacs, aphasics, and in general by all those discredited in words and speech, the Pariahs of thought. I speak only for them" (I**, 46–47). Needless to say, he was no longer speaking for the group, but against them: Artaud's desublimatory position was in marked contrast with Breton's highly refined mode of poetic sublimation. The Surrealists would not long acquiesce with this position: Artaud was denounced in Au grand jour (1927), where he is berated for his "veritable bestiality" and criticized because "he wanted to see in the revolution only a metamorphosis of the interior conditions of the soul, which is characteristic of the mentally defective, the impotent, and the cowardly." This terrible invective concludes: "Today we vomited out this scoundral. We no longer see why this carrion waits any longer to convert, or, as he would no doubt say, to declare himself Christian."[5] Little did they know how literally this prediction of conversion would come true, and how painfully their metaphoric reference to death would become a central trope in Artaud's own autobiographic accounts of his mental "defects."

Artaud's response, in "A la grande nuit, ou le bluff Surréaliste" ("In Darkest Night, or The Surrealist Bluff"), centered on the political interpretation of Surrealism. Artaud believed that human existence could only be changed by "a metamorphosis of the interior conditions of the soul" (I**, 60), and he denied the efficacy of any possible social, material revolution. Thus the Surrealists were "revolutionaries who revolutionize nothing," mere creators of "grotesque simulacra" (I**, 59–63). But Artaud himself did not escape the grotesque.

After his break with the Surrealists, Artaud devoted himself primarily to cinematic and theatrical projects, which culminated in the publication of his most influential work, *Le Théâtre et son double* (*The Theater and Its Double*) (1938). This work outlines the project for a new theatrical art that would be religious, magical, mystical, hieratic, and where theatrical events would no longer be subordinated to a written text, as was the case with Western theater up until that time. This was to be an antinaturalist, antirealist, antipsychological theater, where screams, cries, groans, and all of the dissonant sounds of the human body would bear equal importance with the spoken word, and where language itself would be utilized as a sort of incantation to create a theater of dramatic and curative magic. This desublimatory spectacle, this antitheater, is compared to the plague on the grounds that "the theater is a disease because it is the supreme equilibrium, which cannot be achieved without destruction. It invites the mind to share a delirium that exalts its energies" (IV, 39). The primacy of the expression of *force*, earlier made in relation to Artaud's own poetry, is now generalized for theatrical production; hence the famed notion of a "theater of cruelty," where cosmic force becomes libidinal production and where the symbolic is transformed into the corporeal rhythms of human passions and torments.

The theater is an exorcism, a summoning of energy. It is a means of channeling the passions, of making them serve something, but it must be understood not as an art or a distraction but rather as a solemn act, and this paroxysm, this solemnity, this danger must be restored to it. In order to do that it must abandon individual psychology, enter into mass passions, into the conditions of the collective spirit, grasp the collective wavelengths, in short, change the subject. (V,153; from a letter of August 1933 to Natalie Clifford Barney.)

For Artaud, the double of the theater is life, where life itself is understood according to the exigencies of cruel necessity. Thus *Le Théâtre et son double* proposes not only a theory of theatrical and poetic production but also a hermeneutic of Artaud's own existence. It might be said that the true "theater of cruelty" was played out in Artaud's own imaginary, on his own body, during his stay at the asylum of Rodez, where the cosmic and paranoid struggle against God's judgment was finally to take place.

In 1936 Artaud voyaged to Mexico, to visit the land of the Tarahumaras, where he became steeped in religion, myth, and magic, all of which were subsequently transposed into his own idiosyncratic and snycretic mythopoeia. This quest became the subject of the posthumously published book *Les Tarahumaras* (IX), which is composed of texts written from the time of the trip up until his death, including the source of a section of *Pour en finir avec le jugement de dieu,* "Tutuguri, le rite du soleil noir." Here, for example, he transposes part of the Indian myth and ritual into his own mythopoetic system, so that "the major tone of the Rite is precisely THE ABOLITION OF THE CROSS" (XIII,79). But art proved to be quite different from ritual.

His next voyage marked the catastrophic turning point of his life, where his actual conversion to Christianity was contemporaneous with the onset of madness. His lifelong fascination with religious mysteries reached a participatory culmination when in 1937 he journeyed to Dublin carrying what he believed to be St. Patrick's (or Christ's) staff, wishing to return it to its native land. In September of that year he confessed and took communion on a Sunday morning at the Church of Jesus Christ in Dublin. Soon after, he was arrested after a fit of violence and deported to France, at which time he lost his precious cane (a terrible symbolic disaster) as well as his sanity. Thus he was to begin nine years of incarceration in French asylums, and it was only in February 1945 that he began to write continuously again, the *Cahiers de Rodez.*[6] Characteristically, the text that opens these notebooks is entitled, "Le Retour de la France aux principes sacrés" ("The Return of France to Sacred Principles") (XV, 9nn). But soon afterward, in a letter to Henri Parisot dated 9 September 1945, he definitively renounced his bap-

tism and Christianity, and the stage was set for the works that he created upon his return to Paris in May 1946, especially *Pour en finir avec
le jugement de dieu.*

This century no longer understands the fecal poetry,

    the intestinal ills,

    of that one,

    Madame Death...

                Antonin Artaud

The written project for *Pour en finir avec le jugement de dieu* begins
with a short text containing glossolalia typical of Artaud's writing at
Rodez and after:

kré	Everything	*puc te*
kré	must be arranged	*puk te*
pek	to a hair	*li le*
kre	in a fulminating	*pek ti le*
e	order.	*kruk*
pte		

Glossolalia is a type of speech or babble characteristic of certain discourses of infants, poets, schizophrenics, mediums, charismatics.[7] It is
the manifestation of language at the level of its pure materiality, the
realm of pure sound, where there obtains a total disjunction of signifier and signified. As such, the relation between sound and meaning
breaks down through the glossolalic utterance; it is the image of language inscribed in its excess, at the threshold of nonsense. Thus, as a
pure manifestation of expression, the meaning of glossolalia depends
upon the performative, dramatic, contextual aspects of such utterances within discourse and action; meaning becomes a function of
the enthusiastic expression of the body, of kinetic, gestural behavior.

In *Le Théâtre et son double* Artaud already provides the rationale for the utilization of such enunciations in his theater of cruelty:

To make metaphysics out of a spoken language is to make language express what it usually does not express: this is to make use of it in a new, exceptional, and unaccustomed fashion; to reveal its possibilities of physical shock; to actively divide and distribute it in space; to handle intonations in an absolutely concrete manner, restoring their power to tear asunder and to really manifest something; to turn against language and its basely utilitarian, one could even say alimentary, sources, against its hunted beast origins; this is finally to consider language in its form as Incantation. *(IV, 56)*

Updating these remarks upon his return to Paris after Rodez, he writes:

> *And shit on psalmody,*
> *bomba fulta*
> *enough seeking the true poetic psalmody,*
> *caca futra*
> *ça suffira*
> *mai danba*
> *debi davida*
> *imai davidu*
> *ebe vidu*
> *by repeating* I annul   *(XXIII, 16)*

And in another text (also punctuated by glossolalia, or rather glossograph, omitted here) that may serve as an explanation of the use of glossolalia in *Pour en finir avec le jugement de dieu*, he says: "To be rid of the idiotic and perishable stamp of baptism ... it does not suffice to say it, but I said it and I say it again, I repeat: I renounce my baptism. And the incomprehensible words that precede this are at most imprecations against the fact of having been baptised" (XXII, 377–378). Artaud proposes the religious, magical use of glossolalia as catharsis, as a mode of exorcism: to rid himself of God's influence and judgment.

Allen S. Weiss

The phonetic structures of glossolalia generally parallel those of the speaker's mother tongue (one rarely, if ever, creates a truly new language), though such enunciations are often marked by features idiosyncratic to the speaker. In Artaud's case, there is an extremely high frequency of the letter *k* in his glossolalia/glossographia, as well as of the phonetic equivalents of this sound, the hard *c*, *ck*, and *ch*. (We should note that the letter *k* is one of the least frequent in the French language, yet one of the most frequent consonents in Artaud's glossolalia; it is thus transformed into a highly pertinent feature of this language, and its significance must be sought.)[8]

The scatological signification of the instance of the letter/sound /k/ in Artaud's glossolalia is apparent.[9] Once again in terms of an incantatory exorcism, he writes from Rodez:

The expulsion of the spirits has been effected one day,
not in order to protect the body, for it is spirit, but
to save the soul.

cou cou la ni le ri
ca ca lo lo lo lo
cou cou roti moza (XVIII, 190)

And from the same period he explains that the soul is cacophony while the text is stylistics, harkening back to the distinctions established in his correspondance with Jacques Rivière. But such scatological pronouncements are far more than sheer expletives; they bear an ontological signification, which Artaud explains in a letter written from Rodez dating from the same month as the previous citation:

The name of his matter is caca, and caca is the matter of the soul, which I have seen so many coffins spill out in puddles before me. The breath of bones has a center, and this center is the abyss Kah-Kah, Kah the corporeal breath of shit, which is the opium of eternal survival. (IX, 192)

Excrement, as a sign of death, is formless matter excluded from the organization of the symbolic order. It poses a threat to cultural formations both because it signifies a wasteful expenditure that circumvents societal modes of production and because it is an originary sign of autonomous production, of sovereign creativity bypassing societal structure of exchange. Excrement marks the body, and not the socius, as the center of production, whence comes the necessity, in the process of socializing the infant, of controlling the anal functions and establishing the anus as the place of possession and exclusion. This exclusion entails, in the major irony of human ontogenesis, the rejection of one's own body, a rejection which is the very origin of sublimation. Any desublimated return to anality in adult life marks a return of the repressed and serves as a contestation of the symbolic law.[10]

Artaud pits his own creativity against that of God, where the two are nevertheless mediated by death: "The Word is not made flesh, the flesh will be made shit and, this will henceforth be the only word of imprecation" (XVII, 214). In restating the Johanine myth of creation, Artaud specifies the corporeal origins, the "latrines of sublimity" (XII,41), the chaotic magma of existence where life and death are in constant struggle and where the soul is torn between angelic purity and diabolic filth and corruption. In a moment of hyperbolic hubris and blasphemy, Artaud proclaims that

> *When I say caca, prison, poison, penal servitude,*
> *sodomisation, assassination, urgency, thirst, a quick piss,*
> *scurvy of thirst,*
> *Sodom, Gomorrha,*
> *assassination, urgency, thirst, a quick piss,*
> *god responds inflamed logos.*　　　*(XIV, 178)*

Yet Artaud wishes to preclude even this response, to finally end God's judgment altogether. The diatribe becomes even more vicious, more blasphemous, in *Pour en finir avec le jugement de dieu,* where in the text of "La recherche de la fécalité" he poses the question, "Is God a being? If he is it is made of shit" (XIII, 86). (We might note that, perhaps not coincidentally, this work was published in a journal simply entitled *K*.) Struggling against the return of the repressed, trying to resist and scorn the judgment of god and the judgment of man (which was perhaps even harsher), this final work would become a sort of epitaph, destined (in its very absence) to mark an unfulfilled possibility of radiophonic art and an unclaimed moment in the history of poetry.

... the limbo of a nightmare

of bones and muscle ...

Antonin Artaud

All expression is informed by language *and* the body, bounded by signs *and* the libido. The figuration of force—in what might be termed the "visceral imagination"—always attempts to escape the hermeneutic circle within which force is transformed into form, into meaning. This significative evasion, beneath the threshold of sense, is precisely the level at which Artaud's texts must be read. Given the paranoid, theological deliria specific to Artaud's condition, these corporeal/semiotic restraints must be interpreted in a very specific manner. In an early text entitled "Sur le suicide," ("On Suicide") (1925), Artaud explains,

If I kill myself, it will not be in order to destroy myself, but in order to reconstitute myself; suicide will be for me only a means of violently regaining myself, of brutally bursting into my own being, of forestalling the uncertain advances of God. By means of suicide, I reintroduce my own plan into nature, and instill for the first time the form of my volition into things. (I**, 26)

Thus the force/form distinction is a matter of life and death, and the corporeal/semiotic restraint is transformed into a classic double bind, expressed on the cosmic level:

Even to be able to arrive at the point of suicide, I must await the return of my self, I need the free play of all the articulations of my being. God placed within hopelessness as within a constellation of impasses whose radiation ended in myself. I can neither live nor die, neither not wish to die nor to live. And all men are like me. (I**, 28)

The existence of God creates a double bind for Artaud: the negation at the core of the self, that which separates the self from itself, is God. As Derrida, writing on Artaud, explains, "God is thus the proper name of that which deprives us of our own nature, of our own birth; consequently he will always have spoken before us, on the sly. He is the difference which insinuates itself between myself and myself as death. This is why—such is the concept of true suicide according to Artaud—I must die away from my death in order to be reborn 'immortal' at the eye of my birth."[11] From this comes the need to kill God, to be done with his judgment, in order to gain one's own autonomy, in order to conquer the work of the negative by means of life's creative forces. The torment of my flesh, the dispossession of my self, the bewitching of my soul, the theft of my voice, all must be overcome; the task is to reduce the difference between force and form and thus transform the stigmata of God's judgment into the expression—and not the betrayal—of life. This is to be the goal of the theater of cruelty; however, an ontological pessimism reigns: "When we speak the word life, it must be understood that this does not pertain to life as we know it from its factual exterior but rather from that sort of fragile and fluctuating core untouched by forms" (IV, 18).

The psychological effects of this double-bind system upon Artaud are explained by Guy Rosolato: "Expulsion, for Artaud, was to be situated neither on the exterior nor in the interior of the system, as ineluctable as it might be; neither on the side of life nor on the side of death; but, through the quest for total mastery, by maintaining what became for him the impasse, the double-bind, of the simultaneous and absolute *injunctions to live and to die,* that is to say by means of the single thought incarnate in the infinite instant of passage within the circumscribed immensity of the theater: a scream."[12] The scream is the expulsion of an unbearable, impossible internal polarization between life's force and death's negation, simultaneously signifying and simulating creation and destruction. Parallel to the antithetical sense of excrement for the infant—gift or weapon—the scream, as the nonmaterial double of excrement, may be both expression and expulsion, a sign of both creation and frustration.

In one of the first texts written after his release from Rodez, *Suppôts et supplications* (*Henchmen and Supplications*) (1946) Artaud poses the question, "Isn't the mouth of the current human race, following the anatomical survey of the present human body, this hole of being situated just at the outlet of the hemorrhoids of Artaud's ass?" (XIV★★, 153). This conflation of humanity's mouth with Artaud's asshole is not simply a scabrous affront; this anatomical symbolism also reveals the desublimatory trajectory of Artaud's expression, of a body caught within the symbolic web and wishing to escape, of an anatomy trying to undo its own destiny. Psychoanalytic theory teaches us that speech is invested with narcissistic libido; this is true in regard to both the meaning of enunciations and the psychophysical manifestations of the speech act itself. The pleasures of speech are not merely phatic, communicative, seductive, but also autoerotic; the oral play of sensations, the very grain of the voice, creates and indicates the various pleasures and displeasures of vocal acts of expression. Spoken sounds have a primary libidinal value, for both speaker and (through identificatory introjection) auditor, before ever becoming meaningful: rhythm, harmony, euphony, even dissonance and cacophony have a passional, often erotic, quality. Ultimately, this question reaches beyond the differences between logocentrism and melocentrism, with the latter being only a trope (musication) of the former. Rather, Artaud's poetics is formed beneath the thresholds of both, in the sensate body worked through by the active libido.

What Roland Barthes spoke of as the "grain of the voice" reveals the very materiality of the body within that sublimation known as speech, or song. The scream is the desublimation of speech into the body, in opposition to the sublimation of body into meaningful speech. Barthes insists that "there is no human voice in the world that is not the object of desire, or of repulsion; there is no neutral voice, and if occasionally this neuter, this whiteness of the voice appears, it is a great terror for us, as if we were to fearfully discover a frozen world, where desire is dead."[13] For Artaud, death is not heard in the voice through such a "white terror"; Artaud's terror was dark, filthy, emanating from the deepest recesses of his body, a body that his discourse tried, always unsuccessfully, to rejoin.

Reducing the mouth/anus conflation to the purely physiological level, Artaud notes,

> *The honey kernel of the cyst*
> *of the lingual gum*
> *of the anal tongue*
> *of the hard palate,*
> *glottis,*
> *larynx,*
> *pharynx. (XXIII, 328)*

Here the connection is not merely symbolic: contemporary psycholinguistics teaches that the pronunciation of glottal occlusives (sounds created by closure of the glottis) creates a direct subglottal pressure on the diaphragm and the intestines, thus facilitating defecation.[14] This vortex of force is indicated by Artaud in the corporeal trajectory of gums, tongue, palate, glottis, larynx, pharynx, which explains the meaning of the apparent oxymoron of an "anal tongue" (where the translation of "langue anale" by "anal language" would be linguistically more logical but would break the physiognomic chain of expression). Thus glottal sounds are symbolic—and physiognomic—reflection of defecation: speech, as *flatus voci,* is the ejection of a dematerialized substance, the inverse of the anal *flatus.* Such a relation is often found in psychopathological symptoms, as in the following case of a patient of Sandor Ferenczi, cited by Ivan Fónagy: "Another patient (a hysteric) suffered from two symptoms, simultaneously and with the same intensity: a glottic spasm and a spasm of the anal sphincter. If he is in a good mood, his voice is strong and flows freely and his defecation is normal, "satisfying." During a state of depression—especially if it is due to an insufficiency—or in his relations with his superiors, there is a simultaneously aphonia and tenesmus."[15] The glottic sphincter permits the physical and symbolic articulation of oral and anal rejection (and retention). This is primally and hyperbolically expressed by the glottal occlusive /k/, universally signified in its popular scatological form of *kaka* or *caca,* from which comes the general condemnation of the sound /k/ as ugly, filthy; this is a direct result of the corporeal displacement of anal libido directly onto such sounds.[16]

As such, these glottal vocalizations are screams of the entire body and not just the mouth. Yet these screams never fall below the threshold of meaning, since even the subglottal regions of the body are full of signification and overtly expressive. The interior of the soul speaks through the interior of the body. The realization of the intimate ties between body and language became central to Artaud's poetics:

> *The least that I sought was for words to surpass the text, for the text to leave the writing, so that plain language, habitual words, and spoken syntax are forgotten; perhaps going from word to word the reader will find that I have accomplished this.*
>
> *I don't give a damn if my sentences sound French or Papuan, but if I drive in a violent word, I want it to suppurate in the sentence like hundred-holed ecchymosis; a writer is not reproached for an obscene word because it is obscene, but because it is gratuitous, flat gris-gris.*
>
> *But who will say that it suffices for a word to sweat out its violence in the severed sentence that trails it like a severed living member; within infinity it is perhaps a fine skewer for a poet to burst forth a scream, but this is comforting only from the day that he succeeds in barding his words in such a manner that, parting from him, they would respond within the sentences of a written text as if without him, and when in rereading them he feels*

that these words summon him to them just as he called them to him. (XXIII, 46–47)

Rhetorically creating a "body" of the text (with its corresponding diseases and torments), Artaud wishes to recuperate a poetic or literary level to his work, beyond the raw, brutal scream. In themselves, screams might be effective to jolt us out of our commonplace literary and linguistic habits, but they in no way suffice to create a style, or a poem. Ultimately, the poetic text (including its screams) must distance itself from the poet (it must go beyond the level of sheer expression), only to return to him as an external summons. It is only in leaving the poet that the word can call out to the other and attain its own destiny.

...petrified by the summum

of ourselves. .

Antonin Artaud

Writing of the historical incorporation of phonetics in linguistics, Roman Jakobson cites a text that describes "a particular laryngal articulation which would, had this description been accurate, have inevitably resulted in the fatal strangulation of the speaker."[17] Yet this error is only a hyperbolic statement of the truth pertaining to the expression of anger. The state of anger or hatred considerably increases muscular tension; in regard to its verbal expression, Fónagy explains, "We also observe that anger and especially hatred prolong the duration of the occlusion, and narrow the buccal canal during the articulation of frictive consonants. The evidence of glottal tomography is even clearer and more decisive. Following a hyperfunction of the sphincter muscles of the glottis, the passage of air becomes difficult. Aggressive or hateful phonation often produces a *strangled* voice. This metaphor contains the key to the explication of the gesture: one strangles oneself in order to prefigure homicide. According to a magical conception of the world, this would operate as an action that

Allen S. Weiss

would in itself suffice to eliminate the adversary."[18] Yet on the psychophonetic level, this sort of expression is doomed to failure, since when anger erupts, the vocal cords aren't sufficiently close to vibrate, and in suppressed anger they are too tightly compressed to vibrate normally. The result of such violent muscular contractions is often a state where the vibrations of the vocal cords are "replaced by the sound of air turbulence—a *flatus vocis*—passing through the narrowed glottis."[19] To follow out, in this context, the symbolic relation between the desire to murder and the excremental expression of the *flatus vocis*, we need only consider Elias Canetti's explanation that excrement "is loaded with our whole blood guilt. By it we know what we have murdered. It is the compressed sum of all the evidence against us."[20]

An essential element of the expression of anger or hatred is the simultaneous stimulation and contraction of antagonistic muscle groups, a sort of internal battle within the body.[21] These conflicts are more than metaphoric: they express the profoundly heterogeneous functioning of what appears to be a unified, holistic body, a gestalt organization of the corporeal sensorium. Certain psychopathological conditions raise this heterogeneity, this dysfunction, to a higher and more explicit level, such as the phantasms of *disjecta membra* (the body torn apart) characteristic of schizophrenia, or the personal and cosmic apocalypses found in paranoid discourse. In a letter written from Rodez, Artaud writes of the state of sleep, where we seek ourselves "within that sort of piercing immanence, that space of unfathomable immanence where our unconscious is woven" (XI, 103).

The man who just lives his life never experiences himself, never really lives; like a fire that lives through the entire body in its total expanse, by dint of consuming that body, man does not live through his entire self at each moment his body, in an absolute space of the body; he is sometimes knee and sometimes foot, sometimes occiput and sometimes ear, sometimes lungs and sometimes liver, sometimes membrane and sometimes uterus, sometimes anus and sometimes nose, sometimes sex and sometimes heart, sometimes saliva and sometimes urine, sometimes aliment and sometimes sperm, sometimes excrement and sometimes idea; what I mean is that the ego or the self is not centered on a unique perception, and that the ego is not unique because it is dispersed throughout the body instead of the body being gathered around itself in an absolute sensorial equality, and composing a perception of the absolute. For man is not only dispersed in his body, he is also dispersed in the outside of things, like a corpse who forgot his own body and who swims around his body because he forgot his body and because his body forgot itself; and the man who does not live through all of himself at each instant commits the error of believing himself to be this self, mind, idea, conception, notion, which floats upon a point of the body, instead of being at every instant his entire body. (XI, 103–104)[22]

Once again, Artaud's perception of his own body was to serve as the basis of his theorization of the theatrical spectacle. "Even if the theater is a conflict of gestures, words, movements and noises, it is above all a conflict, a summoning of opposing forces, of clashes, resolved in time rather than space" (IV, 320).

Prefiguring psychoanalytic theory and Freud's claim that ego is body ego, Nietzsche already had a similar understanding of the body: "The body is a great reason, a plurality with one sense, a war and peace, a herd and a shepherd. An instrument of your body is also your little reason, my brother, which you call 'spirit'—a little instrument and toy of your great reason."[23] Yet this body, once civilized and overcivilized, bespeaks a distinct pathology, both as hypertrophied and hypotrophied:

But this is what matters least to me since I have been among men: to see that this one lacks an eye and that one an ear and a third a leg, while there are others who have lost their tongues or their noses or their heads. I see, and have seen, what is worse, and many things so vile that I do not want to speak of everything; and concerning some things I do not even like to be silent: for there are human beings who lack everything, except one thing of which they have too much—human beings who are nothing but a big eye or a big mouth or a big belly or anything at all that is big. Inverse cripples I call them.

Allen S. Weiss

And when I came out of my solitude and crossed over this bridge for the first time I did not trust my eyes and looked and looked again, and said at last: "An ear! An ear as big as a man!" I looked still more closely—and indeed, underneath the ear something was moving, something pitifully small and wretched and slender. And, no doubt of it, the tremendous ear was attached to a small, thin stalk—but this stalk was a human being! If one used a magnifying glass one could even recognize a tiny envious face; also, that a bloated little soul was dangling from the stalk. The people, however, told me that this great ear was not only a human being, but a great one, a genius. But I never believed the people when they spoke of great men; and I maintained my belief that it was an inverse cripple who had too little of everything and too much of one thing."[24]

We might use this passage as a parable of the effects of radiophonic art, and especially its relation to *Pour en finir avec le jugement de dieu*.

During the early years of sound film (the 1930s), several microphones were scattered around the set to capture the sounds, and the signals were later mixed in the studio to attain a consistent, coherent, intelligible quality of speech and sound. Yet there is an inherent discrepancy between the unique viewpoint of the camera and the multifarious positioning of the microphones, such that the auditory aspect of the spectacle is fragmented and only artificially recombined. In an early article, one critic described the spectatorial position in relation to these films: "When a number of microphones are used, the resultant blend of sound may not be said to represent any given point of audition, but is the sound which would be heard by a man with five or six very long ears, said ears extending in various directions."[25] This confusion, explains Mary Ann Doane, is a confusion of media; it is caused by intermixing the radio industry and the film industry. While radio broadcasting of the epoch sought to present all sounds as coming from approximately the same spatial plane, the film industry needed to create spatial effects through auditory means. "The presentation of all sounds as being emitted from one plane could not be sustained. For the drama played out on the Hollywood screen must be parallelled by the drama played out over the body of the spectator—a body positioned as unified and nonfragmented."[26]

This unified and nonfragmented body constitutes, of course, the "normal" perception of one's own body. The case of Artaud and *Pour en finir avec le jugement de Dieu* is radically different from that of most other radiophonic works, precisely because his relation to his body is essentially different from that of most other radiophonic artists and most other spectators. For Artaud, the shattered, disoriented, delirious, ecstatic body was the norm; the unified body was what he fought, what he saw as being at the base of an insipid Western theatricality based on narrative, psychological drama. Ironically, the failure of sound in those early films indicates what could have been utilized as a structural, technical formula for a successful radiophonic presentation of the theater of cruelty. This was not, however, the case. To a certain extent, *Pour en finir avec le jugement de Dieu* failed due to the structural features of recording: Artaud's screams—initially bloodcurdling despite the theoretically low coefficient of success of the expression of anger—lose their effect upon repeated auditions, and their strength upon regulation of the level of amplitude (one of the dubious benefits of the recorded arts resulting in the retrospective transformation of spontaneity into banality through repetition);[27] his blasphemies, injunctions, and vituperations become texts for the archives; his shattered body becomes whole and normal through the effects of monaural recording; and transmission of his work becomes, finally, not the summit of the theater of cruelty but rather a "primitive" example of the radiophonic arts.

But perhaps this failure was exemplary and characteristic of Artaud's lifework. In response to a survey on suicide published in *La Révolution Surréaliste* 3, Artaud speaks of the hypothetical, incomprehensible, unrepresentable nature of this act. And yet, he writes,

I suffer frightfully from life. There is no state that I can reach. And most certainly I am long dead, I am already suicided. That is to say, I have already been suicided. But what would you think of an anterior *suicide, of a suicide that would make us retrace our steps, but from the other side of existence, and not from the side of death. (I**, 21–22)*

Artaud was already suicided at the very beginning of his existence, and *Pour en finir avec le jugement de dieu* was the completion of this suicide by society, just as Artaud explained that Van Gogh was "the man suicided by society." The recording stole his voice; the radio dissimulated his body; the bureaucracy suppressed the broadcast; and a month later, on 4 March 1948, Artaud died—of rectal cancer. His scatological pronouncements, his accentuation of the phoneme /k/ in his glossolalia, his extreme glottal occlusives—which permitted a violent vocalization of the passions and an even more violent, but secret, anal *flatus vocis*—were all matters of life and death. Artaud was the man suicided by society.

In seeking the absolute

one loses everything.

Antonin Artaud

Upon leaving the studio after the session where the sound effects of *Pour en finir avec le jugement de dieu* were recorded, Artaud declared, laughing, "Well, until now I was only a writer, actor, director, sketcher; now I'm a musician" (XIII, 358). This is indeed true: the percussive, xylophonic, glossolalic, and guttural sounds that he created for this work were indeed music, though of a totally new type, a sort of *musique brute* or *musique pauvre* fully in the spirit of this theater of cruelty. His screams became poetry and his noises became music, in an attempt to express the inexpressible, profound, chaotic essence of human existence.

Listening to this new sort of music presents the greatest difficulty, especially in relation to the classic structures of

Western music. Consider, for example, the fact that a sound engineer wishing to determine the acoustic structure of a sound of a given duration must take 40 times more measures for a noise than for a spoken vowel, and 250 times more measures than for a sung one.[28] Thus the complexity of noise—a practically random sound structure—is inexorably more difficult to listen to and grasp in its intricacies than that of song. The quasihypnotic effect of musical regularity (rhythmic and melodic as well as harmonic) is broken by the shock effect of Artaud's "musical" *bruitage*. This follows from his conception of the theater, expressed in one of his early manifestos, *Le Théâtre Alfred Jarry* (1926): "The spectator who comes to us knows that he has just exposed himself to a true operation, where not only his mind but also his senses and his flesh are at stake. He will henceforth go to the theater as he goes to the surgeon or the dentist" (II, 22). Elsewhere, in the claim prefiguring the electroshock "treatment" that he was to suffer later on in life, he sees "the theater as a bath of psychic electricity where the intellect will be periodically reimmersed" (IV, 321).

Artaud's earliest musical project was the libretto that he wrote for Edgar Varèse's prospective (but never actually written) opera, *L'Astronome*.[29] Artaud's work, *Il n'y a plus de firmament* (circa 1932), opens in a manner such that his sound effects would prelude, merge with, or probably even overpower Varèse's music: The first movement opens:

Darkness. Explosions in this darkness. Harmonies suddenly broken off. Harsh sounds. Depressurized soundings.

The music will give the impression of a distant cataclysm and will fill the room, falling as from vertiginous heights. Chords will originate in the sky and then deteriorate, going from one extreme to the other. Sounds fall as if from very high, then suddenly stop and spread out in bursts, forming vaults and parasols. Tiers of sound....

The sounds and light will surge out in fits and starts with the jolts of magnified Morse code telegraph, but this will be to Morse code what the music of the spheres heard by Bach is to Massenet's Clair de lune. *(II, 107)*

Allen S. Weiss

Furthermore, in an archetypically Artaudian figure, we find the human body transformed into a musical instrument in the third movement:

Then the noise of a bizarre drum envelops everything, a nearly human noise which begins sharply and ends dully, always the same noise; and then we see enter a woman with an enormous belly, upon which two men alternately strike with drumbeats. (II, 118)

During the same period, in an interview regarding his play *Les Cenci* (1935), Artaud explains the staging, which would include the use of the Ondes Martenot (an early electronic musical instrument), recordings of the huge bells of the cathedral of Notre-Dame in Paris, and most shockingly, recordings of factory machine noises, "which would have their place in torture chambers of the Middle Ages" (V, 219).

Nineteen forty-eight, the year in which Artaud wrote *Pour en finir avec le jugement de dieu*, was a pivotal year in the history of twentieth-century music. It was the year in which Olivier Messiaen completed his great *Turangalîla-symphonie*, with its extravagant percussive effects and extended percussion section, extreme dynamic range (he was one of the first composers to write extended moments of silence into his works), "sheets of sound" produced by complex sustained chords, use of the Ondes Martenot (Messiaen pioneered the use of this instrument, and this symphony provides its major presence as a lead instrument), sacred inspiration, trance effects, and exotic influences (Hindu and ancient Greek scales, Balinese sonorities, Gregorian plainchant aspects, etc.). The parallels with Artaud's projects are striking, yet the intent was diametrically opposed: Messiaen's goal was to incorporate these foreign effects into the Western musical canon and thus expand it. Artaud wished to subvert that very same musical canon by introducing radically foreign musical forms that would maintain their disruptive stylistic and metaphysical alterity within the new cultural context.

In fact, Artaud briefly worked with Messiaen in 1932, during rehearsals of *La Pâtissière du village*, staged by Louis Jouvet. In regard to the attempt to create some nonmusical sound effects on the organ, Artaud's remarks about Messiaen were less than flattering: "I insist, moreover, that not being a musician myself, I can only convey ideas to the organist, yet he resists with all the forces of his unconscious the idea of isolating non-musical sonorities; also, because of this tendancy which he cannot overcome, his interpretation of even precise points is never what had been agreed upon" (III, 322–323).

The year 1948 also saw the birth of *musique concrète,* created by Pierre Schaeffer working in the studios of *Radiodiffusion-télévision française.*[30] The continual perfecting of recording techniques permitted the high-quality reproduction of everyday sounds; Schaeffer utilized these possibilities to create a sort of "sound object," not a musical composition but a musical drama of sound effects, where the playback capabilities of the gramophone would make it the most general musical instrument. The earliest piece of musique concrète was the *Etude aux chemins de fer* (broadcast May 1948), a three-minute piece of manipulated recordings of trains; later that year there was a broadcast of his *Concert of Noises* (5 October 1948) consisting of sounds derived from saucepans and piano chords (the latter played by none other than Pierre Boulez, a student of Messiaen).

Boulez himself, in a 1958 article, reveals the importance of Artaud's work for the musical experimentation of the period:

The name Artaud immediately comes to mind when questions of vocal emission or the dissociation of words and their explosion are evoked; an actor and poet, he was naturally provoked by the material problems of interpretation, just like a composer who plays or conducts. I am not qualified to thoroughly investigate Artaud's language, but I can find in his writings the fundamental preoccupations of current music; having heard him read his own texts, accompanying them with screams, noises, rhythms, he showed us how to achieve a fusion of sound and word, how to splash out the phoneme when the word no longer can, in short, how to organize delirium. What nonsense and what an absurd alliance of terms, you'll say! Would you believe only in the vertigo of improvisation and the powers of an "elementary" sacralization? More and more, I imagine that to effectively create this we must consider delirium and, yes, organize it.[31]

And earlier, in "Propositions" (1948), Boulez explains that "I think that music must be hysteria and collective bewitchment, violently present—following the direction of Antonin Artaud, and not in the sense of a simple ethnographic reconstitution in the image of civilizations more or less distant from us."[32] More in the tradition of Rimbaud's poetic dictum, "The poet makes himself a *visionary* through a long, prodigious and rational disordering of *all* the senses"[33] than Boulez proved to be, Artaud writes in his "Manifeste en langage clair" ("Manifesto in Clear Language") (1925) against the demands of discursive reason:

This Meaning lost in the disorder of drugs and which appears as a profound intelligence to the contradictory phantasms of sleep. This Meaning is a conquest of the mind by itself, and although it is irreducible by reason, it exists, but only in the interior of the mind. *It is order, it is intelligence, it is the signification of chaos. But it does not accept this chaos as such, it interprets it, and because it interprets it, it loses it. It is the logic of Illogic. And this is to say everything. My lucid unreason does not fear chaos. (I**, 53)*

These observations were to become part of his program for a theater of cruelty, where we must remember that the theater, "like the plague, is delirium and communicative" (IV, 33).

Though *Pour en finir avec le jugement de dieu* does indeed participate in that creative delirium of which Artaud speaks, often revealing the chaotic, terrifying underside of human life, it is hardly an example of the *Gesamtkunstwerk*, the total artwork incorporating and expanding all the artistic media that he intended the theater of cruelty to be. Here, he was simultaneously torn between the contradictory demands of his own poetics *and* the conflicts between the structural features of radio and recording and the necessities of the theater. He provides the rationale for this broadcast in terms of "THE OBLIGATION of the writer, the poet, not to cowardly close himself up in text, a book, a review from which he will never again depart, but to the contrary to go outside, to shake up, to attack the public spirit, otherwise what's the use?" (XIII, 136–137).

He had already understood that for a writer the book is a tomb, and he leaves a great part of the creative act to his readers; he explains of his glossolalia that they can only be read, scanned, stressed, rhythmically, and that each reader must discover his own reading (IX, 188–189). The writer and readers must go beyond the dead letter of the text and bring the word to life. But is the radio any less a tomb? Is it not in a sense the tomb of the book, creating another sort of "dead letter" that vibrates? But this leads to the paradox of all representation, the internal contradiction of all spectacle: the more complete the spectacle, the less is left for the imagination; the more that is left for the imagination, the more impoverished the spectacle. Furthermore, because of the very nature of expression itself—the inadequacies of which Artaud had already charted in his letters to Jacques Rivière and continued to expound upon throughout his entire career—all representation can be but a mere shadow of the conditions of the interior life, the passions and torments of the soul.

In recording, the organic rhythms of the human voice are hypostatized and ultimately destroyed by mechanical reproduction, and then ironically these lost body rhythms are returned by electromechanical means. Thus recording produces an exteriorization and transformation of the voice, a sort of dispossession of the self. Recording and radio—through a sort of sympathetic magic—entail a theft of the voice and a disappearance of the body, a radical accentuation of the mind/body split, with its concomitant anguish. Whence came the terrible, tragic irony of Artaud's creation of this recorded radiophonic piece: *Pour en finir avec le jugement de dieu* reduplicated, in the artwork, the very structure of the theological and psychopathological conditions that he fought so long to overcome.

Recording the voice poses an ontological risk: the recorded voice is the stolen voice that returns to me as the hallucinatory presence of the voice of another. This other's voice may be the voice of God, as is often the case in paranoid experiences, and as was the case for Artaud during the period of his madness. In paranoid projections, one's own voice is hallucinated as coming from without,

Allen S. Weiss

as a divine or diabolic presence speaking the forbidden thoughts of unspeakable desires or unbearable prohibitions. The quotidian, empirical aspects of such an exteriorization of sound without image are outlined by Pierre Schaeffer, and discussed by Michel Chion, in terms of the notion of an *acousmetre*.[34] Radio is, *a fortiori*, the acousmetric medium, where the sound always appears without a corresponding image. This concrete presence and generality of the pure materiality of sounds by themselves bears all of the features traditionally attributed to the Judeo-Christian God and proffers the oftentimes paranoid invitation for us to lose ourselves in its totality. These features of the disincarnate voice—ubiquity, panopticism, omniscience, omnipotence—cause the radiophonic work to return as hallucination and phantasm; it is thus not unusual to find the radio fantasized as receiving messages from the beyond, serving as a spiritual transmitter in overcompensation for a psychotic dissociation from one's own body. With no visible body emitting the sound, and with no image whatsoever to anchor the sound, the radiophonic work leaves a sufficient space for fantasizing, a space large enough to contain the megalomaniacal projections of the most severe paranoia, the theological projections of the most severe paranoia, the theological projections of the grandest God. Thus in terms of *Pour en finir avec le jugement de dieu,* we must ask whether this work achieved the successful exorcism of God, so that it was the voices of Artaud's muse that we heard, or whether this work ironically presented yet one more stage of his paranoid struggle against God, yet one more instance of the voice of divine judgment.

Psychoanalytic theory teaches that figures of style and modes of expression are remotivated and reformalized in order to serve as ego-defense mechanisms, especially in the case of schizophrenia. Thus figurative uses may be taken literally, or literal statements may be rhetorically transformed, as verbal signs of unconscious thought processes. The very problem of style as formalization or demotivation must be considered in its function as a mechanism of defense, in direct relation to libidinal, corporeal operations.[35] What does it mean that Artaud, in the final mix for the broadcast of *Pour en finir avec le jugement de dieu,* suppressed the glossolalia and sentence ("Everything must be arranged to a hair in a fulminating order") with which the work was to have begun according to the written project? And that he didn't replace it with either the screams or the bruitage with which he would punctuate the later articulations of the texts but rather began with a drumroll, followed immediately by the diatribe of the introductory text? Why were his screams of "rage" (hardly stifled) in fact highly theatrical and neither particularly incantatory nor shocking but rather somewhat poetic? Artaud certainly wished to create a broadcast that would break with conventions. But if to a certain extent recording and broadcast technologies conventionalize performance—by fixing it for endless repetition, and by flattening it out to exclude extreme effects undesirable for the exigencies of the apparatus and the aesthetics of the recording and broadcast bureaucracies—then the paradox of Artaud's attempt is evident. This is its ultimate failure: an antirepresentational representation; a spontaneous fixing; a nonbroadcast broadcast; an affront against the public "spirit," which was also a disfiguration of Artaud's own work. The return of the repressed was transfigured according to the exigencies of the radiophonic art, where Artaud's voice was severed from his body, made an autonomous object in the world, and cast off to pursue its own destiny.

Artaud's expectations about the aesthetic possibilities of radiophonic transmission were betrayed both by the suppression of the broadcast *and* by the radiophonic specificity of this new art form. The sheer numerical and geographical advantages of radio over theater were offset by the loss of visual presence and the terrible potential of unchanging repetition. "Cruelty" is thus to be redefined and redirected—but it always returns to haunt and define Artaud. His final work offered no escape. The fate of this work, *Pour en finir avec le jugement de dieu,* is now an integral part of the history of modernist art and philosophy.[36] Perhaps it can finally be heard.

NOTES

1. Anaïs Nin, *The Diary, 1931-1934* (New York: The Swallow Press and Harcourt Brace & World), 1966, pp. 191–192. The narrative position from the point of view of the dead is utilized in several modern texts such as William Faulkner, *As I Lay Dying;* Claude Lanzmann, *Shoah;* Edgar Allan Poe, "The Facts in the Case of M. Valdemar"; etc.

2. Susan Sontag, *Illness as Metaphor* (New York: Vintage, 1979), passim.

3. *Pour en finir avec le jugement de dieu* appears in Antonin Artaud, *Oeuvres complètes,* vol. 13 (Paris: Gallimard, 1974); all references to Artaud's *Oeuvres complètes* will follow the citations in parentheses, with the volume number in Roman numerals followed by the page number in Arabic numerals. All translations are my own, unless otherwise stated.

4. Other versions of this work, and further renunciations of his Christianity, include "Lettre ouverte à Pie Xii" (XXII, 381); "Adresse au Pape" (XXIII, 155–158); (XXIII, 410–411); (XXIII, 451–453); (XXIII, 454–455); see also "L'Evêque de Rodez" (IX, 217–222).

5. Cited in notes to Artaud, *Oeuvres complètes* 1, p. 241.

6. On the linguistic and theological aspects of the *Cahiers de Rodez,* see Allen S. Weiss, "Psychopompomania," *Art & Text* 27, 1977; reprinted in Allen S. Weiss, *The Aesthetics of Excess* (Albany: State University of New York Press, 1989).

7. On glossolalia, see the works cited in Allen S. Weiss, "Psychopompomania"; Allen S. Weiss, "The Other as Muse: On the Ontology and Aesthetics of Narcissism," in *Psychosis and Sexual Identity* (Albany: State Univeristy Press, 1988). See also the two issues of *Le Discours Psychoanalytique* 6 and 7 (March and June 1983), edited by Jean-Jacques Courtine; and the issue of *Langages* 91 (Paris: Larousse, 1988), also edited by Courtine; Gilles Deleuze, in *Logique du sens* (Paris: Minuit, 1969), offers an important comparison of Artaud and Lewis Carroll, in the chapter entitled "Du schizophrène et de la petite fille," pp. 101–114. Despite the radical differences between the glossolalia and "nonsense" texts of children, poets, and schizophrenics, it is of interest at least to note the structural similarities. Compare to Artaud's glossolalia the following sound poem of Tristan Tzara, "Toto-vaca":

> *Ka tanga te kivi*
> *kivi*
> *Ka tangi te moho*
> *moho*
> *Ka tangi te tike*
> *Ka tangi te tike*
> *tike*
> *he poko anahe*

to tikoko tikoko
haere i te hara

(From Tzara, *Oeuvres complètes* [Paris: Gallimard, 1975], p. 454.) Childrens' counting rhymes provide a rich source of examples bordering on both poetry and nonsense.

Emelesi
Petri, Petera
Rupetera
Pétecnol

(From Pierre Roy, *Cent comptines* [Paris: Henri Jonquières et Co., 1926], n.p. On sound poetry, see Henri Chopin, *Poésie sonore internationale* [Paris: Jean-Michel Place, 1979].)

8. Artaud's pronunciation of his glossolalia (whose written phonetic structure borrowed from Turkish and Greek, his mother's "mother tongue") was not quite French, as Paule Thévenin explains in a note to *Artaud le mômo:* for the most part his pronunciation was closer to the Italian than to the French. For example, the *e* is never mute; *u* is pronounced *ou*; *z* is pronounced *dz*; *g* is always hard, and slightly guttural when folowed by *h*; the final *ch* is pronouced somewhat like the german *ch* (XII, 267). These transformations of the French language become pertinent and distinctive features of Artaud's written and spoken texts, thus a highly marked feature of his theatrical (and not only psychopathological) enunciations.

9. On the scatological implications of early modernist poetic glossolalia, see Annette

Michelson, "De Stijl, Its Other Face: Abstraction and Cacophony, or What Was the Matter with Hegel?" *October* 22 (Fall 1982).

10. On the excremental symbolism and Surrealist poetics, see Allen S. Weiss, "Between the Sign of the Scorpion and the Sign of the Cross: *L'Age d'or*," *Dada/Surrealism* 15 (1986); reprinted in Allen S. Weiss, *The Aesthetics of Excess.*

11. Jacques Derrida, "La Parole soufflée," in *Writing and Difference,* trans. Alan Bass (Chicago: University of Chicago Press, 1978), p. 181.

12. Guy Rosolato, "L'Expulsion" in *La Relation d'inconnu* (Paris: Gallimard, 1978), pp. 141–142.

13. Roland Barthes, "La musique, la voix, la langue," in *L'Obvie et l'obtus* (Paris: Seuil, 1982), p. 247.

14. The section on psychophonetics in this article is deeply indebted to Ivan Fónagy, *La Vive Voix: Essai de psychophonique* (Paris: Payot, 1983) which provides an excellent synthesis and rich interpretation of current research.

15. Cited in Fónagy, *La Vive Voix,* p. 91.

16. See Fónagy, *La Vive Voix,* passim, for the empirical research on the relations between sound and meaning; this statistical research provides strong evidence for the nonarbitrary relation between signifier and signified.

17. Roman Jakobson, *Six Lectures on Sound and Meaning*, trans. John Mepham (Cambridge, MA: MIT Press, 1978), p. 6.

18. Fónagy, *La Vive Voix*, p. 89.

19. Ibid., p. 112.

20. Elias Canetti, *Crowds and Power*, trans. Carol Stewart (New York: Continuum, 1981), p. 211.

21. Fónagy, *La Vive Voix*, p. 113.

22. Compare this text with the following passage from the opening pages of Witold Gombrowicz, *Ferdydurke*, trans. Eric Mosbacher (New York: Grove Press, 1968), pp. 12–14: "Half-asleep, I even imagined that my body was not entirely homogeneous, and that parts of it were not yet mature, that my head was laughing at and mocking my thigh, that my thigh was making merry at my head, that my finger was ridiculing my heart and my heart my brain, while my eye made sport of my nose and my nose of my eye, all to the accompaniment of loud bursts of crazy laughter—my limbs and the various parts of my body violently ridiculing each other in a general atmosphere of caustic and wounding raillery."

23. Friedrich Nietzsche, *Thus Spoke Zarathustra*, trans. Walter Kaufmann, in *The Portable Nietzsche*. (New York: Penguin, 1980), p. 146.

24. Ibid., pp. 249–250

25. Cited in Mary Ann Doane, "Ideology and the Practice of Sound Editing and Mixing," in *The Cinematic Apparatus*, eds. Teresa De Lauretis and Stephen Heath (London: Macmillan, 1980), p. 54.

26. Ibid., p. 55. We should note that the development of stereophonic and quadraphonic recording and broadcasting was intended, for the most part, not to further the fragmentation of the senses but rather to unify them: the spatial differential play is unified by the temporal (melodic, narrative) aspect of the music, which performs a synthesizing functon. In certain experimental works, such as those of Karlheinz Stockhousen, the multiplicity of sound channels is indeed foregrounded; but this is a studio or concert-hall effect much more than a radiophonic effect, given both the limitations of home two- or four-channel systems, and the usually less-than-ideal listening conditions in the average household.

27. One should consider Glenn Gould's seminal article, "The Prospects of Recording," in *The Glenn Gould Reader*, ed. Tim Page (New York: Alfred A. Knopf, 1984) for a discussion of the implications of both recording and playback technology for the future of music. He argues for the home listener's creative control by means of adjusting the sound of the stereophonic equipment, in striking parallel to Du-

champ's infamous claim that it is the spectator who completes the work of art.

28. Fónagy, *La Vive Voix*, p. 118.

29. See Edgar Varèse, *Ecrits* (Paris: Christian Bourgeois, 1983), pp. 53–54; see also Artaud (II, 108–124, and the notes on pp. 335–337).

30. On *musique concrète*, electroacoustic music, and experimental music, see Michel Chinon, *La Musique électro-acoustique* (Paris: Presses Universitaires de France, 1982); and Paul Griffiths, *Modern Music: The Avant-Garde Since 1945* (New York: Braziller, 1981). A striking case of censorship in the field of music is that of Luciano Berio's *Visage* (1961), an electroacoustic work sung by Cathy Berberian. This piece, with its radical disarticulation of language and extreme vocal effects, ranging from the violent to the erotic, from the peaceful to the agitated, was evidently received by some as quite obscene, since originally it was only partially broadcast on the radio. See Ivanka Stoianova, "Les Voies de la voix," *Traverses* 20, 1980. This recording can be heard on VOX-Turnabout TV 331 027.

31. Pierre Boulez, "Son et verbe," in *Relèves d'apprenti*, ed. Paule Thévenin (Paris: Seuil, 1966), p. 62. Note that this volume was edited by Paule Thévenin, the editor of the *Oeuvres complètes* of Artaud.

32. Pierre Boulez, "Propositions," in *Relèves d' apprenti*, p. 74. This claim might

be seen to be in some contradiction with Boulez's musical practice of that period; in 1948 he had just completed his *Second Piano Sonata*, which is an epitome of the rationalizing tendencies of dodecaphonic music; it was perhaps not until his composition *Le Marteau sans maître* (1954) that, in setting to music the poetry of René Char, a certain controlled delirium enters into his preeminently controlled rationalism.

33. Arthur Rimbaud, "Letter to Paul Demeny," in *Illuminations*, trans. Louise Varèse (New York: New Directions, 1957). Louise Varèse was the wife of Edgar Varèse.

34. See Michel Chion, *La Voix au cinéma* (Paris: Editions de l'Etoile, 1982), pp. 25–33. These particular qualities of radiophonic reception permit the radio to function as a paranoid or poetic mechanism; for example, Varèse's *L'Astronome* begins with the reception of signals from the star Sirius; the protaganist in Jean Cocteau's *Orphée* (1950) receives poetic inspiration from incoherent messages transmitted through his car radio, a curious muse; Allen Ginsberg's paranoid mother hears spies on the radio, as recounted in his poem "Kaddish" (1959); and also in many cases of spiritualism, the medium receives transmissions of voices of the dead. Artaud was concerned about the problems of dubbing in the cinema—especially the incompatibilities between certain types of gesture and certain voices—as early as 1933, when he wrote "Les souffrances du 'dubbing'" (III, 108–111).

35. Fónagy, *La Vive Voix*, pp. 209–210.

36. Two major theoretical issues are raised by the study of glossolalia in general and Artaud's recording in particular.

1. The investigation of glossolalia provides the test case for any structuralist, especially Saussurian, theory of the linguistic sign, necessitating a revision of the notation of the arbitrary relation between signifier and signified, as well as of the idea of language as a pure system of differences. Jakobson shows how linguistic structures must be considered according to not only their differential but also (and especially) their distinctive features, which differ from language to language and even dialect to dialect; furthermore, as we have seen, the meanings of sounds are not completely arbitrary, but are in part corporeally and libidinally motivated.

2. The influence of Artaud on poststructuralist libido theory, especially Deleuze/Guattari in *Anti-Oedipus,* has yet to be fully studied. Suffice it to say for the moment that the notation of a "body without organs" originates in *Pour en finir avec le jugement de Dieu* (XIII, 104; XIII, 287). Both of these problems will be investigated in a future work.

TO HAVE DONE WITH THE JUDGMENT OF GOD (1947)

Antonin Artaud ———————————————

translated from the French

by Clayton Eshleman

kré	Everything	**puc te**
kré	must be arranged	**puk te**
pek	to a hair	**li le**
kre	in a fulminating	**pek ti le**
e	order.	**kruk**
pte		

I learned yesterday

(you must think that I am very slow, or perhaps it is only a false rumor,
some of that dirty gossip that is peddled between the sink and the
latrines at the hour when the tubs are filled with meals once again
ingurgitated),

I learned yesterday

about one of the most sensational official practices of the American
public schools

which no doubt make that country consider itself at the head of progress.

Apparently, among the examinations or tests that a child has to undergo on
his entry to a public school for the first time is the one called the
seminal liquid or sperm test,

which consists of asking this newly-enrolled child for a little of his sperm in
order to put it into a glass jar

and of thereby keeping it ready for all the attempts at artificial insemination
which might eventually take place.

For the Americans keep on discovering how low they are on manpower
and children,

that is, not workers

but soldiers,

and at all costs and by all possible means they want to make and
manufacture soldiers

in view of all the planetary wars which might subsequently take place,

and which would be destined to *demonstrate* by the crushing
efficacity of force

the superexcellence of American products,

and the fruits of American sweat on all the fronts of activity and potential
dynamics of force.

Because there must be production,

nature must be replaced wherever it can be replaced by every possible
manner of activity,

a major field must be found for human inertia,

the worker must be kept busy at something,

Antonin Artaud

new fields of activity must be created,

where all the false manufactured products,

all the vile synthetic ersatzes will finally reign,

where glorious true nature will just have to withdraw,

and give up its place once and for all and shamefully to all the triumphant
replacement products,

where the sperm from all the artificial insemination factories

will work miracles

to produce armies and battleships.

No more fruit, no more trees, no more vegetables, no more ordinary or
pharmaceutical plants and consequently no more nourishment,

but synthetic products to repletion,

in vapors,

in special humors of the atmosphere, on particular axes of atmospheres
drawn by force and by synthesis from the resistance of a nature that
has never known anything about war except fear.

And long live war, right?

For by doing this it is war, isn't it, that the Americans have prepared for
and are thus preparing for step by step.

To defend this insane machining against all the competition which would
inevitably break out on all sides,

there must be soldiers, armies, airplanes, battleships,

therefore this sperm

which the American government has apparently had the nerve to consider.

For we have more than one enemy

and one who watches us, kid,

us, the born capitalists,

and among these enemies

Stalin's Russia

which is not short of armed men either.

All this is very fine,

but I did not know that the Americans were such a warlike people.

To fight you must accept blows

and perhaps I have seen many Americans at war

but in front of them they always had incommensurable armies of tanks,
        planes, battleships

serving as a shield.

I saw much fighting between machines

but I saw only in the infinite
        rear

the men who drove them.

Confronted by a people who make their horses, oxen and donkeys eat the
        last tons of real morphine which may be left to them in order to
        replace it with billows of ersatz smoke,

I prefer the people who eat right out of the earth the delirium that gave birth
        to them,

I am speaking of the Tarahumaras

who eat Peyote straight from the soil

while it is born,

and who kill the sun in order to establish the kingdom of black night,

and who split the cross so that the spaces of space will never again
        meet or join.

In this way you will hear the dance of the TUTUGURI.

        Antonin Artaud

TUTUGURI

The Rite of the Black Sun

And below, as at the bottom of the bitter
direfully despondent slope of the heart,
the circle of the six crosses opens,
                        far below,
as if embedded in the mother earth,
deembedded from the filthy embrace of the mother
                        who slobbers.

The earth of black coal
is the only humid site
in this cleft of rock.

The Rite is that the new sun passes through seven points before
            exploding at the earth's orifice.

And there are six men,
one for each sun,
and a seventh man
who is the sun completely
                raw
dressed in black and in red flesh.

Now, this seventh man
is a horse,
a horse with a man leading him.

But it is the horse
that is the sun
and not the man.

On the rending of a drum and of a long
peculiar trumpet,
the six men,
who were lying down,
rolled up flush with the ground,
shoot up successively like sunflowers,
not suns at all
but turning soils,
lotuses of water,
and at every upshooting
sounds the increasingly gloomy and *suppressed*

       gong
       of the drum
until suddenly we see galloping headlong toward us, at vertiginous
      speed,
the last sun,
the first man,
the black horse with a

       man naked
       absolutely naked
       and *virgin*
       on it.

Having bounded, they advance following circular meanders
and the horse whose flesh is bloody panics
and caracoles without stopping
on the pinnacle of its rock
until the six men
have finished encircling
completely
the six crosses.

      Antonin Artaud

Now, the major key of the Rite is precisely
THE ABOLITION OF THE CROSS.

Having finished turning
they dig up
the earthen crosses
and the man naked
on the horse
raises high
an immense horseshoe
which he has tempered in a slice of his blood.

The Search for Fecality

There where it smells of shit
it smells of being.
Man could very well have avoided shitting
and kept his anal pocket closed,
but he chose to shit
as he had chosen to live
instead of consenting to live dead.

The fact is that in order not to make caca
he would have had to consent
not to be,
but he could not resolve to lose
      being,
in other words to die alive.
There is in being
something particularly tempting for man
and that something is precisely
      CACA
      (Roarings here.)

In order to exist you need only let yourself go until you are,
but in order to live
you must be somebody,
in order to be somebody,
you must have a BONE,
not be afraid of showing the bone,
and of losing the meat on the way.

Man has always preferred the meat
to the earth of the bones.
The fact is there was only earth and bone timber,
and he had to earn his meat,
there was only iron and fire
and no shit,
and man was afraid of losing shit
or rather he *desired* shit
and, for that, sacrificed blood.

In order to have shit,
in other words meat,
where there was only blood
and scrap-iron bones
and where there was no question of earning being
but where there was a question of losing life.

o reche modo
to edire
di za
tau dari
do padera coco

There, man withdrew and fled.

Then the beasts ate him.

Antonin Artaud

It was not rape,
he lent himself to the obscene meal.

He found it tasty,
he even learned
to play the beast
and to eat rat
daintily.

And what explains this filthy abasement?

Either the world is not yet formed,
or man has only a faint idea of the world
and he wants to protect it forever?

The explanation is that man,
one fine day,
stopped
        the idea of the world.

Two roads were open to him:
that of the infinite outside,
that of the infinitesimal inside.

And he chose the infinitesimal inside.
Where it is only a question of squeezing
the rat,
the tongue,
the anus
or the glans.

And god, god himself hastened the movement.

Is god a being?
If he is it is made of shit.
If he is not
he's not.
Now, he is not,
but like the void which advances with all its forms
whose most perfect representation
is the march of an incalculable squadron of crab-lice.

"You are mad, Monsieur Artaud, what about the Mass?"

I abjure baptism and the Mass.
There is no human act
which, on the internal erotic plane,
proves more pernicious than the descent
of the so-called Jesus-christ
onto the altars.

No one will believe me
and even from here I see the public shrugging its shoulders
but the one named christ is no other than he
who facing the crab-louse god
consented to live without body,
while an army of men,
descended from a cross
where god believed he had long ago nailed them,
rebelled,
and, barbed in iron,
in blood,
in fire, and bone scrap,
advance, reviling the Invisible
in order to end GOD'S JUDGMENT there.

Antonin Artaud

To Raise the Question of ...

What is serious
is that we know
that after the order
of this world
there is another.

What is this order?

We do not know.

The number and order of possible suppositions in this domain
is precisely
infinity!

And what is infinity!

We do not exactly know!

It is a word
we employ
to indicate
the opening
of our consciousness
towards an inordinate
indefatigable and inordinate
possibility.

And what exactly is consciousness?

We do not exactly know.

To Have Done with the Judgment of God

It is nothingness.

A nothingness
we employ
to indicate
when we do not know something
from what side
we do not know it
and so
we say
consciousness,
from the side of consciousness,
but there are a hundred thousand other sides.

So what?

It seems that consciousness
is in us
linked
to sexual desire
and hunger;

but it could
very well
not be
linked to them.

It is said,
it can be said,
there are those who say
that consciousness
is an appetite,
the appetite for life;

and immediately
beside the appetite for life,
the appetite for food
comes immediately to mind;

as though there were not people who eat
without any appetite at all
and who are hungry.

For that also
occurs
to be hungry
without appetite;

so what?

So

the space of possibility
was given me one day
like a loud fart
that I will let;

but neither the space,
nor the possibility,
I didn't know exactly what they were,

and I did not feel the need to think about it,

they were words
invented to define things
which existed
or did not exist
confronted by
the pressing urgency
of a need:
that of abolishing the idea,
the idea and its myth,
and of enthroning in its place
the thundering manifestation
of this explosive necessity:
to dilate the body of my internal night,

of the internal nothingness
of my self

which is night,
nothingness,
irreflection,
but which is an explosive assertion
that there is
something
to make way for:

my body.

And really
reduce my body
to this stinking gas?

To think that I have a body
because I have a stinking gas
which forms
inside me?

I do not know
but
I do know that

       space,

       time,

       dimension,

       development,

       the future,

       posterity,

       being,

       non-being,

       the self,

       the non-self,

are nothing to me;

but there is one thing
which is something,
only one thing
which is really something,
and I feel
how much it wants to
BURST OUT:
the presence of my corporal
pain,
the menacing,
never tiring
presence
of my
body;

however much I am pressed with questions
and deny all questions,
there is a point
when I find myself forced
to say no,

        NO

and so
to negation;

and this point,
it's when I am pressed,

when I am squeezed out
and am milked
until the departure
within me
of food,
of my food
and its milk,

and what remains?

That I am suffocated;

and I don't know if it is an action
but by pressing me thus with questions
even to the absence
and the nothingness
of the question
I was pressed
right to the suffocation
within me

       Antonin Artaud

of the idea of body
and of being a body,
and it is then that I smelled the obscene

and that I farted
in the folly
and excess
and revolt
of my suffocation.

The fact is I was being pressed
right up to my body
and right up to the body

and it is then
that I shattered everything
because my body
is never to be touched.

Conclusion

—And what has been your purpose, Monsieur Artaud, in this
    radio broadcast?

—Mainly to denounce a certain number of officially
    authorized and acknowledged social filths:
First, this emission of infantile sperm given voluntarily by
    children with a view to the artificial insemination of
    latent foetuses
that will see the light of day in a century or more.

Second, to denounce, in this same American people who
    occupy the entire surface of the former Indian continent, a
    revival of the warlike imperialism of ancient America
    which caused the pre-Columbian Indians to be despised by
    all precedent mankind.

—You are expressing here, Monsieur Artaud, some very bizarre things.

—Yes, I am saying something bizarre,
the fact is that the pre-Columbian Indians were, contrary
    to all subsequent opinions about them,
    a strangely civilized people
who had in fact known a form of civilization based on the
    exclusive principle of cruelty.

—And do you know exactly what cruelty is?

—Just like that, no, I don't know.

Antonin Artaud

—Cruelty, it's to extirpate through the blood and as far as the
        blood god, the bestial risk of unconscious human
        animality, wherever it may be encountered.

—Man, when he is not held back, is an erotic animal,
he has within him an inspired tremor,
a sort of pulsation
producing innumerable beasts which are the form the
        ancient terrestrial peoples universally attributed to god.
That made what is called a spirit.
Now, this spirit which came from the American Indians is
        reappearing almost everywhere today in scientific guise
        which serves only to reveal this spirit's morbid infectious
        hold, the revealed state of vice, but a vice which pullulates
        with diseases,
for, laugh as much as you wish to,
what men have called microbes
                is in fact god,
and do you know what the Americans and the Russians make
                their atoms with?
They make them with the microbes of god.

—You are raving, Monsieur Artaud.
You're mad.

—I am not raving.
I'm not mad.
I'm telling you that microbes have been reinvented in order to
        impose a new idea of god.

A new way has been found to make god come out again and to
catch him in the act of his microbial noxiousness.
It's to nail him to the heart,
there where men love him best,
in the form of sickly sexuality,
in that sinister guise of morbid cruelty which he assumes during
the moments when it pleases him as it does now to
tetanize and madden humanity.

He uses the spirit of purity of a consciousness that has remained
ingenuous like mine in order to asphyxiate it with all the
false appearances which he spreads universally through
the spaces and it is thus that Artaud the Mômo can be
dismissed as a crank.

—What do you mean, Monsieur Artaud?

—I mean that I have found the way to have done once and for
all with this monkey
and that if nobody believes any more in god everybody believes
more and more in man.

And it is man that we must now decide to emasculate.

—How so?
            How so?
From whatever angle one approaches you, you are mad, mad
enough to be tied down.

—By having him undergo once more but for the last time a
session on the autopsy table in order to remake his anatomy.

Antonin Artaud

I say, in order to remake his anatomy.
Man is sick because he is badly constructed.
We must decide to strip him in order to scratch out this
      animalcule which makes him itch to death,

        god,
        and with god
        his organs.

For tie me down if you want to,
but there is nothing more useless than an organ.

When you have given him a body without organs,
then you will have delivered him from all his automatisms and
      restored him to his true liberty.

Then you will teach him again to dance inside out
as in the delirium of our accordion dance halls
and that inside out will be his true side out.

MARK E. CORY

In the mid-1960s, the Bavarian Broadcasting Network, one of the nine public broadcasters established in the Federal Republic after World War II, introduced a remarkable work written for radio by Paul Pörtner. *Schallspielstudie*, literally "Soundplaystudy," was a collage of voice and sound effects taken through a series of electronic manipulations until the sound effects begin to speak, the voice to drip like water and shatter like glass. Pörtner's experiment was extraordinary for several reasons. In aesthetic terms, it bared the problematical nexus of verbal and nonverbal elements that has been the most vexing and yet most exciting stimulus for radio art. In historical terms, it ripped the fabric of Germany's highly successful establishment Hörspiel, fundamentally changing the way radio "drama" in that country would be created. And in critical terms, it linked a forgotten chapter of avant-garde experiments from Weimar Germany with the developing aesthetic of today's New Hörspiel in a fascinating pattern of continuity and discontinuity.

When Pörtner reflected upon his experiments, he explained the novelty in his approach by saying, "I trade the desk of an author for the studio of the sound engineer, my new syntax is the cut, my product is recorded over microphones, mixers, and filters on magnetic tape, the principle of montage creates a playful composition [Spielwerk] out of hundreds of particles."[1] Critics initially dismissed Pörtner's *Schallspielstudien* and the works of contemporaries such as Franz Mon, Ludwig Harig, Peter Handke, and Gerhard Rühm as empty experimentation at best and antihumanistic verbal acrobatics at worst. The dramatic vignettes of Friedrich Dürrenmatt, the lyricism of Günter Eich had been milestones in the development of a postwar literary Hörspiel of great subtlety, and that tradition now seemed threatened. The medium whose swift ascent to power and prestige among the nation's foremost literati had paralleled Germany's economic rebirth from the ashes of World War II seemed bent upon a suicidal flight away from plot, theme, and character, and poised for surrender to peripheral areas such as electronic music and sound poetry. Defenders of the New Hörspiel (das Neue Hörspiel), as the experiments eventually were to be called, argued that the traditional radio play tapped merely one part of the medium's potential, and that only when that medium ceased to reproduce a form of text-based literature and to produce instead art forms created with the tools of the electronic medium itself could we speak of radio art.

The heat kindled by the debate from the 1960s still smokes the contemporary critical and dramaturgical scene after twenty-five years, making radio art in West Germany (and to a lesser extent in the other German-speaking countries) a particularly lively forum for the avant-garde. This debate has been carried on in the public sphere, particularly with respect to the awarding of prestigious prizes for new productions (such as the annual Radio Drama Prize of the War Blind).[2] It has also figured significantly within the cultural and political institutions where new forms of radio art are arbitrated, that is, within the radio drama departments of the broadcast stations themselves. The emergence of avant-garde radio art during the sixties was in fact so tropic that for the next decade no broadcaster in the Federal Republic, Austria, or German-speaking Switzerland was without its quotient of experimental radio plays. By 1968 the Austrians Ernst Jandl and Friederike Mayröcker captured the Radio Drama Prize of the War Blind for the avant-garde with their stereophonic experiment *Fünf Mann Menschen*, and the following year the term *New Hörspiel* made its debut in anthologies and criticism. Two decades later the real issue of this debate is the subtle question of

Mark E. Cory

whether by its very successes avant-garde radio art in Germany has become so institutionalized that it has lost its oppositional character.

For reasons that will emerge in this essay, the particular achievement in Germany has been to establish a practice of radio art in all relevant domains: artistic, institutional, historical, and theoretical. With respect to the avant-garde, that practice has had a particularly interesting evolution. Historians, for instance, have begun to look with renewed interest at the early years of radio and to question many of the postwar assumptions about the exclusivity of the traditional lyrical Hörspiel with which the New Hörspiel collided so forcefully. Among other things, historians have redirected attention to a remarkable cadre of innovative theorists and practitioners, figures such as Walter Benjamin, Kurt Schwitters, and Bertolt Brecht, whose early insights into the fundamental changes wrought in our century by photography, film, and the infant medium of radio on the way art is created, transmitted, and evaluated have yet to be equalled in the development of media aesthetics. Avant-garde radio artists during the 1960s worked largely in ignorance of this theory and practice. The most readily apparent reason for this aesthetic amnesia has to do with the political turbulence of National Socialism within a decade of the birth of radio, and of course with the chaos of the Second World War. Careful scholarship and archival work over the past few years have reconstructed much of what was long assumed lost or destroyed during the period of Weimar Germany, however, and have radically revised our understanding of the experimental Hörspiel of the 1960s and its successor, the New Hörspiel.[3]

As in every country, German radio in its earliest years was synonymous with experimentation.[4] From the beginnings of regular transmissions in Germany on 29 October 1923, every broadcast was an experiment, every production an attempt to improve the quality of the sound, to find ways to balance music, sound effects, and voice, to create and enhance illusion. As wax recordings were developed, early attempts to capitalize on the spontaneity of live performances gave way to dramaturgical experiments with cut and mix. Once broadcasts could be recorded (the earliest examples in the German Radio Archive in Frankfurt date from 1928), the concept of a repertoire of radio art and a concomitant theoretical and critical apparatus began to emerge.

The experimental nature of the new technology itself, plus the remarkable pluralism characteristic of Weimar culture, gave rise to at least three distinct types of radio art before the war.[5] The first was a logical extension of the stage, radio perceived as a theater of the blind. The second took radio "drama" beyond the staging of works for the blind and sought to develop an imaginative literature written expressly for the new medium. The third understood something even broader: radio art as acoustical art, a radical and short-lived breaking away from literary conventions that was to signal the debut of the avant-garde tradition resurrected with such success in the 1960s.

Although the first general type, adaptations of stage drama, seems simplistic in its aesthetic now, it offered at least two advantages as a medium for drama, namely independence from the limited number of established theaters and the accompanying freedom to attempt works whose demands upon the imagination exceeded the technical limits of existing stages.[6] These advantages are real and persist to a certain extent today, which accounts in part for the consistent popularity of such readings and adaptations throughout the history of radio art. In Germany the earliest programming marking the transition of radio from a military tool to a cultural medium included music and the recitation of poetry.[7] Poetry recitations gave way to dramatic monologues from classic works by Shakespeare and Goethe, soon to be followed by well-known dialogues and dramatic scenes. By 1924 Radio Berlin had organized separate "playhouses" for broadcasts of opera and drama ("Sendespiel-Bühne, Abteilung Oper" and "Sendespiel-Bühne, Abteilung Schauspiel"). The first production of this prototype radio drama department was Alfred Braun's 1924 live broadcast of Friedrich Schiller's drama of the Thirty Years' War, *Wallensteins Lager* (*Wallenstein's Camp*) with actors brought before the microphone in clanking armor costumed as if for the stage. This initial aesthetic response to the new medium was understandably defensive. Sets, props, costumes—all those customary visual determinants of theatrical action—could be brought before the microphone, but scarcely transmitted. To compensate for the missing visual dimension, early radio plays of this first type relied heavily upon exaggerated "sound scenery" (*Geräuschkulissen*) and the use of gongs to signal scene changes. In looking back on these pioneer efforts, the influential critic Heinz Schwitzke has remarked that the early broadcast studios were so dependent upon gongs for the representation of movement in dramatic action that they came to resemble oriental temples.[8]

The second type of radio art is much more complex and includes both adaptations and original works written expressly for the acoustical medium of radio. Within the first few years of experimentation, the simple *reproduction* of plays for the imaginary stage of the radio gradually gave way to using the new medium in a *productive* manner, that is, to creating art forms that would somehow turn the absence of a visual stimulus into an aesthetic advantage. This was not yet the kind of critical and didactically "productive" relationship Brecht was to demand in his 1930 essay "Der Rundfunk als Kommunikationsapparat" (Radio as a Means of Communication) but rather what Rudolf Arnheim was to celebrate a few years later as an "acoustic bridge": "By the disappearance of the visual, an acoustic bridge arises between all sounds: voices, whether connected with a stage scene or not, are now of the same flesh as recitation, discussion, song and music. What hitherto could exist only separately now fits organically together: the human being in the corporeal world talks with disembodied spirits, music meets speech on equal terms."[9]

Somewhat ironically, the most-often-cited example of this type in the history of the German Hörspiel is an English radio play, inspired in turn by reports in the *General Electric Revue* of similar experiments conducted in the infancy of American radio art. Richard Hughes's *A Comedy of Danger*, first broadcast by the BBC in

January 1924 and in German translation in Hamburg a year and a half later, takes place in a mine shaft. When the lights in the mine unexpectedly go out, the radio audience "sees" exactly as much, or as little, as the three stranded tourists whose plight constitutes the drama.[10] Setting a radio drama in an environment where the visual dimension is eliminated was an imaginative solution to the challenge of creating radiophonic art, a solution often imitated both before and after the war.[11] As critics have pointed out, however, this particular solution, although a definite advance over reciting traditional stage drama before the microphone, still depended upon a primarily visual aesthetic.[12] The discrepancy between the visual information of the listener and that of the character was eliminated, but only by reducing the visual world of the fictional characters to the same impoverished level as that of the listener.

Several pioneers of the Weimar period tried a different approach by incorporating the medium of radio as one of the players. Struggling to create a drama about the rescue attempts surrounding the crash of the airship *Italia* as it attempted a flight over the North Pole in 1928, Friedrich Wolf drew upon the ancient dramatic device of the messenger, now brought up-to-date with radio. Wolf's *SOS Rao-Rao-Foyn / Krassin rettet Italia* imitated a live broadcast of a rescue attempt by the crew of the *Krassin*, as reported over radio. The radio feature was born.

This clever innovation coincided with an era of enormous interest in the heroic adventures of men equipped with new technology as they conquered what were perceived to be the last frontiers on earth. Polar expeditions, jungle explorations, and transatlantic flights had captured the popular imagination, and these heroic lays of modern technology came to dominate the Hörspiel between 1929 and 1935.[13] By dramatizing these exploits through a fictional radio announcer, these works could bridge the physical distance between listener and the exotic event in a completely natural way. The missing visual dimension was neatly parlayed into a kind of visceral excitement, an excitement not merely transmitted by radio but in fact created by it.

Wolf's *Krassin* was accompanied in this period by Walter Erich Schäfer's *Malmgreen*, Arno Schirokauer's *Magnet-Pol,* Hans Braun's *Station D im Eismeer* and Hermann W. Anders's *Polarkantate*—all located in the icy remove of polar explorations—by Bertolt Brecht's very important *Ozeanflug (Lindbergh's Flight)*, and by the most popular Hörspiel of Weimar Germany, Ernst Johannsen's *Brigadevermittlung (Brigade Report)*. The latter is a variation on this solution, in that it relies upon the fiction of a military field telephone during the First World War to suspend the optical disadvantage of the listener. The aesthetic principle, however, is the same. By 1929 a congruity of form and content was achieved in these Hörspiele, and in some a degree of verisimilitude, that would be exceeded only by the most famous radio drama in the history of the medium, Orson Welles's 1938 broadcast of *War of the Worlds.*

The pursuit of perfect illusion in the spirit of *War of the Worlds* was actually not characteristic of most Weimar radio art, however.[14] In fact, Brecht's *Ozeanflug* is consciously designed to inhibit verisimilitude. Although the idea of incorporating the technical feature of radio itself as one of the dramatic partners persisted throughout much of this period, an alternative approach to reality came to be much more important in the Hörspiele of this second major category and in fact went on to dominate radio art in Germany after the Second World War.

This alternative approach to reality relied upon the suggestive power of sound and began to recast the acoustical dimension of radio drama in symbolic, rather than realistic, terms. Whereas the function of sound effects in the early experiments had been to create an acoustical "set" that could substitute for the missing visual props of staged drama, that function was now modified and the sound effects themselves stylized. The most-often-cited example is Eduard Reinacher's *Der Narr mit der Hacke (The Fool with the Pickaxe)*. In this 1930 Hörspiel, a Japanese monk stubbornly and single-handedly hacks a tunnel through the granite face of a mountain isolating a coastal village from the outside world. For years, the only sign the villagers have of the monk is the sound of his pick ringing as a leitmotif throughout the play. As he breaks through to the other side, opening a safe passage for the people of the village with his last strength, we learn that in his youth this solitary laborer had killed a man with such a pickaxe. The work is the propitiation for his sin, the sound of the pick an acoustical symbol of his guilt.

Early theorists such as Richard Kolb correctly perceived that something of lasting importance had been created in Reinacher's work.[15] Now stylized, sound effects could have a totally different structural function. Instead of motivating or compensating for the missing visual dimension, they could function symbolically to suspend the classical theatrical unities of time, place, and action. Instead of contributing to an external verisimilitude, they could lead inward to realms of thought and emotion more characteristic of the internalized monologues of prose fiction than of the dialogues of drama. In the years between 1934 and the war, many attempts were made to develop this aesthetic shift,[16] but Reinacher's innovation would not bear its most mature fruit until the postwar period.

What was long obscured by the enthusiasm of theorists for this last type of radio art is that all the Hörspiele of this second broad category still share a literary model. Although they may or may not be highly dramatic, lyrical, balladlike or epic in style, each was conceived primarily as text-based literature. The third category of radio art in Weimar Germany developed at the same time but differs from the first two categories in that it issued from a crucially different starting point. In an era of active experimentation in radio art, this elusive category stands out precisely because that starting point was not conventional literature. And this category furnishes the most direct link to the sound of the avant-garde in German-language radio today.

The difference is captured in these remarks by Hans Flesch, founding director of the Berlin Radio Hour, on the dedication of his new studio in 1929: "We need to fashion not only a new medium, but a new content as well: Our program cannot be created at a desk."[17] Unconsciously echoed by Paul Pörtner nearly forty years later, Flesch brought an extraordinary originality to the earliest practice of German radio art. His *Zauberei auf dem Sender* (*Microphone Magic*) was broadcast in Frankfurt in October of 1924, only one year after regular broadcasts began in Germany.[18] Calling his work *An Attempt at a Radio Grotesque*, Flesch deliberately challenges "normal" (though very young) broadcasting conventions with interruptions, unmotivated sound effects, and distortions of musical tempi, which are ultimately unmasked as a power struggle between an artistic director and a "magician" determined to show the radio audience the magical aspects of this new medium.

Flesch and his fellow director at Hamburg Radio Hans Bodenstedt also experimented in 1924 with "sound portraits" (Hörbilder) of cityscapes (*Die Straße* [*The Street*] and *Hamburger Hafen* [*Hamburg Harbor*]). Bodenstedt saw especially exciting possibilities for radio art in capturing sounds from the widest possible spectrum of sources: "A room large or small, a theater, a recital hall, an athletic arena, a speaker's podium, classroom, factory, street, ship, zoo…the whole world offers itself as studio."[19] By 1926 Bodenstedt had expanded his cityscape to a larger acoustical portrait he called *Der Herr der Erde* (*The Lord of the World*). In the same year, Alfred Braun broadcast *Der tönende Stein* (*The Sounding Stone*), a work he very significantly called an "acoustical film."

Acoustical films—so we called a piece for radio in those days in Berlin in which a radio director had to create both his own original material and his working script—were works which transferred quite consciously the techniques of cinema to the radio, so that images both flowed dreamily and flitted by in quickest succession, abbreviated images, superimposed images, alternating and blending close-ups and distant shots. Each of the short images was positioned on a particular acoustical plane, surrounded by a particular acoustical set:

1 minute street with the loud music of Leipzig Square;

1 minute protest march;

1 minute stock market on the day of the crash;
1 minute factory with its machine symphony;
1 minute soccer stadium;
1 minute train station;
1 minute train underway, etc.[20]

The influence of the slightly more mature medium of film on its younger technological sibling has long been acknowledged, even by those critics hostile to the avant-garde impulse common to both media.[21] The cinematic technique of the mix was embraced regardless of whether an extant drama was being adapted for radio, a literary piece created especially for the new medium, or a series of sound images assembled into an acoustical film. The technique of the hard cut seemed just as promising. Rudolf Arnheim, writing from the perspective of 1936, praises "filmic wireless plays," by which he means works using prerecorded material on film strips "cut properly afterwards and mounted as a sound-film."[22] The advantage of this new technique over wax recordings, namely the ability to cut and manipulate stored sounds more precisely and predictably, would remain unexploited until long after the development of magnetic tape recording after the war, however, as the process of working with filmstrips proved too expensive.[23]

The only German filmmaker of note to contribute directly to radio art during the Weimar period was Walter Ruttmann, whose 1927 documentary *Berlin—Symphony of a Great City* (*Berlin—Symphonie einer Großstadt*) has become a cinematic milestone for its skillful use of montage. Ruttmann came to film, and hence to radio, from painting. He understood what made visual rhythm in the plastic arts and was practiced in the language of abstraction characteristic of the "absolute film." In 1928 Ruttmann recorded a brief sound montage (300 feet), which was broadcast as *Wochenende* (*Weekend*). His admirer and fellow filmmaker Hans Richter published the following description of *Weekend*: There was no picture, just sound (which was broadcast). It was the story of a weekend, from the moment the train leaves the city until the whispering lovers are separated by the approaching, home-struggling crowd. It was a symphony of sound, speech-fragments and silence woven into a poem. If I had to choose between all of Ruttmann's works, I would give this one the prize as the most inspired. It re-created with perfect ease in sound the principles of picture poetry which was the characteristic of the "absolute film."[24]

In one of his own radio essays, the contemporary critic and theorist Reinhard Döhl has pointed out that *Weekend* proceeds from the same basic thematic impulse as Ruttmann's film *Berlin—Symphony of a Great City* but abstracts from this material an acoustical mosaic whose economy, brevity, and precision were to become key signatures of avant-garde radio art.[25] The individuals whom Döhl credits with earliest advocacy for incorporating the lessons of avant-garde film into the production of radio art are Friedrich Bischoff from Breslau and Hans Flesch, author of *Zauberei auf dem Sender*. Flesch in particular argued as early as 1928 for the "absolute precision" afforded by sound film, an argument published in 1931: "Only the sound film is in a position to fulfill this wish [for absolute precision] and to carry out the intention of the director to its fullest extent. A radio play recorded on sound film can be reviewed and perfected by cutting and mixing until it is complete in the opinion of the director, and only then offered to the listening audience."[26]

It was as director of the Berlin Radio Hour that Hans Flesch commissioned Walter Ruttmann to record *Weekend* as an acoustical film. At the same time, Flesch commissioned a second work with the same Tri-Ergon process, this time from Friedrich Walther Bischoff. For his acoustical film, Bischoff chose to repeat a work originally produced in Breslau in 1927, then apparently redone on wax recording, perhaps for broadcast in 1928.[27] Bischoff called his work *Hallo! Hier Welle Erdball!!* (*Hello! You're Tuned to Radio Earth!!*), and gave it the subtitle "sound symphony." Judging from the available information, this too was an acoustical mosaic more concerned with exploiting the aesthetic and technical opportunities of the new medium of radio than with adapting the conventions of another (literary) genre. One of the preserved sequences is entitled "A Day in the Life of a Man Named K." ("Zeitablauf des Mannes K."). Other sequences were called "Sensations—Catastrophies," and were set in a soccer stadium in England, in a remote jungle, on an ocean steamer, or in Japan. The introduction explains the title: "Treat this like a newspaper. Pick out what pleases you best. The earth reports in! Symphony of the world!" Clearly Bischoff wanted in part to demonstrate and celebrate the ability of radio to move effortlessly and convincingly across time and distance. Clearly, too, he wanted to capitalize on the fascination of the period with radio coverage of sensational events, spectacular accidents, and heroic pioneers. Just as clearly, however, this early work was an experiment with the new medium itself, with its capacity for combining news and entertainment, poetry and music, and also with its suitability for the kind of montage, cut, and mix pioneered by film.

As exciting as these early works for radio were (and still are, although none thus far has been translated for an English-speaking audience), their impact during the Weimar years was marginal. One limiting factor, cost, has already been mentioned. At a time when radio audiences were small and primitive receivers made *any* reception an adventure, the extra costs associated with the kind of filmic precision sought by Alfred Braun, Hans Flesch, Hans Bodenstedt, Friedrich Bischoff, and Walter Ruttmann proved prohibitive. But another limiting factor was just as clearly the avant-garde nature of this third type of Hörspiel. Radio adaptations of classical works and original radio compositions such as Eduard Reinacher's *Der Narr mit der Hacke* and Ernst Johannsen's *Brigadevermittlung* were simply more popular, with critics and apparently with radio audiences. The situation in radio was not very different from that in film, where there was also great tension between the art films of Ruttmann and Hans Richter on the one hand, and the commercially successful films of G. W. Pabst and Fritz Lang with their more traditional story-based aesthetic on the other.[28]

A third factor limiting the impact of the avant-garde in the politically fragile circumstances of Weimar Germany was its oppositional character. Friedrich Bischoff was branded a "cultural Bolshevik" by hostile criticism in 1930. Hans Flesch and Alfred Braun were both dismissed from their posts in Berlin in 1932 and imprisoned by the SS in August of 1933. Ernst Hardt, the brilliant director of Eduard Reinacher's popular works and of Brecht's didactic experiments, died in 1947 as a result of complications suffered during his imprisonment under the National Socialists.[29] As John Willet has shown in his analysis of the relationship between art and politics in Weimar Germany, many avant-garde artists were caught between reactionary pressures on the right and equal intolerance on the radical left.[30] Because wireless broadcasting did not simply appear as a perfected technological miracle but evolved very much as a social product of a highly politicized period in German history, radio art was shaped by political forces as surely as theater, film, and the other arts. Some would argue that the political character of German broadcasting was particularly conspicuous, precisely because it was a state-controlled medium. Writing for a volume on the Weimar artist as social critic, Friedrich Knilli notes that "radio was not comparable as a means of communication to the theater, books, magazines, newspapers, films, records and other media that could be used by everyone—by Jews as well as by Christians, by Communists as well as by Nazis, by the proletariat as well as by the bourgeoisie. Broadcasting authority was vested solely in the state."[31] As Knilli points out, this power structure resulted in a struggle for codetermination, with the working class organizing its own radio press, amateur radio clubs, and even strike actions to force a reduction of license fees and to influence program content.

The point at which this struggle for codetermination becomes especially significant for the development of avant-garde radio art is its illustration in the early work of Bertolt Brecht. Because of his stature in German letters, Brecht's radio plays have always attracted keen interest.[32] His first involvement was through adaptations for Alfred Braun's Radio Berlin, both of his own *Man Is Man* and of several Shakespeare plays. His collaboration with Ernst Hardt, by then director of Radio Cologne, led to Brecht's first original work for the new medium, *Der Lindberghflug* (*The Lindbergh Flight*), presented at the Baden-Baden Music Festival in 1929 and broadcast on that occasion over every station in Germany, save Munich.

As has been mentioned, Brecht's *Lindbergh Flight* is an example of the enthusiasm of the period for the heroic extension of the human spirit through new technologies. The solo flight of Charles Lindbergh in 1927 was transformed by Brecht into a didactic ballad for chorus and individual voices, with music by Kurt Weill (for the American scenes) and Paul Hindemith (the over-water and European scenes). Because of the prominence of its musical component, the *Lindbergh Flight* is often cited as an early example of radio cantata; because of its subtitle (*A Radio Learning Play for Boys and Girls*), it is sometimes classified as a school oratorio for radio. Both classifications are accurate as far as they go, but they miss the deeper point that Brecht was attempting something quite revolutionary with this play, something that would flicker out in radio practice to survive only in the theory of avant-garde radio art until its rediscovery in the late 1960s.

As Stuart Hood has pointed out, Brecht's instructions for the performance of this work make it clear that he conceived of it as a duet between a group of participating listeners and the radio, which for its part would broadcast the music, sound effects, and certain of the choruses:

[The Lindbergh Flight] *is a didactic piece and falls into two parts. One part (the songs of the elements, the choruses, the noises of the water and the motors, and so on) has the function of making the exercise possible—that is to say, of prefacing and interrupting it, which is best achieved by the use of a radio set. The other pedagogic part (the part of the airmen) is the text for the exercise; the person taking part in the exercise listens to one part of the text and speaks the other. In this way the set and the person taking part begin to work together, the stress being rather on accuracy than on expressiveness.*[33]

The distinctive feature of this radio experiment is that it was designed for audience participation. In his *Theory of the Lehrstück*, Brecht stresses that "the Lehrstück is based on the expectation that the person who acts the piece can be socially influenced by the execution of particular actions, by adopting particular attitudes, by reproducing particular speeches and so on."[34] In Brecht's conception for this piece, Lindbergh's struggle against the elements and against his own fatigue was not to be understood as a triumph of one individual but rather as a collective triumph of the human spirit. Consequently the boys and girls in his idealized audience were to recite the part of the airmen, learning by their participation the important lessons of overcoming fatigue and adversity. Brecht was very clear on the dangers of passive listening, "concert" listening, which he felt could lead to a mind-numbing identification with a heroic individual. His insistence on choral recitation, on activating the audience in a critical and didactic exercise, on interfering with verisimilitude through the "alienation" effect—all were designed to transform the art of radio the way his theory of the epic theater was to transform the stage.

By 1932, and despite successive adaptations of his *Lindberghflug*, Brecht could see little effect of his call for change. The belligerence of his initial (1927) assessment—"Everyone justifies the shameful results of radio so far by pointing to its 'unlimited possibilities,' and so radio is a 'good thing.' It is a very bad thing."[35]—had mellowed by the time of his last published theoretical writing on radio, "Radio as a Means of Communication." The Marxist premise that the purpose of art is to help change society undergirds this "talk on the function of radio" and forms the context for Brecht's proposal that radio be converted from a "distribution system" for traditional bourgeois culture to a "communication system" connecting all mankind in a way that would stimulate debate about social issues. His purpose is unchanged and is nothing short of a fundamental restructuring of art and artistic media, but by 1932 Brecht had realized this would be accomplished only when society itself had been changed.

Brecht's theory and practice are consistent with other important contributions of the same period, at least in the extent to which they argued for a radio art that embraced a variety of literary and nonliterary forms, exploited the technological aspects of the new medium for creative, rather than adaptive purposes, and actively challenged the conservative aesthetic that came to dominate the Hörspiel by the close of the Weimar era.[36] Thus the novelist Alfred Döblin (*Berlin Alexanderplatz*) insisted that future radio art would necessarily involve the elimination of traditional genre distinctions and would incorporate music and sound effects as equal partners. Brecht's collaborator, the composer Kurt Weill, foresaw "an absolute radio art,"[37] which would bring to the rhythms and melodies of music new sounds such as human and animal cries, natural sounds of wind and water, and artificial sounds generated by manipulations of frequencies before the microphone. The poet Kurt Schwitters broadcast his sound poems "To Anna Blume" and "Sonata in Archetypal Sounds" as examples of an absolute poetry emancipated from the traditional dependence upon written, syntactically coherent language. And Walter Benjamin, whose essay "Art in the Age of Mechanical Reproduction" would become seminal in postwar aesthetics, created "listening models" (Hörmodelle) designed to harness the didactic potential of an art form whose effect could be enhanced through the popularity of its technology.[38]

It is important to reiterate that these examples of avant-garde radio theory and practice coexisted during the Weimar period with examples of the first two types of radio art discussed, namely with a primitive theater of the blind and with a much more sophisticated, but basically still plot-oriented, radio literature. Our present understanding of the social and political pressures culminating in the collapse of the Weimar government in 1932–1933 makes it transparently clear why these voices of the avant-garde fell silent or were silenced. It is less obvious, however, why this silence lasted so long after 1945. To better comprehend what prolonged the disconti-

Mark E. Cory

nuity in avant-garde radio art, it is necessary to know something of the extraordinary continuity of its rival, the literary Hörspiel.

That such a continuity existed has been a matter for debate. The key postwar historical and theoretical writers on the Hörspiel (Heinz Schwitzke, E. Kurt Fischer) argued in the early 1960s that the literary Hörspiel had not survived the politicized climate of National Socialism and its deliberate, methodical, and successful transformation of all cultural activities to instruments of state policy (*Gleichschaltung*). "The period just before those twelve years, years in which radio was obliged to play the role of motivator of the masses, piper's pipe, and finally trumpet of earthly judgment, was undoubtedly the first significant high point of the Hörspiel. Then came the decade in which a radio art concerned with the 'individual in his living room' was of no further interest. The 'individual' marched in rank and file, and his 'living room' lay buried, despite triumphant fanfares, in ashes and rubble. At the very outbreak of the war, the Hörspiel appeared to be dead."[39]

What took the place of the Hörspiel proper, according to this view, was a radio version of the irrational, often mystical, highly sentimental literature characterized by what would become known as the fascist aesthetic.[40] Favorite themes of this "blood and soil" (*Blut und Boden*) literature included heroic figures of Germanic history, tests of manhood, and a certain fascination with pageantry and death. The favorite form became the choral play (*das chorische Sprechstück*), most often a kind of allegory orchestrated with ecstatic choruses and musical overtones designed to foster a purely emotional response. The titles of representative examples give something of the propagandistic flavor of these works: Richard Euringer's *German Passion* (1933), Eberhard Wolfgang Möller's *The Way to Empire* (1934), Otto Heinz Jahn's *Look Whither the Eagle Soars* (1935). In addition to these full-length choral plays, the National Socialists relied heavily upon short dramatized works designed to accomplish specific educational or propagandistic purposes. Lasting between ten and twenty minutes, these short forms gave pragmatic advice on the importance of air raid shelters, the dangers of espionage, and the advantages of reading (official) newspapers.

Although recent scholarship has begun to look more objectively at what may have been achieved aesthetically during this period, it is impossible to ignore the general truth of the Schwitzke-Fischer position, namely that the face of the Hörspiel changed after 1933. Both Schwitzke and Fischer were actively involved, Schwitzke in Berlin (until 1938, at which time he joined the army, to return from Russian imprisonment only in 1949) and Fischer in Cologne. Fischer in fact served as program director for Heinrich Glasmeier, who took over as intendant of the West German Radio in March of 1933 when the contract of the apolitical Ernst Hardt was summarily canceled. Dr. Glasmeier's inaugural remarks made it clear that the period in which an alien aestheticism (*blutfremdes Ästhetentum*) had determined cultural programming in Cologne, was over.[41] Brecht fled Germany that same spring, joined in exile by Döblin, Weill, Benjamin, and others whose contributions to the avant-garde in the pluralistic climate of Weimar Germany had no further voice in a radio conceived as an instrument of state policy.

There is a point, however, at which the general truth of these observations obscures other truths of particular relevance to the fate of the avant-garde in German radio art. The usually cited data showing that the production of Hörspiele declined during the Third Reich from 2.2 percent of overall programming in 1933 to 1.5 percent in 1935 to a low of 0.7 percent in 1939[42] belie the fact, for instance, that these relatively fewer works were given prime-time exposure during the "National Hour" (*Stunde der Nation*) created to further the ideological goals of the National Socialist Party after its ascent to power. The impact of these traditional blood-and-soil works was enhanced still more during this entire period by the increase in the number of listeners, as inexpensive radio receivers (*"Volksempfänger"*; cf. *"Volkswagen"*) were made readily available to exploit the propaganda potential Goebbels saw in the electronic medium. Moreover, since the dominant aesthetic was a word-based drama, the distinction between works written for radio and for the stage (including the giant outdoor "Thing" dramas) blurs to the point where many of the dramas and carefully rehearsed Party festivals broadcast during this same period must also be considered in any contemporary analysis of the actual impact of the Hörspiel under National Socialism. Finally, the popularization of the Hörspiel and its introduction to the postwar generation of critics and scholars fell to three influential practitioners who were able to flourish in the impoverished climate of National Socialist broadcasting and whose ideological and aesthetic orientation was correspondingly conservative: Richard Kolb (*Horoskop des Hörspiels*, 1932); Heinz Schwitzke (*Das Hörspiel: Dramaturgie und Geschichte*, 1963); and Eugen Kurt Fischer (*Das Hörspiel: Form und Funktion*, 1964).

The fact that Schwitzke and Fischer chose to downplay the development of radio art during the period of 1933 to 1945 is less significant for our present purpose, however, than the type of Hörspiel they and practically every other critic championed so effectively during the postwar years. The celebrated rebirth of the genre was a play written by the young Wolfgang Borchert, whose experiences as a front-line soldier and prisoner of war in Russia gave particular poignancy to his veteran's story *Outside the Door* (*Draußen vor der Tür*), broadcast by North West German Radio (Hamburg) in 1947. Originally conceived for the stage, Borchert's play features a soldier named Beckmann, who returns from Russian imprisonment after the war to find his bed occupied by another, his parents deceased, and no work. Everywhere he turns, doors are closed to him. He stands outside, cut off from the society he served in the war and in imprisonment. Still worse, the woman who finally befriends him is the wife of another veteran, who also returns crippled only to find Beckmann in his place. Written with considerable pathos, this drama of guilt and expiation rediscovered by coincidence the formula achieved by Reinacher in 1930 (*The Fool with the Pickaxe*): a literary work with an existential theme, made effective for radio by the symbolic use of a few elegantly stylized sound effects. In Borchert's play two sound effects in particular are played off against each other; the sound of doors being closed and the teck-tock of the crippled spectre's crutches as he haunts Beckmann.

Subsequently produced on the stage as well, Borchert's play is much more effective as Hörspiel, where Beckmann's conversations with Death and the river Elbe and with his own conscience occur effortlessly in a fluid inner realm embracing both allegory and the brittle reality of 1947. Although there had been regular use of radio during the immediate occupation period to entertain and reeducate the German populace in a shattered country now generally without theaters and movie houses, the enormous popular success of this play galvanized broadcasters into concentrating once more on the Hörspiel, albeit on this one literary and allegorical model.

The next creative impetus came in 1951 with the broadcast of Günter Eich's *Dreams* (*Träume*). Heinz Schwitzke is correct when he observes that this second impetus achieved its initial effect with none of the immense popular appeal of Borchert's drama of the returning war veteran.[43] Where Borchert tapped a sentimental motherlode of empathy for the little man trapped in the aftermath of a lost war, Eich forced listeners to identify the dark forces of inhumanity within themselves and to resist the all too easy drift into the next world war. His five *Dreams* (later a sixth was added) occur to contemporary figures on a variety of continents and consist of nightmarish vignettes of cannibalism, deportation, execution, and the general emptiness of material society, each embedded in a lyrical context that deliberately blurs the boundaries between dream and reality. The ethical message of the closing poem, however, is unambiguous: "Sleep not while the organizers of the world work!/ Be uncomfortable, be sand, not oil in the machinery of the world!"[44]

One measure of Eich's achievement was precisely the initial outrage his *Dreams* provoked. People could be moved by these lyrical little playlets, shaken out of the complacent materialism already nascent in the early years of Germany's economic miracle

Mark E. Cory

(*Wirtschaftswunder*). The more telling measure of his achievement for the history of the Hörspiel, however, was the proliferation of dream plays, as studio after studio became a kind of "acoustical dream laboratory."[45] The existential quest invited by the suspension of external reality and the unmasking of an inner self seemed ideally suited to a medium like radio, with its fluid contours of time and space. The incorporeal voices became easy metaphors for the listener's own dream self, yet were vested with a poetic cadence and richness of imagery that transcended the ephemeral nature of either dream or live broadcast. In fact, so perfectly realized were the literary Hörspiele of Günter Eich and the generation of poets who worked in his shadow during the 1950s and early 1960s that the Hörspiel became a literary genre. Texts by Eich, by Ingeborg Bachmann, by Max Frisch, Friedrich Dürrenmatt, Ilse Aichinger, Heinrich Böll, Peter Hirche, Fred von Hoerschelmann, Wolfgang Hildesheimer, Leopold Ahlsen, Wolfgang Weyrauch, and many others found their way into anthologies that were then read and discussed much as any other work of literature, that is, often without any reference to the production itself. The history of radio art in Germany records this as the classical era of the Hörspiel.

The triumph of the literary Hörspiel after the Second World War is of course due in part to the genuine excellence of these classic works. The point to be stressed in any discussion of the avant-garde, however, is that this critical and popular success was associated with a radical narrowing of the pluralistic aesthetic characteristic of the Weimar period. It would be as simplistic to argue that the triumph of the classic literary Hörspiel represents a kind of aesthetic Darwinism as it would to look for single causes in this dense pattern of shifting social, political, technological, and artistic values. The fact remains that the text-based models of radio art survived the political and cultural collapse of the Weimar period, that these proved readily adaptable to the nationalistic and propagandistic needs of National Socialism, and that these remained the forms championed with a single-minded exclusivity by the conservative practitioners and theorists who moved into positions of influence after the war. To speculate how the Hörspiel and its critical literature might have developed differently after the war had Ruttmann, Flesch, Bodenstedt, or Brecht written the first critical histories is idle, but to observe that the histories that emerged in the early 1960s carry a demonstrably conservative bias is not.[46]

There was one exception. As early as 1961, two years before Heinz Schwitzke's massive (488 pages) *Das Hörspiel* and three before E. Kurt Fischer's similarly large (327 pages) *Das Hörspiel: Form und Funktion*, the young Austrian Friedrich Knilli challenged the entire establishment with a slim volume entitled *Das Hörspiel: Mittel und Möglichkeiten eines totalen Schallspiels* (*The Hörspiel: Means and Possibilities of a Total Soundplay*). Born in 1930, Knilli was trained as a literary critic but became fascinated with radio drama, in particular with the psychological response of listeners to radio art. Developing ideas formulated in his 1959 dissertation (Graz), "The Hörspiel in the Imagination of the Listener," Knilli concluded what no other theorist was willing or able to see: The emperor Hörspiel had no clothes, that is, as art it had nothing to do with sound. It was literature like any other; its authors and dramaturges had developed an aversion to nonverbal sounds and regarded any actual exploitation of the technology of radio as an interference with the lyrical power of the all-important text. "The model of the literary Hörspiel today is exhausted. It produces only more of the same: stillborn, boring, sterile phraseology."[47]

Knilli's prescription was straightforward: "The Hörspiel author today can only free himself from the narrowness of the verbal Hörspiel (*Worthörspiel*) by expanding the acoustical dimension of the traditional Hörspiel and by experimenting with the means and possibilities of both electronic music (Meyer-Eppler, Eimert) and musique concrète (Pierre Schaeffer)."[48] Drawing upon the aesthetic theory of Max Bense, Knilli distinguished the *proper domain* (*Eigenwelt*) of radio art, consisting of acoustical events, from the *external domain* (*Außenwelt*), consisting of the listener and those figures, places,

Mark E. Cory

and events signified by the acoustical events of the Hörspiel.[49] The Totalhörspiel would be achieved only when radio art ceased to imitate the external domain and concentrated upon setting acoustical events themselves in play. The stage of the imagination so assiduously cultivated in the traditional literary Hörspiel had to be transformed into a playground in the listener's living room, a place where concrete acoustical events would be heard and enjoyed as sound play.

The Hörspiel establishment reacted with predictable disdain. For Fischer, Knilli was another misguided disciple of technology in the vein of Friedrich Wolf and Bertolt Brecht.[50] While granting that it might one day be possible to create compositions consisting of sounds and noises, Fischer asserts confidently that such a "sound play" would never bring pleasure or joy to a large listening audience, rather at the most a certain mathematical satisfaction to its creator.[51] Heinz Schwitzke, writing in 1963 with all the authority of his long experience and powerful position as head of the Hörspiel department in Hamburg, simply dismisses the notion that music or sound effects should ever be divorced from their traditional roles as handmaidens to plot, theme, and semantic meaning. He labels Knilli's "radical" attempt to fashion an alternative both foolish and destructive.[52]

In the meantime, Knilli's theoretical breakthrough was finding its practical analogue in the experiences of Paul Pörtner with Pierre Schaeffer's "Club d'Essai" in Paris.[53] The flavor of the Parisian renaissance of prewar avant-garde experimentation and pluralism is captured in Pörtner's recollection of his encounter with the "Club d'Essai":

At that time I came to Tardieu through literature, through translation. I documented Dada, Expressionism, then Surrealism and finally Lettrism and so to the contemporary experimental poetic movements in Paris. And these all ran together in the "Club d'Essai." I wandered in, wanting to look up Tardieu, who at that time was the director of the "Club d'Essai." Rue de l'Université 37, a beautiful old villa in which every room resounded with experimental music and sounds. At that time Lettrism had added to the normal alphabet a phonetic speech register of 52 new characters: the entire articulation of the human mouth, including clearing the throat, smacking the lips, snorting, gar-

*gling, gurgling, squeaking, the ahems and ahums—all these vocal sounds
which find their way into speech, not only to fill pauses, not only to cover
embarrassment and signal emphasis, but which can have the widest range of
meaning. I found in these various starting points—with Tardieu and the
Lettrists—an important indication of the semantic difference between the languages of speech and writing, of the potential for expression in the human
voice through word-less utterances, a potential far greater than one assumes
from the standpoint of a written literature. So I turned my attention to the
acoustical quality of language and came in this way—including musique concrète, which was also developed in the "Club d'Essai"—to my initial
experiments with the medium of radio.*[54]

This expanded alphabet of the Lettrists, together
with the compositional principles of musique concrète and the vastly
improved technical possibilities for cutting, mixing, and electronically
manipulating acoustical phenomena on tape, led Pörtner to the seminal experiments of the Schallspiel studies of 1964–1969. Pörtner's
initial *Schallspielstudie* was a deliberate attempt to take verbal material
and nonverbal sound effects as far as possible in the direction of pure
sound. Systematic compression and extension of sounds, abstraction
of nonverbal sounds from verbal material (words), filtration, modulation, permutation—these techniques for manipulating sound as pure
acoustical material opened a new range of creative possibilities once
the conceptual fetters of the traditional literary, that is, semantically
organized, radio play had been loosened.

Pörtner found the equipment for his initial experiment with language deformation in a small sound studio outfitted
with a vocoder in the *Hochschule für Gestaltung* (design academy) in
Ulm.[55] Since he knew Friedrich Knilli, it seems likely that Pörtner
adopted the title "Schallspiel" for his experiments from Knilli's work.
The opportunity to have the experiments performed came from the
support of Hansjörg Schmitthenner, chief dramaturge and later director of radio drama for Munich's Bavarian Radio. In describing the
interaction between Schmitthenner and Pörtner, Reinhard Döhl jus-
tifiably praises the former's courage.[56] Nothing like Pörtner's work

had been broadcast as a Hörspiel since the war. And although Paul Pörtner was to retreat significantly from the threshold of electronic music in his subsequent Schallspiel studies (2 and 3), the Hörspiel became accessible and interesting again to the avant-garde through this constellation of Knilli, Pörtner, and Schmitthenner.

Schmitthenner's openness to Pörtner's experiments stemmed from an active interest in the related movement of concrete poetry, founded simultaneously on two continents by the Brazilian de Campos brothers and by the Swiss Eugen Gomringer. The recognition on the part of concrete poets in the 1960s that artistic expression was possible through the tangible, concrete material of language—its graphemes and its sounds—as well as through the semantic meaning shaped by that material, was instrumental in developing both artists and an audience for a revitalized avant-garde Hörspiel. It was, of course, more the acoustical poets than their visually oriented brethren whose work was most readily applicable to radio. Chief among these was the Austrian Ernst Jandl. Jandl's texts reverberate through the extraordinary conjunction of his impish playfulness with a keen sense of the profound. Short, economical, and memorable, these texts explore tensions within words, between the sounds of words and their semantic meanings, or find new levels of meaning by shifting the focus from language as a medium to language as material.

In 1968 Stuttgart's Southwestern Radio broadcast a brief (fifteen-minute) radio play by Jandl and Friederike Mayröcker entitled *Fünf Mann Menschen* (*Five Man Mankind*). In a series of minimalist vignettes, birth, life, and death in contemporary Western society are evoked, celebrated, and simultaneously criticized. The seduction of drugs, the narcotic of popular music, the pervasive influence of violence—all are evoked by sounds, language, and music treated as equal components and distributed playfully across the left-right axis in one of the first effective uses of stereophonic broadcasting. One scene from the published score for the original broadcast is worth including here as an example of this radical new approach to organizing acoustical material for radio art:[57]

SPEAKER: The youth becomes a man.

Films turn him on.

Young Men 1–5 Pos. 1–5 facing away from listener

Voices from the film Pos. 3 ca. 20 meters from listener

precise sound effects *(music and film text)*

FILM ----- *(music)* ---

------------------------------- *(m u s i c   f a d e - o u t)*

GANGSTER: # Boss!

(sound effect: *fist striking face*)

YM3: k.o.

FILM --

------------- **BOSS:** . . . . .betrayal. . . . . .punished.

YM5: O.K.

FILM ---

------------- **DRUGTAKER:** (sound effect: *unmistakable inhalation,*

then, slowly and

with great pleasure)

YM1: Coke

YM2: O.K.

FILM ---

------------- **BOSS:** *You bastard!* (sound effect: *fist striking face*)

YM4: k.o.

FILM ------------------- (fade-in: *Music*) ---

--- *(Music breaks off)*

In a surprising decision marking one of those rare moments when a traditional arbiter of aesthetic norms embraces an avant-garde work so completely as to begin a fresh chapter in cultural history, the jury conferred upon Ernst Jandl and Friederike Mayröcker the prestigious Hörspiel Prize of the War Blind for this cunningly crafted minimasterpiece. Citing *Fünf Mann Menschen* as a work that appropriated for the Hörspiel the means and possibilities of concrete poetry in exemplary fashion, the jury legitimized an approach to language and sound effects that had become fairly ubiquitous by 1968 but that had been relegated to the gray periphery of "experimentation." Jandl, whose career as a sound poet was well established by 1967, credits Hansjörg Schmitthenner and, ironically, Günter Eich for the encouragement to apply the principles of his speak-poems (*Sprechgedichte*) and sound-poems (*Lautgedichte*) to the medium of radio.[58] To his genius for systematically deforming individual words and phrases by subtle changes that simultaneously wake the listener from the drone of everyday language and seduce him or her to a new and richer linguistic reality, the Hörspiel brought the even more complex acoustical environment of sound effects and music. Moreover, the novel technique of stereo broadcasting introduced a whole new dimension of playful permutations and manipulations. To an extent unsurpassed in German radio art, Jandl and Mayröcker exploited the Hörspiel (from *hören*—"to hear"—and s*pielen*—"to play") as a double imperative.[59]

The only dissenting vote among the eighteen-member jury in that historic decision of 1969 was a holdout for an equally avant-garde work by Ludwig Harig. Of the same generation as Jandl and, like Jandl, a teacher, Harig began publishing his own texts in the early 1960s. *Ein Blumenstück* (*Flower Piece*) fits into the German postwar literary tradition of *Vergangenheitsbewältigung* (coming to terms with the past), but it does so in unconventional fashion, completely forsaking plot and substituting instead a stereophonic permutation of nursery rhymes, children's songs, quotations from fairy tales and nature guides, and fragments from the diary of Auschwitz commandant

Rudolf Höß, whose predilection for flowers and for the sentimental legacy of Germany's cultural heritage was notorious. In approaching this most difficult subject for any German artist after 1945, Harig eschews both description and commentary to allow elements of an extant acoustical world to reshape our perceptions of innocence and to challenge comfortable notions of beauty. What one hears in this acoustical bouquet is a chilling juxtaposition of the violence latent in folk song and nursery rhyme with the quiet admiration expressed by Höß for the simple beauty of a blossoming tree or a window box in flower. In the words of Harig's contemporary Jürek Becker, the point of this work is not to make the nursery rhymes of nineteenth-century German romanticism responsible for the crimes of the Third Reich; it is however the case that this language had a formative influence on the ideological framework of National Socialism. In such a framework where aggression is mixed with the idyllic, and contemplation with ferocity, children's language can lose its neutrality and become a political instrument.[60]

Neither Harig's *Flower Piece* nor Jandl and Mayröcker's *Five Man Mankind* displays the methodical deformation of language or deliberate blurring of the boundaries between verbal and nonverbal material explored by Pörtner's initial Schallspiel. The single technical innovation in these works is the use of stereo, employed not to enhance verisimilitude but to accomplish the opposite, to alienate the listener from normal dramatic expectations of plot, to create new structures for the arrangement and distribution of acoustical material, and to permit the perception of simultaneous aural events. By 1968–1969, Pörtner, too, had added stereo to his palette. Drawn again by his interest in the Lettrists, he turned to the late Mallarmé for his second and third Schallspiel studies. His purpose in *Alea,* as he was to call the last of these experiments, was no longer to probe the limits of sound play but to replicate, enhance, and reveal with the electroacoustical means at his disposal the range of verbal effects latent in the expressive typography of Mallarmé's 1896 *Un Coup de dés jamais n'abolira le hasard.* Working now not only with the vocoder but with the more elaborate equipment for manipulating sounds at his disposal in the studio for electronic music at the University of Utrecht, Pörtner gave parts of the translated text to different voices, shaped these voices in turn for new and unexpected effect through modulation and filtration, added emphasis with rhythmic and melodic patterns, broke up sounds and their conventional meanings by stereophonic juxtaposition, and gave new dramatic emphasis by the introduction of "cry rhythms" (by the Roy Hart Singers). Pörtner describes his intent as follows: "I took Mallarmé's sentence, "Thought will never triumph over chance," as an aphorism of profound despair, as a prophecy of catastrophe. What this Schallspiel gained through its electronic realization was a transformation of language and sound effects to an acoustical unity, a rhythmical and tonal structuring of acoustical values derived from the act of speaking, and the expansion of expressive potential extending from prearticulate speech to abstract signs."[61]

Pörtner's *Alea* was broadcast as a coproduction in 1970 of the Bavarian Radio, the West German Radio in Cologne, and Radio Saarland. The latter station was the locus of extensive experimentation in this resurgence of the avant-garde in the late 1960s, both with stereo broadcasting and with aleatoric operations. One of the older generation attracted to the medium of radio at this time was Max Bense, professor of philosophy at the Technical University of Stuttgart and founder of the influential Stuttgart School, with its *Rot* (Red) publications series. In 1968 Bense collaborated with Ludwig Harig to translate insights from current information theory into radio art. The *Monolog der Terry Jo* (*Monologue of Terry Jo*) is based on an actual event in which a young girl is rescued from a suspicious boating accident. Initially unconscious, Terry Jo grows gradually more coherent in her monologue, until she makes more sense than the conflicting statements of those persons attending her. In the Hörspiel, the monologue is introduced by a vocoder synthesis of human speech. To translate the movement from unconsciousness to consciousness into acoustical terms, the synthetic speech begins with computer-generated prearticulate utterances that then move gradually into random syllables and finally into grammatical patterns before being substituted for by human speech. The gradual distillation of semantic meaning out of chaotic sound is simultaneously a fascinating insight into the operation of the human psyche and a convincing demonstration of the powerful potential in acoustical art for structures employing chance operations.

Implicit in the examples cited so far is a skepticism about traditional language consistent with a venerable avant-garde tradition dating back at least to Mallarmé and conspicuous in the experiments of Dada. In the same heady years of 1968–1969 that produced *Five Man Mankind, Flower Piece*, and *Monologue of Terry Jo*, the enfant terrible of Austrian letters, Peter Handke, brought to radio a work that made skepticism about the traditional Hörspiel its theme. Handke entitled his piece *Hörspiel*, the first of a series of three works for radio to bear that title. Loosely patterned after a political interrogation in an undetermined totalitarian state, Handke's "play" begins to play with the acoustical reality of the genre itself. Voices invoke patterns of interrogation, a new voice responds without connecting meaningfully with the questions asked, sound effects are employed as if to illustrate an unseen action where no action is involved or a landscape with no relevance to the dialogue, music is played to accompany nothing, words are repeated, sounds are repeated, laughter turns to inarticulate but audible signs of impatience, silence sets in, persists, and triumphs.

Handke's *Hörspiel* is an exercise in the defeat of expectations. Listeners who were conditioned to expect congruence between the semantic meaning of the dialogue in a radio play and the sound effects or background music employed find instead an ironic disjuncture. Like the other experiments of this period, Handke's work consciously seeks to liberate text, sound effects, and music as coequal elements for the acoustical artist, elements that in his case can then be reshaped to isolate and expose clichés and to invest shopworn sound effects with new meaning.

A different approach to the common aesthetic problem of refocusing attention on an acoustically approachable world is that of the *Hörtexte* or "listening texts" of Handke's contemporary Ferdinand Kriwet. A mixed-media artist, Kriwet concentrates in his acoustical works on the systematic registration and exploitation of all possible forms of human utterance, a "phenomenology of language and of speech."[62] He concentrates for his most interesting work on an acoustical analogue to Duchamp's "found objects," that is, on the organization of prerecorded speech from a variety of usually trivial sources for new and surprising aesthetic effect. His *One Two Two*, broadcast by the West German Radio in 1968, employed recorded fragments from four distinct language areas: foreign languages, including extensive quotations from English and American popular music, but also Russian, Italian, and Latin excerpts (the last from recorded speeches by the Pope); dialect excerpts from various regions in Germany; jargon, especially the jargon of popular culture as expressed in comic book slang, Radio Luxemburg spots, etc.; and political speeches. In contradistinction to Bense and Pörtner, Kriwet is not interested in chance operations. He arranges his lengthy collages with meticulous precision, clustering excerpts thematically and moving from and to them by associations suggested by the content or sound or rhythm of the acoustical material itself.

Part of Kriwet's intent is to make aesthetic use of throw-away language, language that before the advent of tape and wax recordings was lost to later artists at the moment of utterance. In part, however, his is a critical and didactic intent. "*Training und Aufklärung*" ("training and enlightenment") describe this intent, by which Kriwet means a schooled ability for concentrated listening. The desired result is not so much the crystallization of single bits of information from the bombardment of simultaneous and disparate sounds but more the ability to synthesize new associations, relations, and structures as antidote to the reduced levels of spontaneous speech he finds in today's saturated acoustical environment. Some of Kriwet's more critical works for radio are those in which he focuses on the role radio and television have played in diminishing real communication through the trivialization of superlatives and emotional speech in general. His Hörtexte *Voice of America, Apollo America,* and *Campaign* draw upon the particularly crass examples of commercial broadcasting in the United States, where as *Modell Fortuna, Radioball, Radio,* and *Radioselbst* play with broadcasting clichés in West Germany. All of these sound collages are rhythmically fascinating, technically exciting acoustical compositions in their own right. The critical function they serve is the natural concomitant of the heightened acoustical perception they foster.

The tendency of Kriwet's Hörtexte to document certain media events, such as election campaigns, soccer matches, moon landings, etc., draws them close to the radio form developed in the 1970s called *O-Ton,* or Original Sound. An experimental form of documentary radio, O-Ton differed from the features of the past by virtue of its compositional technique. Instead of beginning with a script and then taping interviews to illustrate and give depth to the various points the author wishes to make, the O-Ton artist simply begins recording and then assembles out of the recorded original material a coherent, and sometimes surprising, sound portrait. In a very real sense, the O-Ton Hörspiel was the first to employ postwar technology (the tape recorder) to implement Brecht's prewar hope that radio would go beyond mere distribution (*Lieferantentum*) to organize its listeners into coproducers.[63] The most productive source material for O-Ton has proved to be the voices of those otherwise disenfranchised by traditional radio art. The men in the street, prisoners, workers, apprentices—those whose distinctly nonliterary voices and nonstandard diction had seldom figured in the Hörspiel— became its staple. Often heavily didactic (for example, Günter Wallraff and Jens Hagen's early ecological protest, *Das Kraftwerk* [*The Powerplant*]), these works could sometimes attain a lyricism and subtlety equal to the finest traditional Hörspiel. One of the masters of this form was Paul Wühr, recognized with the Hörspiel Prize of the War Blind in 1972 for his *Preislied* (*Hymn of Praise*). Although the

Mark E. Cory

piece consists exclusively of positive statements by a multitude of citizens toward their state, when these positive expressions are isolated from their original context, grouped thematically, and arranged by inflection, the result is profoundly critical. By separating individual words and sentence fragments from their usual fluid context, by listening to the concern latent in hesitation and aggressive inflection, by allowing the original voices to recombine according to principles transparent only in the language as raw material, Wühr uncovers a discordant malaise beneath the superficial harmony of everyday praise.[64]

Hörspiel Prize of the War Blind was awarded within four years to such disparate works as Jandl and Mayröcker's *Five Man Mankind* and Paul Wühr's *Preislied*, each as far removed from the traditional Hörspiel as from each other, which meant that extraordinary new life had been breathed into a fifty-year-old genre. The experiments of Paul Pörtner, testing the semantic boundaries between shaped sound and deformed language; the introduction of play as an organizing principle in concrete poetry by Jandl and Mayröcker; the use of stereo, synthesizers, and vocoders to manipulate acoustical material and even to generate sounds not found in nature; the flirtation with chance operations; the substitution of musical principles of composition for traditional approaches to organizing a text; the deliberate exploitation of nonliterary language in O-Ton and the equally deliberate and provocative critique of the Hörspiel and its medium by Handke and Kriwet—all these phenomena seemed so fresh and radical that a new body of theory was called for as well as a new name by which these experiments and their successors could be identified.

The person who more than any other individual has contributed both is Klaus Schöning. Born in 1936, Schöning came to the Hörspiel like many others from an initial interest and experience in theater. He joined Cologne's West German Radio (WDR) in 1961, the same year in which Friedrich Knilli urged the creation of a "total Schallspiel." Together with the Saarland Radio under the directorship of Heinz Hostnig and the pioneer work of the Bavarian Radio, the WDR was one of the more hospitable broadcasters for the new wave of experimentation. What was to make its contribution to the development of avant-garde radio art in Germany singularly important was the seriousness with which it took the task of educating its audience through a series of radio essays broadcast along with the experimental works in its Third Program.[65] In 1969 Schöning edited an elaborate anthology of experimental texts for Suhrkamp Verlag, arguably the premier literary publishing house in the Federal Republic. Entitled *Neues Hörspiel. Texte, Partituren* (*New Hörspiel: Texts, Scores*), the 462-page volume contained the texts of fifteen of the most radical pieces broadcast in the preceding few years, including works by Kriwet, Handke, Pörtner, Bense, and Harig. With this single anthology Schöning accomplished two crucial things: he coined the term *Neues Hörspiel* as a collective designation for the full range of what was unfolding in Germany, and he demonstrated throughout the very inadequacy of the printed texts, scores, and renotations how close this New Hörspiel had come to an actual acoustical art form.[66]

Schöning has complemented this crucial anthology of primary works with a series of theoretical collections.[67] The most important of these to date is the 1970 companion volume, *Neues Hörspiel. Essays, Analysen, Gespräche* (*New Hörspiel: Essays, Analyses, Conversations*), to which radio artists, polyartists, practitioners, and critics contributed in equal measure. Heinz Hostnig comments on stereophonic broadcasting, Peter O. Chotjewitz on the new relationship between "author" and director, Bazon Brock on the development of a grammar of acoustical perception, and Schöning himself reopens the issue of artistic freedom in a genre traditionally dependent upon a "public," that is, state-controlled, medium. Schöning's essay is seminal in several respects, key among these being the critical vocabulary he develops for describing and contrasting the acoustical phenomena of both the old and the new Hörspiel. Second, he posits for the New Hörspiel a relationship between the artist, his material, the available technology, and the means of production and distribution of the creative product that is more typical of music than literature. Third, he makes explicit the theoretical and historical link between the New Hörspiel and the prewar experiments of Weimar radio. And finally, he lays the groundwork for the open aesthetic still unfolding today.

The relationship between New Music and the New Hörspiel already mentioned in connection with Pierre Schaeffer's influence on Paul Pörtner and posited in theoretical terms by Klaus Schöning came into full measure during the next decade. By 1970 Cologne was the locus not only of the most active experimentation with Hörspiel but of experimental music as well. The interest of the composer Mauricio Kagel in writing music for radio plays led to the experimental structuring of a rehearsal *as* a Hörspiel (*Hörspiel—Ein Aufnahmezustand*), in which he probes the extent to which the spoken word is as important in a musical rehearsal as the musical sounds played. Kagel became fascinated with the prospects of composing with ambient sounds, both music and sound effects or spoken words, and hence was intrigued by the traditional distinction drawn between music and Hörspiel. He dedicated the 1970 Cologne Seminar for New Music, conducted in conjunction with the WDR Hörspiel department, to the topic "Music as Hörspiel" and has been active ever since in systematically blurring the conventional distinctions between these art forms to the mutual benefit of each.[68] In fact, one of the principal contributions of Kagel's redefinition of the Hörspiel-music nexus has been to illustrate that the "New" Hörspiel has its aesthetic roots in the avant-garde achievements of the Weimar period. As Reinhard Döhl has pointed out, Kagel actually achieved in 1969 what Kurt Weill held out as a goal in 1925, namely "to search through the entire acoustical landscape for sources and means—regardless of whether they be called music or sounds—to structure one's own art."[69]

1. Paul Pörtner, as cited by Reinhard Döhl, *Das Neue Hörspiel: Geschichte und Typologie des Hörspiels 5* (Darmstadt: Wissenschaftliche Buchgesellschaft, 1988), p. 58. Unless otherwise noted, translations used are my own.

2. The *Hörspielpreis der Kriegsblinden* was founded in 1951 by the Federation of the War Blind of Germany (Bund der Kriegsblinden Deutschlands e.V.) in tribute to radio in general and to radio drama in particular. The prize, which is honorary only and involves no money, is awarded annually for the most significant original radio play composed in German and premiered by a broadcaster of the the German Broadcasters Association (ARD) during the previous year. See Stefan Bodo Würffel, *Das deutsche Hörspiel* (Stuttgart: Metzler, 1978), p. 106n.

3. Especially important has been the work of the Deutsches Rundfunk Archiv (German Radio Archive) in Frankfurt. The extremely valuable materials of this archive are accessible to students and scholars upon application and are catalogued in the volume H. Joachim Schauss and Reinhard Döhl, eds., *Tondokumente des deutschsprachigen Hörspiels 1928–1945* (Frankfurt: Deutsches Rundfunk Archiv, 1975). The indebtedness to the DRA and to the scholarship of Professor Döhl for many insights extending my own previous work will, I trust, be clear from the references in the present study. I am also indebted to the Deutscher Akademischer Austausch Dienst (German Academic Exchange Service) and to Fulbright College for the financial support of my research during the spring of 1989.

4. Würffel, *Das deutsche Hörspiel*, p. 10, traces the development of radio from its beginnings as an instrument of war on the western front in 1917 to its first peaceful uses as a communications device under the auspices of the national postal service by 1919. Dr. Hans Bredow is credited with having organized the earliest military transmissions and then, as Commissioner of Radio for the Postal Ministry, with having protected the concept of public radio from the attempts to commercialize the medium in the early years of the Weimar Republic.

5. I rely here on the paradigm sketched by Döhl, *Das Neue Hörspiel*, p. 122n. Different and often vastly more complicated paradigms are offered by nearly every historian of the genre. For a typical alternative, see Würffel, *Das deutsche Hörspiel*, p. 22n.

6. Writing in 1936, Rudolf Arnheim cites both symbolic figures, "which, realized on the stage, are visually presentable but not without an involuntary comic effect," and extended monologues, where the "entire content lies in words, and no external action has to be indirectly represented," as examples of radio's superiority as a me-

dium. Rudolf Arnheim, *Radio. An Art of Sound* (London: Faber & Faber Ltd., 1936), pp. 181, 178. Sometimes the advantage was political, as when in the turbulent days of the crumbling Weimar Republic Brecht's *St. Joan of the Stockyards* was rejected by the Berlin *Volksbühne* and other theaters but was broadcast over radio. See John Willet, *Art and Politics in the Weimar Period: The New Sobriety. 1917–1933* (New York: Pantheon, 1978), p. 204.

7. Würffel cites the recitation on 3 November 1923, by the actor Peter Ihle of Heine's "Seegespenst" as the birth of literary programming in Germany. Würffel, *Das deutsche Hörspiel*, p. 11.

8. Schwitzke, *Das Hörspiel: Dramaturgie und Geschichte* (Cologne and Berlin: Kiepenheuer & Witsch, 1963), p. 41.

9. Arnheim, *Radio*, p. 195.

10. For an excellent description of *A Comedy of Danger* see Schwitzke, *Das Hörspiel*, p. 49n.

11. Cf. Rolf Gunold's 1925 ghost play *Spuk* and the long-running American postwar series *The Shadow*.

12. Würffel, *Das deutsche Hörspiel*, p. 15.

13. From the introduction to the archival broadcast of Friedrich Wolf's *Krassin rettet Italia*: "Das alles ist wohl das erste Heldenlied unserer Zeit, unserer Technik…"

14. See Schwitzke, *Das Hörspiel*, pp. 141–144.

15. Kolb's 1932 *Das Horoskop des Hörspiels* is generally considered to be the first substantive theoretical work on the genre.

16. See Schwitzke, *Das Hörspiel*, p. 179, on Alfred Braun's experimental studio.

17. "Nicht nur das übermittelnde Instrument, auch das zu Übermittelnde ist neu zu formen: Das Programm kann nicht am Schreibtisch gemacht werden." (Quoted in Döhl, *Das Neue Hörspiel*, p. 128.)

18. Opinions differ as to whether or not *Zauberei auf dem Sender* was ever actually broadcast. Schwitzke cites it with a precise date (*Das Hörspiel*, p. 443); Friedrich Knilli among others suggests that this cannot be verified (Knilli, *Das Hörspiel. Mittel und Möglichkeiten eines totalen Schallspiels* [Stuttgart: Kohlhammer, 1961], p. 12). The text, at least, is available: Hans Flesch, *Zauberei auf dem Sender und andere Hörspiele*, ed. Ulrich Lauterbach (Frankfurt am Main: Waldemar Kramer, 1962).

19. Quoted in Döhl, *Das Neue Hörspiel*, p. 127.

20. Quoted in Knilli, *Mittel und Möglichkeiten*, p. 12.

21. Cf. Heinz Schwitzke, who concedes that cinematic techniques, characteristic of the "monsterous" subgenre of the acoustical film, stimulated many of the pioneer pieces of early Hörspiel history. See Schwitzke, *Das Hörspiel*, p. 63.

22. Arnheim, *Radio*, p. 126.

23. Döhl, *Das Neue Hörspiel,* p. 133.

24. Hans Richter, "Experiments with Celluloid," *The Penguin Film Review* 9 (1949), p. 114.

25. Reinhard Döhl, "Neues vom alten Hörspiel," radio essay broadcast by the West German Radio (WDR) on 29 December 1980. Quoted from typescript, p. 26.

26. Flesch, *Rundfunkjahrbuch* (1931, p. 36), quoted by Döhl, "Neues vom alten Hörspiel," p. 22.

27. Two segments of about twenty minutes total length are available in the Deutsches Rundfunk Archiv and constitute the oldest available sound document in Germany. My synopsis and quotations are taken from the analysis in Döhl's radio essay, "Neues vom alten Hörspiel."

28. See Willett, *Art and Politics in the Weimar Period,* p. 147nn.

29. See Schwitzke, *Das Hörspiel,* p. 47; Döhl, "Neues vom alten Hörspiel," p. 23; Knilli, *Mittel und Möglichkeiten,* p. 16.

30. See Willett, *Art and Politics in the Weimar Period,* esp. p. 185nn.

31. Knilli, "The Radio Culture of the German Working Class in the Weimar Republic," *Germany in the Twenties: The Artist as Social Critic,* ed. Frank D. Hirschbach (New York and London: Holmes & Meier, 1980), p. 99.

32. In his eminently readable introduction to "Brecht on Radio," *Screen* 20 (Winter 1979–1980), pp. 16–23, Stuart Hood corroborates Knilli's analysis of the institutionalization of broadcasting in Germany.

33. The translation is by Stuart Hood, introduction to "Brecht on Radio," p. 21. By the time he composed these notes, Brecht had changed the title twice, once to *Flug der Lindberghs* (Flight of the Lindberghs), which shifted the stress from heroic individualism to a collective heroism, and then to *Ozeanflug* (Ocean Flight). In the last version, the voice of Lindbergh has been changed to a chorus of airmen. Distressed by the political stance of the historical Charles Lindbergh, Brecht insisted upon these later changes. The version in the German Radio Archives is not the original broadcast, but a recording of a 1930 broadcast.

34. Translated and quoted by Stuart Hood, introduction to "Brecht on Radio," p. 21.

35. From Berthold Brecht, "Radio—eine vorsintflutliche Erfindung," in "Radiotheorie 1927–1932," *Werkausgabe Edition Suhrkamp, Gesammelte Werke 18, Schriften zur Literatur und Kunst* (Frankfurt: Suhrkamp, 1967), p. 120.

36. For a summary of the earliest theoretical statements on the Hörspiel, dating from the Kassel conference on "Poetry and Radio" ("Dichtung und Rundfunk") in 1929, see Würffel, *Das deutsche Hörspiel,* pp. 46–53, as well as the several references in Döhl, *Das Neue Hörspiel.*

37. Kurt Weill, "Möglichkeiten absoluter Radiokunst," written in 1925. Cited in Döhl, *Das Neue Hörspiel,* p. 81.

38. Only fragments of a piece for children have been discovered and are available in the German Radio Archives. The fullest discussion to date of Benjamin's contribution to radio art, both in theory and practice, is Reinhard Döhl's radio essay, "Walter Benjamins Hörspielarbeiten," WDR (nd).

39. Heinz Schwitzke, "Bericht über eine junge Kunstform" ("Report on a young art form"), in *Sprich, damit ich dich sehe,* an anthology of six radio plays (Munich: List, 1960), p. 13.

40. See Susan Sontag, "Fascinating Fascism," *New York Review of Books* 22 (6 February 1975), pp. 23–28; also Klaus Vondung, *Völkisch-nationale und national-sozialistische Literaturtheorie* (Munich: List, 1973); J. M. Ritchie, *German Literature under National Socialism* (London: Croom Helm, 1983); and Uwe-K. Ketelsen, *Völkisch-nationale und Nationalsozialistische Literatur in Deutschland 1890–1945* (Stuttgart: Metzler, 1976).

41. Reported in the Dortmund *Tremonia* of 19 April 1933, and quoted in Döhl, "1933: Das Nationalsozialistische Hörspiel. Ein Exkurs mit Beispielen," radio essay broadcast on 27 December 1973 by WDR. Quoted from typescript, p. 11n.

42. Döhl, "Das Nationalsozialistische Hörspiel," p. 22. I follow Döhl's arguments closely in this discussion.

43. Schwitzke reports that the archives of the North West German Radio still contain a tape of listener telephone calls received after the broadcast, a response nearly as large numerically as for the Borchert play, but hostile, rather than grateful. (Schwitzke, *Das Hörspiel,* p. 301.)

44. Günter Eich, *Träume* (Frankfurt: Suhrkamp, 1953), p. 190.

45. Werner Klose, *Didaktik des Hörspiels* (Stuttgart: Reclam, 1977), p. 39.

46. The argument that follows is restricted to the development of radio art in West Germany after the war. The Hörspiel charted a different course in the German Democratic Republic, where it was influenced by the socialist realist aesthetic affecting all the arts. The much slower reemergence of the avant-garde in East Germany would merit a separate study.

47. Knilli, *Mittel und Möglichkeiten,* p. 21.

48. Ibid., p. 21.

49. Ibid., pp. 23, 114.

50. Fischer, *Das Hörspiel. Form und Funktion* (Stuttgart: Kröner, 1964), p. 195.

51. Ibid., pp. 117, 292.

52. Schwitzke, *Das Hörspiel,* p. 236.

53. Schaeffer began to experiment with recorded sounds in the archives of Radio Paris as early as 1942. The "Club d'Essai" grew out of these experiments and became a regular feature of the O.R.T.F. under the direction of the avant-garde playwright Jean Tardieu. See Döhl, *Das Neue Hörspiel*, p. 46n.

54. Quoted in ibid., p. 48.

55. See the description in ibid., p. 52.

56. Ibid., p. 53. I supplement Döhl, who is the most articulate champion of Pörtner, with my own observations from a year spent with the Bavarian Radio in 1968–1969.

57. The following excerpt is translated from the renotation published in Klaus Schöning, ed., *Neues Hörspiel. Texte, Partituren* (Frankfurt: Suhrkamp, 1969), pp. 116–117.

58. In a radio interview with Jörg Drews, published in Klaus Schöning ed., *Hörspielmacher. Autorenporträts und Essays* (Königstein/Ts.: Athenäum, 1983), p. 201.

59. From the poem by Ernst Jandl on the cover of the Jandl/Mayröcker anthology *Fünf Mann Menschen. Hörspiele* (Berlin: Luchterhand, 1971).

60. From Becker's introduction to the score of Harig's *Ein Blumenstück* in Klaus Schöning, *Neues Hörspiel. Texte Partituren* (Frankfurt: Suhrkamp, 1969), p. 445.

61. Quoted in Döhl, *Das Neue Hörspiel,* p. 56n.

62. The quotations from Kriwet are translated from portions of a published interview with Klaus Schöning, "Training und Aufklärung. Hörspielmacher Ferdinand Kriwet," *Hörspielmacher* (Königstein/Ts: Athenäum, 1983), pp. 239–256.

63. Würffel, quoting Brecht's "The Radio as Communication Apparatus," *Das deutsche Hörspiel*, p. 175.

64. I have discussed *Preislied* in detail in Mark E. Cory, "The O-Ton Hörspiel: An Analysis of Paul Wühr's *Preislied,*" *Monatshefte* 58 (Winter 1976), pp. 418–424.

65. Reinhard Döhl, one of the most prolific radio essayists, reviews the awakening of interest in the experimental Hörspiel among the various broadcasters in *Das Neue Hörspiel*, pp. 5–25. This is the first of a planned series of volumes bringing out in printed form the radio essays of more than a decade. The second volume in the series, due soon, will discuss the Hörspiel of National Socialism.

66. The latter point was handsomely underscored by featuring both the printed renotation of the Jandl and Mayröcker *Five Man Mankind* and a vinyl recording of the broadcast packaged inside the rear cover.

67. These include, in addition to the anthologies already cited, three additional anthologies: *Neues Hörspiel. Essays, Analysen, Gespräche* (Frankfurt: Suhrkamp, 1970); *Neues Hörspiel. O-Ton* (Frankfurt: Suhrkamp, 1974); and *Schriftsteller und*

*Hörspiel. Reden zum Hörspielpreis der
Kriegsblinden* (Königstein/Ts.: Athenäum,
1981).

68. Döhl, *Das Neue Hörspiel,* esp. p. 89n,
for a summary of Kagel's own Hörspiele,
including *Der Tribun* (*The Tribune*), for
which he received the 1980 Hörspiel Prize
of the War Blind. My own article, Mark
E. Cory and Barbara Haggh, "Hörspiel as
Music: The Creative Dialog between
Experimental Radio Drama and Avant-
Garde Music," *German Studies Review* 4
(1981), pp. 257–279, offers a fuller introduction to this relationship in English.

69. Kurt Weill and Lothar Band, "Musik
im Rundfunk," cited in Döhl, *Das Neue
Hörspiel,* p. 89.

FRANCES DYSON

As a composer, writer, artist, philosopher, guru of the avant-garde, John Cage's impact on the thought and artistic practices of contemporary culture can hardly be overstated. Described both as an exploder of traditions and a neotranscendentalist, Cage has certainly hurled music and its premises into the stormy mass of the postmodern present, yet at the same time he can be charged with recuperating music's content, sound, within a neoromantic nostalgia for the prediscursive "in itself" of Nature. The tension between the liberatory and the conservative elements in Cage's oeuvre has rarely been made apparent. Beneath the surface play of his aesthetic reflections, however, one can glimpse an anchoring of his philosophy of sound and life within the darker folds of a mystical and metaphysical notion of existence, which, located beyond either music or philosophy, can only be articulated through recourse to a poetics of ambiguity. Expressed emblematically in the form of the koan, this ambiguity has particular implications for an emerging theory and practice of sound art. On the one hand, it is testament to the difficulty Cage had in developing a discourse of sound in terms of its phenomenality rather than (musical) organization; on the other, it grounds Cage's aesthetics in the peculiar question of sonic representation and musical meaning.

Because the question of representation is antithetical to "the thing itself," Cage is forced into a paradoxical play between the phenomenal and metaphorical determinations of aurality, both in its natural and "organized" states, both "in itself" and as perceived by the listening subject, and as a result the discursive and disruptive potential of his aurally oriented contributions to the field remain mute, silenced in the vacuum that exists between the literal and metaphorical. This essay investigates the sonic and cultural dimensions of this "in between"; the spaces prohibited by accepted notions of music that Cage sought to open, inhabit, and name, and that must themselves be loosened from the knotted monopoly of his sonorous and metaphysical (dis)order. In so doing it will examine the period 1935–1965, during which Cage developed his major compositional and philosophical strategies, taking as its point of departure his well-known desideratum: "Let sounds be themselves." From these four words Cage opened the musical establishment to the democratic ambience and semiotic ambivalence of aurality, while at the same time inaugurating the disappearance of the received category "music" for which he is now so famous. Yet a serious commitment to the project of letting sounds be themselves also involves a hubristic attempt to represent the unrepresentable and to confront not only the boundaries of music but the very demarcations that constitute the self. To his credit Cage embraces such a confrontation, but in doing so he invokes metaphors of absence, such as silence, selflessness, and nothingness, forcing those who would "let" sounds be themselves to occupy an impossible existential position and to speak an impossibly ambiguous and stunted discourse. Cage's prescriptions concerning Sound, Art, the Self, and Life, while resonant and poetic, nonetheless envelop sound within a semantically silent recantation. Situating the configurations of Cage's retreat into this silence—as it manifests between sound as phenomenon and sound as metaphor, self as lived and self as represented, and locating the spaces and moments of its resolution—will be the major concern of what follows.

CONSTITUTING SOUND

At the very outset of his career Cage fashioned a notion of silence that was both phenomenal and abstract in order to constitute and legitimate his preferred sonic and aesthetic domain. In 1933 at the age of twenty-one he became a pupil of Arnold Schoenberg but soon discovered that he had "no feeling for harmony" and in fact wanted "to find a way of making music that was free of the theory of harmony, of tonality."[1] This involved abandoning the primary principle of Western tonality—pitch—as a means of structuring compositions, and by implication: melodic development, expressivity, and the ideal of musical movement. With neither the sonic material nor the structural devices to compose what in 1933 would normally count as music, Cage's only option was to create a new form of music utilizing a new structural means. And this he did by using silence "to separate one section of a composition from another" (CC, p. 51), instead of the traditional structural device of harmonic cadence. Realigning the parameters of the tone (pitch, amplitude, timbre, and duration), Cage placed duration in the position pitch normally occupies within the tonal hierarchy. Duration, substituting for pitch, was then the "correct" structuring principle of musical composition, correct not on the basis of a contingency (Cage happened to like silence or he didn't happen to have a good ear) but on the basis of necessity:

Sound has four characteristics: pitch, timbre, loudness, and duration. The opposite and necessary coexistent of sound is silence. Of the four characteristics of sound, only duration involves both sound and silence. Therefore, a structure based on durations (rhythmic: phrase, time lengths) is correct (corresponds with the nature of the material), whereas harmonic structure is incorrect (derived from pitch, which has no being in silence).[2]

A peculiar logic is at work here. Firstly, the existence of sound—as abstract a concept as that of the tone—is made dependent upon the existence of its "opposite": silence. Second, since the existence of sound and silence share only one characteristic in common, that of duration, then duration, according to Cage, "corresponds with" or is "true to" "the nature of the material," that is, sound. Furthermore, since pitch is a characteristic of sound but not of silence, a structure based on pitch (tonality) does not correspond

The Ear That Would Hear Sounds in Themselves

to, is not true to, sound. What is occurring here is a confusion of categories; logically if pitch is a subset of sound, and silence its necessary condition, then silence bears a relation to pitch. The problem arises because Cage insists on equating sound and music, as if they belong to similar categories; however, the latter pertains to a particular system (composition) that is symbolic, independent of aural realization, and arbitrarily produced, whereas the former is generally understood as phenomenal, nonsystemic, and bearing an indexical relation to the lived environment. Cage conflates these categories, thereby musicating *silence*, since it now functions as a metaphor for a structural absence, yet this new definition also contains the sense of silence as an actual absence of sound. Silence thus becomes a metaphor for a structural and phenomenal absence, and as such it signifies both phenomenally and symbolically. Amid this kind of confusion *sound*'s meaning, and particularly its autonomy from *music,* is almost impossible to define.

THE OBJECTHOOD OF SOUND

Using silence as a structural device for organizing sonic material, Cage was able to expand his musical domain to include what lies beyond the consideration of music as an art form: the world of noise.[3] In his hands noise became both a polysemic, multifunctional lever suitable for inching open the closure tonality and serialism presented and a palimpsest for the deeper philosophical regions he was now exploring. Profoundly influenced by the abstract filmmaker Oskar Fischinger, Cage's understanding of sound, indeed his fundamental ontology, veered toward the animistic and transcendentalist view of objects Fischinger held. According to William Moritz, "In the summer of 1932 Fischinger heard his wife drop a key in an adjacent room. He became fascinated by the idea that he could tell this noise—just an ordinary "plink"—was made by a key and not a tea spoon, scissors, knife, nail file or other comparable object in terms of size and material."[4] The idea that the sound of objects is capable of a certain articulation was interpreted by Cage as evidence of the deeper reality:

When I was introduced to him, he began to talk with me about the spirit which is inside each of the objects of this world. So, he told me, all we need to do to liberate that spirit is to brush past the object, and to draw forth its sound. That's the idea which led me to percussion. In all the many years which followed up to the war, I never stopped touching things, making them sound and resound, to discover what sounds they could produce. Wherever I went, I always listened to objects. (FTB, p. 74)

Through percussion Cage melded sound, object, and spirit in a material unity, the unity of the object, which has its architectonic correlate in the unity of his new rhythmic structure: "The whole has as many parts as each unit has parts, and these, large and small, are in the same proportion."[5] Thus beginning in 1937 with *First Construction (in Metal)*,[6] the animism of Fischinger and the organicism of the romantics were fully embodied in his compositions.

With silence, sound, spirit, object, and organic rhythmic structure in hand, Cage confronted not only the structural mechanisms but the very space and instrumentation of tonality. For instance, finding himself in a space that simply could not hold all his percussion instruments, he created the prepared piano, adapting his score for *Bacchanale*, Sylvia Fort's dance piece, to suit its mellow, percussively transformed tones. This was a particularly significant act, for the parting and muting of the strings, first with a pie plate and more successfully with screws, also symbolized the parting of the instrument with its history. The piano's "preparation" suggested also a readying for death, death of the crowning technology of tonality, annihilation of its fixed and claustrophobic temperament, and marginalization of its once precise, notatable, and interpretable borders. Although the symbolic end of the piano would later be enacted through its literal destruction by members of the avant-garde, at that time it was enough that its performance yield a different spirit; not the spirit of the romantics, for whom music served as a vehicle for the expression of their emotionally charged intentions, but the more subdued and modest spirit of the objects placed within the piano's frame. Substituting spirit for affect, Cage, in muting the strings, de-muted the object, at the same time giving voice to his broader philosophical aim: "What we were looking for was in a way more humble: sounds, quite simply. Sounds, pure and simple" (*FTB*, p. 74).

SOUND IN SPACE: RADIO AND THE OTHER

The origin of "sounds pure and simple," however, cannot be found in the concrete object as such. Like Cage's concept of silence, the sound/object/spirit nexus is prone to ambiguity: it remains unclear exactly what it is or where it might be situated. Only through the abstracted space of technology can the ontological void that "sound/object/spirit" suggests double as an opening, providing a locus for the aural/object thus reconfigured. Cage explores this transformative space in *Living Room Music* (1940), a percussion and speech quartet using "instruments to be found in a living room: furniture, papers, windows, walls, doors," in which the domestic sphere, now vacated of the petit-bourgeois piano, is presented as a site for musical production rather than mere reception.[7] In contemplating a possible music of the living room it is difficult, however, not to consider also those sounds originating from other, quasi-object, in fact technological, sources—television, radio, and the phonograph—which have traditionally inhabited the living room and which would presumably form part of its new instrumentality. Indeed, in the absence of such technologies the music of the living room becomes, oddly enough, simply part of the furniture. Yet in their presence it is reconfigured, transferred to the diaphanous field of the quasi-object, the object whose origins and ontology can be found in what Cage, referring to compositions produced "when I was using electric or electronic technology" (*CC*, p. 158) called "Imaginary Landscapes." From the prepared piano, to the living room, to the imaginary landscape, one can trace the course of both real and metaphorical space, phenomenal and symbolic being, as it continually abstracts and then redetermines what sounds, being themselves, might be. Sound is released first by an acoustic instrument, then by an electronic device; its being is connected first with silence, then with objects, and finally with technology; it is located at first in the orchestra, then in the living room, and finally, as the title of the compositions suggests, in the imagination.

The first Imaginary Landscape, *Imaginary Landscape No. 1*, developed from an opportunity that brought Cage in close contact not only with a large collection of percussion instruments but with a radio station able to broadcast "small sounds that required amplification" to an adjacent theater in the Cornish School (Seattle). *Imaginary Landscape No. 1* is a score for two phonographs, one Chinese cymbal, and piano. Of all the instruments, only the cymbal remains relatively unaltered (it is however, through transmission via microphone and radio studio, made radiophonic). The piano is played by "sweeping the bass strings with a gong beater," at times muting the strings with the palm of the hand; the speed of the turntables changes from 33 1/3 to 78 RPM depending on the score's instructions; and the styluses are raised or lowered to produce a sense of elongated rhythm.[8] By choosing test tone records (Victor Frequency and Constant Note records) as the sonic material the phonographs would play, Cage transformed not only the phonographs but the entire radio studio into an instrument, an effect that led him in 1942 to propose a synthesis between the percussion orchestra and the radio studio in order to facilitate the production of "hitherto unheard or even unimagined sounds" through the development of "compact technological boxes, inside which all audible sounds, including noise, would be ready to come forth at the command of the composer."[9] As an instrument, however, the radio studio ironically produced not only sound but the "presence" of the radiophonic apparatus itself. For the test tone, the frequency used to standardize both broadcast equipment and the on-air signal, is considered by radio technicians and producers as a standard or measurement more than as a sound. Heard only in the inner sanctum of the studio, employed only to assist the interfacing of technology, when broad-cast, its sound becomes paradoxical, audible yet at the same time placeless, a sound without origin, a pure signal coursing through the airwaves.

In the new space of the studio, Cage's understanding of sound changes. Still connected to the object, still evoking a spirit, sound nonetheless is abstracted, its sonic and metaphorical envelope now adjusting to the shape and meaning of the radio. This change is evident in Cage's response to the inaugural performance of *Imaginary Landscape No. 4* (1951), an indeterminate score for twelve radios and twelve performers. Because of its late scheduling on the night of the performance, very little radio signal could be received and the piece was considered by some as a failure. However, for Cage "the radios did their job that evening quite satisfactorily" (*FTB*, p. 169) by func-tioning as instruments which, while determined (by the radio station) in their sonority, were yet indeterminate in their actual audition. In contrast to the percussive object that, once struck, could only remain silent in a vacuum, the broadcast signal, dependent as it is upon the workings of an already existing technology, can remain silent in the living silence of the yet-to-be-tuned airwaves. As Cage declares, "lis-tening to this music one takes as a spring board the first sound that comes along; the first something springs us into nothing and out of that nothing a-rises [*sic*] the next something; etc. like an al-ternating [*sic*] current" (*S*, p. 135). The "alternating current" can now be seen in the fullness of its electrometaphysical ambiguity. For the electronic airwaves allow the possibility for a silence that is not dead, a silence re-presenting a presence whose essence is actualized even when its sonorous potential is not.

Indeed, the potency of such a presence is contained in the very word *radio* itself: from the Latin "*radius:* a ray, emanating from a center; *radians:* beaming, filled with light, radiation; *irradiatus:* to illuminate, to brighten, to heat with radiant energy, to enlighten intellectually."[10] Although the radios' emanations are inscribed with the theology of light, coming from the cosmos, the Sun or Son, but descending to the material or pseudomateriality of electricity, however, it is not merely a receptacle, as matter is believed to be the inert receptor of the divine and intellectual ether. The radio also emits both the sound and history of audiophony, making audible those mystical traces surrounding the latter's inauguration in the nineteenth century. Like Thomas A. Watson's interest in electricity and the occult amid the early barkings of telephony, like Edison's attempts at thought transference and communication with the dead, like the "eccentric" obsessions of early ham operators conversing on the airwaves with their "magical" crystal sets, the radio studio reconstructs an openness to the unrepresentable, mystical, and sublime heritage of the "ether" to which electronics has culturally been attached.[11] Thus in the imaginary of Imaginary Landscapes, sound occupies the nonspace of electronics, possesses the nonbeing of the invisible and intangible, and releases the spirit, not of objects, but of the quasi-objects that constitute technology and are themselves permeated by the animating force, or spirit, of electricity.[12]

Entering the radio studio, Cage leaves behind the everyday notion of objects and locales, positioning the aural within a continually shifting field where sound fluctuates between the acoustic and the electronic or radiophonic, the object and the quasi-object, the produced and the reproduced.[13] Within the scope of this oscillation, however, a new unity is provided by technology's ability to "liberate" sounds from objects, in the same way perhaps that sound liberates the spirit of the object, therefore providing a neutral avenue toward the essence of the sound itself. Amplification, for instance, allows sounds that otherwise would remain silent to be heard via the action of electronic ears, ears that Cage never suggests might have their own modes of constructing sound. Live and improvised radiophonic transmission liberates sound from the objectification recording imposes: "The phonograph...is a thing—not a musical instrument. A thing leads to other things."[14] And radiophony, even when silent, provides technical assistance in the transformation of "our contemporary awareness of nature's manner of operation into art," allowing the art object (and the object of art) to recoup the flux of life: "The radios did their job that evening quite satisfactorily. So you see, I sometimes manage to bring about pure processes" (*FTB*, p. 169). In this way technology becomes a process within the overall metamorphosis of the cultural into the natural, the entelechy of the natural and sounds in themselves becoming dependent upon and almost overshadowed by its liberating force.

LETTING SOUNDS BE...

When Cage substitutes the "process" for the "thing," he seems to be abandoning the object in favor of the medium, for a record is a thing whereas a radio transmission is not. But for Cage a process is not simply a state of being; it is also a metaphor for ideal artistic practice, a practice that integrates the artist with *sounds in themselves* in a continuum of creativity and creation. And its metaphorical elaboration is intimately connected to the phenomenal characteristics of sound. For instance, sound's continuity, its ability to merge with other sounds, and its lack of borders represent for Cage a phenomenal equivalent to the artistic concepts of interpenetration, unimpededness, and nonobstruction, active processes that ensure the indeterminacy and hence freedom of performance when adopted as a creative strategy.[15] Similarly, sound's invisibility and temporality is interpreted as a characteristic of nonbeing, itself a trope for the "letting go" inherent to the process: "A sound possesses nothing, no more than I possess it. A sound doesn't have a being, it can't be sure of existing in the following second. What's strange is that it came to be there, this very second. And that it goes away. The riddle is the process" (*FTB*, p. 150).

Cage also considers the listener in his aurally oriented *Weltanschauung*. His evacuation of the self through the practise of nonintentionality suggests the kind of subjectivity required to *let* sounds be themselves, and this subjectivity, by embracing sound without imposing intentions or values, is more aligned to listening, to the way in which sound infiltrates the ear and is beyond the ear's control, than to seeing, with its mechanisms for projection directing the seen always to the controlling eye/I of the seer. In this respect Cage's developing philosophy is radical, for through his emphasis on action and process, his critique of the static and fixed work of art and his repudiation of being as presence—"Every something is an echo of Nothing" (S, p. 131)—he reveals an epistemology that does not assimilate the discourse of sound within the visualist notion of being so central to Western thought. Working with concepts such as interpenetration and nonintentionality, Cage articulates the hitherto unimaginable: sound in its semantic and referential ambiguity, the listening subject as fully integrated with the flows of life and aurality. And he does this by way of the equally unrepresentable: the notion of silence and the void. Thus it is possible to hear, in the concepts of nothingness, nonintentionality, nonmeaning, purposelessness, silence, and at-oneness that form Cage's uniquely styled rhetoric, powerful metaphors of *nonbeing,* through which the ephemerality of sound, in its interpenetration and unimpededness, becomes meaningful. Unlike music theorists or speculative philosophers, Cage is then able to articulate the as-yet-unexamined *being* and experience of sound.

The process by which Cage arrives at being through nonbeing and subjectivity through the withdrawal of the intentions, judgments, and perhaps even the consciousness of the subject must be considered also as a practical application of the Hindu and Zen philosophies he internalized.[16] To see this more clearly it is helpful to bear in mind the allegory of Zen enlightenment that Cage applies to music, substituting "music" for "Zen" and "sounds" for "mountains" and concluding that, like enlightenment, the realization that "men are men and sounds are sounds" comes only after "one's feet are a little off the ground," that is, after one has gone through a process of estrangement from the naive, preontological perception (sounds are sounds) to abstract intellection (sounds are tones), in order to see the original perception in its complexity.[17] Thus, sounds are sounds, but, paradoxically, they are also indistinguishable from life, and for Cage "life" is an undifferentiated melange, charged equally by natural and synthetic processes and manifested equally by the chirping birds in the forest, as the traffic sounds of the city, or the cacophony of a dozen radios playing simultaneously. Within this ambience, the phenomenal and the metaphorical, the thing and the process, merge; artistic pursuit, "letting be," can now be defined as "bring[ing] into co-being elements paradoxical by nature the whole forming thereby an organic entity" (*JC*, p. 84). This entity becomes for Cage the function and "final meaning" of a piece of music:

The material of music is sound and silence. Integrating these is composing.

... Activity involving in a single process the many, turning them, even though some seem to be opposites, towards oneness, contributes to a good way of life. (S, p. 62)

As such the "organic entity" is able to penetrate contradictions, both musical and epistemic, that might appear on the surface of thought and language, to touch the more metaphysical, more spiritual, more experiential "oneness" that lies below. There, within the process— art-as-life—sounds are themselves and life is authentically lived, and that which sets life and art apart, including the dichotomies between sound and silence, subject and object, intention and nonintention that form the basis of both tonality and metaphysics, dissolves as the artist adopts the manner of the being or becoming of sound:

Urgent, unique, uninformed about history and theory ... central to a sphere, without surface, its [sound's] becoming is unimpeded, energetically broadcast ... It does not exist as one of a series of discrete steps, but as transmission in all directions from the field's center. (S, p. 14)

Using the being of sound as a metonym for (ideal) being in general, Cage grounds the former in the trope of transmission, where the idea of activity originating in a center and radiating out to interpenetrate with other such centers is reminiscent of the radio studio and the animate essence of phenomena alike. Obviously this condensation derives as much from analogies provided by the mechanical and electronic tools of his trade as meditations on the nature of aurality, particularly since composition, structured according to an organic rhythm and embracing any and all sounds including silence, is also, Cage notes, the domain of sound engineers, who "seemingly by accident" meet the artist "by intersection, becoming aware of the otherwise unknowable (conjunction of the in and the out) imagining brightly a common goal in the world and in the quietness within each human being," (S, p. 62).

Cage had ample opportunity to interact with sound engineers and sound technology in the course of composing. Between 1952 and 1965 he produced five major pieces using magnetic tape and four works for radio, adding to his "electronic" ensemble microphones, loudspeakers, and tape loops, plus the curious "percussive" device of the phonograph cartridge, which appears in *Cartridge Music* (1960), scored in part for "amplified small sounds."[18] During this period Cage's rhetorical register expanded with philosophical insights gleaned from his audiophonically based experiments. In 1957 for instance, he claimed that technics, in this case magnetic tape, could not only alter but generate a "total sound-space...the limits of which are ear-determined only," guiding the composer through the vicissitudes of its workings (the lack of synchronization in tape machines for instance) toward the acceptance of indeterminacy in performance and composition that parallels the multiplicity found in nature. (S, p. 9). For Cage magnetic tape illustrated the continuum of life that tonality and thinking had divided into discrete units, leading him to "renounce the need to control durations at all" and thus to the composition of indeterminate works such as *Music for Piano* and *Variations,* which, beginning anywhere and lasting any length of time, "are...not preconceived objects...[but] occasions for experience" (S, p. 31). Just as the materiality of tape assisted in the development of Cage's "art into life" philosophy, it also reaffirmed his already established views, inspired originally by Fischinger, of sound as some kind of object, the being or "center" of which could be released through the incisions of a razor blade. Commenting on *Williams Mix* in 1958, Cage advocates the method of splicing tape used in its construction as a means for "heighten[ing] the unique element of individual sounds, releasing their delicacy, strength, and special characteristics" (*JC*, p. 127).[19] Similarly, Cage saw the use of amplification as a means of projecting the sound of both sounds and objects outward from their inaudible center toward the human ear:

I want to listen to this ashtray. But I won't strike it as I would a percussion instrument. I'm going to listen to its inner life, thanks to suitable technology ... at the same time I'll be enhancing that technology since I'll be recognizing its full freedom to express itself.... It would be extremely interesting to place [the ashtray] in a little anechoic chamber and to listen to it through a suitable sound system. Object would become process; we would discover, thanks to a procedure borrowed from science, the meaning of nature through the music of objects. (FTB, p. 221)

CAGEAN SUBJECTIVITY

Once again, we are confronted with a complex and circular definition of the being of sound and the practice of letting sounds be themselves; circular because sound moves indiscriminately from object to process, phenomenon to metaphor; complex because "letting be" involves a surrender of intention in the midst of a technologically motivated *poesis*. One wonders how Cage manages to remain stable within these ever transmuting and often antagonistic surfaces. Precisely, it seems, by refusing the barriers of contradiction, moving always beneath the dualisms of appearance, to recoup or construct a unity, a synthesis, from the fragmented materials of his craft. The profundity of these operations lies in the suturing of disparate elements—art to life, subject to object—and is perhaps quintessentially expressed in the metamorphosis of the body into instrument, into art, and finally into aesthetic principle and rationale. This is evident in *0'00"*, Cage's electronic "silent piece," where the body and its actions constitute the instrument and the performance is intended to be merely "the continuation of one's daily work," which, when amplified through loudspeakers, suggests that "everything we do... can become music through the use of microphones" (CC, p. 70). According to many, the most notable performance of this piece was by Cage himself. Placing a contact microphone on his throat and drinking a glass of water, his swallowing reverberated through the performance space "like the pounding of giant surf."[20]

If bodies as well as objects can be made audible through technology, if the prostheses of technology can radiate inward, to the center of being, as well as outward, to the broadcast medium, then the "process" of letting sounds be themselves is also a process of self-realization at its deepest, most painful, and most internalized level. Cage underwent such a transformation in 1952 when, left alone in an anechoic chamber, he was directly confronted with the sounds of his nervous system working and his blood circulating (S, p. 8). Cage often acknowledges that this experience radically altered his conception of sound and silence, for hearing the internal workings of his body instead of the silence he had anticipated, he understood the impossibility of hearing pure silence, since one always hears with one's body and that body is itself permeated with sound. Based in the flesh rather than the intellect, this realization marked a surrender of the absolute—pure silence, pure absence—and the dichotomy sound/silence upon which Cage had previously argued for the "correct" basis of musical structure.[21] Silence is now no longer an abstract quantity, no longer the "opposite" of sound by virtue of an absence, but has become substantial, filled, so to speak, with the echoes of experience. As Cage's ear turned inward to hear the sounds of his body, so his concept of silence turned outward; "Silence" is now "the aspect of sound that can be either expressed by sound or by its absence" (CC, p. 52) and with this new latitude has an entirely different structural role. Since "the essential meaning of silence is the giving up of intention" (CC, p. 189), it is now the absence of the latter rather than the absence of sound that constitutes the "correct" basis for musical composition.

To ensure that this new silence, metonym for nonintentionality, would govern the structuring of a composition, Cage turned to chance operations, most notably the I Ching, hoping to introduce different means of decision making uninfluenced by conscious or unconscious interference ("psychology"). Chance, particularly in its oriental demeanor, is a perfect tool for this since in contrast to Western rationality, it is considered aleatory, contingent, accidental, coming from nowhere, grounded in the irrational and therefore without meaning or intention. In the immediacy of chance, nothing is ever before the fact, there is no work before the work, no prior intention to delimit the musical goal. More fundamentally, while the surrender to chance may open one's life to a benign serendipity, equally the caprice of circumstance may deliver death. Such a loss of self would foreclose the possibility of realizing the "narrative of man," represented in music by the A-B-A of tonality, in culture by the idea of existential progress. Yet Cage embraces this very possibility:

Life is one. Without beginning, without middle, without ending. The concept; beginning, middle and meaning comes from a sense of self which separates itself from what it considers to be the rest of life. But this attitude is untenable unless one insists on stopping life and bringing it to an end. That thought is in itself an attempt to stop life, for life goes on, indifferent to the deaths that are part of its no beginning, no middle, no meaning.... The acceptance of death is the source of all life.... Not one sound fears the silence that extinguishes it. And no silence exists which is not pregnant with sound. (S, pp. 134–135)

In living life authentically, in being aware of its continuity, one must accept death, nothingness, in the manner in which sound accepts silence, that is, without fear. But how can one avoid fearing death? Perhaps only by knowing that it does not exist: life goes on, silence is pregnant with sound, and nothingness is always potentially something. A comforting thought and for Cage a cushion against the incisive demands his rhetoric of selfless existence might make. Just as there is no absolute silence, there is no absolute death, and, at the same time, there is no causality, no meaning, no possible narrative, only undifferentiated being known through the simple fact of noise, the body's continuous hum, which, when potentially audible, guarantees that one is alive, when impossible to hear, signals the collapse of hearing, of the body itself. For Cage the noise of the body now represents both life and the arche of unintentionality, since "no one *means* to circulate his blood" (*S*, p. 80).

With noise-as-unintentionality so cathected to the body, the transcendental pursuit of the ear that would hear "sounds in themselves" is substantially curtailed, driven into the only locale available for hearing the body: the anechoic chamber. Outside, in the noise of everyday life, the ear rarely turns inward to hear the sounds of its own existence, nor does it detach itself from the body and its noisy psycho/physiological circulations in order to hear a sound "in itself." The deafness of the ear in hearing the arche of unintentionality means that it cannot be certain of the impossibility of silence, and by implication, of death. And if its hearing is always imbued with the uncertainty of the "unheard," then in what sense can it claim to hear fullness, the "themselves" of sounds? Only an ear detached from the mind, and therefore capable of a "pure" hearing unsullied by preconception or uncertainty, or conversely, detached from the body and able to penetrate the essences of things themselves, could ever know what sounds in themselves are in order to let them be. Cage finds this ear in technology; perfectly disembodied and supposedly neutral, it possesses the pure hearing that the human ear lacks and incorporates a kind of surrogate subjectivity capable of action but not, presumably, intention. The operations of this ear are complimented by another technology—chance operations—that ensures the work's production originates from a subject that is also endowed with neutrality and therefore is not responsible for the meaning or intention of its actions. Through these surrogates the composer inherits not only neutrality but all that "neuter" encompasses: neither body nor mind, neither mortal nor immortal, but infinitely present in the infinite permutations of aleatory and electronic transmissions. There is now no need to fear the silence, for as Cage realized late at night with the help of twelve radios, an electronic silence ensures that Silence as such, Silence as Death, will remain a convenient metaphor only.

THE PROBLEM OF REPRESENTATION

With silence as nonintentional sound and nothingness as nonintentional action, nonintentionality, it could be said, is formed from absences, the absence of will that constitutes the composer/performer/audience *as such*, that is, as the controller, director, creator, interpreter, definer, and, Cage implies, destroyer of the sound or the action. Although it might seem that within this schema everything is bound to disappearance, the ideal of nonintentionality does not demand the *actual* nonpresence of the composer, performer, or listener, but only that a certain rupture-provoking distance be inserted between an action (whether performative or perceptual) and its eventual sedimentation as meaning-laden representation. This distance is palpably guaranteed by the quasi or surrogate subjectivity Cage constructs through the mediating mechanisms of chance and technology. *Sounds in themselves* (including the sounds of the body) can then be known by subjects who ironically are not, or do not perceive as, "themselves"; however, Cage relies as much upon rhetorical as technical devices to distance, "reframe," and resituate the perceptual/cognitive perspective so that it does not infer meaning, will, or intent upon sound being itself. This strategy is nowhere more evident than in Cage's "silent" piece *4'33"*, the most controversial work in his history and the one most preferred by the composer himself. In *4'33"* *no* sounds are produced by the performer, who simply sits quietly in front of the piano for four minutes and thirty-three seconds, opening and closing the piano lid to indicate the piece's three "movements." Commenting on the philosophical position this piece embodies, Daniel Herwitz remarks, "We cannot construct, even in the imagination, a kind of half-person who both is like us and embodies the

Frances Dyson

Cagean perceptual position. Yet *4'33"*, once constructed, takes on the aura of being iconic precisely of that person we cannot imagine. ... Its silence (lack of performed sounds) becomes a metaphor for dis-structuring the ordinary, for producing a hearing of it in a way more immediate than the way we ordinarily hear—as if the sounds now heard were suddenly heard prior to mediation."[22]

The possibility of sounds being heard "prior to mediation" is evoked through an extremely inventive synthesis of two traditional incommensurables; the pure ear of the unthinking, un-representing body—the ear that "could hear [noises] directly and didn't have to go through any abstraction" (*S*, p. 116)—and the dis-embodied ear of an irredeemably objectifying technology. Yet the "dis-structuring of the ordinary" only occurs through a shift in per-spective brought about by a reflexive interrogation of the act of per-formance itself.[23] When in *4'33"* the background (ambience) takes the place of what is usually considered to be the foreground (the per-formance of a piano work), the audience is shaken from its conven-tional modes of aesthetic appreciation and forced to consider the object, in this case both the performance and "silence," in its com-plex richness.[24] Part of the brilliance of *4'33"* is the way it reveals the presence of meaning and culture in the reception of sound, present-ing its figure/ground reversal as a necessarily artistic, that is, *nonlin-guistic,* representation of sound and silence removed from certain cultural preconceptions. In keeping with the Zen parable, sounds are returned from the fixed (mis)conceptions of language to the unbounded processes of art not simply as sounds but "a little off the ground," suspended in quotation marks, so to speak. The quotation marks are provided by the "frame" of performance—the presence of the piano, stage, score, audience, and performer—which suggests not only that ambient sound can be music but that a series of silent actions can also be a performance. As a result, the meaning of the concepts *music, silence, sound,* and *performance* is ruptured, scattered in the winds of poetic expression—where discrepancies exist between a term and itself (*silence* is not silent), where the operations of language are opened to interrogation, and where the listener is forced to recognize the terms *silence* and *music* as metaphors *only*. The statement *4'33"* makes is therefore as much about systems of representation as about the nature of sound and music, and it implies that when these systems falter, what remains is only a lack of meaning, a diffusion and proliferation of metaphor, and nothing else. As Cage suggests, "no one loses nothing be-cause [*sic*] nothing is se-curely [*sic*] possessed" (*S*, p. 132). Indeed, nothing *can* be possessed when words disembark from the real, assuming the levity of performance, the fluidity of music, and a measure of arbitrariness sufficient to meet Cage's approval:

"Well...about Symbolism: I have never particularly liked it...I don't like it when it is a one to one relationship. That is to say, that a particular thing is a symbol of a particular other thing. But if each thing in the world can be seen as a symbol of every other thing in the world, then I do like it" (*EP*, p. 46).

In destabilizing concepts and conventions that have existed for centuries within Western culture, Cage suggests that the familiar ground of the real is in fact diaphanous. Segments of this unsteady terrain are revealed in *4'33"*, where the inherent responsibility of the perceiver in determining the nature and meaning of silence, music, or performance is rendered visible. There is a point, however, at which *4'33"* stops short, exposing the tyranny of culturally prescribed meaning in the reified context of art, but not in the more mundane world of sound. Before considering this foreclosure, it is important to recall another one, evident when Cage redefined *silence* after the anechoic chamber experience as "nonintentional," that is, nonmusicated and especially nonpitched, sound. If, however, *pitch* were to be replaced by the now more common term *frequency*, the material distinction between a noise or ambient sound and a tone would disappear, since both tones and noises have a certain frequency range. The distinction obviously has less to do with the materiality of sound than the *meaning* of noise and music; it is not the absence of pitch but the absence of the musical signifier, metaphor for intention-

Frances Dyson

ality, that makes noise, ambient sound, *silence*, so appealing. In the Cagean complex such aurality, being free from tonality, is free from any relational structure whatsoever, and therefore free from meaning anything other than itself. Yet, as *4'33"* reveals, the possibility of meaning returns to inhabit even this uncharted region, for even where sound means nothing, its appearance, on the stage or in the street, is still bound by symbolic representation. Just as Fischinger realized that a sound could be referred to a specific object, the Cagean sound, set adrift from the grid of musical signification, lands solidly in the weave of an equally structured and equally meaningful net, a net that perpetually interrupts Cage's transcendental movement toward the in-itself of sound by refusing to let sounds—known by objects, defined according to object criteria, and in fact so wrapped in the object that they cannot be understood, or perhaps even perceived, apart from it—be or express "themselves."[25] Consequently, within Western culture at least, the in-itself of sound is entirely dependent upon visually based systems of representation; sounds are described as "delicate" like the glass or "hollow" like the urn. Yet in what sense can sound be said to be "hollow"? Obviously, only in a sense that conceals sound within the shadow of the object.[26] This shadow is the mark of representation casting meaning, the meaning that haunts Cage even when object disappears into process, even when the innocent muteness of ambience frames and usurps the rational and articulate rhetoric of art.

An operation similar to *4'33"* occurs again in Cage's multimedia piece *HPSCHD,* a work for seven harpsichords, fifty-two tape machines, eight film projectors, and sixty-four slide projectors, which he produced in collaboration with the engineer-composer Lejaren Hiller and performed for an audience of 9,000 in the Assembly Hall of the University of Illinois, Urbana (May 1969).[27] The magnitude of this event was not simply a result of its size and complexity, for in *HPSCHD* the multitude of chance determinations that Cage, using the *I Ching,* had to perform were consigned to the computer, while the barely discernable and strangely archaic strains of

The Ear That Would Hear Sounds in Themselves

Mozart, including his *Introduction to the Composition of Waltzes by Means of Dice*, provided much of the "musical" content of the work.[28] Moving to the computer, and returning to Mozart, Cage in a sense completed a circuit; in the mass of disparate events and musical/visual references gathered together in the Assembly Hall, there existed an elevated unity, coherence, and organization, found not so much in the images or sounds themselves but in the media and mechanisms responsible for their generation and integration. As Daniel Charles remarks, "Ironically, in *HPSCHD the nontransparency and nonneutrality of the medium itself* becomes—thanks to the innumerable interferences between the various media involved—the very "subject" of the work,"[29] and this is heightened by the fact that the most identifiable sounds were, according to Virgil Thompson, "occasional shrieks of ear-piercing feedback."[30] The "irony" here is produced by a shift in reference, the foregrounding of that which had previously remained in the background as the "silent," invisible, and neutral actions of technology. And media and technology, now the "subject of the work," displaces sound by a double irony, silencing it through cacophony. In a mirroring of *4'33"* the "silence" is given voice *as* unintentional yet electronic sound, as the distortion and feedback produced by multiple amplifiers generating an electronic din, a thickened wall of sound/noise, in which sounds as such are either obliterated or become the "frame" within which the metaphor of technology, and the technology itself, assumes meaning.

Unlike *4'33"* however, the "framing" that occurs in *HPSCHD* goes unacknowledged; there is no hint that the use of audio technologies might insinuate a distance between sounds and their "pure" audition, no admission of the sonic and cultural transformations that audio technologies effect. Yet such a refusal is perfectly consistent within a Cagean aesthetic and indeed demonstrates his absolute reliance upon technology and all it represents. For an acknowledgment of the role of technology requires some degree of distance, of separation of the self from the technological milieu, and such a distance, separation, or departure might bring one face-to-face

Frances Dyson

with the possibility that nonintentionality implies: the possibility of human nonexistence, of silence and nothingness as such. And as Cage divined from the anechoic chamber and the circumstances surrounding the performance of *Imaginary Landscape No. 4,* a meeting with either of these states could only occur at death. But whereas death is a human inevitability, it makes no sense to speak of the finitude of the airwaves, or the mortality of the automata, or for that matter, of the perceptual limitations of a cyborg—the "half-person" who, like the electronic ether, is always potentially capable of being there— either in and with the "sound itself" or on the radio station ever ready to be tuned. Consequently, the metaphors of the electronic otherworld are able to represent those absolute, transcendental concepts—silence, nothingness, and nonintentionality—upon which Cage's aesthetic and philosophical arguments are grounded, whereas its mediums, by establishing an electronic intimacy with objects, can provide access to the conceptual essence of "sounds themselves."

REPRESENTING THE UNREPRESENTABLE

The importance of these concepts and their techno/tropic foundations is evident in the essay *Rhythm Etc.* (1962), where Cage makes a surprisingly lucid bid for the necessity of transparency:

There was a time...when, in Music, there was a glimmer of perfection—a relationship between the unit and the whole, down to the last detail: so elegant. How did that come about (it was an object)? It was an icon. It was an illustration of belief. Now do you see why what we do now is not at all what it was then? Everything now is in a state of confusing us, for, for one thing, we're not certain of the names of things that we see directly in front of us.

...when we say as one artist to another, "The unit and its relationship to the whole," we speak of an object, and it is well to remember that the only time the idea of movement on the part of an object entered his head, except as farfetched analogy to music of previous times, was when he was forced to accept errors in his calculations.

The Ear That Would Hear Sounds in Themselves

... (He had not made mistakes: it was just that circumstances were overwhelmingly different than the idea with which he was attempting to cloak them. And his idea, actually, he said, was a tool, an instrument—not an object. But it had all the elements (present only as measurements) that the object, once made, was to have. Thus it was not a tool... but an instrument, like the piano, which, used, leaves its notes scattered all over the music that was played.

... The problem is more serious: we must dispense with instruments altogether and get used to working with tools.... It can be put this way too: find ways of using instruments as though they were tools, i.e., so that they leave no traces. That's precisely what our tape-recorders, amplifiers, microphones, loud-speakers, photo-electric cells, etc., are: things to be used which don't necessarily determine the nature of what is done. (AYFM, pp. 123–124)

In 1962 Cage is ready to identify the "traces" that electronics do not leave: "We live in a global village (Buckminster Fuller, H. Marshall McLuhan).... One of the things we nowadays know is that something that happens (anything) can be experienced by means of technique (electronic) as some other (any other) thing (happening)" (AYFM, p. 33). In 1965 Cage relates this simultaneity and lack of differentiation to the archaic elegance that music was before words got in the way: "All technology must move toward [the] way things were before man began changing them: identification with nature in the manner of operation, complete mystery... Science and technology... lead to many more ways so that we become Imagination personified."[31] And in 1966 he concludes that "Nowadays everything happens at once and our souls are conveniently electronic." (JC, p. 167)

It is possible to discern a certain resignation in these reflections. Music, once so elegant, has been transformed by representation into an object, cluttered and confused not only by notation and tonality, its once-accepted discourse, but by the words and the theories used to prescribe its very being. And these prescriptions are themselves shrouded in a language that, disconnected from the world "as it is," is no longer useful. To recapture that connection, it is necessary to find and use a "tool" that will "leave no traces," that, in other words, will allow an unmediated relationship with the thing in itself. For Cage that "tool" is first and foremost a system, embodied initially in the *I Ching,* and later in electronics, that represents a means of organization whereby the absence of the composer's intention can be conceived as the corollary of technology's neutrality and can thus be absorbed within its multiple, unknowable, and traceless configurations. Once the subject has been diffused in the simultaneous and insubstantial sphere of electronic circuitry, the gap between subject and object, or word and thing, no longer matters, since everything and everyone is everywhere all at once. Within this sublime sphere, free from material commitments and unfettered by signification, sound becomes for Cage what music once was, a thing that represents only itself, of which nothing can be said with any certainty, which, as Schopenhauer insisted of music,

never expresses the phenomenon, but only the inner nature, the in-itself of all phenomena.

*   ... in its language, which is understood with absolute directness, but which is yet untranslatable into that of the reason, the inner nature of all life and existence expresses itself.*[32]

Traditionally, the Sublime has been featured in metaphysics as the domain of the "absolute" and therefore unrepresentable; in the musical hermeneutics of the classical and romantic era (which includes twentieth-century tonality) it was expressed in the purely instrumental compositions of "absolute" music. According to Carl Dahlhaus, the paradigm of absolute music is music without words, free from "extramusical" associations, self-sufficient and providing a direct avenue to the true, the beautiful, and the divine, whose contemplation alone allows one to escape the bounds of mortality in moments of self-forgetting.[33] Instrumental music has been considered best suited to the concept of the absolute since it "purely and clearly expresses the true nature of music by its very lack of concept, object and purpose. Not its existence, but what it stands for, is decisive. Instrumental music, as pure 'structure,' represents itself."[34] Representing only itself, absolute music is therefore above or beyond language, referring to the divine "essence" rather than the mere "appearance" of phenomena, and revealing this essence to the soul in the privacy of aesthetic and often ascetic contemplation. As Nietzsche says, [Words symbolize] only representations.... [Yet] Confronted with the supreme revelations of music, we even feel, willy-nilly, the *crudeness* of all imagery and of every emotion that might be adduced by way of analogy.... In the face of the supreme deity revealing himself, the symbol no longer has any significance; indeed, it comes to be seen as an insulting externality."[35] Dissolved from the constraints of reference, instrumental music, in the words of Dahlhaus, "'sublimates' or 'exalts' itself above the boundedness of the finite to an intimation of the infinite," thus ascending to the sublime. Here also, "the symbol no longer has any significance," for the simple reason that the sublime, defined as "unspeakable," ceases to exist the moment it is spoken. If music is devoid of symbolic associations, however, as was thought at the time, the "unspeakable" can be given a nonlinguistic expression.[36]

It is not my object to bury Cage's aesthetic within the hermeneutics of absolute music, for certainly he argued against the system of tonality such music embodied; however, his critique of tonality has been motivated in part by the fact that its current discourse, musicology, confers meaning upon music in the same way that tonality itself confers meaning upon sounds. Thus tonality "speaks," ceasing to represent only itself, referring to things outside itself (emotions, intentions, histories, intellectual schemas) and becoming an object of interpretation. As such, it can no longer serve the rhetorics of both absolute music and "sounds in themselves," for not only does it lack the silence Cage is looking for—the silence of sound in its nonsignificatory, nondiscursive muteness—but it cannot

Frances Dyson

guarantee the detachment of the observer from the sublime object of contemplation, since both object and observer are now involved in language and representation. Ernst Kurth characterizes the situation well: "Hence we can see clearly that the word 'absolute' has a double meaning. In a technical sense it means dissolved from song [that is, language]; in a spiritual sense, dissolved from man."[37] Cage's notion of "sound being itself" satisfies both meanings of the term, in that it refers to an observer possessing a quasi-subjectivity itself constituted via technology and thus "dissolved from man," and an object that, formed by silence as the absence of intention, is without meaning and therefore "dissolved from song."

After confinement in the anechoic chamber, Cage discovers that the possibilities for transcendence that sounds-without-meaning present are possibilities expressed only through paradox, that *Silence* is an extremely full metaphor of lack not of material sound but of intention/mind/discourse/culture/meaning, which has resonance only through the equally enigmatic concept of nothingness: "No thing in life requires a symbol since it is clearly what it is: a visible manifestation of an invisible nothing."[38] It is here that Cage's relationship to the sublime assumes added significance, for the problem of meaning and reference, of representation as such, is intimately connected to the impossibility of representing the absolute—death—with which both unintentionality and the notion of "sound in itself" is associated. The perspective from which one could speak either of the sounds of one's body or the inner sonorous life of an ashtray is necessarily detached from life. At the same time, the representation of these sounds is essential to Cage's philosophy; he must "speak" them, yet at the moment they are spoken Cage himself becomes disembodied. As Daniel Charles remarks with some anguish,

DC:
But there's nothing more to say about it....
We are always led back to this: there is nothing to say.

That is, to silence—to the world of sounds.

If I had something to say, I would say it with words. (FTB, p. 151)

The problem is, however, that Cage does "say it with words" and in so doing hubristically occupies the space of his own nonexistence: the sublime, the unrepresentable. It seems that the ear Cage is looking for is the ear that could hear the sound of its bodily existence, could hear, and thus allow to be spoken, the body of which it is a part. This hearing is possible only in a space of no sound, and where sound is a metonym for life, and silence a metonym for one's nonreflective, nonintentional immersion in life, such a space would be very close to death. To speak such a hearing one would have to occupy the space of death—one would have to *be* dead. The only way to redeem this space for the living is to describe it in terms of a "pseudovoid," a void that is not nothing, which shares the essential divinity of the sublime yet can be inhabited by mortals. The Cagean subject can occupy and internalize this space. By inhabiting the netherworld of electronics on the one hand, and the metaphorical/paradoxical interstices of language, the very limits of representation, on the other, it is able to represent both the Ur-silence, the sound of unintentionality, and the sound in itself, as it represents only itself, from a still living but also detached perspective. Thus there is "no more discourse. Instead...electronics," (*FTB*, p. 173).

Let us review this development in the context of the dictum that began this essay, *Let sounds be themselves.* A very schematic account could proceed as follows: first, Cage replaces pitch relations with rhythmic articulation as the "correct" structuring principle for composition; second, since rhythm is unaffected by pitch and therefore open to noise, he dissolves the distinction between music and noise, at the same time declaring noise to be music; and, third, he associates noise with objects, giving the latter both a sonority and a "spirit." In the next series of progressions, heralded by *Imaginary Landscape No. 1,* Cage redefines the object, both aural and material, to include the sphere of electronic sounds and devices. Thus no sooner does the object appear as liberator of sound from music (just as the sound of the object liberates its spirit) than it disappears, becoming less material than technological; no sooner is its noise amplified than it is eclipsed by the sound of technology, adding to this metaphonic dimension both the irony and reflexivity of the aestheticized signal and also the promise of the pure sound unsullied by worldly associations. These parallel aspects of Cage's utopianism inaugurate the third, and, for the purposes of this essay, final, movement, in which electronics becomes a favored existential and metaphorical mode. Representing a sphere that can only be expressed through the "language" of ambiguity, supplemented by the actual invisibility of sound and the seeming invisibility of technology, electronics provides a perfect avenue to the sublime.

Within this configuration the perceiver is also rendered invisible, becoming a subject who, lacking intentionality, is bound to act only via the prostheses and spaces that technology supplies: the loudspeaker, the computer, and the audiophonic and informational interface. Yet by those same prostheses the subject is able to inhabit a domain usually reserved for the dead, able to speak the unspeakable usually reserved, as Nietzsche said, for the deific or for music. In the meaninglessness of sounds and noise, in the chance-play of audio technologies, and, as evident in 4'33", in the metacritical and reflexive distance resulting from the erasure of the performer and the work as such, Cage develops a system for the representation of nonintentionality. And the quasi-subjectivities, or technological disembodies, which he inserts in the place that pure absence might have occupied, allows that concept, like silence, to conveniently function as metaphor only, ensuring that no void, no silence, no death need actually occur. Speaking of *sounds in themselves* from such a position, Cage presses against the limits of discourse; skirting the phenomenal ground of sound, he articulates with metaphors what is in fact realized through electronics: the limits of silence, the limits of embodiment.

NOTES

1. The latter seems to have always eluded Cage: "I have, so to speak, no ear for music, and never did have. I loved music but had no ear for it. I haven't any of that thing that some people speak of having— knowing what a pitch is." Additionally, "I might even say, or someone else may say of me, that my whole dedication to music has been an attempt to free music from the clutches of the A-B-A." (Richard Kostelanetz, *Conversing with Cage* [New York: Limelight, 1988], pp. 60, 59. Hereafter cited in text as *CC*.)

2. John Cage, "Forerunners of Modern Music," in *Silence* (Middletown, CT: Wesleyan University Press, 1961), p. 63, n. 2. Hereafter cited in text as *S*.

3. "I realized that a structure based on rhythm or time, on duration, could be just as hospitable to noises as to so-called musical sounds." (John Cage quoted in Daniel Charles, *For the Birds* [London: Marion Boyars, 1981], p. 73. Hereafter cited in text as *FTB*.)

4. William Moritz, "The Films of Oscar Fischinger," *Film Culture* 58, 59, 60 (1974), p. 50. Cage worked with Fischinger on animation and may have provided a percussion score for the film *Organic Fragment* (1941).

5. Richard Kostelanetz, ed., *John Cage* (New York: Praeger, 1968), p. 127. Hereafter cited in text as *JC*.

6. Prior to this piece Cage composed *Quartet* (1935) composed of fixed rhythmic patterns and *Trio* (1936) using skin and wood.

7. Edition Peters catalogue of *John Cage* (New York: Henmar Press, 1962), p. 37. Hereafter cited in text as *EP*.

8. Sleeve notes from the record album, *25-Year Retrospective Concert of The Music of John Cage* (New York: George Avakian, 1959).

9. John Cage, "For More New Sounds," in *John Cage,* ed. Richard Kostelanetz, pp. 64–66. *Imaginary Landscape No. 1,* while composed in 1939, was conceptually dated as early as 1937 in "The Future of Music: Credo," where Cage proposes that the word "music" be replaced by "organization of sound," and where he declares that "the use of noise to make music will continue and increase until we reach a music produced through the aid of electrical instruments." (John Cage, "The Future of Music: Credo," in *Silence,* p. 3.)

10. *Webster's New Universal Dictionary,* s.v. "radio."

11. For an account of Watson's mystical inclinations see Avital Ronell, *The Telephone Book* (Lincoln: University of Nebraska Press, 1989). For Edison's formulations of telepathy and otherworldly communication see Thomas A. Edison,

The Diary and Sundry Observations of Thomas A. Edison, ed. Dagobert D. Runes (New York: Philosophical Library, 1948).

12. As Kathleen Woodward writes, "Just as the technology of electronics transfigures the material world, so the metaphor of the invisible transforms our way of interpreting the world.... Thus for Cage electronics is much more than a concrete phenomenon. It is also a metaphor for what is also invisible and thus spiritual.... It is the wireless technology which can turn man towards his original harmony with nature." (Kathleen Woodward, "Art and Technics: John Cage, Electronics and World Improvement," in *The Myths of Information,* ed. Kathleen Woodward [Madison, WI: Coda Press, Inc., 1980], pp. 175, 184.)

13. For Cage the field acts as a potent metaphor for the continuum of life. As he says in an interview with Roger Reynolds, Edition Peters catalogue of *John Cage,* p. 50, "The difference is specifically the difference, say, between an ashtray and the whole room. Ash tray can be seen as having beginning and end.... But when you begin to experience the whole room—not object, but many things—then, where is the beginning? where is the middle?... it is clearly a question not of an object but rather of a process."

14. Cage, *Silence,* p. 125. Similarly, in 1952, when Cage first worked with magnetic tape, he discovered that sounds could occupy determinate spaces, measured in lengths of tape that corresponded to specific durations, and this correspondence was interpreted as a technologically motivated synesthesia: "In the late forties and early fifties it became clear that there's a physical correspondence between time and space. And music is not isolated from painting because one second of sound is so many inches on tape.... Therefore, I began doing graphic notations." (Kostelanetz, *Conversing with Cage,* p. 184.)

15. See John Cage, "Lecture on Nothing" and "Lecture on Something," in *Silence.* "Unimpededness" appears again in "Julliard Lecture," (a composite of collaged fragments from the two) given in 1952 at the Julliard School of Music, as an index of the development of Cage's ideas. Later, in conversation with Daniel Charles, Cage adds, "I like to think that each thing has not only its own life but also its center, and that its center is always the very center of the Universe.... there are a plurality of centers, a multiplicity of centers. And they are all interpenetrating and, as Zen would add, non-obstructing.... There must be nothing between the things which you have separated so they wouldn't obstruct each other. Well, that *nothing* is what permits all things to exist." (Charles, *For the Birds,* p. 91.)

16. In 1945 Cage's profound questioning of the purpose of writing music led him from a once-only encounter with psychoanalysis to study the philosophy and classical music of India with Gita Sarabhai and Zen Buddhism with Dr. Daisetz Suzuki.

17. "Before studying music, men are men and sounds are sounds. While studying music things aren't clear. After studying music men are men and sounds are sounds. That is to say: at the beginning one can hear a sound and tell immediately that it isn't a human being or something to look at.... While studying music things get a little confused. Sounds are no longer just sounds but are letters: A,B,C,D,E,F,G....If a sound is unfortunate enough not to have a letter or if it seems too complex, it is tossed out of the system. [In composition] the sounds themselves are no longer of consequence; what "count" are their relationships. [In understanding a musical idea]...you think that a sound is not something to hear but rather something to look at. In the case of a musical feeling ... [one] has to confuse himself to the final extent that the composer did and imagine that sounds are not sounds at all but are Beethoven and that men are not men but are sounds....this is simply not the case. A man is a man and a sound is a sound. To realize this...one has to stop all the thinking that separates music from living.... Sounds are sounds and men are men, but now our feet are a little off the ground." (From John Cage, "Julliard Lecture," in *A Year from Monday* [Middletown, CT: Wesleyan University Press, 1967], p. 96. Hereafter cited in text as *AYFM*.)

18. His pieces using magnetic tape were *Williams Mix* (1953) and *Fontana Mix* (1958), a score for the production of any number of tracks, performers, and instruments, and through the use of transparen-

cies, indeterminate of its performance. Its tape realization was also used in subsequent works such as *Water Walk* and *Sounds of Venice* (1959) and *WBAI* (1960), an auxiliary score for performance with lecture, parts of *Concert for Piano and Orchestra,* recordings, and radios. Cage's works for radio included *Imaginary Landscape No. 5* (1952), a score composed using the *I Ching* for the recording and mixing of various elements of forty-two phonograph records on tape; *Speech* (1955), an indeterminate score for five radios and newsreader; *Radio Music* (1956), for one to eight performers each at one radio; and *Music Walk* (1958). During this period Cage also composed for piano, prepared piano, toy piano, orchestra, voice, percussion instruments, and "any sound-producing means" (*Variations* 1–7). (Edition Peters catalogue of *John Cage,* pp. 33–41.)

19. *Williams Mix* took about one year to make; was produced on eight tracks; involved the recording of six hundred sounds divided into six categories (city, country, electronic, wind produced, manually produced, and small sounds requiring amplification), which are further catalogued in terms of pitch, timbre, and amplitude and organized according to the *I Ching;* and lasted a little over four minutes. (Kostelanetz, *John Cage,* p. 111; Edition Peters catalogue of *John Cage,* p. 41.) Speaking in a later publication, Cage expresses excitement over the fact that, with tape, time is measurable in inches, one second being equivalent to fifteen inches of tape. As a result, sound's temporal ephemerality is no longer a problem. With sound so easily manipulated, it is understandable that Cage would begin to consider it an object that can be "entered" in some way or another. (Kostelanetz, *Conversing with Cage,* p. 164.)

20. Cited in Michael Nyman, *Experimental Music* (New York: Schirmer Books, 1974), p. 78.

21. This happened fairly quickly. In *Lecture on Nothing* (1950) the argumentation remains dualistic—apophanticly establishing the "correct" grounds of musical structure (rhythm) and then proceeding to separate the ear and the mind, aligning the ear with noises and the possibility of hearing "fresh" sounds that had not yet been "intellectualized," the mind with the suffocation or "wearing out" of sound: "Thinking had worn them out." (Cage, *Silence,* p. 117.) In *Lecture on Something* (published in 1959 but "prepared some years earlier") Cage positions the creativity of unthinking perception, the ear, within the now problematic (post-anechoic-chamber) notion of silence.

22. Daniel Herwitz, "The Security of the Obvious: On John Cage's Musical Radicalism," in *Critical Inquiry* 14 (Summer 1988), p. 801.

23. This is evident also in *Imaginary Landscape No. 1,* where the broadcast of the test tone, despite its musicalization, is automatically straddled with the radio-phonic apparatus, as if the radio were airing itself in its prebroadcast state, as if the radio studio were no longer the hidden and effaced enclave of mainstream media but, now instrument, presented itself on the radio stage.

24. For an excellent account of the "phenomenological attitude" that *4'33"* engenders see Don Ihde, *Existential Technics* (Albany: State University of New York Press), 1983, p. 95.

25. Think, for instance, of the generally onomatopoetic linguistic representation of sounds; *crash* or *clatter* are entirely ambiguous terms until "grounded" in the object presumed to be their source: the breaking glass or the disturbed crockery. This point has been raised by Christian Metz, whose seminal text *Aural Objects* (*Yale French Studies* 60) poses the problem of sound's existence in terms of its status in Western epistemology as a "secondary characteristic" of concrete, visible objects. Like Cage's advocacy of noise, Metz's redress calls for the recognition of "aural objects" as ontologically equal to objects that happen to be present to sight, implying that such an admission would radically alter the foundations of an epistemology based on the Greek confluence of seeing and knowing. Although extremely original, Metz's rehabilitation of sound, as his neologism "aural object" suggests, encloses the aural within a metaphysics the existential criteria of which are inappropriate to aurality. No longer a characteristic, sound becomes an "object" at odds with the meaning of the term; autonomous perhaps, but for what and in what sense? It could be argued that the objectification of sound, its assimilation of visualist criteria, does little either to challenge the origins of those criteria or to represent sound outside visualist discourse. The same argument could be directed at Cage, which is not to deny the strategic importance of recognizing the musicality of sounds distinct from the musical context. Although the "aural object" and the "musical noise" are truly fresh and necessary concepts, left on their own they stand as oxymoronic, leaving unanswered the question of *why* sound should be assimilated in terms of either music or the object.

26. Don Ihde gives two useful examples of our determination of the aural: first, in the anthropomorphic description of the cries of a bird or whale as a "song"; second, in the notion that sound is unitary, belonging to "an object," whereas it is in actuality already a "complex polyphony": "When I use a pen to strike the water pitcher, you hear both the sound of the glass and of the plastic, simultaneously in a duet of voices of things." In order to isolate and name a particular sound within that polyphony, a reduction must occur; the particular object (the pitcher or the pen) must become the center of focus and the sound mix (described perhaps as a muted "ting") attributed to that object alone. Once isolated and named, the sound mix is referred to as *the* sound of *that* object—no longer sound as such, its characteristics are described in terms of

the material characteristics of the object; it is "delicate" like the glass or "hollow" like the urn. (See Don Ihde, *Consequences of Phenomenology* [Albany: State University of New York Press, 1986], p. 28.)

27. According to Thompson, this performance also included "59 power amplifiers, 59 loud speakers, and 208 computer generated tapes. The visual contributions... employed 64 slide projectors showing 6,400 slides and 8 moving-picture projectors using 40 cinematographic films." (See Virgil Thompson, *A Virgil Thompson Reader* [Boston: Houghton Mifflin, 1981], p. 475). Cage remembers the event as using "80 slide projectors with 8000 slides [many of which] dealt with space travel... the central theme was [surprisingly] interplanetary travel." (Charles, *For the Birds,* p. 195.)

28. Daniel Charles, "Music and Technology Today" in *Art and Technology,* ed. Rene Berger and Lloyd Eby (New York: Paragon House Publishers, 1986), p. 154. While speaking from the audience with Earl Brown, who sat on the "composers panel" at the *Cage at Wesleyan* Symposium (1988), Cage mentioned that he preferred Mozart to Bach, since Mozart was concerned with multiplicity whereas Bach was concerned with unity. Many thanks to Douglas Kahn for the recordings of this symposium.

29. Ibid., p. 160.

30. Thompson, *A Virgil Thompson Reader* p. 476.

31. Charles, "Music and Technology Today," p. 93.

32. Arthur Schopenhauer, "Art and the Art of Music," in *Readings in Philosophy,* ed. Justus Buchler, John Herman Randall, Jr., and Evelyn Urban Shirk (New York: Barnes and Noble, 1950), p. 247.

33. Carl Dahlhaus, *The Idea of Absolute Music,* trans. by Roger Lustig (Chicago: University of Chicago Press, 1989). Citing Karl Philipp Moritz (1788), "As long as the beautiful draws our attention completely to itself, it shifts it away from ourselves for a while, and makes us seem to lose ourselves in the beautiful object; just this losing, this forgetting of the self, is the highest degree of the pure and unselfish pleasure that beauty grants us. At that moment we give up our individual, limited existence in favour of a kind of higher existence" (p. 5).

34. Ibid., p. 7.

35. Friedrich Nietzsche, "On Music and Words," trans. Walter Kaufmann, in Carl Dahlhaus, *Between Romanticism and Modernism* (Berkeley: University of California Press, 1989), pp. 107, 112. Note that Nietzsche also believed music to be "an imitation of nature."

36. According to Dahlhaus, though this removal developed music's romantic aesthetic, its motivation was primarily literary: "Paradoxically enough, the discovery that music—specifically instrumental music free of object or of concrete concept—was a language 'above' language occurred 'in' language itself.... The pathos used to praise instrumental music was inspired by literature: were it not for the poetic conceit of unspeakability, there would have been no words available for reinterpreting the musically confusing or empty into the sublime or wonderful." Dahlhaus, *The Idea of Absolute Music,* p. 63.

37. Ernst Kurth, *Bruckner* (Berlin, 1925), p. 258, cited in Dahlhaus, *The Idea of Absolute Music,* p. 40.

38. Cage, *Silence,* p. 136. Thus, the opening comments of *Lecture on Something* (Cage, Silence, p. 129) are devoted to

- the unity of opposites: "Something and nothing are not opposed to each other but need each other to keep on going."
- the problem of language: "It is difficult to talk when you have something to say precisely because of the words which keep making us say in the way which words need to stick to and not in the way which we need for living."
- the development of a negative ontology: "It is of the utmost importance not to make a thing but rather to make nothing.... Done by making something which then goes in and reminds us of nothing."

ROBIN LYDENBERG

SOUND IDENTITY FADING OUT
WILLIAM BURROUGHS' TAPE EXPERIMENTS

Most writers don't use their voices in their work. . . But Burroughs writes with his voice. . . .One cannot simply read his texts; one must, in reading them, also hear them. It is necessary to throw oneself into the voice.

Philippe Mikriammos, "Vox Williami, vox monstrorum"

For thirty years reviewers of William Burroughs' fiction have acknowledged the power of his literary voice. In her 1966 review of *The Soft Machine*, Joan Didion ridicules critics who judge Burroughs' work on the basis of its moral, political, or thematic content. In Burroughs' case, Didion argues, "the medium *is* the message: the point is not what the voice says but the voice itself, a voice so direct and original and versatile as to disarm close scrutiny of what it is saying."[1] Like many of Burroughs's readers, Didion appreciates his brilliance as an impersonator—he mimics T. S. Eliot in one phrase and a young street hustler or aging junky in the next; but she also hears the complexity of his *own* voice, "hard, derisive, inventive, free, funny, serious, poetic, indelibly American" (p. 3). She hears, too, the way his writing captures and transforms the acoustic environment we all inhabit: "[His is] a voice in which one hears transistor radios and old movies and all the clichés and all the cons and all the newspapers, all the peculiar optimism, all the failure" (p. 3). In what is surely a unique expression of admiration, Didion declares, "Burroughs is less a writer than a 'sound'" (p. 2).

Burroughs' earliest writings are grounded in that sound, in the immediacy of voice and performance. "Twilight's Last Gleamings"—Burroughs' first routine—was composed in collaboration with his childhood friend Kells Elvins in 1938, the two acting out the characters who came to them as voices. Developing the routines for *Naked Lunch* fifteen years later, Burroughs liked to read them aloud to friends, emerging from the excruciating isolation of his writing—as Kafka had done—to test and enjoy its comic effects. Not until he began giving public readings in the 1970s did Burroughs rediscover the pleasures of direct contact and collaboration with a sympathetic audience that had fueled his earliest creative ventures.

Between acting out routines for his friends in the 1950s and emerging as a public performer in the 1970s, Burroughs spent several years intensely engaged in an interrogation of language and the voice. With Brion Gysin, Antony Balch, Ian Sommerville, and other collaborators in London, Paris, and New York, Burroughs experimented with cut-ups, fold-ins, and permutations of word and image. His raw material included not only written and illustrated texts but tape recordings and film sequences as well. The tape recorder experiments of this period represent most explicitly his exploration of voice, of the word's relationship to the body, of the proliferation of the word by the mass media, and of the word as a weapon of illusion and control. Burroughs' goal in these experiments is always "break through"—the explosion of "prerecorded" words, asssociations, and identity. The titles of two collections of Burroughs' tape experiments indicate the direction in which he is headed: *Break Through in Grey Room* and *Nothing Here Now but the Recordings*.[2]

From the experimental detour of his text and tape cut-ups Burroughs returns not only to voice but also to the more conventional narratives of *Cities of the Red Night* (1981), *The Place of Dead Roads* (1984), and *The Western Lands* (1987). This return indicates not a failure but a choice; no longer condemned to language, body, and narrative, Burroughs may *choose* to inhabit them—a tourist without itinerary, free to pack up and take the next flight out. In this essay I will explore in some detail what happens along the route of this experimental detour—in Burroughs' actual tape cut-ups, in his cut-up novels (*The Soft Machine* [1961], *The Ticket That Exploded* [1962], and *Nova Express* [1964]), and in his theoretical essays.

Burroughs' experiments with voice and sound can best be understood in the broader context of his theories about language. He views Western culture as ruled by a system of mass ventriloquy in which disembodied voices invade and occupy each individual. The basic pattern of such domination and control is uncovered by Burroughs in primitive and modern cultures alike: in primitive societies where the priest king ruled by "produc[ing] his voice in the brains of his loyal subjects,"[3] or in modern societies where the "mass media of newspapers, radio, television, magazines form a ceremonial calendar to which all citizens are subjected."[4] By alternating subliminal contradictory commands—"an integral part of the modern industrial environment: Stop. Go.... Come in. Stay out.... Rebel Submit. RIGHT. WRONG" (*Job,* p. 45)—this modern system of control is able to "limit and stultify on a mass scale" (*Job,* p. 193).

In an early permutation exercise, Burroughs stumbles on several variants that strangely resemble the speech of Lacan's signifier: "Words are what is not. Knot is what are words. Words knot are what is? What knot words?... What words knot our is?"[5] Because he insists on the arbitrary relationship of "verbal labels" to what they supposedly represent (*Job,* p. 201), and because he associates the word with absence or lack, Burroughs' use of *word* here corresponds closely to Lacan's signifier. Like Lacan, Burroughs acknowledges that the individual is indeed constituted by the signifier, by his or her existence within the predetermined (and knotted) structure of language. The permutation exercise is a way of tracing the loops of the knot, a way of becoming conscious of the system's susceptibility to variation, but without leaving its imposed parameters.

Burroughs perceives similar patterns of restriction or domination in interpersonal relations as well, the impact of any strong personality producing a sinister form of ventriloquy: "You think of someone and you can hear their voice in your throat feel their face in yours and their eyes looking out"(*AM*, pp. 131–132); "If you are listening to someone, that person's voice is inside your head. It has to some extent invaded and occupied your brain."[6] The primary invading and occupying voice, however, is always that of language itself, and Burroughs' experimental work with cut-up tapes is designed to ferret the word out of its hiding place. He reasons that once we see that "Word is another voice" (*BF*, p. 198), we will recognize language as an alien invader threatening individual will and spontaneous evolution. Personal or impersonal, internal or external, voice itself is always the weapon of coercion and control. In the cut-ups, as Brion Gysin puts it, "It speaks."[7]

MAKING THE WORD CONCRETE

The resistance strategy Burroughs proposes is to force the word to reveal its concrete form so that the enemy can be seen and expelled: "*Communication must become total and conscious before we can stop it.*"[8] Establishing itself in the subject's body, insinuating itself as necessary for that body's survival, the alien word or voice becomes the "Other Half" of its human host, an invisible parasitic invader. Burroughs traces all parasitic relations back to a primitive stage of life at which what he calls the "word virus" was first produced and thereafter "genetically conveyed" (*Job*, p. 13). Burroughs often describes this function of the word virus as a conveyor of predetermined aspects of human life through the metaphor of electronic transmissions on magnetic tape—an invisible writing that imposes absolute control. He makes both this metaphor and the process it represents concrete and literal in *The Ticket That Exploded*, where the narrator is trapped in an uncomfortable fusion with the anonymous parasitic "other rider" on his "long trip": "the sound of his voice and his image flickering over the tape recorder are as familiar to me as the movement of my intestines the sound of my breathing the beating of my heart.... In fact his voice has been spliced in 24 times per second with the sound of my breathing and the beating of my heart so that my body is convinced that my breathing and heart will stop if his voice stops" (*T,* pp. 1–3). Like genetically coded material that circumvents all individual thought and will, the tape recording works directly on the body and mind, invisibly, from within. The notion of language as an uncontrollably proliferating viral infection thus finds expression also in the notion of the technological mass reproduction and manipulation of human identity by tape recordings and film images.

The cure, Burroughs argues, is to "splice your body sounds in with air hammers. Blast jolt vibrate the 'Other Half' right out into the street" (*T,* p. 50). Such cut-up experiments with magnetic tape and flesh constitute a concrete embodiment of Burroughs' cut-up writing methods. The cut-up technique, like the visual artist's use of collage or montage, offers the advantage of making the writer's medium tangible: "The writer does not yet know what words are. He deals only with abstractions from the source points of words.... These [cut-up] techniques can show the writer what words are and put him in tactile communication with his medium" (*Job,* pp. 27–28). The technique itself is simple: "Cut right through the pages of any book or newsprint...lengthwise, for example, and shuffle the columns of text. Put them together at hazard and read the newly constituted message" (*TM,* p. 34). The basic method for cut-up tapes is similar: spin or click the wheel of the recorder back and forth to record and erase at random, creating new juxtapositions.

Whether cutting up written texts with scissors or splicing, overlapping, and distorting recorded voices on tape, Burroughs is engaged in the physical handling of language. Gysin describes Burroughs' excitement during the early experiments with cut-ups: "When you handle the stuff yourself, you get the feel of it. William loved the idea of getting his hands on his own words.... Burroughs was busy punching to death a series of cheap Japanese plastic tape recorders to which he applied himself with such force that he could punch one of them to death inside a matter of weeks, days even."[9] After spending the better part of a year cutting and splicing the tape recordings that make up "Williams Mix" (1953), John

Cage expressed a similar pleasure in this physical handling of sound, which he called "making music manually."[10]

Burroughs was aware that cut-ups produced with tape recordings could extend the process of making the word concrete by transforming sound frequencies into actual patterns of magnetic dust on plastic tape. In his critical study *A la recherche d'un corps: Langage et silence dans l'oeuvre de William S. Burroughs,* Serge Grunberg offers an elaborate analysis of the "metaphor of magnetic tape" in Burroughs' work, a metaphor that nevertheless retains its *literal* force. Grunberg traces the circuit of the recorded human voice into electronic frequencies, which are then coded as magnetic dust patterns on tape and returned by playback to sonic vibrations. He argues that Burroughs' attention to this process underscores the nature of voice as mere semblance. With the voice "inscribed" on magnetic tape—visible, reproducible, and independent of the speaker—the distinction between speech and writing and the privileging of the former over the latter is undermined. Language is a virus produced by the machine, and voice is nothing but an electronic signal which can be produced, reproduced, and counterfeited. The tape cut-ups in particular, Grunberg argues, expose the most repressed levels of the psyche: as sound on the tapes is spliced, erased, or buried beneath new recordings, the unconscious effects of castration and loss are made literal and concrete. This "scandal of writing," its exposure of the effects of the unconscious at work or "in labor," are thus reproduced on the tape recordings, which become a metaphor for all textual deployment.[11] Burroughs has thus displaced the uncanniness of the psyche, of language and voice, onto the machine where it can be exposed, explored, and exorcised.

THE TECHNOLOGY OF WARFARE

Burroughs' exploration of language with the aid of tape recorder technology, however, is only part of a larger project, which he conceives of most often not in terms of experiment or play but of warfare. For example, the science fiction scenarios of his cut-up trilogy, in which technology often plays a major role, focus on intergalactic as well as internal conflicts. Much of the fictional material Burroughs reads in the cut-up recordings is drawn from these adversarial dramas of cosmic and local struggle, and the intensity and immediacy of battle are reinforced by his vocal delivery. In a clipped and insistent monotone, often repeating the same orders ("Shift Coordinate Points," "Recalling All Active Agents," "Cut all tape"), Burroughs produces the effect of messages crackling through battle with the "walkie-talkie immediacy" that characterizes the cut-up style (*BF*, p. 34).

The conflicts Burroughs obsessively rehearses in his fiction are not familiar disputes over territorial borders fought with conventional weapons of destruction; instead, he imagines more subtle and insidious struggles over the power to manipulate information codes and communication systems. The French writer Jean-Joseph Goux situates Burroughs's experimental work at the turning point in the modern age when the machine as a source of energy and speed (as the Futurists celebrated it) has given way to the machine as an information system coding and controlling all knowledge.[12] Julia Kristeva, Michel Serres, François Lyotard, and others have similarly characterized post–World War II modernity by the rise of information systems,[13] and they see computers and the mass media as providing the arena in which issues of power and control are played out.

From his earliest experiments with tape and text cut-ups, Burroughs perceived their potential use "as a decoding operation" (*BF*, p. 34) for strategic deployment in interplanetary warfare. In science fiction novels such as *The Ticket That Exploded*, the manipulative power of modern media technology is wielded by enemy forces from other planets who program the earth's inhabitants through vast switchboards of prerecorded tapes and film images. Cut-up interventions by revolutionary agents are designed to obstruct

Sound Identity Fading Out

such habitual and imposed patterns of decoding (that is, decoding information into binary oppositions, hierarchies, or linear sequence), and to replace them with an infinite variety of modes of reception that would open up rather than restrict options.

One version of Burroughs' revolutionary strategy is outlined in "Electronic Revolution": "*As a long range weapon to scramble and nullify association lines put down by mass media....* You can cut the mutter line of the mass media and put the altered mutter line out in the streets with a tape recorder.... For example, prepare cut ups of the ugliest reactionary statements you can find and surround them with the ugliest pictures. Now give it the drool, slobber, animal-noise treatment and put it out on the mutter line with recorders" (*Job*, pp. 176–177). He imagines, that with such "scrambling" of texts, images and recorded sound, the underground movement could weaken and possibly defeat conventional methods of control. This theoretical proposal is approximated on some of the cut-up tapes where Burroughs introduces fragments of newscasts reporting on actual military battles as well as local fires or industrial explosions.[14] Often the line between real news reports and Burroughs' fictional elaborations is blurred, exposing the authority of news reporting as merely a form of manipulative creative writing.

The kind of thematic and even syntactic scrambling proposed in such texts as "Electronic Revolution," however, is still operating on a relatively accessible level. Beneath this surface level, Burroughs perceives a more threatening conflict, the effects of more subtle and invisible methods of control that call for correspondingly subtle methods of resistance. In *The Job*, for example, Burroughs describes a new weapon he has read about that uses magnified sound frequencies. The experimentors seem less interested in the weapon's conventional powers (at full blast these frequencies could destroy a building) than in its more insidious effects: "'It not only affects the ears,' Professor Gavreau says, 'but it works directly on the internal organs. There is a rubbing between the various organs because of a sort of resonance. It provokes an irritation so intense that for hours afterwards any low-pitched sound seems to echo through one's body'" (*Job*, p. 62).[15] This sound weapon, which shifts the battlefield to the internal arena of the body itself, typifies for Burroughs the new adversarial mode of parasitic invasion and occupation that has replaced more traditional and overt military destruction of property and life. Control is imposed not only at the level of subliminal suggestion by prerecorded word and image but at the deeper level of rhythmic sound waves attacking flesh molecules.

If language and even the sound frequencies that constitute it have invaded the human body, Burroughs' proposal to use tape recorder cut-ups to vibrate word and sound out of the body seems almost logical. In effects similar to those of Professor Gavreau's sound weapon, Burroughs' tape cut-ups often produce an assaultive pulsation that "ululate[s] rhythmically" (*Job*, p. 62), leaving the listener unable to construct context, linear sequence, or even syntax from what he hears and thus liberating him or her from these imposed patterns of thought. As he explains in *Ticket*, "The content of the tape doesn't seem to effect the result" (*T*, p. 18); the power resides instead in the rhythm, in patterns of alternation at specific intervals.

In his film "Towers Open Fire,"[16] Antony Balch dramatizes Burroughs' mythology of conflict and utilizes many of the resistance strategies Burroughs outlines in his fiction and theory. The soundtrack of the film includes cut-ups of resistance messages spliced at such short intervals that one hears only an incomprehensible pulsing. In the visual images accompanying these sound effects, Balch often cuts in footage of Brion Gysin's Dream Machine, a stroboscopic invention that regulates light frequencies "complementing the alpha rhythms in the brain [to produce] changes of pattern...in apparent random order...dream images, imaginary events."[17] This rhythmic manipulation of sound and image assaults the viewer selectively: as these techniques cut off the viewer's access to continuity, logic, and even "alleged content," he or she gains access to the infinite potential of chance, dream, and imagination.

Burroughs is eager to "reach the Front"[18] in this war, and willing to use even the enemy's own devices to achieve freedom from control. He is not unaware of the irony of this situation, but he has always insisted that any technique is only good or bad according to who is using it, and for what purpose. His goal in understanding how the control machine operates is to reprogram the machine in order to liberate individuals from all programming, from all modes of control. Unlike the repressive forces who are thoroughly dependent on their devices of control, Burroughs' revolutionary cadets are advised to train voice, body, and consciousness to achieve technological breakthroughs without the aid of drugs or technology.

ESCAPING THE SELF

In Burroughs' mythology, therefore, issues of political and cosmic warfare are eventually played out in a personal context—in the body and mind of each individual. On the actual cut-up tapes, fragments of intensely personal and familiar voices often emerge unexpectedly in the midst of radio broadcasts or mechanical sounds. The clipped, emotionless voice in which Burroughs reads the news reports of various disasters (sometimes repeating a death count with the insistence of an incantation) is undermined by these eruptions of despair, fear, and loneliness: "all through, can't do another thing," "but I'm dying ...open this up so I can touch you," "please don't ask me to go there," "help me get out."[19] Many of these phrases are taken from the transcript of Dutch Schultz's dying words, and they carry the weight of those final moments, echoing obsessively a lifetime of regrets, terrors, and desires.

Burroughs proposes that one might escape these nagging, frightened voices by feeding all emotional habits, all obsessive association lines of fear, hate, and memory into a "cement mixer" of tape recorders: "Whatever your problem is just throw it into the machines and let them chew it around a while" (*T*, p. 163). After being repeatedly filtered through the machine, these "prob-

Robin Lydenberg

lems" are neutralized and evaporate: "the more you run the tapes through and cut them up the less power they will have cut the pre-recordings into air into thin air" (*T*, p. 217). Burroughs had encountered the metaphor of mental tape recordings during his brief study of Scientology; he extends that metaphor to argue that the "memory tapes" and "mind tapes" that constitute our prerecorded identity, our past and future, can be wiped clean. He insists that we can learn more from such technological experiments than from years of analysis or meditation.

In "Just Checking Your Summer Recordings" Burroughs explains patiently to a silent or absent listener, "When you spliced yourself in with another recorder you activated all your sex recordings in me and deactivated the recordings in yourself and transferred them to another machine." Filtered through the literal mechanism of the tape recorder and the metaphorical mechanism of human desire as a prerecording, desire and betrayal are distanced and depersonalized. Burroughs' voice in this segment is slow and sad, but the cut fades out in an exaggerated parody of sentimentality with a long instrumental solo of "Buddy Can You Spare a Dime." In "Silver Smoke of Dreams" and "Summer Will," two soft voices have been so closely spliced that one can make out only a few phrases returning like a lyrical lament or a painful memory: "smell of late morning," "still, stale," "dreams of Billy," "desolate markets," "found him." The voices stumble and stutter, often unable to finish even a single phrase, sometimes catching on the hopeless call, "Billy... Billy... Billy." In one version the lonely voices are intercepted and undercut by the throbbing drums and flutes of the Joujouka Festival or the scraping sound of the tape being inched across the tape head—interruptions that break the sentimental spell of the recurring laments and allow for the intermittent and inexplicable cries of "Joy!"

These experiments seem to stem from an effort to exhaust and then move beyond human sentiments and identity, and in that context conventional psychoanalysis has little application. As Goux argues, in our technological moment there is no more

Lacanian "mirror stage" but only a "phonograph stage, a television stage, a video stage, a photocopier stage." With no guarantee of any narcissistic return of his own image in the present, the individual receives back only the reflection of an obstructed, delayed, and deformed self (C, p. 136). In order to see more clearly the alienated and fictive nature of the self, Burroughs approaches it from outside with the detachment of a technical observer. In the recordings of this period he often affects an inhuman voice and delivery, speaking as an alien visitor in what Goux describes as an "incomprehensible Morse code from interstellar space...in a sort of mechanical and coded bi-bip...no longer human but cosmic" (C, p. 139).

The farewell litanies that dominate *Ticket* and *Nova Express* can be heard as Burroughs' parting words to a human condition he hopes to leave behind: "'Remember i was a battery of tape recorders at the door—...sound identity fading out—'" (T, p. 68), "Nothing here now but the recordings."[20] Technology provides both the metaphor for the artificial falsity of the self and the literal mechanism for an escape from that constricting identity. The measure of Burroughs' achievement of a total indifference to his "sound identity" may be seen in his recent practice of giving away recordings of his voice—no strings attached—to musicians who will follow his own lead in distorting or fragmenting that voice at will or at random.[21] This abdication of self-possession characterizes the kind of anonymous collaborative venture which has been extremely important to Burroughs throughout his career.

The merging or exchanging of identities that takes place in collaboration finds a dramatic analogue in Burroughs' fiction, in scenes staging a more literal escape from the self and its limits. In *The Soft Machine,* one character may enter the body of another through magic rituals involving drugs and incantations; in *Ticket* and *Nova Express*, the dissolving of body outlines is achieved by more technological procedures using tape recordings and film. Burroughs was involved in some actual experiments along these lines. In the short film "Bill and Tony," for example, Burroughs and Antony Balch each give a deadpan recitation of a short text, and then each moves his lips while the other's voice comes out of his mouth. They exchange names, faces, and set speeches without any visible effort, surprise, or anxiety. One of the recited texts is a set of directions on how to climb out the back of your head and move around the room; in a carnival barker's harangue, the other text promises to reveal "the most amazing living monstrosity of all time." Both speeches suggest ways of breaking out of the cover or cover-up of conventional identity and achieving a freedom that may also seem monstrous.

One of the appeals of the cut-up technique, as Brion Gysin puts it, is that it offers "ways *out*—out of identity habit, perhaps out of the human form itself" (*RE,* p. 40). In the sound track to Balch's film "Cut-Ups," distinctly different voices are manipulated so that they blur, combine, overlap, and separate again. Because the actual content of what is repeated continuously on the soundtrack is staggeringly banal ("Yes." "Hello." "Thank you"), the listener's attention is drawn to the weaving and overlapping of the voices themselves. One effect of these permutations and variations is to replace patterns of domination (in which one speaker inevitably silences all others) with a collaborative practice, a variation on the game of musical chairs in which individuals move freely from one identity to another, never at rest in any single self-image or "sound identity." For Burroughs, writing in general provides access to this sort of metamorphosis and collaboration. He describes, for example, the pleasures of taking off on another writer's "shining" words, escaping one's own habits and obsessions, and he reports experiencing the activity of composing and then reading his work as "hearing other voices"—"muttering phantom voices waiting for a role." If writers would give their characters "a chance to talk back,"[22] he advises, the writer and his identity might dissolve into the very life of the work.

The recordings of Burroughs' formal readings of extended "straight" routines offer convincing evidence of his consummate ability to move effortlessly through a motley crew of identities, shifting voices like a one-man vocal band: the robotlike voice blurting out combat directives and warnings; the droning voice of the lecturer, detached and impersonal; the threatening voice of a gangster; the slow hypnotic voice of the "Doctor" brought in to soothe the marks into passivity; the evil insinuations of the "Green Nun."[23] James Grauerholz describes Burroughs' enjoyment in creating personalities through "voices," in "giving life to a fictional universe" (*RCF,* p. 27), and one hears his pleasure clearly in those public readings where he is working the crowd with a finely honed routine. When he hits his stride, he reads in a voice that never breaks off but slides from word to word, carefully paced and inflected. He feels his way around each word, each consonant (especially *l*'s and *r*'s), with a sensuous care and attention. In these rare moments word and body seem to operate in harmony.

These moments of pleasure, however, are quite different from the experience produced on and by the cut-up tapes. Many of the familiar character voices can be recognized, but they are spliced, distorted, jarred constantly by eruptions of loud drum music, electronic screeching, traffic sounds, subway noise, radio static. Burroughs never fully enters or establishes any character, he never "soars" on another writer's words or even on his own. In fact, one is constantly aware of constraint—the constraint of the machinery used (the clicking of recorder buttons, the speaker fumbling with the microphone), and the constraints of Burroughs' own "soft machine"—the alien body through which he must speak. At times his voice sounds as though he is speaking from inside a box or echo chamber, as if from deep within his own body. In the film sequences when he reads a text in front of the camera, Burroughs parts and moves his lips just enough to let the sound out—the constraint and discomfort of speaking made visible. On a few of the tapes Burroughs affects the tight-throated voice of the junkie trapped in his addiction and his isolation.

There is a peculiar quality in Burroughs' delivery that makes one acutely aware of the passage of the voice through the body. In this context, Henri Chopin compares Burroughs to the sound poets in France for whom the body is always the beginning point.[24] But while the sound poets seem to celebrate this language of the body as opposed to the artificial limits of the page, Burroughs perceives the body itself as a prerecorded script, a prewritten "ticket" to be exploded.

On "Throat Microphone Experiments" we have an example of Burroughs's efforts to record "subvocal speech." A vague voice snarls incomprehensible words, but the tone of hostility and suffering comes through clearly. The vocal bursts and softer mutterings suggest some internal, unedited language, closer to the body and perhaps also to unprocessed raw emotion. Burroughs elaborates on these experiments in *Ticket*: "Small microphones were attached to the two sides of [Bradly's] body the sounds recorded on two tape recorders—He heard the beating of his heart, the gurgle of shifting secretions and food, the rattle of breath and scratches of throat gristle" (*T*, p. 72). With calculated manipulation of "feedback between the two body halves," Bradly finally breaks free of body, identity, and word. Assessing his own experiments with contact microphones more realistically, Burroughs admits, "All we got were some interesting noises."[25]

Similar interesting noises are produced by inching the tape, "taking a recorded text.... and rubbing the tape back and forth across the head" or "playing a tape back and switching the mike control stop start on and off at short intervals which gives an effect of stuttering" (*J*, p. 161). The results of inching on the "Sound Piece" resemble a bubbling, underwater sound, as if words were gurgling up through the body's liquids and out at the lips. Made aware of mouth and tongue, the listener may imagine he or she hears the body itself speaking its own secret language. This is perhaps the same sound that

Roland Barthes has called the "grain of the voice"—a language "lined with flesh, a text where we can hear the grain of the throat, the patina of consonants, the voluptuousness of vowels, a whole carnal stereophony: the articulation of the body, of the tongue, not that of meaning."[26]

Whereas for Barthes this immersion in the body, in the materiality of the "mother tongue," is a source of gendered and erotic bliss, Burroughs descends into the realm of the body of language only to work his way through and out. When Burroughs inches his recorded voice through the tape recorder, the patina of meaning is scraped away and words are laid bare in their most primitive essence. As he describes similar techniques in *Ticket*, "The words were smudged together. They snarled and whined and barked. It was as if the words themselves were called into question" (*T,* p. 18) "and were scarcely recognizable as human voices" (*T,* p. 187). The familiar sound of the word in the body and in the very air we breathe ("I had heard it for years barely audible"[*T,* p. 19]) is forced to the surface in these experiments: "loud and clear now a muttering hypnotic cadence" (*T,* p. 19). The word takes on body, and its body is monstrous.

AGONY TO BREATHE HERE

Where one becomes most aware of the body in Burroughs' voice, however, is in the absence of voice—in the preliminary intake of breath that often precedes his speech. Chopin has remarked that what most expresses Burroughs is not the body but the "souffle," the breath that passes through the body (*PSI,* p. 136). That "souffle" has been most thoroughly analyzed by Philippe Mikriammos in his essay "Vox Williami, vox monstrorum."[27] He describes the "labial preliminary," conscious and labored, with which Burroughs often begins his phrases: "he breathes in [before speaking] noisily, making the air he breathes in rattle, almost whistle through his lips. Thus before it is heard, Burroughs' voice precedes itself, it announces itself.... Burroughs breathes in noisily as one does when about to spit or blow violently"

(*Vox*, pp. 101–102). This sound makes us aware, he argues, of the passage of the voice through the body, the passage between the self and the external world. For Mikriammos, that intake or sigh or hiss says it all: Burroughs' boredom at repeating the same unheeded messages or prerecorded routines, and his ambivalence at having to speak at all, having to give in to the inadequate machinery of language.

On the tapes, the intake of breath often comes before a curse or warning ("and—cursed—be—he—who—moves—it"), before final words of farewell ("Nothing here now but the recordings"); before a line that functions as a repeated refrain, a bit of continuity in an otherwise fractured cut-up ("We see Tibet through the binoculars of the people").[28] In "Silver Smoke of Dreams," one of the moments where the tape catches and repeats is on that intake of breath. The effect is disturbing and painful, as though one is hearing the actual sound of the struggle to communicate; in that repeated gasp is the *effort* to begin without the relief of beginning. In a similar moment in the long cut-up film "Ghosts at #9," Burroughs' labored breathing into the microphone begins to sound like an urgent but incomprehensible whisper or the amplified trembling breath of someone weeping silently. This sound is magnified and prolonged until its bare intimacy is almost intolerable. In a conversation with friends, Burroughs puts it simply and without self-pity: "I think it's just hard to be myself. It's hard to draw breath on this bloody planet" (*WWB*, p. 50).

We are reminded of the difficulty of breathing with every audible intake on the tapes, and Burroughs' theory that the word parasite exists within the body on "an air line" of survival is thus dramatized. The breathing circuit, the passage between inside and outside, is where the individual is most vulnerable and where the word insinuates itself most effectively. Both Gysin and Burroughs warn against this "symbiosis con" by which language devours human life: "You breathe in words. Words breath you IN" (*TM*, p. 61), or "Words are made from breath. Your breath" (*BF*, p. 197). In Burroughs' view of the language virus, each word emitted uses up breath and survives by depleting the life supply of the host individual.

Carl Weissner gives an account of a meeting with Burroughs in 1966 at which they "compare[d] tapes." "We played his tapes, then some of mine. Nothing was said....Then we put a microphone on the table and took turns talking to the tape recorder switching back and forth between tracks at random intervals. We played it all back and sat there listening to our conversation" (*WWB*, p. 8). Among the results of the experiment were the following phrases: "Agony to breathe here. *Muy* alone in such tense and awful silence and *por eso* have I survived" (*WWB*, p. 9). To counteract the silence and isolation of writing (or living), this sort of cut-up collaboration allows the unspoken and unspeakable to find expression, the most intimate struggle and pain of survival to speak up in phantom voices out of the tape recorder.

The effect of the cut-up method in writing or taping, then, is to create breathing spaces, gaps between words and broken continuities providing ways out of predetermined patterns of thinking and speaking. In *Nova Express*, Uranian Willy leads a resistance attack after he has "rubbed off the word shackles" and "[thrown] up a Silence Screen...Coating word patterns":

The grey smoke drifted the grey that stops shift cut tangle they breathe medium the word cut shift patterns words cut the insect tangle cut shift that coats word cut breath silence shift abdominal cut tangle stop word holes. (NX, p. 58)

While the Silence Screen closes off the "abdominal breathing holes" of the enemy, the cut-up opens *new* breathing space through which "partisans" might escape and "never look back" (*NX*, p. 58).

ACROSS THE WOUNDED GALAXIES WE INTERSECT

Burroughs creates breathing spaces in the cut-up text by blasting holes in continuity. In the written cut-ups, these holes are indicated by dashes, ellipses, slashes, or blank spaces. In the tape cut-ups, breathing spaces are indicated primarily by the audible *click* of the machine as a cut-in segment interrupts the underlying sequence. For the listener, the *click* has a surprise effect, undermining the expectation of continuity; but it also invites a new way of listening in which discontinuity and fragmentation demand more active participation. Laszlo K. Géfin has described the collaborative work of the reader of the written cut-up who executes a "'jump' *over* the invisible yet perceptible 'seam'... while also attempting a semantic reconciliation *across* the 'seam.'" Reading a cut-up text produces a "mind jolt" that brings the reader to the very limits of language.[29] In the tape cut-ups, that "jump across" seems more like a stumble or stutter. Because the material of these cut-ups is more heterogeneous (alternating voices with electronic sounds, street noise, scraps of music), the discontinuities dominate and for the most part resist semantic closure or resolution. The fragmentation of voice in the cut-up tapes often reduces it to a series of purely phonemic gestures, a level at which language as meaning is virtually eradicated. A similar effect is produced in the visual context by Brion Gysin's calligraphic writing, where words are transformed from signs into designs.

As Burroughs explains in *The Job,* thinking may seem continuous, but it is actually constituted by such leaps and breaks: "Actually the thoughts flow stop change and flow again. At the point where one flow stops there is a split-second hiatus. The new way of thinking grows in this hiatus between thoughts" (*Job,* p. 91). To adopt this new way of thinking, then, is to be attentive to the hole or cut or *click* between texts: to proceed poised for unexpected scraps of meaning reaching across the break, but also to proceed without any such expectations, giving in to the hypnotic incantatory rhythms of the cut-up, the pleasures offered by a language without meaning or syntax.

In "We See the Future through the Binoculars of the People" our attention is drawn to these points of interruption or intersection by the frequent *clicks* of the machine. There are incongruities, as when an apocalyptic voice ("IT IS THE GREAT AWAKENING!") *clicks* into the detached and patient drone of the lecturing researcher ("recordings made with no apparent input"); but there are also odd moments of coherence, as in the sequence "who are you?/ knew just where he cut in/ put you in touch/ the connection is to...." Here the unrelated voices intersect at a common desire for human contact, a desire which survives all experimentation, even the most radical attempts to dissolve continuity and identity. Such contact has always been Burroughs' goal, and the cut-up experiments merely offer new ways of making contact without domination or control, in a collective anonymity: "*Across the wounded galaxies we intersect* bits and pieces of P.B....so many others...so many voices" (*TM*, p. 93).

Such points of intersection or contact may occur within the cut-up text (which Burroughs describes in the Foreword Note to *Nova Express* as "a composite of many writers living and dead"), or between the cut-up and its audience. In a handwritten note that accompanies the scrapbook layout of "Afternoon Ticker-tape," for example, Burroughs invites the viewer to "Put any picture that fits from your time into this space";[30] and he advises confused readers of this cut-up to read for "points of intersection, a decoding operation...relating the text to external coordinates" (*TM*, p. 136). Such attentiveness, Burroughs argues, must be extended to daily life as well, where word and image, external world and subjective mind, are continually moving in and out of sync, where no given set of coordinates is stable or correct.

In his essay "Precise Intersection Points," Burroughs describes the experience of encountering in reality a picture which seems to refer to something he has written: "When I saw the picture, something clicked in my head like a camera shutter. /*take*/....Now, the intersection may be a picture or it may be a text...not all that much difference for words *are* pictures and vice versa....In either case, you know it is happening when something clicks. For a picture, the *click* is like a camera shutter. For a text, it's more like the *click* of a tape-recorder switch. Listen for that *click*" (*TM*, p. 135). The *click* that connects things is, of course, intermittent—in cut-ups as in lived experience; and listening *for* the *click* often slides into listening *to* the *click* and the rhythms it produces as pictures move in and out of focus and words move in and out of meaning.

Grunberg has compared this rhythm, as manifested particularly in the back and forth movement of the manipulated tape, to an erotic rhythm, an "ejaculatory movement" of the text that gives birth to new words on tape (*SG,* p. 126). Burroughs has certainly explored the erotic potential of tape experiments in his fiction where he describes both the pleasures and the dangers of such sexual-technological experimentation: "The voices of Harrison and 'Genial' alternated. They both recorded a short text then the two tapes were cut into short sections and spliced in together. This produces a strong erotic reaction.... so long as the spliced tape finds an outlet in actual sex contact it acts as an aphrodisiac... nothing more.... But when a susceptible subject is spliced in with someone who is not there then it acts as a destructive virus" (*T*, pp. 18–20). Making actual contact is, once again, essential to the productive and creative use of cut-up techniques.

MAGIC AND ART

Early practitioners of collage such as Max Ernst and Jean Arp noticed both the erotic and the magical potential of cutting up and recombining disparate elements. Ernst, in particular, celebrated the alchemical powers of verbal and visual collage or cut-up. Similarly, Burroughs creates scenes in his novels in which characters experiment simultaneously with sex and magic in order to extend levels of consciousness and dissolve the boundaries of the individual self. These multimedia experiments with tape recordings, radio static, music, and film images are often staged as magic rituals or incantations.

Just as Burroughs keeps himself open to the creative potential of modern technology, he has always remained receptive to the possibilities offered by magic or the supernatural. Tracing this influence back to his earliest days, Burroughs recalls that his mother possessed some psychic gifts and that he himself had several strange visions as a child—visions that filled him sometimes with wonder, sometimes with fear (*WWB*, pp. xiv, xvi). Living in Tangier, in a culture where magic is a part of daily life, and working closely for many years with Brion Gysin, Burroughs found his early interest in psychic or spiritual powers reinforced. He was particularly interested in the Joujouka musicians living in the hills of Morocco, musicians Brion Gysin describes as having a secret language, a means of communication beyond the constraints of word and voice (*RE*, p. 50). Cutting his Joujouka tapes into recordings of electronic sounds and human voices, Burroughs is perhaps attempting to break up conventional modes of language and open other levels of communication.

Gysin has probably contributed more than anyone else to the view of Burroughs in his cut-up period as a somewhat demonic character who supposedly carried around with him tape-recorded ritual curses for protection. He also enjoys telling the story of at least one occasion on which Burroughs seemed to have successfully cast a fatal spell on a rude newspaper vendor. We do have on tape one recording of Burroughs reciting a protective anticurse, spitting out its chantlike phrases with venomous insistence: "Curse go back curse go back/ Back with double pain and lack/ Curse go back" (*RE*, p. 45). In the film "Towers Open Fire," this same tape is used in a sequence where Burroughs waves his hands as if casting a spell over a pile of canned films. This segment is rather stagey and exaggerated, and it is difficult to take it seriously. More effective and convincing, perhaps, are the sequences in "Cut-Ups" showing Gysin's calligraphic paintings forming the double grid pattern in which certain ritual curses are written. Often accompanied on the soundtrack by the Joujouka musicians' drums and flutes, these images gradually accelerate until they explode into a frightening and urgent blur of electronic static.

In Burroughs' work, magic is never far from technology, and writing is never totally divorced from magic. In his most recent trilogy, magic still figures in the narrative plot. In *Cities of the Red Night*, for example, the private eye Clem Snide practices a kind of technological magic for locating missing persons. His method is to tape record the subject's environment—the rattle of dishes in the kitchen sink, the flushing toilet, the sounds from the street—and then to cut in various texts at random: The *Magus*, the official files on the subject, any recordings of the subject's voice. By paying "special attention to the cut-ins" or intersection points, information about subjects missing or dead may be revealed to the technician.[31]

Whereas Burroughs elaborates on the magic potential of tape recorder cut-ups in his fiction, he is quite circumspect about actual experiments. When the tape recorder research of Konstantin Raudive and others came to his attention in the 1970s, for example, he recognized their similarity to some of his own earlier experiments. Raudive's basic procedure involves recording in a silent room onto factory-fresh blank tapes and then listening to the playback with sensitive equipment that seems to pick up "faint voices of unknown origin" (*AM*, p. 53). What interests Burroughs is that these voices often come through speeded up and pulsing rhythmically like incantations or poetry, a style that he has generated with cut-up techniques and that he also recognizes in the language of dreams and in the speech of some schizophrenics. Burroughs remains skeptical about Raudive's conclusion that the voices on tape are coming from the dead, and he speculates instead that they are imprints produced by the "memory banks" of the present experimenters.

In spite of his cautious skepticism, however, we cannot be certain that Burroughs is speaking only metaphorically when he describes the tape cut-up technique as "electronic table tapping" (*AM*, p. 55). By cutting up and recombining fragments of texts by Shakespeare and Rimbaud, Burroughs tells us, you will hear new poems by Shakespeare and Rimbaud. Yet he certainly mocks the idea of "medium" poetry that claims to produce the "personal appearance" of dead writers: "Anybody who is anybody is there, many of them having undergone a marked deterioration of their mental and artistic faculties. Goethe isn't what he used to be....Shakespeare is announced to be followed by some excruciatingly bad poetry" (*AM*, p. 55). Brion Gysin may be correct in his assertion that the cut-ups make exorcism explicit (*RE*, p. 45), but they also seem to demystify it, and even at his most susceptible, Burroughs is never duped by magic. On "Creepy Letters" we hear an unedited recording of an actual incident in which he has just received a letter and proposes to cut it up in order to find out "what it is rrreeeallly saying." Burroughs hums away as he cuts up the letter, but after reading aloud the results, he merely dismisses the experiment laconically, "Well, that doesn't make any sense."

Burroughs' interest in magic does persist in his belief that writing and painting have a common origin in ancient rituals designed "to produce very definite effects" (*AM*, p. 61), to make things happen. Writers still operate, Burroughs declares, "in a magical universe" (*AM*, p. 101), which is always providing messages, completing thoughts—if only we would keep our eyes and ears open. Cut-up procedures with texts or tape recordings enhance the magical powers of chance; leaving behind the artist's own subjective habits, the cut-up allows him or her simply to "read and transcribe" (*BF*, p. 189). But unlike the figure of the possessed poet transcribing from the car radio in Cocteau's film *Orpheus*, Burroughs never romanticizes the role of magic in the creative process. He insists on the necessity of discipline, rigor, and control. There is no shortcut to creativity, and there are no guarantees. "People who are into ritual magic like Aleister Crowley," he explains, "—he may have been a competent black magician but he is not a good writer."[32]

Burroughs' own association of writing with magic moves in a more pragmatic direction: "All writers are involved in ESP. If you're not to some extent telepathic, then you can't be a writer, at least not a novelist where you have to be able to get into someone else's mind" (*WWB*, p. 18). Generalizing and domesticating the idea of magical or psychic powers even further, he concludes, "Anybody who is good at anything uses ESP" (*WWB*, p. 18). The real magic, as he puts it in *The Place of Dead Roads*, is when characters and settings "live and breathe in a writer's prose, in the care, love and dedication that evoke them."[33] As Oliver Harris points out, "Burroughs appraises writers according to the presence of magical flashes" in their work (*LW*, p. 305). and Burroughs remembers those moments with gratitude and admiration: "I can think of writers I read years ago and have forgotten the writer's name and the title. But I can remember a chapter, a paragraph, maybe just a phrase, that really shines...with the writer's gift of life" (*AM*, pp. 71–72).

Burroughs launched into his cut-up tape experiments believing that they could produce superior effects, "effects of simultaneity, echoes, speed-ups, slowdowns...all sorts of things you can do on a tape recorder that cannot possibly be indicated on a printed page" (*Job*, p. 29). He did at one time believe that tape experiments offered the greatest promise for a genuine breakthrough. In an interview with Nicholas Zurbrugg in 1982, however, he states unequivocally that tape recorders are "of *no use whatsoever* to the *writer*" (*RCF*, p. 21), and by this time he has ruled out using the tape recorder even in the most conventional way: "Using a tape recorder for composition has never worked for me....talking and writing are quite different. So far as writing goes I do need a typewriter. I have to write it down and see it" (*WWB*, p. 6).[34]

So the 1980s have brought Burroughs back to seeing, back to the visual impact of his images rather than the sound of his voice. In the past decade he has entered new creative territory as a painter and collagist, and his recent trilogy has given us some of his most vivid pictures. But that inimitable "sound" Didion identified is still there, and one can still hear in his recordings and film appearances the voice Emmet Williams likened to "a slow but faithful old Ford, with out-of-date St. Louis plates, a buggy somewhat the worse for international wear and tear on rocky roads." It may no longer be the voice of one "hell-bent for interplanetary travel,"[35] but it is the voice of one who—with the help of cut-up technology—has traversed language, the body, and identity and returned to tell the tale.

NOTES

1. Joan Didion, "Wired for Shock Treatments," *Book Week,* 27 March 1966, p. 2. Further page references will appear in the text.

2. *From the Archives of William S. Burroughs: "Nothing Here Now but the Recordings"* (Industrial Records, Ltd.), is a selection made from hours of cut-up tape recorder experiments carried out mostly in the 1960s. I will refer to the following cuts from this recording: "Just Checking Your Summer Recordings," "Summer Will," "Throat Microphone Experiments," "We See the Future through the Binoculars of the People," and "Creepy Letters." From *William S. Burroughs/Break Through in Grey Room* (Sub Rosa Records, Sub 33005–8. Documents, n.d.), I will refer to "Working with the Popular Forces," "K9 Was in Combat with the Alien Mind-Screens," "Recalling All Active Agents," "Silver Smoke of Dreams," and "Sound Piece."

3. William Burroughs, *The Adding Machine: Selected Essays* (New York: Seaver-Holt, 1986), 91. Further references in the text will be to *AM.*

4. Daniel Odier, *The Job: Interviews with William S. Burroughs* (New York: Grove Press, 1970), p. 44. Further references in the text will be to *Job.*

5. William S. Burroughs, *The Burroughs File* (San Francisco: City Lights Books, 1984), p. 197. Further references in the text will be to *BF.*

6. Victor Bockris, *With William Burroughs: A Report from the Bunker* (New York: Seaver Books, 1981), p. 187. Further references in the text will be to *WWB.*

7. William S. Burroughs and Brion Gysin, *The Third Mind* (New York: The Viking Press, 1978), p. 44. Further references in the text will be to *TM.*

8. William S. Burroughs, *The Ticket That Exploded* (New York: Grove Press, 1967), p. 51. Further references in the text will be to *T.*

9. *RE/SEARCH 4/5: A Special Book Issue: William S. Burroughs, Brion Gysin and Throbbing Gristle* (San Francisco: ReSearch Publications, 1982), p. 44. Further references in the text will be to *RE.*

10. Richard Kostelanetz, *Conversing with Cage* (New York: Limelight Editions, 1988), p. 162.

11. Serge Grunberg, *"A la recherche d'un corps": Langage et silence dans l'oeuvre de William S. Burroughs* (Paris: Editions du Seuil, 1979). I have summarized pp. 126–143 here. Quotations in English are my own translations. Further references in the text will be to *SG*.

12. Jean-Joseph Goux, "Téléscripteur W.B." in *Le Colloque de Tanger,* vol. 1, ed. Gérard-Georges Lemaire (Paris: Christian Bourgois, 1976), p. 131. Further references in the text will be to *C,* and all translations are my own.

13. See Julia Kristeva, "Women's Time," trans. Alice Jardine and Harry Blake, *Signs* 7 (Autumn 1981), p. 1; Michel Serres, *The Parasite,* trans. Lawrence R. Schehr (Baltimore: Johns Hopkins University Press, 1982); and François Lyotard, *The Postmodern Condition: A Report on Knowledge,* trans. Geoff Bennington and Brian Massumi (Minneapolis: University of Minnesota Press, 1981).

14. Examples of this can be heard in "Recalling All Active Agents," "K9 Was in Combat with the Alien Mind-Screens," and "Working with the Popular Forces." Burroughs traces his earliest exposure to sound cut-ups to the hilarious incongruities of "The Drunken Newscaster" tape, a scrambled cut-up of several newscasts that he first heard in 1953. Whereas this original tape revealed to him the pure entertainment potential of tape cut-ups, Burroughs' choice of material seems more heavily oriented toward issues of political conflict and social repression.

15. Henri Chopin asserts that "thanks to sound poetry and electronics, which enter our bodily resonators, we hear sounds more fully than by the ear alone" ("Voix Off," in *Colloque de Tanger,* p. 61). This seems further evidence of Burroughs' theory that the same technique can be used for repressive or liberating effects.

16. "Towers Open Fire," *Three Films: 1950's–1960's: Films by Antony Balch,* (London issue from archives of Psychick Television, VHS–TOPTV 002). This film also includes "William Buys a Parrot," "The Cut-Ups," "Bill and Tony," and "Ghosts at #9."

17. Robert Palmer, "William Burroughs," *Rolling Stone* 11 (May 1972), p. 51. In this quote Burroughs describes Gysin's invention.

18. Letter from Burroughs quoted in Alan Ansen, "Anyone Who Can Pick Up a Frying Pan Owns Death," *Big Table* 2 (Summer 1959), p. 41.

19. This excerpt from "The Valentine's Day Reading (1965)" (phonodisc of *Revue Où* 40–41, 1971, ed. Henri Chopin, Paris) is a version of the recording "Working with the Popular Forces."

20. William S. Burroughs, *Nova Express* (New York: Grove Press, 1964), p. 154. Further references in the text will be to *NX.*

21. In Nicholas Zurbrugg, "Burroughs, Grauerholz, and *Cities of the Red Night:* An

Interview with James Grauerholz," *Review of Contemporary Fiction* (Spring 1984), pp. 19–32, Grauerholz explains, "William has been getting a little involved with music in the sense that he has been allowing tapes of his voice to be used in produced pieces by other people, collaborations where basically he says, 'This tape is my contribution, you do with it what you will,' and they cut it up and do this or that and that makes it interesting" (p. 28). Further references in the text will be to *RCF*.

22. This and the previous phrases in this paragraph are from "The Valentine's Day Reading (1965)," in which Burroughs describes the technique he calls "Boarding a Writer."

23. Aside from the footage of Burroughs giving public readings in Howard Brookner's *Burroughs: The Movie* (New York: Giorno Poetry Systems, 1985), see the cuts on the phonodiscs *You're the Guy I Want to Share My Money With,* with John Giorno and Laurie Anderson (New York: Giorno Poetry Systems, 1981) and *William Burroughs/ John Giorno* (New York: Giorno Poetry Systems, 1975). Since the completion of this article, Burroughs has released the finest collection of his recorded readings: *William S. Burroughs: Dead City Radio* (New York: Island Records, 1990).

24. Henri Chopin, "William Burroughs," in *Poésie sonore internationale,* ed. Henri Chopin (Paris: Jean-Michel Place, 1979),

p. 136. Further references in the text will be to *PSI*.

25. Quoted on the jacket notes to *From the Archives of William S. Burroughs.*

26. Roland Barthes, *The Pleasure of the Text,* trans. by Richard Miller (New York: Hill and Wang, 1975), pp. 66–67.

27. Philippe Mikriammos, "Vox Williami, vox monstrorum," in *Colloque de Tanger.* Further references in the text will be to *Vox*.

28. These three quotes are from the album *From the archives of William S. Burroughs,* cuts 2, 1, and 7.

29. Laszlo K. Géfin, "Collage Theory, Reception, and the Cut-ups of William Burroughs," *Literature and the Other Arts: Perspectives on Contemporary Literature* 13 (1987), pp. 96–97.

30. Quoted in Oliver C. Harris, *The Last Words of William Burroughs* (Ph.D. diss., Oxford University, 1988), p. 265. Further references in the text will be to *LW*.

31. William S. Burroughs, *Cities of the Red Night* (New York: Holt, Rinehart and Winston, 1981), pp. 43–45.

32. John Tytell, "An Interview with William S. Burroughs" in *Kerouac and the Beats: A Primary Sourcebook* (New York: Paragon House, 1988), p. 38.

33. William S. Burroughs, *The Place of Dead Roads* (New York: Holt, Rinehart and Winston, 1984), p. 201.

34. Ironically, on several tapes one hears a typewriter clacking away in the background, as though the cut-up sounds and their transcription were simultaneous. Neither tape cut-ups nor typed transcript would thus be given any clear precedence or priority.

35. This phrase and the previous one are from Emmet Williams' sleeve notes to *Call Me Burroughs* (Paris: The English Bookshop, 1965), as quoted in Zurbrugg, "Interview with James Grauerholz," p. 19.

CRAIG ADCOCK is Professor of Art History at the University of Notre Dame, specializing in nineteenth- and twentieth-century art. He has published essays about Dadaism and its influence, and numerous essays about Marcel Duchamp. His most recent book is *James Turrell: The Art of Light and Space.*

MARK E. CORY is Professor of German at the Unversity of Arkansas. His main research interest for more than twenty years has been German radio art; he also writes about experimental poetry, contemporary prose fiction, and Holocaust literature.

FRANCES DYSON is an Australian media artist and independent scholar residing in Phoenix. Her radio artwork has been commissioned and aired internationally, and she has produced audio for installation, performance, and video.

MEL GORDON is Professor of Dramatic Art at the University of California, Berkeley, and the author of many books and articles on American, French, German, Italian, Russian, and Yiddish theater. His most recent book, coauthored with Alma Law, is *Meyerhold, Eisenstein, and Biomechanics.*

CHARLES GRIVEL is Professor of Modern and Contemporary French Literature at the University of Mannheim. His works include numerous texts on avant-garde literature, fear and fantasy, the sociological analysis of texts, the phenomenology of reading, and text-image relationships.

DOUGLAS KAHN is Associate Professor of Media Arts at Arizona State University West in Phoenix. His audio works have been broadcast internationally. His essays on sound in the avant-garde have appeared in such journals as *October, Public, Art & Text, Musicworks,* and *New Music Articles* and in *Sound by Artists* and *The Spirit of Fluxus.*

ROBIN LYDENBERG is Professor of English at Boston College, author of *Word Cultures: Radical Theory and Practice in William S. Burroughs' Fiction* and coeditor of *William S. Burroughs at the Front: Critical Reception, 1959–1989.*

CHRISTOPHER SCHIFF is an independent scholar and performer living in Colorado Springs. He received his graduate degree in Experimental Music from Wesleyan University, where he studied with Alvin Lucier and wrote his thesis on the history of Erik Satie's *Parade.*

ALLEN S. WEISS is a writer, translator, and editor working in the fields of film studies, art history, philosophy, and psychoanalytic theory. He is author of *The Aesthetics of Excess* and coeditor of both *Psychosis and Sexual Identity* and *Sade Beyond Measure.*

GREGORY WHITEHEAD is a writer, radiomaker, and audio artist. Since 1982 he has produced more than fifty radioworks and live-to-air performances in North America, Europe, and Australia. He is also the author of numerous essays on subjects relating to language, technology, and the politics of broadcasting.